Taulus

Taulus

**Over eight decades , a French orphan's
Rollicking saga of survival and victory:
war, women, Africa**

© 2006   René Dassac and Patrick K. Robbins

Copyright © René Dassac and Patrick K. Robbins. 2006
ISBN 978-1-4303-0000-7
Printed in the United States of America

Without limiting the rights under copyright reserved above, no part of this publication may be reproduced, stored in or introduced into a retrieval system, or transmitted, in any form or by any means (electronic, mechanical, photocopying, recording, or otherwise), without the prior written permission of the copyright owners

DEDICATION

Taulus is dedicated to my wife Anna and our son Philip without whose unlimited love and encouragement my life would not have been as rich as what we have shared and to Genevieve, Paulette and Juliette, my three sisters for ensuring that I always had a loving family in France. Georges and Christianne Leclerc helped me get started with a new life when I returned to Paris in the early 1950's and I will always be in their debt.

ACKNOWLEDGEMENT

Books don't just happen to get written. Pat and I learned that it takes time and a lot of hard work to capture fleeting ideas and transform them into words. Once the words started to flow we had to work even harder to push them into honest paragraphs.

Taulus is my story but Pat `dragged it out of me. Many times he probed and encouraged me to develop ideas and I was often reluctant to follow him. Either what he was asking me to do was too hard or it was too painful. Often he needled me to deal with both the difficulty and the pain until I got out what had to be said. Pat's patience, persistence, and good humor over many months and hundreds of pages kept me motivated and happy and I acknowledge that Taulus would not have been written without his pushing, pulling, prodding and laughter. Thanks, Pat

INTRODUCTION

When I turned eighty in 2002 the 'age factor' really hit me. There is nothing wrong with my health except for a few aches and pains associated with having clocked eight decades on the face of this earth. I chop wood and steer the wheelbarrow through the garden trying to keep up with my wife, Anna. I've stopped climbing our olive trees to trim them every year; they look quite nice now that they are 'full' and the olive harvest doesn't seem to have suffered from me deciding not to play Tarzan. Mentally I am still sharp and I read a lot to keep up with world affairs.

Looking at television and watching the world start to unravel got me thinking seriously about putting my life's story on paper. I have been an actor in some of the most tumultuous decades of the twentieth century and I knew I had a story that I wanted to tell to my family and close friends. The idea of writing my autobiography was great but I knew the task could easily overwhelm me. I had tried a couple of times but after a few weeks my interest petered out. I simply could not stick to the daily grind of emptying my mind into my computer and my inability to persist bothered me. Was I going nuts or going senile, or both? Others wrote their life stories but my story remained locked inside my head. My notes and diaries were a great source of fact and inspiration. All the mechanics were in place but I could still not get going.

In April 2004 our neighbors had a lunch party for a lot of their friends. I knew many of them but there were more new faces around the tables than I recall having seen in our village, Callian. After a nice long aperitif hour we served ourselves and sat at long tables wherever there was a place free. I forget who I was seated next to but I remember I was at the end of my table. It was a good lunch. We ate well and drank well. After the main course the tables split up before starting dessert. Guests mingled and sat down at other tables and started new conversations but I was comfortable so I didn't move.

I was looking out over our host's garden probably thinking long thoughts about nothing in particular when a tall man with a white beard sat down next to me. We started talking in French and then we switched to English, something he wasn't expecting because most Frenchmen my age can't speak English. He was easy to talk to and we introduced ourselves. When I told him my name, Rene Dassac and John Powell, he looked me straight in the face and asked, "Are you kidding me?" I told him I wasn't. He asked me why I had two names and I replied, "It's a long story and you really wouldn't be interested." He persisted and got me going. I gave him my standard fifteen-minute short version answer to his question. While I was talking I watched his face and I could tell he was genuinely interested. When I finished he sat staring out in space and then asked me, "Why don't you write your memoirs?"

His question made me uncomfortable because before he sat down next to me, among all my thoughts, I was probably struggling again about "really getting serious" and finally settling down to grind out my autobiography. His question wasn't new. Others had already asked me the same question. I knew that I was spending a lot of time thinking about how to get started and then actually stick with the project to the end. But, when I met him I was still stuck in the thinking phase. The hard part, the 'doing phase,' was ahead of me. One thing was certain: the last thing I wanted to do was start and stop again. Life is getting too short to start playing around with time and his question made me edgy.

I asked him if he thought my story would be interesting; he assured me it would. "What's holding you back?" I told him I had started a couple of times but I couldn't bring myself to come up with a simple satisfactory answer of what I didn't continue. I hemmed and hawed and finally blurted my confession: "I'm not sure I know how to write it." That was the truth. He thought for a couple of moments and then made me an offer: "You draft your book and I will ghost write it with you. And, don't get your hopes up. I'm no pro. We're both learners." At least, I thought, he sounds honest.

Maybe both of us had drunk too much of Jean Pierre's good wine because his proposition seemed perfectly natural. He explained that he had wanted to tackle a writing project for a long time. That was good news because it meant the idea of working together also met his needs. He assured me that we would be moving forward together because he had never completed a project as big as a book, especially an autobiography. We shook hands and I agreed to call him if I wanted to proceed.

It took me a couple of weeks to digest his offer. Two strangers were thinking about making a huge commitment to each other. At least from my side I wanted time to think about what I was getting into. In early May I called him. I was half expecting him to ask me to remind him who I was and how we met but my name rang a bell and we agreed to meet at my house in Callian to layout the project.

We agreed on a basic format: I would write the first draft and he would expand on my draft using my input and getting my approval every step of the way. In this era of computer technology, I agreed to hunt-and-peck a few pages and send them to him. We began immediately, "Full speed ahead." Once he finished working on what I sent over we met and reviewed the fruits of our labors, caught any glaring mistakes, and agreed on the date for our next meeting. He was a taskmaster but I managed to stay ahead of him. Our sessions in my house were all work and no play. A few jokes, a few comments on world events and we got down to work.

Counting my original draft, we wrote four complete drafts. At times it was tough going because he pushed me to reveal things about myself that I had bottled up and sealed off. He made me break the seals. Sometimes my eyes started smarting but we worked through the hard parts because they were so important for me to tell a true story. We started off as total strangers but we grew closer the longer we worked together. A couple of times when he showed me his drafts of sections I had struggled with I had the feeling that he had been there to experience the event with me. He began climbing inside my head. My descriptions of what happened came to life the way I wanted them to without me having to make any excuses. He helped me find my voice. I became more confident writing my story and I think that helped him drag out of me thoughts, reactions, emotions, and experiences that I might have omitted had I struggled on my own.

In the end, we wrote my life story and I am proud of our book. Two strangers met over lunch, two strangers decided to undertake a journey into the unknown. Could we really write a book together? Neither of us believed we'd get this far and have so much fun. It's taken us two years. My story is told and I have made a friend for life. Not a bad accomplishment for a scrawny little French - English man in his mid-eighties.

Can any man tell a complete story of his life? Writing an autobiography is hard work. Events trigger memories and memories often made me ask questions about myself that were often difficult to answer. Why have I always been so hardheaded and persistent? Were those traits in my genes or did Fate intervene and have a hand in making me the man I am today? When you are orphaned at any early age, when you spend six years at war, watch a marriage fail, go to Africa and build a business, raise a son, when you succeed despite the odds, you begin to wonder: "Why have I made it when others failed?" Answers to those questions were not easy and they took time. Writing reminded me that I have roamed the world and explored the deepest reaches of my mind and soul. I have laughed and cried, cursed and cajoled, been wildly optimistic and savagely depressed, made money only to lose it and make it again, made friends and seen some of them killed. I loved and lost and loved again.

My autobiography is by no means complete. Some omissions are unintended lapses in my ability to recollect but others are intentional. Out of deference to the living, sometimes I have changed family names in order to protect their identities. I wrote honestly and candidly and, as far as I can remember, accurately. Despite weeks trying to root them out, there are probably some errors of fact and syntax still buried in the text. I accept responsibility for them; they are unintentional and I hope they do not offend the reader.

To the best of my knowledge, there are no distortions. I have written neither to harm nor hurt anyone or settle any scores. I wrote about events the way they happened to me. When my family reads this in its entirety they will have questions and hopefully I will have answers.

My story begins in France soon after the end of the Great War.

John Powell   Rene Dassac
Callian, France 2006

CHAPTER ONE: EARLY YEARS

Tarascon, where I was born in 1922, is a sleepy farming town in the south of France. It was, and still is, a bump in the road midway between Avignon and Arles. Even then there was nothing noteworthy about Tarascon. For centuries its economy depended on vineyards, fruit and vegetable cultivation. Farmers knew their land and loved it. Most farms were passed from father to son for generations. Life was so dependable that you could almost set your watch on when the seasons and crops would change. Every year the Rhone flooded some of the adjacent farmland. Flooding was part of the life cycle. Some years it was worse than others but everyone accepted the mighty Rhone had its own mind.

Villagers stayed close to their land, played cards on the main square, and watched the sky to predict when the weather would change. The Mistral, blowing furnace hot in summer and bitterly cold in winter, pounded the wooden shutters and the walls of the solid stone houses. Few villagers ever ventured down river as far as the Mediterranean Sea. The Camargue was a foreign land for most of them. Tarascon was a world unto itself.

There are no great historical or architectural monuments in Tarascon but there is a chateau, le chateau du roi Rene. Since there were no Renes in either my father or mother's families, I guess my father named me after the chateau when I was born on 4 April 1922, the third in line in a family that would eventually include five children. Following custom, and in recognition of my father who was a local notable, the church bells were rung to celebrate my arrival.

It was at Sainte Marthe with its thundering bells where my sisters, older brother and I went to mass every Sunday whether we wanted to or not. In the summer the days were hot and humid because the Rhone flowed through town. Inside the church there was some relief from the heat but cooling off inside meant having to sit through services that, for me at least, seemed like they were droning on forever. Time stopped when I went to church. As a kid I wanted to stay outside and play but attending church every Sunday was a ritual that I could not escape no matter how hard I tried. My parents were practicing Catholics and our family had been in southern France for centuries.

Until my parents died life was uneventful and happy. When I was born my family still had some of the fortune my father inherited from his parents. I'm not sure, in money terms how big it was, but it was enough to keep the family fed and properly housed. We lived in a large stone house at the edge of town. The back of the house opened onto a field where there were a couple of horses my parents used to ride on outings with their friends. They weren't grand fancy horses but big solid animals strong enough to carry both of them riding bareback.

A photo of them riding together on their favorite horse hangs at the end of our bedroom corridor and I pass them many times a day. The photo was taken before the war. Father is wearing a suit, collar, tie and bowler hat; mother is wearing a full dress with just a bit of white petticoat showing above her high black lace boots. My father, Pierre, holds the reins in a manner typical of a man who raised with horses. Marguerite, my mother, looks as if she wants to burst out laughing but photographers in those days did not approve of their subjects smiling, especially a fine couple on a good horse. But I can hear her laughter and smell my father's warmth.

Father was always well dressed. His boots were shined, his collar starched, and his suits looked as if their creases had been designed into the tailoring. Nothing fancy, but he dressed in a manner consistent with being the son of wealthy landowners. The farmer landowner class was a social milieu in rural France situated above the average peasant farmer and distinct from the urban middle class. When I look at a photo of him on horseback he still radiates a sense of quiet purpose and determination, staring into the photographer's camera as if daring him to trip the lens. I am not sure whose side of the family they came from but somewhere along the line he inherited a pair of arresting steel blue eyes. When I was acting up he brought me back into line with only a quick riveting glance. His eyes spoke volumes and I usually got his message without him raising his voice. It was the fashion in those days for men to part their hair down the middle and comb it back. He was fashionable and handsome: clean parted wavy auburn hair, a dark moustache and a square jaw. He had fine hands, almost as graceful as a piano player's but he didn't play. Sometime in the few short years we shared, I think he must have laughed but I can't remember anything like hilarity erupting from him. He wasn't glum by nature but when I was born, nearly four years after the end of World War I, he was very sick.

While we were living in Tarascon my father spent a lot of time on the large farms he owned in Boulbon and Beaucaire. Unfortunately, the riverbanks adjacent to the land were low and in a poor state of repair. In the post World War I years when the national budget was coping with the after effects of the war there weren't enough public funds to spend shoring up riverbanks. For as many centuries as man farmed next to the Rhone, flooding was a recognized danger. Father's lands were spared most of the time but in the early 1920's his riverbanks were weak and vulnerable. Most of the male population had been away at war and there weren't enough able bodied men left in the villages and towns to maintain the riverbanks. Inevitably, at a time when he couldn't afford repairs, the Rhone repeatedly burst its banks and flooded his farms. The first big flood was bad but he somehow managed to drain the land and keep farming. The second flood was devastating. On paper he was wealthy but in real terms, in cold hard cash, he didn't have enough money to repair the riverbanks and pay off all the loans he had taken to finance his crops. Bowing to the inevitable, after the second flood he sold the farms and we moved to Nimes in 1926 where I went to school for the first time.

In our new home there was the usual squabbling among the kids, going to school and running errands. Mother made sure we were fed and not too much under foot. By local standards we were an average size family. There were two boys: Jean was six years older than me. He was the oldest child, a sister Genevieve was born between us in

Rene Dassac (in collaboration with Patrick K. Robbins)

1918 and two sisters, Paulette (1923) and Juliette (1928), were born after me.

Mother came from a well-established vineyard and wine making family in Macon. She was a petite brunette, with fine features and very pretty. Perhaps I am idealizing, but her face reminded me of a cameo painting. She was serene and gentle but she was also strong enough to keep her brood in line.

Characteristic of their generation and class, my parents raised us in what would now be called a 'strict household.' Lunch was the big meal of the day. In addition to our seven family members, there were occasional guests. We sat at a rectangular table. My parents sat on one side; the children were distributed on the other three sides. I think Jean and Genevieve were each given a side because they were older. The three squirming young ones were parked opposite our parents. Meals were traditional. In the winter we began with soup, followed by meat and vegetables, cheese and a sweet. When summer came mother replaced the soup course with a huge platter of fresh vegetables and vinaigrette. Sometimes there was fresh fruit instead of a dessert.

As far as the children were concerned, when we went to the table we were expected to eat and behave. Conversation was reserved for the adults; children listened. When the meal was finished we were allowed to speak but not before. As long as food was on the table the children's purpose in life was clear: eat and be quiet. From today's perspective that may seem awfully strict but when I look back on those meals I realize there was great comfort and security living with that kind of routine. I don't think I felt oppressed. All my friends and their families ate their meals just like us.

Being a child I was bound to test the limits of proper behavior and get into trouble. One time at lunch I had been thinking a lot about some of the mysteries of nature and I blurted out, "Where do babies come from?" My father was furious. I guess I was about seven or eight at the time and I was beginning to ask questions. Silence, leaden silence fell across the table. My brothers and sisters stared at their plates; I was sent upstairs. As I was leaving the dining room I heard my mother admonish my father, "He's just a little boy." Later, while I was sitting on the edge of my bed staring out the window trying to understand what had made him so angry, I heard my father come in. He sat down next to me, cleared his throat, and apologized. I can't remember the exact details of what he said but I felt better knowing that, as he put it, "one day when you are grown up you will understand." Of course his answer only made me want to find out more but at least I knew that I was not to bring up that topic again in his presence.

*****

By the time I turned twelve we were orphans; both my parents were dead. My father died first in 1931. I guess you could call it a miracle that he lasted as long as he did. Like so many men his age, he was an infantryman in World War I. When he returned home in 1918 he was a broken and sick thirty-five year old. He was gassed in Flanders and he contracted malaria in the Dardanelles. Although he was a physical wreck, often coughing huge gobs of phlegm from his rotten lungs, he refused to sit quietly by the fire waiting for death. No, he had seen so much in the trenches that he returned with a great urge to live his remaining days to the fullest. He wasn't silly; he knew that his years were numbered.

When we moved to Nimes we were nearer the military hospital and father made friends with another veteran who was also in bad shape. He called his friend, Monsieur Trompe la Mort. Together, they wheezed their way to the military clinic for their weekly check ups. For a couple of years he tried to augment his meager disability pension by working as a traveling salesman. He sold wool and cotton yard goods to customers located between Nimes and Montpellier. It didn't bring in much money but at least it gave him the semblance of a 'normal' life.

He tried not to miss the well-known bullfighters during the corrida season. Once he took my mother to a special fight. She was dressed to the nines and even an old man with poor eyesight could see that she was a beautiful woman. Defending his beautiful wife almost landed my father in jail. A policeman took a fancy to her and pinched her behind. She let out a yelp and my father turned on the cop and threatened to smash him into little pieces. Fortunately cooler heads in the crowd managed to separate the two men before any damage was

Rene Dassac (in collaboration with Patrick K. Robbins)

done. My father's honor was preserved; I bet my mother was secretly rather proud of him.

In the village there were other men his age and in a physical and mental condition similar to his. They met to play cards and while away the hours, drink a little wine and reminisce. No medicine could cure them; their time was running out. Years in the trenches had taken their toll. After the war they were not going to get better. They died slowly and each often left a sad story.

There was a retired colonel living close to our house. Some of his children went to the same school with us. One day I heard my brother ask my father, "Why does the colonel drink so much. Is he an alcoholic?" My father waited a few moments before replying. When he began it was as if floodgates in his mind, firmly shut for years, suddenly burst open. "The war made them drunkards," he began. Trench warfare was more awful than he could bear to describe but he tried. Killing wasn't done at long distance. Sure, there were times the allies let loose artillery barrages but when they lifted, and even sometimes under a barrage, you had to move forward and bayonet men who rose out of the mud to shoot or bayonet you. It wasn't always the case, but father explained one of the ways officers and men managed to strengthen their resolve before an assault was to drink heavily. Trench life demanded an animal like instinct for survival. Staying alive was a struggle that took its toll. Alcohol, exhaustion, damp stinking uniforms, rotting feet, bad food and diarrhea were realities from which there was no escape.

Day after day, often on the verge of madness, sometimes even toppling into insanity, many men drank and drank and drank. When the Armistice was declared they took their broken bodies home but they didn't leave the horror of the trenches behind in Flanders. It went with them, an invisible wound eating into their souls. Too sick to work, they gambled, talked and coughed, and shuffled their well-worn deck of cards. Small wagers led to bigger bets. Not everyone could win. Inevitably my father's losses ate into the family fortune. By the time he died in 1931`my parents assets, all the land and property that had been left to him by my grandfather, had been sold to pay off his debts. In the end, it was malaria eating into my father's skinny frame that proved too much for his doctors.

The family sank deeper into debt until we were broke. I don't begrudge him for what he did. In my own time I would learn that war changes men in many ways. It's not only the body that changes. Something inside, maybe it's what philosophers call the "Spirit", that changes. When you survive a war you are not the same person you were before the war. So it was with my father. The Great War was over but the battle inside my father lasted for nearly two decades before he wasted away. Only once or twice do I remember him telling me something about the war without being prodded. Even then, if he chose, he would deflect the question onto another topic and I was wise enough not to pester him.

One memory is still vivid. He was walking me to school, holding my hand and listening to me chirp. A Zeppelin flew over us. I heard the noise and saw it cast its long shadow down our street. My father's head snapped back and he stared into the sky. His body was shaking but it wasn't from any tremors I had learned to recognize. This time it was different and he almost swayed when he blurted, "It's the Boche again! Look at them. They'll be back in France. I promise you!" I had rarely seen him so angry. I stared into the sky until the great gray cigar droned out of sight. He was right on both counts. It was the Germans and they would be back but he would be long dead.

He didn't die suddenly. While he weakened on his way to death, the entire burden of raising his young children fell to my mother. My most vivid memories of my mother during that period are those of a quiet woman, very gentle, someone who did not complain, a woman with great patience. I guess she must have been upset with my father. She married a wealthy man who became poor in a few short years. But, as he withered into death, I cannot recall her raising her voice at him. Even now I think she understood her husband's need to struggle, in his own destructive way, against his constant pain and despair.

*****

While I was still quite small it was becoming obvious to other adults in the family that our family could not live together on my father's meager veteran's pension. He stopped working; there was no more land to sell. Five growing children had to be fed and cared for and there was not enough money. Before my father died, in the depths of the Depression, my mother and aunts and uncles took the only decision that they could: we were farmed out to live with relatives.

My sister Paulette and I were sent to live with one of my father's sisters, tante Francoise. She was a widow but her nineteen-year-old son Henri was still home. Her husband had been general manager of the Banque de France in Ales where they lived in a lovely large apartment above the bank. The bank was downtown; the front windows of the apartment overlooked the main square. I'm not sure how she was lucky enough to continue living there after her husband's death, maybe the apartment belonged to them instead of the bank, but one thing I am certain about: she left the house exactly the way it was the day he died. He collected swords, sabers, rifles, muskets, bayonets and helmets beginning with the Napoleonic era. One entire wall of the living room was covered with his fine collection. There were a couple of pieces of armor and various helmets including a German helmet with a huge spike in the middle and a French cavalry helmet with a lovely red brush.

I had my own bedroom with a high ceiling and a big heavy walnut armoire for me to hang my clothing in. The armoire was handy but at night it creaked and groaned, as if it were alive and stretching before pouncing on me. My imagination never allowed me to completely trust it. I was convinced that if it ever broke loose from its moorings and fell on me it would take four men to lift it off me and by the time they got it off I would be dead.

Life had the potential for being quite pleasant with my aunt but there was a problem. She wanted me to become a priest. Following her conviction that I would make a splendid cure, she sent me to a parochial preparatory school. The teaching brothers quickly got into my preparation for the cloth. Almost before I sat down at my desk they had me learning Latin and Greek. I had other ideas about what I wanted to do.

I ran away from the seminary three times before she finally understood that I was not going to become a priest. For starters, priests didn't run around in armor, brandish swords, shoulder muskets and shoot people. Instead of Latin verbs sailing through my mind, my thoughts drifted to that magical wall in her living room. For me dreaming of using weapons was much more exciting than learning, "Watch out for the dog" in Latin. My aunt didn't mind when I played with some of the old muskets and I even managed to put on a metal breastplate. My skinny arms stuck out the huge arm openings like twigs stuck into the bottom of a rainspout. Of course the helmets were too large but I found one that I liked. It was silver with a large brass strip down the middle with a place for a huge red plume.

Later, when I returned to Nimes, our house which was known as the 'Villa des 3 Ponts on the Route d'Uzes, was on the road used by the artillery corps when they hauled their cannons out to the firing range. Whenever I heard the horses straining to pull the caissons up our road I would rush out the front door and stand to attention. There I was: a skinny little kid wearing a breastplate that came almost to his knees, a helmet that I could barely see out of and two thin arms holding a small musket to attention. The horsemen would snap me a salute. That made my day. Was it about then that I started to feel a pull toward a military life?

Without a doubt, my forays into and out of the seminary, meant life with my aunt was strained. I was unhappy. I missed my other sisters and brother and my parents. I knew father was not getting any better. Time wasn't on his side. Every few days my mother would send me a letter or a small parcel with some chocolate bars. Inside each bar there was a picture of a famous French warship. Sometimes they were sailing vessels but the pictures that really appealed to me were the World War I ships: dreadnaughts, destroyers, cruisers, ships bigger than I could imagine. For that matter, I couldn't imagine the ocean because I was born inland and there was no reason for me to go out to the coast.

Other than the occasional brief chance to play soldier, life was pretty grim. Lunch never varied because, according to Aunt Francoise, Paulette and I needed to be fattened up. Every day she bought a scrawny piece of beef, cooked it into steel-like peg and clunked it down on our plates. We were allowed to leave the table only after when we finished the meat. Paulette, although younger than me, quickly learned how to chew the meat into a small wad, cover her mouth and spit it into her cupped hand. Very carefully, so as not to arouse my aunt's attention, Paulette wedged the meat under the edge of the table. After lunch when we had the run of the house, she sneaked into the dining room, scraped off her stash, and flushed it down the loo. I wasn't as quick as my sister; I chewed every miserable bite into a mush and washed it down with lots of water. To this day I am a bit nervous when I'm served a thin well-cooked steak. Some childhood experiences become lessons lasting a lifetime.

I was homesick; I wanted my mother. Tension between my aunt and me was so thick that I thought it was a way of life. Nothing I did was 'right' and the list of things that I did wrong was too long for me to remember so I kept making the same irritating mistakes over and over again. Fortunately, Henri was an understanding lad and I found myself opening up to him. Somehow he had survived her good intentions; maybe I could too. Could he give me a few tips? All he managed to do was hug me and assure me that even though she was a pain in the backside, she wasn't nasty. That was a heady statement of philosophy and it probably whistled right over my head. All I remembered was the pain part.

Although I was under my aunt's roof, mother was still the center of my life. I knew she was 'there' but I also knew that she had no time to care for her children. All her waking hours were taken up with caring for my father who grew thinner and coughed more. One day at lunch, it was sometime in 1931, my aunt answered the phone and came back into the dining room where we had been eating our lunch. "Your father is dead," she stated coldly. She didn't try to wrap me up in her apron, sit me on her knee, and break the news to me gently. It was the same tone of voice she used when she reminded me to close the front door, clean off my shoes, go to bed, sit up straight, and wipe my mouth. I exploded with grief. In my rage I grabbed my knife and sank it into the table, shouting and crying.

Despite my pleas and tears, I was not allowed to go to my father's funeral. After all, funerals were not for children. I tried to remember the last time I saw him, what he looked like, where he was sitting, but my mind was whirling and all I could think of was going home to mother.

At his funeral there was another meeting of the family members who had been looking after us. My mother wanted us back and we wanted to return. It was not a question about her children being ungrateful where we had been sent because I think we probably understood and accepted why we had been farmed out. Mother's wanting us back was more of a need to rally us and come under one roof so we could face an uncertain future together as best we could. I didn't begrudge my aunt; she meant well, but she wasn't my mother.

Soon after father's funeral we went home again. At least, his death at age forty-eight wasn't a total loss: what was left of the family was back together. After the first couple of weeks when everything was still new, we settled into a routine but I couldn't fail to recognize that mother was sick. Someone told me she was suffering from cancer but that meant nothing to me. I was ten years old.

With no money to pay for my education, my sisters and I became 'Pupilles de la Nation'. This meant that, for the purposes of education, we were wards of the state. The Pupils program was established at the end of the war to help families where men could no longer work and pay for their children's education. All my education fees were paid for by the state, a welcome relief because mother barely survived on her meager widow's pension. There was no money left for our education.

What little fortune my father had owned was long gone. Later, I found out that even my mother's jewelry had to be sold. Stoic as ever, mother refused to complain but, after a couple of months, I suspected that something was seriously wrong but I was too young to understand the gravity of the situation. And, that was a time when, in old conservative families, children were not really kept informed about what was going on in the family. Today children are handled differently. Then, it was normal for parents to draw down a curtain between themselves and their children.

Old enough to know something was wrong, too young to understand, I went through the daily motions of trying to survive as best as I could. Often I would sit on the floor and lean my head on mother's knees. Together we would recite poems written by Victor Hugo. His famous "Waterloo" was our favorite. She would stroke my head making me promise, "Never to gamble." I did not know what she meant. It was just another big word but I solemnly gave her my word that I would not gamble. All my life I have kept that promise.

Mother became sicker and she was tired all the time. She had a breast removed. After the operation she looked normal but soon the cancer returned. This time we could see it. A tumor appeared at her temple, at first no bigger than a bad bump but it grew and grew. Her doctors had few options and surgery wasn't one of them. The doctors used heavy radiation to fry it into submission. Their treatment scarred her beautiful face and partially paralyzed some of her facial muscles. Toward the end, when she spoke to us she turned her head so that all we could see was the good side of her face.

She was going down hill; the doctor came often, cleaned her bulging tumor and gave her injections. She spent more and more time in bed. One day, perhaps eighteen months after father died, I answered the doorbell. It was the postman. He had a registered letter that my mother needed to sign for. She was in bed and I called out to her. She did not answer. Frightened, I raced into her room yelling, "Wake up!" My sister began screaming and the postman rushed into mother's room behind us.

Mother was dead, propped up in bed, her head tilted to the side as if she had just nodded off for a moment. The postman ran out and called the neighbors.

*****

The next few days were a blur. Friends and family filled the house. I don't mean it to sound callous, but in the first couple of days it seemed as if my parent's children were getting in the way of all the grieving adults. They had their emotions to deal with but we knew that death robbed us of the one person who had managed to hold our family together. In financial terms we were poor. No one could dispute that. But we were rich beyond belief because my mother made sure her children were given her unending love. Adored and loved almost to the point of veneration, for a long time after her death I often caught myself talking to her.

For as long as I can remember her empty armchair, where we had spent so many quiet and gentle hours, wasn't really empty. It just seemed that way. I could see her and if I tried very hard, I could still smell her serenity that had rubbed off onto the upholstery. Sometimes I whispered or talked to myself in the quiet of my mind, a very private space where nobody could come. Sometimes I would even steal away to talk aloud to her when no one could hear and maybe think I was crazy. As usual in a family, my sisters and I quarreled and I couldn't turn to them for help. My older brother Jean was a conscript in the army and I rarely saw him. Years after her death he and I would be reunited but by then we were both men.

When my mother died I was just a kid, lonely and very sad. Perhaps it was because of those days when I was so alone, days when I was forced to rely on no one but myself, I began developing a character trait that would mature quickly in the coming years. When I could not reach out to someone and get help, instead of sitting and moping, I began learning how to rely upon myself. "What can I do?" was the question that started nagging at me instead of "What is someone going to do for me?" Maybe modern child psychologists have a theory but for me, self-reliance was another form of survival.

The changes in me were too profound for me to understand what was going on inside my little head. I didn't know that I was learning to cope with adversity. Little by little, I was turning into a survivor. Mother's death and the loss of our family life, as pitiful as it was, began breeding a fiercely independent spirit in me. What happened was too much for me to understand; mother was living one minute and dead the next. I didn't have a chance to say good-bye. It was too much for a little kid. I couldn't understand a lot of what was happening but I did know that I was lost, an orphan, just when the world was starting to rush into another war just like the one that ruined my father. It was 1933 and I was barely eleven years old.

Distant family met to decide what to do with my sisters and me. Of course I was too young to participate in the meeting but Jean was old enough to be involved. It was from him that I learned my sisters and I had barely escaped being sent to an orphanage. My father's oldest brother, Francois, was a notaire in Avignon. He looked at the world differently than the rest of the family. For him what happened to us was a question of numbers and facts.

The fact of the matter was clear for all to see: no one family had the money and the space to feed, school and house, four children. According to him, we were better off in a state run institution. There the government would provide food, clothing, housing and education.

Rene Dassac (in collaboration with Patrick K. Robbins)

In the beginning no one wanted to talk about love and family life. Those were intangibles; we were very real hungry little problems that needed solutions.

Fortunately, my mother's brother Joseph, who owned a vineyard in Macon, took up our cause and argued that we should be placed with different family members who were able to handle a couple of kids at a time. It was a good idea but he and his wife weren't candidates. Unfortunately, his wife was sort of nuts and they already had two children. But, the idea took hold and we four children were sent to live with different aunts and uncles. Genevieve went to one of my mother's cousins who was a well-known barrister in Ales. After much huffing and puffing, my mother's brother who lived in Lyon, took charge of my two younger sisters and me.

Uncle Gaby was a gentleman, a retired banker, someone respected in the local community. He wore a beard to hide a huge goiter that occasionally poked out of his whiskers and frightened me until I learned to live with it. Uncle Gaby was a widower who lived alone and his lifestyle was not the kind of family environment three little kids needed. Being a widower without a live-in housekeeper meant we lost even the remotest chance to have a woman act like a stepmother. Sadly, his wife died giving birth to their only child, a son four years older than me. Gaby was a well-meaning man but he was bitter about how Fate had dealt him a double blow. First, he lost his wife when their son was born and second, early into a rather comfortable retirement, he was saddled with having to raise three orphans.

I remember him as a good man, courageous to accept the challenge of raising his sister's children, but a man who really didn't know how to relate to three youngsters. There is no doubt in my mind that he assumed his responsibility with considerable misgivings. Although his retirement was comfortable and he had a good position in local society, he was not wealthy. He had enough money to enjoy the fruits of his labors but not enough to afford the additional cost his sister's children represented. Furthermore, educating us was demanding both in terms of time and money. State funding only went so far and we were a financial burden. And his patience had limits that we tested daily.

Because of what I had already gone through in my short eleven years I found that I had become an unusually sensitive boy, a kid who was quickly aware of other's feelings. Sometimes in my uncle I detected what I could only describe to myself as his heavy sense of sacrifice and despair. Sacrifice because the unplanned arrival of three children was too much to handle and despair at the thought of having to shoulder so much responsibility alone. When we were naughty, or more correctly, when I was naughty, he let me know in no uncertain terms that he was 'sacrificing' the best years of his life for me.

I suppose his reaction was normal, an explosion resulting from venting frustration that is the natural by-product of raising children. I couldn't understand it but I was savvy enough to feel my uncle's anguish. Rather soon after we arrived, I concluded that I did not like living with him. That realization didn't drop out of the sky as a crystal clear revelation on one rainy afternoon. It grew out of my torment.

My mind turned into a whirlpool of conflicting emotions that I tried to hide. I was reasonably successful but I kept thinking, "If we are burdens, if this is too much for him, what's going to become of us?" Confused and unhappy I had no one to turn to, absolutely no one to confide in, no one but myself.

No matter how I looked at the prospect of living with him, it simply was not going to work out, I told myself. Slowly at first, but when the idea caught on inside me, I started to think more clearly. "I want out," I kept repeating to myself, my own private chant that echoed through the reaches of my mind, my own private world.

With hindsight I now realize that he was trying to do as best as he could but at the time, I didn't have the maturity to give him the benefit of the doubt. He placed my two sisters in a girl's convent school and I went to a boarding school in Pont de Vaux, about thirty miles from Lyons. My sisters and I saw each other during the school holidays.

I was fairly happy in boarding school. It was a mixed school and I soon became quite attracted to a girl about three years older than me. She started asking me questions about myself. Imagine, a pretty girl interested in me? She must have been sixteen or seventeen and I was barely thirteen, a skinny little runt. She was beautiful: red cheeks, light brunette hair, a big smile and the button holes on her school blouse seemed to strain, or was that just my lusty little imagination?

Whenever we shared classes I made sure that we sat next to each other and we spent many breaks together. I'm sure from her side it was merely an early manifestation of maternal feelings but I was head-over-heels in love. Trying to handle love and academics is a heavy task. My grades started suffering. Uncle Gaby became concerned. I wasn't dumb and I hadn't got into trouble at school. Something was wrong. To be on the safe side, he took me out of Pont de Vaux and put me in a Catholic boarding school closer to Lyons so that I could spend weekends at home and he could keep a closer eye on me. In the new school I soon let it be known that I was not going to become a priest; a clear line was drawn but I was still not a happy student who got good grades.

I was down in the dumps because of what happened to my love life. His choice of new schools was putting a severe strain on my relations with my beloved Mireille. I know it sounds quaint in this era of e-mail instant communication but in order to stay in touch with her I resorted to the only method I knew that I could afford. It was a method that I figured was absolutely foolproof: We began writing letters. At least I thought it was foolproof. Uncle Gaby had his eyes on me and I had to be careful. I told Mireille to address all her mail to my cousin Raymond, Uncle Gaby's son. In turn, Raymond would give me my envelopes unopened. It was, at least so I thought, a perfect system.

Uncle Gaby's life in rural banking had taught him to be observant. In his mind, "things have to add up." One day the postman pushed the mail through the door slot and rang the bell to let my uncle know that the day's delivery had been made. I was away at school. My uncle looked at the letters and saw one with an unusual post office address: Pont de Vaux. Tiens? Raymond doesn't know anyone there, he thought. Should I be aware of something? He opened Mirielle's letter and read it. I am sure he must have had a good laugh at her innocent profession of love and adoration but he jumped to a simple conclusion: our relationship had to be stopped. I'm not sure what lusty thoughts romped through his mind but he quickly concluded that it was not healthy for a young boy to be so involved at such a young age! And to think, he didn't even know the girl or her family! How dare she seduce his little nephew?

As usual, I came home for the weekend. As soon as my cousin saw me walk through the front door he doubled over with laughter. I glanced into the long mirror hanging in the hall. Nothing was out of place; the front of my pants was buttoned shut. "What's so funny," I asked. He kept laughing but he wouldn't tell me that he knew what was going to happen next. "You'll find out," he gasped. "Wait till papa gets a hold of you." I knew my uncle had a temper; I had provoked it so many times I could almost recite from heart what he was going to say. He may have been old, but when he got it into his head that he was right and I was wrong, all hell broke loose. My cousin stopped laughing when he heard his father thundering down the corridor.

The old man barreled into the living room where we were standing, shaking my letter in the air and began bellowing, "Are you not ashamed of yourself?" I was speechless but he had had a week to work up a head of steam. After seven days, I thought I could see vapors shooting out of his ears. Oh, oh, I didn't like watching my uncle erupting in front of me. My survival in the household, at least for the time being, was at stake. "Is this all the thanks I've got for all the sacrifices I've made to give you a good education?"

If my letter had wings it should have taken off to escape his fist. He stopped bellowing but he was still waving my love's precious words in front of us as if her letter were some kind of a shield that he had to raise to fend off anything I might say or do. Without warning he slapped me hard on the face and then began tearing Mireille's letter into little pieces. He cupped them in one hand, strode into the kitchen, and dumped them into the waste bin. My gentle and carefully nurtured love life soaked up oil from left over lunch scraps.

To this day I don't know what happened to Mireille. In my mind she is always a lovely young girl. But, after that incident, I knew something had to happen to me. I needed to get out of my uncle's house. To his credit, I knew deep inside that he was well meaning but the situation was getting ugly. I was mature enough to know that I wasn't prepared to put up with his heavy-handed attacks on my private life. Not that I had many secrets but what few I had I wanted to keep.

My survival instinct kicked in and I began thinking of what I had to do to protect myself. I kept my head down that weekend but that was the weekend when I began plotting another life. It wasn't clear, but after our blow-up I really started listening to the little voice inside me. His stinging slap across my face succeeded in one thing: it focused my thoughts.

On another occasion we got into an argument and he exploded. "My god, after all the sacrifices I've made for you," and he paused to catch his breath for another volley, "and, you do this." It was another one of "those" incidents, little things that I succeeded in doing, little things that really irritated him. To this day I cannot remember what I had done to provoke him but looking back at that incident, that silly argument, his outburst became another turning point in my life.

I quit making excuses and I backed away so we wouldn't start quarreling. Quietly, I told myself, "That's it. I want a life where I owe no one anything." Deep down I knew what I wanted in life: an education, my independence, and the chance to be responsible for my future. To be on my own became my commitment to myself. Funny, seventy years later, I am still my own man and I have had a hard but a good life.

After much quiet reflection, and perhaps "talking" to mother, I decided that, come what may, I was going to leave my uncle's house. It wasn't a question of packing a suitcase and running away in the middle of the night. That was too easy and quite foolish. I was honest with myself and could admit that my uncle was trying to make our relationship work. He really was trying to do the right thing, but the fit between the two of us was never going to work as long as I was in his custody.

More time wasn't the answer; I knew that no matter how much time I gave us, living with him wouldn't work. In my own very simple way I arrived at a huge conclusion. Because I had lost everything, I had to look out for myself. If I accepted responsibility for myself, that meant I couldn't depend on someone who didn't want me. Uncle Gaby wasn't mean. Maybe he was too heavy handed but his heart was in the right place. He was genuinely concerned about our future but having the responsibility for three kids was too much for him to handle.

During a holiday when I was home from school I went to the gendarmerie and asked for the application papers to become a Pupille de la Marine. The application was long but not too complicated; even I could understand how to fill-in the blanks. By that time I had earned my primary school certificate and I could read and write. Completing the form was the easy part. The hard part involved my uncle: he had to sign the application because he was my legal guardian.

Slowly I began preparing the groundwork to launch my scheme. Time dragged and it took a lot of effort to stay focused and wait for the right moment. Thousands of times I had to remind myself: "You have a plan and you must follow it carefully." One day I caught him in a good mood. "Uncle Gaby," I began with a calm and matter-of-fact voice, "Would you please arrange to send me to naval school?" I handed him the application form that I had partially filled-in with a pencil. I had rehearsed the scene many times in my mind. I was convinced that I was right in asking him to send me away. When I began speaking I knew there was no turning back. Like a hunter who has fired both barrels of his shotgun, I knew that I could never put my words back inside my head and zip my lips shut.

He stared at the papers, then up at me, and back to the application, stunned. For a moment he didn't know how to reply to my request because it hit him with no forewarning. Right out of the blue I asked him a huge question. I watched him carefully and recognized his reactions. He was taking time to think. Softly, he ran his hand over his beard, stroking it down to hide his goiter. "Why the navy and not something else," he asked me. I wasn't prepared for an interrogation; I really didn't have a straight answer for him. But I didn't give in and I must admit, it was a good question. His years as a canny old banker had taught him to ask hard and penetrating questions and now my request was being examined with the same detail he must have devoted to a balance sheet or a loan proposal.

To be truthful, I didn't have a clear and crisp answer. Probably the idea of going into the navy had been planted years before when I remembered hearing my father tell stories about the horrors of living in Flanders' mud with lice and rats, wet through to the bone and cold for days and days. Maybe he and his mates were jealous of the sailors and their good life. Or, maybe it was mother's influence when she sent me the chocolate bars with the navy ships. Being on deck with sea spray washing my face was a damned sight better than conjugating verbs in a language only priests spoke. Or, maybe what motivated my choice was more mundane. The difference between the navy and the army, at least the way I understood it was: in the navy you had three meals, a bed, and a roof over your head. Life was regimented. Boundaries were clearly defined. You knew what was expected of you and you knew what you had to do. As a skinny teenager, that's all I wanted.

Even after all these years I am sure that I wasn't thinking of anything grandiose like becoming an officer and parading about with a sword or a swagger stick. My thoughts were simple and straightforward: With a naval education I would have a career and with a career I would not have to owe anyone anything. I would be my own master. No one would open my letters.

I was probably just thirteen when I made my first request but I stuck with it. Without telling him, I would whisper to my mother, what I really wanted: get out from under his roof. I knew I was running from a 'something' that was fairly well defined in my head toward a 'something' that was probably a pipedream but at least it was my dream. Slowly, direction was coming into my life.

At first uncle Gaby tried to reason with me. I was too young, going to sea was a fantasy, wait and the idea would pass, and something better would come along. I listened quietly and thought about his counter arguments. A funny thing happened: the period leading up to my departure was probably one of the nicest times I spent with him. We shared a topic and most of the time when we discussed my project we managed to listen to each other.

He was persistent but after a few months I caught him returning to the same old arguments. His intractable position was also a measure of my success. Since there was nothing new on his side, I took that to mean that I was wearing him down. At the end of each session I repeated my intention to go to school in Brest. In the end my stubbornness finally won him over and in 1936 I went to Brest.

CHAPTER TWO:
APPRENTICE SEAMAN

We took the night train from Lyon to Brest, lurching across the heartland of France. All night I stared into the dark. Little villages, some with only their street lights on, blurred into the wet night. Rain lashed the carriage window as we approached the coast. Soon after dawn broke I could see the sky as we approached Brest. It was gray; more bad weather was on the way. Steam billowed from behind the locomotive's pistons over the tracks and onto the concourse. I followed my uncle down the quay through the sullen station. Looking around at all the sleepy faces, I had the funny feeling that Uncle Gaby and I were the only people awake.

Outside the station we found a café and ordered breakfast. The cafe was one of those non-descript places that spring up around train stations anywhere in Europe. A large zinc counter ran down most of one wall. Two men, one big and burly and the other thin and bald, worked the counter. It was filled with workers in faded blue denim jackets, gnarled tired men with red rimmed eyes and yellow teeth. I looked around and figured we were the only non-regulars. The air was thick with the smell of wet clothes, cheap tobacco, stale beer, and steaming bowls of chicory-café. We ordered and took our croissants and coffee to the end of the counter. I was the only kid in the place; we ate in silence not daring to look at each other, each lost in thoughts that we did not share until years later. I was in a hurry and I wanted to get the ordeal over with as quickly as possible.

My uncle got directions from the little man behind the counter and we set off for my school. I can still see us, a little boy carrying a small suitcase with shiny silver latches walking behind an old man with a bulging white beard. My uncle trudged ahead across town. His gait was heavy. It had been a long and uncomfortable trip squirming on the narrow wooden benches in our third class wagon. My joints ached but he was older and his real ache came from the constant battle waging between his mind and heart. His worst ache came from the relentless agony he put himself through in the weeks leading up to my departure: was he doing the right thing letting me go off to school? In his mind I was young and innocent. In my own mind, if I could have told him what I was thinking, I probably would have agreed with him, but I was not going to turn back.

His despair grew with each step. He kept shaking his head and muttering to himself. When we got closer to the barracks Uncle Gaby stopped. "Mon cher petit Rene, do you really want to go through with this? You can turn around and go home with me on the afternoon train." A fine rain was beginning to soak us. Rain beaded and fell from his hat brim onto his overcoat. "There's nothing to worry about. I'm happy and I'm going to make something out of my life." The old man grunted and shook his head. Little raindrops flew off the brim of his hat into the cold morning air. His head nodded up and down and then I knew he was finally resigned to the inevitable. In desperation he was probably asking the Lord, one last time, why had He given him, a retired and respectable former banker, such a headstrong nephew?

Years later when we could talk about that eventful morning, he told me that he tried to convince me to pursue a naval career but to start at the top, the officer class, instead of at the bottom as an ordinary seaman. His arguments fell on deaf ears. I had my heart set and nothing was going to dissuade me. We approached the barrack gates and passed the sentries. Outside the red brick walls was the civilian world to which he belonged. Inside was the navy where, for reasons I still don't know, I felt deep in my small bones that I belonged.

The duty officer of the cadet barracks shuffled through his files and found my name. "Dassac, Rene?" "Oui monsieur," I replied and handed him my papers. He stepped aside to let me say goodbye to my uncle. We hugged and he patted me on the head. I can't remember what we said or if we said anything at all. He trudged through the gate, his wet cuffs flapping above his wet shoes. Uncle Gaby paused at the sentry's post, waved, and began his slow trudge back to the station. I waved back, turned and walked through the big steel gates to begin my new life.

*****

The captain of the cadet barracks was a unique officer. He ran a boarding school for seaman cadets who were still children. We were kids who could not be treated like adults but in a very short period he had to turn the kids in his command into responsible seamen capable of handling adult responsibility. He had a challenging task, doubly difficult because he had to lead kids who were naturally inclined to be unruly and mischievous. After eighteen months, provided we passed all the exams and had not got into any serious trouble, we would leave his world of apprentice seamen and enter the adult world as able seamen, young professionals who could be relied upon by our shipmates and our officers. It was a huge transition for us to make. Not only were we leaving our childhood's behind us, we were being groomed for future roles that we were too young to understand when we signed up.

I was determined that I would make it through without too many problems. Discipline was firm and fair, which is what I expected, but discipline also took into account that the captain's crew were not young men but children enroute to adulthood. I adjusted to the routine because the kind of discipline the officers required was similar to what I had already learned at boarding school. Of course, even then there were moments when I got into trouble but somehow I managed to keep on the right side of my headmasters and at the same time play-off my uncle's attempts to keep me on a tight rein. Those survival skills helped me in the barracks.

I really enjoyed my new life. The cadet corps was organized into three companies and each company had four sections. There were one hundred and sixty boys per company, forty per section. We lived in a dormitory building that formed part of the barracks quadrangle. Each floor housed a company. Discipline was drilled into us but it was not beaten into us like what we heard happened in some foreign cadet schools.

Rene Dassac (in collaboration with Patrick K. Robbins)

Our officers, commissioned and non-commissioned, were chosen to serve in the barracks largely on the grounds that they had proven flexibility to work with youngsters. In my company our ages ran between fourteen and eighteen, difficult years for kids and hell for adults unless discipline was taught, practiced, and quickly accepted by each cadet. Rebellion against barrack life was a sure ticket out of the corps. Since we were all volunteers, there was little rebellion. In its place we began to nurture an intense pride in our country, pride in our company, and pride in ourselves.

On general inspection parade we were treated like men even though we were a bunch of gangly pimply faced lads. When we turned out in our full "number one" uniform every inch of our person was inspected by all the officers. Our hair could be no longer than three centimeters. Any button that could be polished had to shine, any piece of leather that was buffed had to shine, and our stiff leather boots with hob nails were shined so bright the sun bounced off them. No detail was overlooked and nothing could be hidden from our mentors. They were demanding; it was their duty to make sure that we learned to follow orders. When we were told to do something, it had to be done. Even if that meant polishing, scrubbing and mending parts of our uniforms no mortal, other than an officer, would ever see.

Being organized into companies did not mean we were left on our own. Each section had a leading seaman instructor. When we had problems he was the person we turned to. Most of the time he could handle our requests, but when he needed help he couldn't provide he bucked the request up through the ranks. What we were learning at this early stage in our naval careers was a vital lesson for life onboard: there are right ways and wrong ways to get things done. Obedience, respect for hierarchy, knowing how to live within the system, those were behaviors that had to be learned until they became second nature.

There was a navy way to get things done and nothing else was tolerated. We were taught that every request had a channel and if you stayed in channels, you'd get an answer. Maybe not as fast as you wanted, or maybe the response would not be what you wanted to hear, but someone would get you an answer. Working out of channels and trying to short circuit the system were punishable offenses. Later, once real life experience tempered the theories I learned in training, I caught on quickly to the real world: every formal system has an informal system. Depending on how you played the systems, you got results. But, that knowledge was a later stage by-product of growing up. In the barracks, I was just a kid learning the ropes and I couldn't imagine doing anything that might incur the wrath of my officers.

As far as I was concerned, life was just what I wanted it to be. There was a routine, I had responsibility, and I wore a uniform. Our day began with a bugle reveille call at 06:00. Right after reveille we made our narrow metal frame beds to naval standards. The sheets were tucked tight at the corners, so tight that on morning inspection a centime piece dropped on the bed had to bounce! Our regulation second blankets were folded and placed at the foot of the bed, properly centered. After making our bunks we raced into an ice cold shower where we lathered and rinsed and then lined up shivering in front of the duty officer for "little carrot" inspection. When I was at home I learned to wash behind my ears and between my toes; no one ever told me to pay attention to my carrot. Every morning it had to be lathered, rinsed and dried. Breakfast consisted of big bowls of café-au-lait and large chunks of white bread slathered with jam. After breakfast we lined up for formation in the courtyard.

The barracks were built in the form of a quadrangle. Standing with the main gate to our backs, we faced the west side of the quad. A tall mast rose in front of the west building. We stood to attention as the school band played the "raising of the colors." As the tricolor was slowly hoisted in place we took off our caps when the order was given, "Attention pour les couleurs.". I can still hear the band wheezing and banging in the cold wet morning chill. I was proud of "La France," my France.

Joking aside, the school band played well. Most of the band members were Alsatians who had learned to play their brass instruments in their native villages. Forget the fact that they were kids because most people shudder when they hear student brass bands. Those guys were true Alsatians and that meant playing drums and brass horns was second nature to them; they were really good and they rarely hit a sour note. Their enthusiasm was so contagious that the first time I heard them I secretly wished that I could play something. Not too long thereafter, I was given the opportunity to learn to play the bugle.

After the flag raising ceremony we were dismissed to attend our academic classes. School lasted until noon break and lunch. Most conscripts complain about military food but we had good cooks and we ate well. My favorite dish was crabs served with mayonnaise or vinaigrette, followed by cheese and a dessert. Each cadet was issued a quarter liter of red wine, "one per man." After lunch we were given about an hour 'free time' and then we had more academic classes until 16:00 when we changed mental gears and were taught the basics of seamanship.

We learned how to row and sail and handle lines. Many hours were spent in the quad learning how to march correctly. The drillmaster would bark out his order and then start us marching to the gait he whistled on his shrill little brass whistle. Fast, fast, slow, whistle blast, turn; fast, fast, slow, whistle blast, turn. It was all very confusing to begin with but I managed to catch on quickly. We drilled with mouscatons which is a shorter version of the British Lee-Enfield .303. Shouldering a mouscaton was easy for the bigger cadets but I was a scrawny little runt. I don't think I'm too far off when I say that my rifle was about two-thirds as tall as I was and it probably weighed about half as much as I did. I never complained and when it came time to snap my bolt during inspection I was as good as the best man in my section. Dinner was served at 19:00 followed by study time and lights out at 22:00. At first it was tough but I liked the discipline and the camaraderie.

I felt great because I was a student in the Ecole des Pupilles de la Marine. Could any kid ask for more? I made good friends and I began learning new skills. The Alsatians, a rowdy and fun loving lot, asked me if I wanted to join the band. "I can't play anything." The student bandleader, a kid called Fritz, asked me if I had ever tried to play any instrument? I thought for a moment and replied, "The violin, but I was no good." He laughed. "We don't need violins but we need another bugle." "Try it and let's see what happens." I jumped at the chance.

Maybe learning to play an instrument was a sign that I was an early achiever because I learned how to play the bugle and soon became the chief bugler for the cadet corps. More responsibility also led to more opportunity. First up in the morning, I was first into the galley. That was a good deal because I was always hungry. The cooks were nice men and quite understanding because they let their scrawny bugler skim off the cream from the milk and make huge jam and butter sandwiches before the rest of the hungry corps marched down to the breakfast tables. The cooks were sailors, men old enough to show compassion and wise enough to look the other way when the boy – men acted their age.

By mid 1937, after eighteen months of discipline and training, I had learned the rudiments of seamanship. Looking back on that period, as the boy turned into a youth, the seeds of patriotism and honor were also planted. To toughen us and get us used to the rigors of military life, we were issued heavy mouscaton and ordered to pack full backpacks. When we got kitted up we marched into the hills singing patriotic songs glorifying France.

During those long marches I also learned something about myself: I hated marching. If nothing else convinced me of the wisdom of my decision to join the navy and not the army, it was marching. Straining under the weight, marching along narrow paths we learned physical and mental endurance. Over and over we sang "La France Nous Appelle" with gusto and conviction. La France needed strong young men.

The cadet corps was no place for complainers or quitters. There was no doubt in my mind: if I were asked, I would die for the Republic. No one shoved that conviction down my throat. I had arrived at that conviction on my own and it has stayed with me all my life. I was proud to be treated like a man and excited about the prospect of finishing my training and getting out into the real world. Just over the horizon there was the prospect of being independent but I was also part of a fine family: the French navy. Yes, the daily routine was tough and I was challenged every step of the way. No, I never quit or half learned something.

If something was hard, I resolved to spend more time until I became competent. To this day, as a man in his eighties, I can understand Morse code when I hear it. Why is that so important now? It really isn't but when I was a cadet I had to learn it and I couldn't learn to read as fast as my classmates. Not once, not twice, maybe a couple of hundred times, my instructor would throw his arms up in despair and I would have to write out the code fifty times. Today, in the back hills of the Var, if the gendarmes ever need someone to read Morse code, I'm their man!

The drums of war were beginning to roll, Hitler was rearming and I knew that whatever the future might hold for me, I would be able to face it with discipline, guts and honor. Honor for my flag, for my country, admiration for my officers, who, at least to our minds, were men representing all that was good and honorable in France. Honor meant a lot to me, perhaps more than for some of the other guys in our barracks. Although my father returned from World War I alive, he was dying and the short period between his return and his death was really a process of dying for the Republic.

I had grown up in a family in which honor and respect for the flag were integral parts of the way we lived as a French family. I was comforted by the fact that throughout the barracks and on the quarterdeck of every ship in the French fleet we were reminded of the importance of honor and discipline. Countless shields were engraved with bold lettering: "Honneur et Patrie" or "Valeur et Discipline." My training in cadet school reinforced those time-honored values.

It seemed as if my cadet life was over before it began. The passing out ceremony was on us before we really had time to stop and think about the huge step we were taking. Life as cadet Dassac was coming to an end. In a few days I knew I would stand my last inspection, march my last parade, salute my officers for the last time, pack my sea bag and get on with my future. As God was my witness, I was proud to be a young naval cadet!

As a cadet in Brest the navy introduced us to every branch of the service. This was done in order to help us to recognize our natural skills and find which branch of the navy we were genuinely interested in. After cadet training we were expected to choose a branch and that choice would become our career.

*****

Even before I went to Brest, I had a natural ability to work with mechanics and electronics. When I had the time I was always fiddling with something mechanical or electrical. It was only logical that when I had to elect a career choice I requested an assignment to the naval mechanical school in Toulon.

Once in Toulon I passed the exams for entrance into the highly specialized torpedo school. My choice of specialty was not based entirely on my proven skills. Perhaps another factor was my real motivator. Torpedoes are mounted on small ships: destroyers, mine chasers, corvettes, patrol boats. Remember, I hated marching. If I had chosen a specialty that was likely to get me assigned to a big ship I knew I would have to run the full length of the ship to get to my battle station. Running and marching, what's the difference? Small ships meant covering short distances. The more I thought about my choice of specialty the more I realized that, despite my youth, I was becoming wiser.

Being a torpedo man was a multi-skilled profession. That meant we learned much than knowing only the mechanics of how to destroy the enemy. By the time we finished our training there was no part of the torpedoes used in the French fleet that we hadn't worked on. We were able to dismantle and reassemble a torpedo: all three meters and however many hundred kilos it weighed. I forget the exact weight but to move them we had to cinch them into a block and tackle and muscle them into position. With my eyes shut I could walk through every step from arming the warhead with two hundred and fifty kilos of TNT to lathing a primer ring or casting a new fin. In the end, there was nothing about a torpedo I didn't know.

We fired dummy torpedoes with floating warheads. Once the warhead hit its target (sometimes we missed and had to row all over hell to find the red floating warhead) we would reload and fire again. As a torpedo man, I was the key man between the bridge and the torpedo. An officer on the bridge calculated the angle of fire and gave me my orders. All I had to do was wait for his order, calibrate the 'fish', and fire when ordered. It sounds simple but when you are in a driving rain and trying to stand upright on a pitching deck, theory meets reality and the shot doesn't always go according to the book.

Rene Dassac (in collaboration with Patrick K. Robbins)

When I reported for duty the doctor in charge of inspecting all new arrivals pulled me out of the line and questioned me about my age. From his point of view, the kid in front of him with ribs sticking out of his puny chest was too short and too skinny to be able to survive the rigors of torpedo school. Finally, convinced that I was not lying about my age, the doctor ordered me to report to the galley every morning at 0900. The cooks, in turn, were ordered to cook me a rare steak sandwich or make a sardine sandwich until my skinny frame began to fill-out. A good prescription; it didn't work. But, I enjoyed those good breakfasts. In fact, I'm in my eighties now and I'm still lean.

I may have looked frail but I was a typical wiry little fellow with great stamina. No fat, just lean muscle covering the small body of a teenager eager to prove himself. It was soon apparent to my instructors that 'the little one' had talent and I moved through the machine shop easily and showed great skill. Shaping, lathing, forging, brazing, I acquired all the skills of a master craftsman. I excelled and when WW II broke out I was a qualified first class torpedo man with many friends.

I completed that school without any major problems. In fact, I realized that I had found something to do that I really enjoyed and I excelled. Of course, I was a teenager and still cocky. A subtle transition had begun in me; it began sometime late in my cadet training. When I started off as a star struck earnest kid, I obeyed every order without question. I may have thought the order was nuts, but, as far as I was concerned, orders were orders and I accepted they had to be obeyed to the letter. As I grew out of my childhood awe into a more confident kid, something began changing in me. Slowly, without much fanfare, I began testing the limits of authority, trying to get by without doing something minor that I felt was a pain, something that seemed stupid for me to have to do just because that was the way the navy did things.

One day we were lined up for inspection. The officers and noncoms worked their way down the ranks, peering, poking, and lifting to see if pockets and buckles were fastened. I felt good. My hair was short, my ears were clean and my uniform was spotless. Admittedly, there was a hole in one of my knee socks that I hadn't darned but, what the hell, no officer would get that picky to catch me, I thought. I almost made it but my hole gave me away. In an explosion of rage, probably theatrical but impressive nevertheless, my inspecting officer gave me a savage dressing down. Cutting through all the verbal bombast, it boiled down to: dereliction of duty!

He wasn't serious; all that for a bloody little hole? I was marched off between two sentries and taken to the brig where I was given a thin wool blanket and told to spend twenty-four hours reflecting on my stupidity. I looked around my cell. My 'bed' consisted of wood planks perched between two sawhorses. There was a bucket for my toilet and a naked light bulb. The door clanged shut and I wrapped up to keep warm. I spent a long night shivering in the cold. When I was released and allowed to return to my barracks I was greeted with jeers and laughter. From the back someone called our mockingly, "Welcome home Taulus." My nickname stuck. In French slang, the term for when you're thrown in prison is, "faire la taule" and my bunk mates weren't going to let me forget my brief encounter with law. With a stretch of the tongue, "la taule" became my new name, "Taulus" Dassac.

The course finished and I had to wait until I was ordered to join a ship of the line. In the meantime I waited, impatiently, onboard the Condorcet, an old battleship that had been turned into a training school and staging point. Waiting is hard and I wasn't comfortable going through the motions of a temporary assignment when what I really wanted was to be onboard my own ship. Hurry up and wait, I had to wait my turn.

One day two Royal Navy destroyers came into port. Later, I would recall their arrival marked another turning point in my young life. While I was looking at those destroyers a thought flashed through my mind, "I can see myself onboard one of those." More than a revelation, it was an exciting certainty, something deep inside me that felt absolutely right. Looking at those two ships it was as if I began defining 'home' in a new way, a ship where I could belong. From then until I was assigned to a destroyer, I knew what I wanted.

The destroyers were escorting the HMS Argus, a towering aircraft carrier. They berthed next to our ship and I was thunderstruck by how differently Britain and France were preparing for war. The

Rene Dassac (in collaboration with Patrick K. Robbins)

British destroyers were weather beaten. Sea spray crusted their funnels, proof of many hours in rough weather. Unlike the French ships, the British ships were already stripped of peacetime refinements. Shiny copper had been painted a dull naval gray. Their crews moved quickly about the deck making sure their ships were ready for war operations anywhere and at anytime. On the French side of the dock we spent time making our ship look pretty.

Seen from a British sailor's point of view, the contrast must have been very stark. Britain was obviously on a war footing while the French ships bobbed at their moorings looking like elegant yachts being primped for an afternoon cruise. Maybe the French were relaxed and casual, I thought, because the French government had stated publicly that if they flexed their muscles enough in the Med, and if Italy kept out of the war, there was no reason for France to begin preparing for events that were surely not going to affect them!

The British destroyers left harbor a few days later and I didn't think too much about them. I was more concerned about where I was going to be posted. Ratings were assigned ships according to their skills and how well they had done in training. I wasn't too worried about getting a good ship because I had excelled in training and I had completed the requirements to become a qualified torpedo able seaman.

In the summer of 1939 Europe was uneasy but at peace. I went on leave to visit one of my mother's brothers, my uncle Theo, in Juan les Pins. He was a successful salesman and a wealthy bachelor who was looked after by a homely Belgian housekeeper who took a liking to me. Nothing illicit or immoral happened between the two of us but she made sure that I knew she was looking out for me. Uncle Theo gave her an allowance every week to cover their meals and the general upkeep of the house. That fine woman knew the ins-and-outs of budgeting. Every now and then she would slip me a few francs and wink, "Here are some more potatoes." Maybe she was cheating on my uncle, I don't know. If I hadn't taken what she offered the francs would have wound up on the table somehow. It wasn't much and I frankly think her little game was about the most exciting daredevil thing she ever did in her boring life. Her life had to be boring because

I can guarantee you; with her looks she couldn't have bought a boy friend!

Theo was good to me. He didn't have children and I think by showing me a good time he was also letting the spirit of my mother know that the family was still capable of looking after me. Just when I was really beginning to enjoy my leave, I was called up to go to the naval depot in Lorient for an eventual assignment to a ship. Typical military: They tell you to go somewhere but don't give any details so I was left wondering what was going to happen next.

By then no one was talking about anything else except war. Toward the end of August I began detecting an almost palpable resignation in almost everyone I came into contact with: for the second time in twenty five years two neighbors, France and Germany, would start killing each other again. Go into a café and have a drink, listen to what people were talking and arguing about and there was only one topic: war.

There were at least two fairly distinct schools of thought. There were optimists who saw the war as an opportunity to settle long-standing scores once and for all and there were pessimists who saw carnage and destruction. I was happy my father was not alive to have to witness what was becoming increasingly clear: Europe had begun a sure descent into another war.

More than once I recalled him walking me to school under the Zeppelin's shadow. Sadly, he was right. I was fiercely patriotic. If war broke out, and I was convinced it would happen very soon, I knew I would see action. Bravery can't be taught; it is a response and a responsibility. As a cadet and in torpedo school our lives were governed by the ethics of honor, loyalty, discipline and patriotism. Those four concepts were riveted into my soul. But, they were still abstract because they hadn't been put to the test. I hadn't been to war and the war games we held were no substitute for the real thing. In the countless conversations I had with myself and with my friends, I quietly vowed that I would act in such a way as to bring honor to my family. Surely, my father's sacrifice had to be repaid.

CHAPTER THREE: AT WAR

War broke out in September 1939. No longer was the threat of armed conflict a topic of heated debate. Now there was shooting and killing which was another way of saying an abstract idea had become a reality. As far as we seamen were concerned, it was still too early to talk about casualties and destruction. The fronts were somewhere 'out there' or the front page of Le Figaro. Talk was cheap in those early days of the war.

One day I went ashore with some shipmates. We headed into a local bar and began shooting off our mouths about the war. "France was strong, France had a good navy, good officers, and of course, excellent seaman." We drank as if tomorrow would never come. Our drunken boasting became too much for the barmaid. Swirling on us she gave us a tongue-lashing. I am not too sure how old she was, but I guess she was probably old enough to have known the First World War. "Drunken little fools," she snapped. "Talk about winning the war? You're crazy, silly. Wrong! France will get overrun. She'll be beaten and occupied." She was so mad I thought for a minute she was going to throw her wet table rag in our faces.

We had drunk too much to try and argue with her. Furthermore, she wasn't worth it. We burst out laughing, mocking her. We were so right and she was so wrong. Why waste valuable drinking time on such a silly woman? How could that old cow know what we know? We were sailors, members of the glorious French navy and we were simply the best seamen on the Seven Seas. That afternoon the might of the nation and the navy was in good hands. That is, if only we could we could stop the floor from rocking.

On the way back to our base we stopped by the local brothel, thought twice, and decided to save the cost of a few moments of pleasure in order to pay for Christmas leave. Our side trip reminded me of a funny story that I shared with my mates. It happened several years earlier when I was going on home leave with some of my fellow cadets in Brest. I can't remember the details but I was probably fifteen at the time and the others were about the same age. We were in uniform and we looked like sailors except we were obviously kids. When we got to Rennes we had to change trains to head to our respective homes.

Nobody had a tight connection so we decided to wander through the brothel area located near the train station. In those days it was perfectly normal to go into a brothel and sit at the bar and talk with the girls. If talk led to a commercial transaction that was legal provided, of course, the client was of age. We were all underage. Finally, one of my mates summoned up his courage and went upstairs with a big Alsatian girl. She was tall and blond with huge cannonball size breasts and her shoulders were wide enough to hoist a beer keg over her head. They reappeared after a few minutes. Rather, she thundered down the steep stairs cradling her young charge tightly to her bosom. She stopped at the foot of the stairs and rocked his hapless body in deep dramatic sweeps pretending she was his mother calming her crying baby. "He's a man…. and what a man," she announced loudly to the cheering room.

A few days later I received my draft sheet ordering me to proceed to the naval barracks in Lorient for an eventual assignment to a ship. At last, I thought, I will finally get to sea in a fighting ship. By Christmas 1939 the summer dreams of an easy war had given way to reality. No nice little war was unfolding. Men were dying and I was an able seaman torpedo man itching for action.

Military life is regimented and often irrational. When I reported to the duty officer in January 1940 I squared my shoulders and looked directly at him. He eyed me up and down and scowled. Only seventeen, I was still a wiry, scrawny looking kid. When I stretched I was 1.60 tall. Soaking wet, I might have weighed 55 kilos but only if I had been weighed after a big lunch. The officer scowled at me and asked, "How old are you?" "Eighteen," I replied evenly and confidently. I was positively brimming with confidence.

Taulus

No one could deny me my achievements. I was a qualified able seaman torpedo man who knew everything that could be taught about how to arm and fire torpedoes, mines and depth charges. I think I conveyed an attitude of, "Give me a chance and I'll blow the enemy to hell." Certainly it wasn't my size but I knew there was something about me that must have appealed to him. Maybe he was thinking, "This cocksure kid looks good and acts trustworthy. With all the deadbeats I've seen onboard, I think I'll take him under my wing." He also could have been thinking a whole lot of other thoughts but somehow I think I am right in my assessment of what was going through his mind.

He smiled and glanced at his watch. "It's lunch time. Come down to the mess with me." Over lunch he grilled me about my background. At first I thought that this was a routine interrogation step but as we talked I began to understand some of his concerns. "You're different than a lot of men your age on this ship because you're a seaman who has come up through the ranks, done well in rigorous schools, someone who has accepted discipline, and someone who is proud to serve his flag." I must have looked puzzled because this was the first time I had ever heard an officer talk that way. He lowered his voice and quickly explained that he had a lot of young ratings that he could not trust. "They're conscripts, many are leftists who fought for the communists in the Spanish civil war, most despise their officers and almost to a man, they loathe every moment they have to conform to naval law and order."

There it was. I understood why he had taken a keen interest in me. Without coming outright and saying it, he had told me there were two types of sailors: dedicated young men like me who had volunteered, trained, and wanted to serve their country, and conscripts who often did not share my dedication. He trusted the first lot but he could not trust the others. In view of my long apprenticeship and excellent record, he assigned me to duty as a night sentry in the dockyard. It wasn't quite what I imagined my first real assumption of responsibility would be, but it was a chance for me to prove myself.

I was proud to have that opportunity. It was the first time I could prove my worth to an officer who hadn't watched me for months in training. I liked the responsibility but I was also struggling to understand what he revealed over lunch. The way I heard him, his concerns translated into two messages. First, he trusted me and second, I had to watch my back and keep an eye out for other sailors who were the complete opposite of me. My naiveté staggered me; I could not get over the first shock of realizing that all seamen were not happy to be in the navy, happy to be French, happy to be called to arms. I was still very green, a kid in a sailor's uniform and I still had much to learn about the real world.

I spent the next two weeks on sentry duty. Long hours, it was cold, wet, boring and potentially dangerous. Rumors flew about saboteurs who were probably lurking in the shadows waiting to pounce on unsuspecting guards. But from midnight until six in the morning another enemy arrived every night. Mr. Boredom crept through the night wearing soft slippers. I told myself that it would be so easy to lean up against a wall or the guardhouse, lock my knees, and go to sleep standing up.

During the night nothing moved except cats, rats, and petty officers trying in vain to catch me sleeping. Others were caught dozing but I remained awake and vigilant, staring into the night. A persistent rumor, always there like the bitter night cold, would not go away. German paratroops were supposed to land one night close to Lorient and capture the base. Perhaps it was a way for the admiralty to keep their sailor sentinels on their toes while on guard duty, or perhaps enemy agents spread the rumors to demoralize us. Whatever the source, the scare tactic worked on me. I remained vigilant but it was hard. To keep awake I tried every trick in the book including counting everything that could be counted, shifting my weight from one foot to the other, and even trying to stare holes into the night, pretending that my eyes had some kind of magical power that could turn darkness into light.

While I mounted guard on a dock in France, the Royal navy was fighting the German navy in Norway. For a time it looked as if the Brits had the upper hand but it was another false hope. The German navy suffered a heavy loss when they battled a combined force of British and Polish destroyers but it was not a one-sided victory. The Royal Navy lost a couple of destroyers in the encounter. The battleship Resolution had some small bomb damage but it was not serious enough to take her out of action. A French light cruiser was dusted by dive-bombers but stayed on the line.

But, on the ground, British troops were being pounded from the air. Soon it became clear that the allied forces would be forced to withdraw from Norway and re-deploy to help the Netherlands and Belgium repel the German invasion. The allies were performing a strategic defeat in the face of an overwhelming enemy. No matter how hard we searched the newspapers, the news from every front was uniformly bad.

As the war swirled beyond my horizon, I found that I was getting more and more edgy about the possibility of not getting into the conflict. There were times that I thought the war would happen around me and be over before I got my chance to fight. Frustration and boredom were hard to manage. And, to make life more difficult, not everyone in the barracks shared my eagerness to start fighting. Many conscripts were happy to stay safe in harbor, as far as possible from the fighting.

I was different but there was nothing I could do to speed up getting my ship. My transfer drifted through the huge naval bureaucracy, just a few more sheets bobbing in a white paper sea. There was no way to neither speed up their transit through the system nor slow it down if I had wanted to. The cogs of war ground slowly while battles raged and men died. I was in a hurry; I had to wait.

Finally, in late March 1940 two shipmates, leading seaman Pineau and rating Lafont and I were called to the drafting office and given our orders. Three good friends, we managed to stick together. Maybe it was luck, maybe it was part of a grander design, we didn't know and didn't care. What was important to us was the fact that onboard our new ship we would know someone and that was bound to help us get adjusted. We were excited. At long last, we were leaving Lorient and we were heading into action.

After all the time wasted waiting, our orders were simple: take the train to La Rochelle and join the colonial light cruiser Savorgnan de Brazza that was undergoing a refit. She was a colonial light cruiser brought back from the Far East. We thought that after her refit she would be sent back to Saigon in French Indochina but the Ministry of Defense had other plans for her.

A new ship and the prospect of finally getting into the war were both good news and bad news. We wanted to start fighting but we had mixed feelings about our new ship. Already there were rumors in the barracks about her and we did not like what we heard. She had just returned from the Far East to be modernized and rearmed before being ordered to join the Atlantic fleet. You don't have to be supremely intelligent to know that refits, no matter how carefully they are carried out, never really produce a ship in which everything new works well from the start.

It takes time for parts to work into place, for washers to lock, pistons to slip without slapping their drive shafts, gun mounts to swivel and train smoothly and quickly, bulkhead doors to shut, wiring not too short, millions of tiny details that have to come together. Everyone knew that the only way for a refit to find its soul was to run it at sea for many weeks. During sea trials we would be expected to run down everything that went wrong.

That was the theory of how a refit/sea trial worked in peacetime but that theory didn't fit with reality: we were at war and time was not on our side. Our refit had to be correct right from the start. In short, we had to build her sea soul into her from the beginning because time was running out. She had to go to sea as quickly as the last bolt was tightened and the last tonne of bunker was loaded. Whatever we did for the first time had to work because we were not going to be given a second opportunity.

We arrived at La Rochelle on a bright and sunny day in April just in time for lunch. We could have been three teenagers taking a trip to an amusement park for the first time in our lives. The gate to the base at La Rochelle was the entrance to our 'amusement' park. Shouldering our sea bags we tried to act nonchalant as we approached our ship. Anyone watching us would have seen three scrawny kids, gawking and stumbling over cables and lines as we made our way to the officer on duty at the gangplank.

Halfway across the dock we stopped dead in our tracks. The noise was deafening, metal clanged on metal, steam hissed into clouds, men's voices shouting and cursing sliced across the dock, growling diesel trucks spewed thick black exhaust, crane hawsers twanged taught as they swung huge jute nets laden with supplies over our heads. For an instant I remember thinking, a man could get killed if he stood still. It was as if all the rides in our amusement park had been taken apart and heaped into one huge swirl of men and machines. We knew we had to board our ship but what in God's name had we got into? Training hadn't prepared us for this kind of situation.

It was chaotic on deck. Gaping holes in her thick hull and superstructure were being fitted with guns, ladders, windows, and doors. Before returning to France the dockyard crew had removed all the old rails that had been used to drop mines around the coast of Indochina. New railing was being fitted. A large empty space on the fantail meant that their seaplane and its catapult had already been removed. Something else was going to be fitted but we couldn't figure it out just by looking at the stacks of crates and pipes that had been pushed into place waiting for assembly. Men lugged pieces across the deck and out of sight. Below deck sailors yelled, cursed and grunted in the hot spring sun.

None of this made sense to our untrained eyes. We'd come from the well-ordered world of our cadet barracks through various training schools. At each stage of our lives "back then," there was an established routine, a precise way of doing something, clear orders and strict discipline. Our lives were parts of a series of processes designed to take a raw recruit in the beginning and turn out a finished product. Each step in our evolution from recruit to able seaman was thoroughly thought through with infinite care. We knew what direction we were headed in and how a particular training step would end. Was there method in the mayhem unfolding in front of us? Did anyone know what in horrible hell was going on? Someone had to believe there was order behind the apparent chaos strewn in our way. Good for him; we couldn't figure it out. This was the first time we had seen a refit and we were understandably convinced that all the pieces would never be made to fit, let alone work. And we were going to ship out on ……….this?

Probably someone yelled at us to get out of the way and that shook us out of the clutches of paralyzed astonishment. We boarded and reported to the duty officer who sent us to our mess to have lunch. Entering the mess we heard a familiar roar and we began to relax. This first introduction was good, we thought. The crew appeared relaxed and jovial, a welcome change from the sullen and surly conscript seamen we had lived with in Lorient.

Immediately after lunch we were assigned to duty stations. There is a lot of difference between watching something happen and making something happen. Our observer status ended when we marched up the gangplank. Except for sleeping and meals, we worked around the clock; there was no shore leave. It took a week of hard work cleaning, painting and rearming before the de Brazza was ready to put to sea. To our astonishment, all the pieces really did fit. The ship belonged to us.

Today, when I read about ships going in for refits, I can't help laughing when I remember that furious week in April. We didn't have computers, mechanized trolleys, pneumatic jacks and back-friendly hoists. All we had was muscle and guts, a few cranes, spanners, and a lot of grunting and cursing.

Capitaine de Fregate Baden was the de Brazza's captain. He was widely respected as a seafarer but he was a cold and aloof leader who did not show his feelings or share his opinions with his officers. He was even more remote with his crew. Seamanship and leadership are two separate qualities and only rarely are the two found in a captain. In his thoughts, and by his actions, he was his own commander, answering to no one onboard, only to his superiors.

Disliked as a person, but respected as a mariner, the crew was uneasy with Captaine de Fregate Baden. Years later, as I scratched through dark corners of my mind, I've tried to find the right words to describe his command style. Maybe he thought of himself as a reincarnation of a mythical sea god and we were his subjects. He acted as if he believed there was a hierarchy of humans onboard. Ratings were subhuman but necessary beings, best when they were out of his sight and out of his mind. Officers were vital appendages he needed to buffer him from the ratings. He was the Supreme Being onboard, master of his universe. His authority was absolute; his wisdom was complete, his decisions were divine in our world at sea.

Signals pipes screeched through the loudspeakers. The first lieutenant called the ship's company to attention: "We will sail tomorrow morning at 0800 for Brest where we will be fitted with two sets of twin 40mm anti aircraft guns. Then we will re-supply the ammunition magazines and sail for our new mission. I am sure I can rely on you all to do your duty as you have done it in the past." Short and sweet. We knew when we were leaving, where we were going, what we were going to do and how it might end.

Or did we? Rumors flew but none were lurid enough to be taken seriously. Excitement replaced fear; we were ready to go. Deep inside, each of us was probably glad to know we were heading out to sea, getting ready to fight the same old enemy whom our fathers, grandfathers, and great-great grandfathers had also fought.

On the last night in port I felt as ready as I ever would be to face the unknown called war. Until now, war was a game. During all our training sessions, when we finished playing war, we showered, ate a warm meal and watched a film or played cards, secure in our world of order and routine. But, I knew tomorrow was the beginning of something different in my life. We could just as easily be blown out of the water as we could drink a cup of coffee or throw a cigarette butt overboard. In a few hours, I told myself before drifting off to sleep in my hammock, when I wake up we might kill or be killed, and that's the way my life is going to be until the end of the war. Briefly, I wondered if my father felt the same way in the face of such uncertainty.

Spirits were high as the de Brazza left La Rochelle the next day. The big ship plowed through the mirror-like sea under a dark blue sky. Once out to sea the captain ordered gunnery exercises and engine trials. The crew and the ship came together quickly; the run up to Brest was uneventful. We reached our mooring on time. As soon as the ship arrived in the port area it was immediately sent into the gunnery dockyard to have our guns fitted. Nonstop, day and night, there was the now familiar and constant deafening noise of men yelling, rivet guns banging, metal sheets clanging into place, cranes groaning, men shoving, and the incessant din of continuous pounding.

Rene Dassac (in collaboration with Patrick K. Robbins)

Within four days our ship put to sea to test its new guns and fire a few depth charges on the way north to Cherbourg. On that test run I took the first step into the real world of life onboard a fighting ship. This wasn't school anymore. We weren't firing dummies. If there had been an enemy sub in the area we would have done our best to sink him.

The war on the ground was going from bad to worse while the de Brazza was going through sea trials. The Germans broke through Dutch defenses and were slicing into Belgium. No one seemed to have any accurate information; rumors became facts in the absence of official word. After a while I quit listening and stayed focused on my job. But, it struck me that in the face of all the bad rumors that were eventually followed by accurate news when we finally got it from BBC or the French government, there were no signs of panic. We were too busy to have the luxury of free time in which probe our emotions.

In Cherbourg we heard our first bombs and saw German dive-bombers pounding French defenses. Conscripts manned the newly mounted AA guns. Even though our firing was accurate, it still looked as if our rounds were going through the enemy flights and exploding on the other side of the dive-bombers. Worse, some weren't exploding at all. It was eerie to be tied up to a wharf and see bombs falling not far from the de Brazza.

It was my first time under enemy fire and I felt strangely calm. Maybe my calm came from training; maybe it also came from the comfort of being surrounded by others who were calm, at least on the outside. I kept telling myself that I was in the war now but I knew I was kidding myself. I was still playing at war; I was too far removed. Firing and dying weren't close enough yet. I didn't act as if I were a target, at least not yet. For me, the war was still "out there."

If Fate had me in its crosshairs, he or she was a lousy shot that day. Quietly, I prayed for those crosshairs never to stop and pick me out. "Please, when the war's over let me still be alive and in one piece." That was a tall order for a prayer but I wasn't in a mood to beat around the bush talking with God. But what a strange thought, I said to myself: the war would be over? The thought that the war would end seemed crazy but I knew that it would end one day just as it ended for my father. We would either be victors or we would be occupied. The war was creeping up on me fast and time had run out for a kid to play sailor. My play days were over. I was a young man, part of a lethal machine and I was fiercely proud my machine was French.

The de Brazza refueled and put to sea. Off the coast we began receiving signals: the front lines were collapsing. Orders were given to lay down a bombardment on German panzers sighted near Saint Valerie. Another French warship, the Leopard, took up station next to us. Above our ships an aircraft spotter circled the tank formation. He called down strikes with deadly accuracy. The de Brazza was firing three 138mm and the Leopard fired her five 130mm guns. Sheets of fire and smoke belched from our ships while the spotter circled for better advantage.

Suddenly, after an hour of non-stop firing we received another signal: Stop all firing! "The tanks are French," yelled a gunnery officer. Captain Baden was almost speechless with rage. "What's gone wrong," he managed to scream at no one in particular? Answers weren't lying around on the deck like spent shell casings. Later we learned behind the tragedy lay a stark fact: panic had set in among the French army units facing overwhelming odds. The Germans were everywhere. The lines were fluid; in some cases there were no lines. There were just masses of soldiers and equipment piled on top of each other. With so much confusion and no clear means of communication, the chains of command had broken down. Offshore we did our job. A deadly accurate barrage was well executed. Tragically, the front was so fluid that we managed to hit the wrong column.

Onboard the de Brazza we were bitter when we found out what had happened. What a helluva way to fight a war! Killing our own guys wasn't what we had signed up to do. I heard someone mutter, "c'est la vie." Maybe our horribly accurate barrage was, "la vie." Or maybe what the guy who said that was trying to do was make a feeble stab at gallows humor; no one was listening. We were struggling to understand the enormity of the chaos unfolding on land. The Germans were killing our troops and now, so were we. Before leaving port we knew that the land war was going badly; our army and the Brits were getting torn apart. How in the hell were we supposed to feel? Our first time in action and we help the enemy. Our mess was sullen and bitter but the de Brazza stayed on station.

The next day we returned to Saint Valerie with orders to disrupt a column of German motorcycles and light armored cars advancing on a narrow road parallel to Saint Valerie. No one questioned our orders but there was considerable muttering about the nationality of the targets that had been selected for us. The gunnery crews stood at the ready waiting for their orders. The spotter plane circled over the target and then confirmed it. This time there was no mistaken identity. Yes, our targets were Germans. Intense firing erupted. Our gunnery officers trained their binoculars on the German vehicles and made sure they were blown to bits. A few vehicles managed to make an about turn and dashed into a small forest for cover. We shredded the forest. By the time we stopped firing I don't know how anyone could have survived the barrage we laid down.

There was no time to savor our small victory. Whining in on top of us, Luftwaffe dive-bombers made several passes but could not break through the ferocious wall of fire we were sending up at them. But, they were tough and determined pilots and there were several near misses. Their bombs blew columns of water high into the air and I shuddered to think of how it would feel if they hit their target and their target was the de Brazza. Our big guns continued to hurl shells onto the shore. We were firing a lot but our rounds were probably not going to change the course of the war.

On land disaster loomed. All the fronts were breaking down and the allied troops encircled at Dunkirk were stranded waiting for evacuation. There was no possibility of a land column slicing through the German defenses to open a corridor for an orderly retreat. Hour by hour, the disaster was getting bigger and our response was becoming more futile.

We were detailed to go to Le Havre with some British destroyers to blow-up fuel tanks and destroy war materiel left in the docks. I couldn't believe my ears when we received our orders. Okay, I admitted that the war was going badly for us, but I had enough respect for the French general staff to assume that they had alternatives. Surely, wasn't our run up to Le Havre just another ploy? The closer we got Le Havre the more I began to fear that our mission was not a ploy but a definite commitment of French men and resources to destroy French resources. My head was spinning.

Can you imagine what it felt like to steam toward a French port and receive an order to destroy vital materiel? Even a simple rating like me knew fuel and materiel were hard to come by in the best of times and these were certainly the worst of times. Our order was impossible to understand. We could have covered long enough to load some, if not all, of the materiel onto our ships and then race back to safer lines. But, what I did not know, or at least it seemed to me this is what happened, in the twenty-four hours prior to receiving our orders to proceed to Le Havre, panic replaced reason. Crates containing Curtis aircraft and other war materiel were smashed and pushed into the sea.

We got the job done in record time and steamed away from the coast back to our newly assigned battle station. There was a lot of grumbling among the crew. For the first time I detected a note of bitterness at what was happening and even contempt for the government and the minister of Defense. What a waste! Destroying our means of fighting the war was, in my mind, an admission that neither the government nor the armed forces had used the months after September 1939 to plan ahead. France had been caught unprepared.

By June 1940 the Funny War was no longer a laughing matter. Bad news came in waves. Hour after hour bad rumors turned to facts, facts fed more rumors, fifth columnists had penetrated throughout France, and the government had sold out. No, wait! New orders came and de Brazza moved to a new battle station.

Off Boulogne the de Brazza was ordered to cover three British destroyers entering the port to evacuate troops that had managed to escape the German onslaught. The soldiers were a pitiful and sorry lot but we didn't have time to commiserate. Luftwaffe dive-bombers controlled the air space over our ships. Two of the British destroyers were badly damaged, but we still managed to evacuate hundreds of exhausted and wounded men. While we were pulling men bobbing helplessly from the water, or pulling them out of swamped boats and rickety barges, German pilots swarmed over us like angry bees.

Their fighters roared in at us from every angle, holding their bombs until the last possible moment before releasing and darting away through holes in our covering fire. Maybe we hit some, maybe we didn't. Who took time to keep score? We were too busy fighting and staying alive to count our hits. We were fighting for our lives; we desperately needed help but there was none. The Germans owned the sky. No allied fighters scrambled to engage them. The Luftwaffe just kept coming, wave after wave, trying to blow us to shreds.

We were alone, sitting ducks. I hated the way I thought but I gave them credit: the Luftwaffe was damned good. They were disciplined, aggressive and too often, deadly accurate. It seemed as if everyone was getting hit. Falling shells and exploding ships beat the sea into froth. We'd no sooner survive one run when another, or maybe two, started in on us. Maybe all the planes in the German air force were over us that day or maybe not. From what I could see I was convinced their whole damned air force was above us. Their planes kept coming and coming.

When we passed Boulogne captain Baden received orders to swing west to head to Dover to provide cover and offer assistance to the vast motley armada streaming back from Dunkirk with evacuees. The surface of the Channel was strewn with the most extraordinary array of floating vessels I had ever seen. Anything that could float was used to help our troops flee the Germans. At one point we managed to rescue three soldiers who were wedged into a lorry inner tube. They were paddling toward Dover with their hands. All around us fishing boats bobbed in the swells. Their fish nets were hung over the sides of the boats to help soldiers clamber up and then collapse exhausted on the little boat's crowded decks. There were vessels for as far as the eye could see, some small, some large, some seaworthy, and some leaking wrecks that should never have left the safety of their harbor in England. Skippers pointed their boats toward France, plowing through the cold gray sea apparently oblivious to the risks they were running. Their sole goal was to get their craft over to Dunkirk and return, God willing and the Luftwaffe unwilling, with countless soldiers. The spectacle unfolding before us had to be one of the greatest mass acts of courage in modern history.

Taulus

There was no let up. Our guns hammered the sky hoping to get a hit. A heavy pall of cordite hung over the deck; even the wind couldn't blow it away. We raced ammunition from the magazines up to the gun crews, stepping over sodden soldiers we fished out from the Channel.

Signals pipe screeched announcing the first officer. "This operation will cease. Our ship has been ordered into Portsmouth." Our guns were still firing while we hoisted another lot of soldiers out of the water and onto the deck. Some wounded were escorted below to our crowded infirmary. We pulled up the loading nets, changed course and headed toward England.

Something was going on. I felt it in my bones. Admittedly, I didn't have the advantage of decades of service at sea to rely on to help me piece together a picture that made sense. Rumors had been floating for the better part of a day, maybe two, that the French army had stopped fighting. At first I fobbed them off, "typical navy versus army bullshit," but they kept coming back with more convincing detail. Apparently the signals ratings were monitoring other channels on the sly. They overheard army units talking. What they heard was insane; the unthinkable had happened. Or, had it? We tried to make ourselves believe the army was still fighting. How could we know we were about to be swamped by a disaster?

The de Brazza plowed toward England. There were fewer enemy aircraft and those we saw were active closer to the French coast. Once again, rumors ripped through the ship, a whitewater of fact, fiction and fear. Someone "had heard" that France was about to stop the carnage and sign an armistice with Germany. My first reaction was to tell everyone to shut up. France is a great country and we don't accept defeat, I both thought and said to anyone who would listen to me. That was what I believed and what I learned in cadet school. A quaint conviction coming from a youngster, perhaps I was one of the last in the crew to finally quit defending information that sounded real, not some rumor, a nasty joke, some misunderstanding from somebody who had got his signals crossed. Disbelief and shocked began slipping into grudging acceptance. As far as France was concerned, did what was happening on land mean the war was over? We were still in the dark because we hadn't heard from the captain but there were other channels of communication. Several reliable seamen had overheard officers murmuring about an "armistice" with Germany.

We edged toward the English coast. One question was on everybody's lips: "Is the war over for us?" What's up? The de Brazza was ordered into Portsmouth where it anchored between the Isle of Wight and the entrance to the Portsmouth dockyard. In the space of a few hours the crew had gone from being a fighting force to an almost spent force. No one could believe what was happening to us. The bosun's pipe screeched over the loudspeakers. "Attention all hands, the captain is to address the crew," an officer's voice droned. It wasn't the normal tone I associated with what might be a routine information announcement.

He spoke slowly and weighed each word. I could imagine the junior officer stepping aside to make way for the captain in front of the microphone. Captain Baden cleared his throat, paused, and began speaking. I stared into the fine mesh covering the loud speaker opposite my battle station. Calmly, perhaps too calmly, he did not acknowledge the rumors and dismiss them. "I have orders to confirm to you that most of France is occupied and the government is negotiating an armistice with the occupiers." He didn't call them Germans. He didn't have to. All the men at my station were silent, deathly silent. No one stirred. I caught myself staring into the speaker wishing he'd lose his voice. What I had heard was not true. Desperately, I wanted to believe he'd gone nuts and this was a macabre joke, a last desperate squawk before they took him away in a straight jacket. He wasn't off his rocker; captains don't play tricks on their crews.

France was beaten? How could it happen; the war had barely started? It didn't make sense but I had to admit, within months Germany had overrun Europe and sent us packing into the relative safety of an English harbor. As I turned my head away from the speaker I heard the captain continue in his slow methodical manner. He spoke about practical matters. The de Brazza would soon weigh anchor for Casablanca and wait for further orders. "Before leaving we will enter the docks to refuel and re-provision." That made sense. We used up a lot of bunker and ammunition off Dunkirk. I had no argument with that. But what got me was his voice. It was too calm, I thought. I kept telling myself, "Here we were facing one of the greatest disasters in the history of France," and he drones on with about as much emotion as a tired petty officer ordering the forward watch to scrape off rust and repaint the chain hoist.

We maneuvered into our mooring position. After securing the ship we were given shore leave for the afternoon in Cowes. It was our first leave since leaving Brest. We came ashore to another world. Cowes was peaceful. Little old ladies in flower print dresses and straw sun hats strode down the high street with their wicker shopping baskets. People greeted each other, stopped and passed the time of day. On this side of the Channel daily was life unfolding as it probably had for centuries? I couldn't tell; this was my first time in England.

To me this quiet little town wasn't the real world. Only for a moment was it possible to forget the tragedy unfolding on the opposite shore. Perhaps only a few miles separated the two countries. On one shore men died and on the other some families were bathing in the warm June sun. My mind kept racing between watching these quiet Brits only to remember the noise and horror of the past few days. Instead of green grocer shops, I saw bleeding men being pulled out of the cold Channel waters onto boats and ships swarming toward Dunkirk to rescue them.

I had gone ashore on my own. I needed time to think, time to try and put together a picture of what the future was going to be but, as hard as I tried, I couldn't make sense out of what had happened. I began walking and I didn't know where I was headed. I was wandering aimlessly, my head following my feet down a street leading from the harbor into Cowes. I desperately needed to be alone with my thoughts. There was no way I could escape the gravity of what had happened to my beloved France or escape what was happening to me.

I tried pulling my thoughts together, to chop up the mess into smaller pieces so that I could understand just a little bit of what was happening around me. No matter how hard I tried, given what little I knew, the situation looked pretty hopeless. Neither France nor I had any place to turn and run and hide until the nightmare was over. I could not escape the awful reality that the Germans had beaten us. And then I almost caught myself snickering out loud. "Funny", and then it struck me so hard that I really did manage a small laugh. "This is absurd. My first time in England and it's a war that gets me here." Everyone else I had ever known who had been to this side of the channel had gone to England on holiday. This was no holiday lark, my dark side told me. I began slipping deeper into the raw aching sadness I felt as a child when I stared my dead mother in the face. Life, at least as far as I had known it, was over. My France was defeated. The country I had been trained to respect and defend was at that very moment being divided and I was alone in a foreign country. Never mind that I was part of a crew and someone would make decisions for my mates and me. The world, as I knew it, was dead.

I didn't see her coming and I think I actually jumped when she spoke to me in French. My mind was bouncing about like a tennis ball, whacked from one thought to another and the last thing I expected was to have a pretty girl stop and speak to me in my language in England, of all places. I guess I stared at her until I regained some composure. It took a moment for me to let her voice register and then I realized she was asking me something. "Please, will you come home for tea with me and my parents?" Was this some kind of a joke? You could have knocked me over with a feather. Here is a nice looking girl who I had never ever seen before, politely asking me to go home with her for tea! For a fleeting moment I thought this was the way British girls would pick up a French sailor but she didn't look the type. No, she was asking me to do something very civil and very gentle, right at a time when I thought my head was going to explode. The world was at war and she was offering me a cup of tea! It didn't add up but I thanked her and walked back with her to her parent's house, a small cottage with a tidy garden. Her parents were warm and kind. Over and over and over they let me know how sad they were for what happened to France.

And then it hit me. Sadness more painful than anything I had ever known, even greater than when father and mother died, battered me harder than storm waves pounding against the sides of our ship. My grief was huge and dark and it smashed deep into every bit of bone and tissue stretched over my puny little frame. I was neither cold nor hot; I was numbed from a pain that began welling up in me until it finally burst through my feeble attempts to restrain myself. Sailors weren't supposed to cry. Wet eyes and sloppy sentimentality like that were supposed to be drilled out of us. It doesn't always work, or at least in my case, it didn't because I was sobbing at the futility and hopelessness of my world. All I could do was to remind myself that I was just eighteen, cut-off from my country, cut-off from my family, a sailor whose navy had been defeated.

It was too much. I couldn't clear my thoughts. As if to taunt me, my brain repeated painful words: defeat, destruction, France, family. I could see France occupied by my great grandfather's enemy. There was no way to get in touch with my sisters, brother, aunts and uncles. But that was in France and I was in England bawling in front of total strangers in their pleasant little cottage. Who are these good people? Why did this family reach out to me, an honest-to-God stranger and welcome me? Why was this happening?

Nearly seventy years later that chance meeting is as clear in my mind as it was the day it happened. Maybe extra human powerful forces were at work, forces greater than I can ever attempt to understand. I have even thought that maybe I imagined that episode but the details are too clear for it to be a figment of my imagination, a hallucination that I created to cope with a reality I could not accept. There was no way for me to measure how long I spent with them but I think it was a couple of hours before I finally got hold of myself and took my leave. For the first time in my life I owed 'the Brits' something. It wouldn't be the last. I waved good-bye and made it back on the last lighter back to the de Brazza.

That afternoon I fought my devils in private. Not quite private but pretty close. Don't ask me how but I managed to wrestle them back into a secure dark private corner of my soul. On the way back to the ship there was no mistaking how I felt: I felt better than when I had started my innocent wander through the picturesque little town of Cowes hours before. In the intervening years I thought often of that little family. Unfortunately, I'll never know anything more about them so I'll never really be able to figure out why they happened to show up when I was pretty close to losing my mind. And, I'll never know whether their little cottage survived the Luftwaffe. Much of Cowes was flattened.

Onboard bitter arguments and wild speculation replaced the usual rough and rollicking banter shared among shipmates. "What's going to happen to us once we land in Casablanca," was on everyone's lips? The prospect of being demobilized was slightly more appealing than being transferred to German POW camps. But that was stretching a point because none of the alternatives we came up with made any sense. The Devil was in our midst. Uncertainty began eating away at our morale. Lafont, Pineau and I began talking, probing, asking each other questions, trying to find out what the other guy was going to do. Pineau was married and he seemed to be the only one with a clear idea of what he wanted to do. "I'll go home and then see what happens," he said. Fine for him but that left Lafont and me arguing late into the night.

The next morning we were ordered to prepare to enter harbor. After securing our mooring we were given shore leave until 2400 hours. Lafont and I went ashore. I hadn't told him about my experience in Cowes. As far as he was concerned, our only mission was to find the nearest pub. We didn't have far to go. The residents of Portsmouth had turned out to give us a tremendous welcome. By mid-morning Portsmouth was bursting with French sailors; many of our ships had been ordered into the dockyard. We couldn't believe our eyes. There was the old battleship Courbet. It was once used as a gunnery school in Brest. The Leopard was there! The feeling didn't last long but for the first time since we went into action, we felt safe. Portsmouth was fast becoming a drunken sailor's idea of heaven.

We weren't the only foreign troops ashore. Every pub was filled with servicemen from all over Europe but the majority was French. As soon as we emptied our glasses someone would refill it and yell, "Vive la France." I may have been just a kid but I was no wallflower so I joined in and began drinking with the heavy quaffers. Pub drinking is an art; I still had a lot to learn from the old masters before I could earn my place. To my credit, in just a few weeks I changed from acting like a peacetime able seaman into a young man at war, someone who knew what cordite smelled like when it was fired in anger and not in peacetime practice, I knew what a ship feels like when it rolls with cannon blasts, had seen death, known fear and loneliness, and had even met nice strangers. Yes, I had learned a lot but my education had not taught me how to drink.

Taulus

I drank too much and found out that a skinny kid's stomach can't hold too much. The pub's toilet and I became well acquainted that afternoon and well into the evening. Certainly, I wasn't alone. When the pubs closed at 2300 Portsmouth must have been home to the largest concentration of drunken sailors in the world. Teetering somewhere in the middle of the crowd stumbling toward our ships, I was one very wet and queasy young sailor.

The officer of the deck heard us before he saw us and when he saw us he knew tomorrow's roll-call would be a painful experience for most, if not all, of his sodden sailors. Some were staggering while others carried mates who had lost their sea legs with the last pint. Some walked stiffly with great determination because they knew that if they stopped they'd fall flat on their faces. I think I was a stiff walker but I'm not sure because I really don't know how I got back onboard.

The officer of the deck steeled himself as the first wave of seaman lurched onboard. From the looks of it, there had been a lot of living in a few hours. I suspect that he probably could have cared less about our drunken state. In fact, it was natural, he must have thought. We had to blow off steam and vent our anger and frustration. Our condition was to be expected. He knew that the entire ship's company, officers included, was shocked by the tragedy unfolding in France.

Hours earlier I'd quit being preoccupied with political questions, by the endless argument of what was going to happen next. I had succeeded in getting myself drunker than I had ever been in my life. At the end of my first night in Portsmouth, all I wanted was to lie down. I managed to clamber into my hammock before passing out but maybe a mate took pity on me and threw me into my canvas cocoon.

During that night of fitful sleep interspersed with retching, snoring, farting and moaning, many of us were having nightmares. War was the dream theme. Uncertainty and fear were digging at us no matter how often we tossed and turn. "What is going to happen to me now that my war is over?" I bet every man onboard, if he had been given the chance and a quiet place, would have welcomed the opportunity to yell his head off with the same question. We heard General de Gaulle make his call to arms. He fired us up, at least most of the seamen were behind him, but his call was short on specifics and that was what we needed. Hard answers to hard questions seemed out of reach. In the absence of fact our minds played games and we started to rationalize.

We caught ourselves telling each other that we weren't being told specifics because the timing was wrong and this was just to confuse the enemy because 'somebody' really knew what was going on. That game didn't last too long because the question on every man's lips was personal: Where could the ship go and how were we going to get to wherever 'there' might be? The navy was the only part of the French armed forces still intact and it was unthinkable to desert the ship and join DeGaulle in London. Furthermore, we had been assured that all the ships would go to ports in the French empire. The de Brazza was slated to go to Casablanca. Everything was too confusing; no amount of beer could wipe away our questions and our need for answers. Too grim to accept, but we had to accept: France had collapsed as a fighting force. We were alone, sailors without a homeport in a war that, for the time being, the allies were losing.

CHAPTER FOUR:
A BRITISH SEAMAN

At 0400 hours the next morning someone switched on all the lights in the mess decks. I shuddered awake. Steel boots clanged on deck. My eyes were burning, my mouth was dry and my head was splitting. I wanted to vomit. As I fought hard to swallow, I peered out over the side of my hammock. A steel bayonet, inches from my nose, glistened in the flickering ship's light. It wasn't a French bayonet. My body convulsed from drunken nausea to fear, the kind of fear that sobers you up very fast. Fifth columnist? No, they're German paratroopers. The bastards have landed and taken over the dockyard! I peered out the other side. There were more bayonets. Making a run for it was not an option. Sitting up was hell but, through the fog of the last pint, I began to sense that something was wrong with my first conclusion. My ears were working better than my brain. Slowly I managed to roll to one side so I could peer out at what was happening on deck. I strained to make sense out of what was going on.

My first attempt failed but I kept trying to recognize noises that I had heard only a few hours before in the pubs. They were almost familiar. There it was! They were talking. The soldiers were speaking English, not German. Slowly, in order not to appear threatening, I raised myself far enough in my hammock to reach out and take a piece of paper that was being handed out by an English seaman. It was in French. It read, or at least what I can remember: "The admiralty regret to have to take over your ship. But, because France signed an armistice with Germany, we cannot take the risk that this ship will fall into the hands of the enemy. All your ships will be returned to France at the end of the present hostilities. You will be asked to make your own choice a) to be repatriated to a port of the

French empire, b) to join the Free French Navy which is going to be formed or, c) to join the Royal Navy until the end of the present hostility." My eyes burned. He continued, "In the latter case, you will keep your own rank and be treated as a British Seaman. Now pack your bags and hammock and fall in on the jetty where your Captain will speak to you."

For a few seconds I thought this was a practical joke but one more look at the Royal Marines in full battle kit with fixed bayonets told me they weren't pranksters. They were taking no chances and I was not going to be the Hero of the Day and do something stupid. I looked at the other hammocks. Some of my mates had begun to swing to the deck, glassy-eyed and struggling to stand without swaying. Some still roared drunken snores and had to be shaken awake.

A raging hangover mixed with what I had just read drove my morale into a hole deeper than the deepest rift at the bottom of the ocean. "My God what have we done to deserve this?" I kept saying to myself. Kids, even teenage sailors, tend to trust their leaders. I thought those guys with their great educations and experience were supposed to steer a course and avoid disasters and mishaps. From what little I saw since we went into action, my life in the navy had become one massive fuck-up. If today was my first day in British hands, I thought, I was not at all happy. And, I was horribly hungover.

My mind was actually racing as I packed my kit bag. A little voice almost reassured me. "Of course in the two admiralties, the British and French have prearranged plans and what's happening is just another cock-up, another firing on our own troops, another bungling that will be set right tomorrow. Surely they saw this mess coming," I kept saying that to myself as I jostled my way through the mess and up on deck. A light cool breeze blew from offshore. It felt and smelled good after the stench below and I caught myself inhaling deeply. My arms were tingling and my legs ached. Was that the effect of too much the day before, or were my jangling nerves tightening my muscles?

About the only officer on the de Brazza daring to look at the crew was last night's duty officer, the poor chap who stared us down as we staggered onboard. Did he know what was going to happen to us? Out on deck I was becoming desperate. I tried to find some idea or an event that I could hang onto and use it to make sense out of what was happening. Later, more combat would teach me that great fear often generates absurd hopes and that by clinging to them you can manage your way back from panic to a survival mode. The turmoil in my mind was producing wishful thinking, a fantasy world in which everything would turn out the way it was supposed to. On that fateful morning I couldn't know that later more facts would be revealed. Events would unfold showing that many French generals and admirals, men we trusted to lead us through war to safety, and those great and lofty human beings were actually quite unprepared for the mess we were in.

Up on deck, captain Baden stormed out of the officer's mess screaming at the top of his voice. For a cold fish, he put on quite an act. We'd never seen him so alive, so human, and so thoroughly out of control. "I've been assaulted," he bellowed, pointing a long trembling finger at a young British sub-lieutenant who minutes before had leveled his revolver at our captain and then marched into his quarters to take him into custody. "What is this?" The young officer offered no explanation. Realizing that he was out of form, captain Baden stepped back, as if to gain distance and composure. Before he could start up again, another officer appeared, a British senior officer who spoke to him in French. He spoke quickly and quietly. We couldn't hear what he said but Captain Baden stiffened to attention, saluted, and appeared to calm down, almost as if he was following an order. From arrogant to almost deferential, he assumed the posture of a senior officer who acknowledged a superior force. Whether rank was right or wrong, rank was always obeyed.

The British officer, we couldn't figure out his rank but he had enough gold on his left arm to mint a few coins, ordered the ship's company to fall in on the jetty. After giving his order, he strode off as if the morning's event was routine light duty. Who in the hell was he? We'd soon find out but one thing was obvious: There was a change of command. We were now under British officers! What a hell-of-a thing to happen to French sailors. Captain Baden trotted at the side of the British officer. Perhaps, was he trying to pretend that he was still in control of this nightmare? Nothing made sense. By now, every set of French eyes followed the two officers down the gangplank. Royal Marines stood at the foot of the gangplank with fixed bayonets. They snapped to attention as the officers stepped ashore.

There was no doubt that the British officer was in command of our ship and our lives. Later, I found out that he was a commodore. From the way he stood on the jetty it was as if he wanted to announce to anyone who could see him that this was his show and he quite enjoyed it. He was neither arrogant nor loud. He stood calmly and radiated authority. I couldn't take my eyes off him. "That man's a leader," I kept saying to myself. Why? I don't know now, and I didn't know then. From a distance he was different than all the other brass on the dockside, including ours. There was something in the way he talked to his officers, the way he walked among the British sailors and Marines, something about him that set him apart.

The difference between him and captain Baden was clear. I'd never seen a British officer up close, let alone a guy that important, but the way he ran the show helped calm me down. Of course, Baden was having a bad morning. In the space of a few minutes he lost his ship, lost his officers, lost his crew and his career to a junior officer in the Royal Navy. Later, I would arrive at my own conclusions: his own government destroyed him. For the time being, victor and vanquished stood side-by-side as if the occasion were nothing out of the ordinary. Only their uniforms were different. What must have been going on inside their heads was another story.

I tried using my sentry eyes to stare into the darkness of the commodore's head, trying to anticipate what he was going to say to us. It seemed to me they were taking their own sweet time to get the show on the road. My confusion grew with each minute we stood in formation. Would I ever understand what was going on? My head was spinning and I felt like vomiting. A funny thought crossed my mind. "If one guy starts to empty his beer savaged guts, how many hundred will follow?" There was no doubt in my mind that our formation would collapse in chaos if someone bent forward and started retching. My first real hangover turned my body into a battle zone. My mind was in hand-to-hand combat with my churning guts. With no place to run, I was the captive audience of the war going on inside me. Those were two firsts in my life I could have done without. My temples had begun to throb and my mouth had gone dry again. I was trying to pucker up some spit but I was afraid the pursing would make me vomit. Mr. Captive Dassac. What in the horrible hell had happened to me? Shit, I was scared, very scared. Fear rattling my bones was worse than anything I had ever known.

The ratings formed up as ordered and the two senior officers talked. Facing us, not close enough to be menacing, Royal Marine guards stood at ease with their legs spread. Their Lee-Enfield rifles were fixed with bayonets. Their rifle steel butt plates were crunched into the jetty. Their gaze never wavered. There was no doubt which side had the upper hand. I quit staring at them and tried to count seagulls.

The French crew was lined up with officers on one side followed by petty officers and ratings. My shipmates and I stood in uneasy silence facing the British officers. There was no shouting and pushing. The whole sad episode was serious but civil. It was also my first introduction into how important 'form' is for the British.

Walking slowly, almost sauntering so he could stand in the middle of his officers, the officer with all the gold introduced himself as Commodore Walker. He spoke French with remarkably little accent. His voice was clear, unwavering, and he had our complete attention. None of the guys in my line were doing more than managing to breathe normally. None of us could believe what was happening. Before anyone could focus, the commodore turned to us and lifted his left arm as if to salute us. That was a strange gesture. Saluting from the left? It didn't make sense but nothing did. But it wasn't his good manners that riveted me. Instead of a hand and a fist he had a hook, a great big hook, big enough to grab you by the scruff of your tunic and pull you out of the water.

He was big enough to drop you back in the drink and maybe dunk you up and down a few times until he got your attention. His tunic was neatly pressed; I could have cleaned the grease out from under my nails on the crease running down the front of his crisp trousers. I said to myself, "Who knows, maybe all officers at his rank have to have a hook." His hook really suited him. He had a smooth pink face, probably what the French called, British Pink Gin. He addressed us calmly but his eyes and face were serious. Radiating from him was a definite no-nonsense air that was neither feigned nor theatrical. He was a professional, a man whose superiors had given him a mission he had every intention of completing. "This is where we are gentlemen," and he paused to give us a look that left no doubt that our lives were in his hands. He wasn't gloating and it struck me that he had probably been through a lot, he knew how to handle men, and he meant business. He would get his way whether we liked it or not. A true leader, as he spoke I had a fleeting thought that he was actually attempting to look every Frenchman in the eyes. On that crisp morning, there was no mistaking who was the master of our fate.

His voice was mellow, a deep baritone that was easily heard. He was matter-of-fact. Was he your friendly village boilermaker telling us our boiler rings needed rescaling? "I apologize for treating you this way but," and he explained that lining us up on the jetty under the control of a detachment of Royal Marines was the best way to avoid unnecessary bloodshed which could have happened if the French Minister of Defense had ordered the French captains to scuttle their ships. I felt my nerves tingling again. I thought, "That's it. We're done for."

Commodore Walker continued in his quiet French. "We are taking over your ships because some of the clauses of the armistice which your government has negotiated with the Germans are not clear. As it stands there is every possibility that the Germans might use these ships," he waved his hook at the small flotilla still flying the tricolor, "if they were to fall into their hands." He paused, weighing each word and then it became clear to me that Britain was not prepared to take any chances. "Britain will continue fighting until the whole of Europe," his hook waved in the sunlight, "is freed." He hacked one of those British officer 'hems', a voice trick I would soon learn to appreciate for its timing and importance, "and, in particular, France."

My knees started shaking. My head and my ears were finally working together because what he was saying was starting to sink in. This guy is going to fight for us!" Without wasting a lot of time on a long speech he got right to the point and let us know whose side he was on. Wait! Something else was coming. I could feel it but when I heard him I was unprepared for the choice he was giving us. He cleared his voice and boomed, "Now, those of you who wish to be repatriated to France or North Africa fall in on the right!"

He was asking us to answer a life or death question. The de Brazza was our only link to France, our families, our navy. Since putting out to sea our ship had become our home and our reason for existing. Defending her was defending everything that we held dear. If we kept her intact through the war there was a good chance we would finish the war alive. I couldn't think of leaving her. After all, I'd worked so hard to qualify to join her, what was left for me to do with my life if I left her? At first no one moved. Then our ranks broke.

First, it was the odd shuffle somewhere out of sight, followed by more shuffles. The ship's company broke ranks. What we knew of France, our ship and its crew, began disintegrating. I began shivering almost uncontrollably; it wasn't because of the early morning chill hanging over the docks. I could not believe my eyes. All our officers and petty officers, except one marine petty officer, moved to the right. A sailor behind me gasped as if he had been hit hard in the stomach. So, there they went! Our leaders, the men who were trained to take us into battle, the men charged with looking after us, the men who swore to defend their country, the men some of us even looked up to and admired, every officer turned and marched into the right column. No looking back, no nods, nothing but backs and bobbing heads moving down the jetty, moving away from the horror of war to live, perhaps, in an occupied France. Or even, worse, join the Nazis and someday fight against their former shipmates.

I stared after them and my eyes were burning again as if they had been seared. Was I fighting instant hatred or tears? If I'd been an older man I might have had a stroke. I stared at Captain Baden. "What in God's name was going on?" I kept asking myself. Captain Baden cleared his throat and began speaking. His voice was shaking. He was unaccustomed to seeing a sea of faces twisted in shock and disbelief. He spoke in a flat, listless, neutral voice. Not admonishing us, he sounded like a tired father instead of a man of decision responsible for his ship and his crew. "I can't give you any advice but you must do what your conscience and sense of duty tells you to do." That was it. Nothing more, no explanation, no thank you for support, no appeal to patriotism, no pride in being French, nothing but a quick 'do what you have to do'. He turned on his heel, stumbling off to join his fellow officers. A young British lieutenant marched at his side. I am not even sure Captain Baden saluted us. He left us alone on the jetty facing the Royal Marines.

Someone moved from among the ranks of my shipmates. A conscript stepped forward and followed captain Baden. No sooner had he turned his back on us shipmates when a voice bellowed, "yellow bastard." No one else moved. The British sailors and marines stared at the French sailors and the French sailors stared back. What next? If there was any certainty at that moment, the only members of the crew who knew where they were going were the men who turned to the right and marched into captivity. At least they were being taken to a camp somewhere until secure transport could be arranged to take them back to North Africa.

We couldn't stand there forever wondering what to do. The morning's events continued to unfold. "Forward march," rasped through the air. A British petty officer took charge of us. If he hadn't given the order we might have stayed there for a very long time. No one knew what "march" meant but we caught on fast when the marines closed ranks on either side of our column and began marching behind the petty officer.

Training and discipline broke us out of our stupors. This wasn't the proper time for an English lesson; we marched off to HMS Victory barracks. The atmosphere was electric. Each of us had taken a major decision with virtually no time to think through the consequences. I've often wondered whether our officers had time to think about what their options were, but for my shipmates and me, there was no time to think and weigh, discuss and argue. It was wartime and in the heat of the moment each of us took a life or death decision.

Not that life in the navy was a guarantee to survive the war. But it was the life I had chosen and the life I intended to lead. Come what may, there was no turning back. I said to myself: only surviving and getting through the war in one piece, somehow going forward, was all that mattered from that point on.

Once inside the gymnasium we stowed our gear and lined up for a British breakfast. Big trays of fried eggs, tomatoes and bacon rashers, butter, toast, jam had been laid on. The smell of the warm rich breakfast made me realize I was ravenously hungry. I'd forgotten about my hangover. Captivity had shocked my system into sobriety.

As the morning wore on, ratings from other ships marched into the barracks. Even French commercial fishermen, known for their fierce independence, managed to make their way to England. Within a couple of hours there were well over a thousand men milling around in the gymnasium. Sailor or simple fisherman, each was eager to join a French ship and fight. The spirit was there but there was no organization, no officer corps, no way to commission a French ship, and it would be months before a Free French Navy could be formed, crews trained, battle plans assigned.

So much had to be done and there was so little time, and there were certainly no signs of forward planning. Our fighting spirit was hot, but it would be a long time before milling seamen were trained and assigned ships with new leadership and a new command structure. Looked at another way, we had the men and the spirit and all we needed was a new navy. Getting from where we were, bumping into each other in an overcrowded gymnasium and then onto ships and out to sea was going to be a Herculean task.

Order emerged from confusion in the course of the following days and weeks. De Gaulle announced the creation of a Free French Navy and all those who wanted to join were sent to the old Battleship Courbet. That tub became the temporary flagship for the Free French Navy. It came as no surprise, given what we had just gone through, life onboard the Courbet was utter hell. Too few officers and petty officers meant discipline could not be enforced. Tempers flared, arguments erupted and fights broke out. It was obvious that something drastic had to be done so the Free French Navy became a reality instead of the General's dream. In other ports fights broke out between British and French sailors while on shore. Onboard the submarine Surcouf, fighting among the allied crew resulted in the deaths of two sailors and many more were injured.

Tension continued to rise. In July news of the Mers El Kebir affair swept through allied ranks like wild fire. The British Navy was understandably shocked. After hearing the complete explanation about what had happened, plus the obvious tension between the

Rene Dassac (in collaboration with Patrick K. Robbins)

French Naval Officers and their British counterparts, I secretly began to wonder whether the French didn't see Britain more as an enemy than an ally. I could not influence events but I was a keen observer and I knew there was something fundamentally wrong and it had to be addressed before it tore us apart even further. As agonizing as my thoughts were, I did not have time to sit and reflect on my plight. My new British superiors were hell bent to turn their Frenchmen into respectable British sailors.

New uniforms and kit were issued, and every day, for hours on end, we drilled on the parade ground while the Marine band played military marches. Iron Hook Walker stood on the review platform resplendent in his commodore's uniform. I hate to think of what was going through his mind. If it hadn't been wartime and serious business, the scene could have been something out of a comic cinema. A bit of Charlie Chaplin, a bit snipped from the Marx brothers, unruly seamen were trying to march like Brits.

Commodore Walker commanded foreign sailors who chose to stay in Britain and fight. As far as we were concerned, that was the right thing to do. But, at this early stage in our new careers, we were men who constantly did the wrong thing. Was getting a Frenchman to execute and order a problem? No, provided he understood the order. Virtually none of us spoke English and what little we spoke was certainly not British Royal Navy English. We could negotiate a pub or straddle a lady of the night but an "about face order" produced collisions, curses and repetitions, hour after hour after hour.

A young Canadian Officer was put in charge of the French company because he spoke French and English. Fine choice in theory, in reality the Canadian was accepted neither by the French nor the British. His French was not the real French the sailors spoke and his English was different than what his British fellow officers spoke. He almost went crazy trying to turn his Frogs into real British sailors. God knows how many time the Commodore bellowed over the loud speaker, "For the Frenchmen, once more!" And under their breaths, barely audible to the French, British sailors in charge of our training pleaded, "For fuck's sake French cunt wake up." In the first few weeks our drilling was bad enough to be funny. Only when the parade was over could we manage to have a good laugh about our capers under the commodore's gaze. That ability to laugh at ourselves and share our shortcomings with the British began proving to us that the Brits were slowly beginning to accept us. Not surprisingly, in spite of our chronic inability to understand our British officers, we actually began to make progress and started to like the Brits. They meant well, at least what we could understand we took to be well intentioned.

One day after a reasonably successful drill the Commodore gathered all the French sailors around him and gave us a thorough briefing on the bloody Mers el Kebir affair. As usual, he was firm and clear. Facts killed rumors and I could feel my spirit improving. The commodore spared no detail. What he said was ugly and it was true. We were stunned. When he finished much to our surprise, the commodore invited us to join him in singing the Marseillaise. Truly, Iron Hook Walker was a leader of men. He made a stirring commitment. "It will take time, but you can be sure, we will soon go back to France." We cheered ourselves hoarse and somehow, deep inside, I knew the Hook was telling the truth. When and how we would return to France was anybody's guess. Iron Hook continued but his tone changed and he was grim. "You know that because France signed an armistice with Germany you have become rebels as far as the Germans are concerned. In the future, if you should be so unlucky as to be taken captive, the Germans have a right to shoot you."

In the back someone muttered, "merde," which pretty much summed up how each of us felt. Commodore Walker pretended not to hear. "We have thought through this matter for you and we have a solution. Tomorrow you will choose an English name." I could not believe my ears. Me, a sailor from the south of France, me an able seaman trained in the French naval schools, me a former bugler, am I to become British? What the commodore said made sense but what he was ordering us to do was to take a big step. Being captured was bad enough but being shot was worse.

The process was simple. Each sailor was ordered to give his company officers any identification proving he was French: identity papers, photographs, and personal letters. If a sailor was captured he had a reasonable chance his interrogation would follow an established procedure protecting him under the Geneva Convention. All he was required to identify was his name and serial number. That was the extent of the Hook's address. By then I had come to accept that he was a leader of few words. When he spoke, he chose his words carefully, got to the point and then moved on. He expected his audience to understand him and follow his orders.

We were at war. In the few moments needed to get his point across to us, commodore Walker changed our lives. Typical of what we were learning to expect from him, he didn't have his say and then walk away leaving us stunned bumbling. He paused, changed his tone ever so slightly to convey another emotion, one he obviously felt very deeply. Somehow he managed to talk to each and every man. He was uniquely capable of making each man, and there must have been hundreds of us, feel as if he alone was being spoken to by the commodore. He told us how much he appreciated the commitment we had already made and the commitment we were about to make. He saluted, "I am proud to have you serving with us. Good luck to you all and God bless you." Somebody muttered behind me, "Tomorrow we'll be born again." That got a good laugh but when we had time to think about his wisecrack, he wasn't too far off the mark!

That night Lafont and I went ashore. All we could talk about was how to choose an English name. Lafont had it all figured out which was more than I could claim. "As from tomorrow I will be Georges Watson," he said with great gravity. "Do you know who that is?" I didn't know and I really didn't care so I couldn't answer his question. "What about you Taulus, have you thought of your new name?" He caught me cold. I didn't have a name, had not really given it any thought, and frankly I didn't really care that much. After all, what's in a name unless you're some noble with a bunch of hyphens and 'de's' tacked together to make you sound important?

As we were talking we stopped in the middle of the sidewalk in front of a shoe shop. The blind on the entrance door was rolled down: "Closed", as if that wasn't already obvious. There was just enough light to make out the lettering on the storefront. The owner's name was printed in shiny gold letters: "J. Powell." I looked at those two words. I repeated them a couple of times to myself to get their feel before I turned to Lafont. "Okay, I've got a name," I blurted out my new name, enormously relieved at my decision. "As of tomorrow I will be known as torpedo man John Powell." That was it. End of story, no more guessing, my new identity was Mr. Everyman, high street Great Britain.

Before we got to the end of the block I looked back at my new name, almost wondered what the real owner was like, but I wasn't going to come back and meet the bloke. We were thirsty and we had something to celebrate. "Now let's go and drink to our new names." We had a few drinks in the "Wheelbarrow, "a little the pub where Frenchmen used to meet. It was located in South Sea, a suburb of Portsmouth facing the Isle of Wight. I caught myself looking in the mirror behind the bar and raised my glass to John Powell. From what I could tell, John Powell was still a skinny kid who really looked like a Frog.

*****

In early July the Luftwaffe started their daylight bombing raids on populated areas of the town causing many civilian casualties. The population reacted courageously. For me, it was a very good example of the difference between scenes of panic on the continent when the population was given the same punishment. The British were different. They took their horrible hits, dug out, and went on living. Watching them, I became absolutely convinced England would fight to the very end. Tough, resolute, cheerful and determined, I could not help but admire their courage. My mind hadn't made the complete switch to my new identity. I'd forgotten. It wasn't a question of "their" courage; it was "our" courage.

One Sunday afternoon I was caught in town when it was attacked. I couldn't see the bombs but I heard them whistling as they fell. One bomb fell on a cinema filled with children watching a matinee. The film was a routine event, a chance for the children to forget the war for a couple of hours and get lost in their fantasy world. I rushed to the site and began clawing at the rubble in the hopes of finding some child alive under the bricks and collapsed walls. NFS ambulances, gyros flashing, lined up to take away the wounded children while hearses loaded stretchers with covered little bodies. Many children were killed.

I was furious and began throwing bricks to one side hoping to find someone alive. White searing rage spurred me on. I was more animal than man, cursing half in English and half in French. "Those bastards," I kept saying. "They murdered kids, miles away from any military targets." I can't remember how long I spent burrowing into that fallen building but I guarantee you I never got over that afternoon. No matter how deep I dig into my soul, I cannot forgive those German pilots. I can still see the kid's mothers and fathers converging on the ruins of that blasted cinema. Yes, we were in war, but those kids weren't fighting. They were just acting like kids do anywhere, innocent and free, hurting no one, just acting like kids.

By the end of July the Luftwaffe had suffered heavy losses during their daylight raids so they began night raids. They caused a lot of damage to the town but in fact they did very little damage to the dockyard. Anti-aircraft defenses had, finally, been organized into an effective protective shield. RAF night fighters managed to intercept many bombers before they had a chance to reach Portsmouth. In the depth of night, searchlights probed the sky with their long white fingers hoping to catch a German bomber and stay on it while the air defenses went to work. AA guns flashed; sometimes they picked out a bomber and helped bring him down. The Germans were getting mauled but the British paid a stiff price on the ground and in the air. The RAF lost many fine young pilots.

While all this was going on, I realized that I was facing another frustration that I hadn't counted on. As a kid in uniform I was an easy-going outward person who enjoyed meeting just about anyone I came across. After smiles and handshakes I became tongue-tied. Shyness and a lack of self-confidence were the culprits. Why was I shy and uncertain of myself? The answer was simple: I couldn't speak English well enough to make myself understood. To my credit, I had made some progress because I had begun to curse in English but I still hadn't learned enough to carry on a normal conversation let alone a decent conversation, one that was nice enough to let me chat up the girls. Progress came slowly but not fast enough for me.

Finally, the day came when we had to sign on and register under our new name and get our official number. Leave it to the British. They made a nice ceremony out of the very important transformation we were about to undergo. The registering officer sat at a large desk that had been placed exactly in the middle of the parade ground. A large bound folio book, the kind you used to see in accountant's offices, was open in front of him. The high drama was accentuated by the simplicity of the setting. There was no doubt the officer and his book were placed to get the attention of every man on the field.

I can't recall but I think we formed up in alphabetical order according to our French names, or did we form up in order of our new British names? By then, hundreds of training hours paid off and I accepted the British military passion for queuing and marching. I waited my turn as the registering officer began with the first French sailor in front of him. "Give all your papers, letters and photographs to the petty officer over there." He pointed to a man soon to be almost buried under a pile of official looking brown envelopes. "These will be returned to you after the war." He sounded so damned sure of himself. Even though we were getting pounded on a daily basis there was no doubt in his mind that the war would be over and Britain would defeat the Germans. I was struck by this certainty and watched with great amusement when my shipmates responded to his order, "And now give me your new name." It was the beginning of my new life.

The fun started with the 'naming' of French sailors. All the great historical names were given: Nelson, Wellington, Churchill, Anthony Eden, and even the names of our favorite cigarettes were also popular: Woodbine, Players. More common names, Johnson, Watson, Jackson, were also popular but we were discouraged to take the name of Smith because the registering officer said there were already too many in England.

Once we had handed in all our papers and given our names we were instructed to use only our new names. Our names given at birth would be removed from all official British documents. My turn came. I snapped a salute and introduced myself: John Powell, I said in the most English accent I could muster. In a flash R. Dassac ceased to exist but he breathed, laughed, and fought as John Powell.

To make sure we understood the full implications of our name change, we were also told not to contact our relatives in France or elsewhere. This meant that we could not write our families via consulates in foreign countries because our letters would probably be intercepted by the enemy and used as an excuse to arrest our relatives.

Taulus vanished and reappeared as John Powell. I thought long and hard about what we had been told, how we needed to conduct our new lives and live our new identities. I swore that I would not converse with other Frenchmen except those who were like me: serving in the Royal Navy. Let's face it I told myself, for the time being the navy is my family. The navy is taking good care of me and now that I was really in the big Royal Navy family I could always ask for advice when in trouble. Certainly, from then on I counted on the navy to help me find a way to solve my problems.

With new names and new futures, all we wanted to do was to be drafted to a ship and get into action. We almost drove our officer-in-charge crazy peppering him with the same question, "When are we going to sea?" Patiently, and for the millionth time, he would reply, "You will be going soon enough." And he was right. We did get drafted, perhaps sooner than any of us expected and for a reason that really hadn't dawned on any of us. The admiralty realized that the best way for us to get a sufficient knowledge of English was to send us out to sea. Drafting rules stipulated that no more than two or three former Frenchmen were to be assigned to the same ship. Admiralty's logic was simple: mix up the Frenchmen and toss them into the middle of English speaking lads and they would soon learn to speak and understand English.

At the end of August we finally began to ship out. A lot of ratings, petty officers, and I were called up to the drafting office and told to get our gear and hammock and be ready to board a train that was coming especially for us. The special train pulled into the back of the barracks gate at 20:00 hours. We boarded and then we were told were going to Greenock by night to board a troop ship to set sail for an unknown destination. No one slept that night. Rumors flew and for every guy who 'knew' where we were going there were six who told him he was wrong because 'they'd heard.' So it went until dawn when we rolled into Greenock docks. We were immediately marched up to a troop ship. On its bow was written, "Empress of Canada".

Once onboard we were told that we were going to Halifax, Canada to commission the first lot of fifty American destroyers that the U.S.

government had made available to Britain. In reality, they had been "sold" to Britain for leases against five bases in the Atlantic for 99 years. It was my first experience with the Lend-Lease program President Roosevelt used to arm Britain without having to go through Congress. For America this was good business and getting these destroyers was vital to protecting Britain.

Everyone in the British government expected an invasion at any time; Britain was not in a position to bargain over prices and terms. Britain desperately needed the destroyers to escort convoys as well as to protect the island in the event the Nazis decided on a ground invasion of the British Isles. During the last few months many British destroyers had been sunk or damaged. Therefore, it was imperative to mobilize all available ships and assign them to the south and southeast coast of England. Once on station, their role was to gun down and ram enemy landing crafts. Britain was fighting for its very life and the Lend-Lease destroyers had to make it across the Atlantic.

The evening of the day we arrived we left port at high speed. My future shipmates and I were assembled and told that we would be commissioning the USS Satterlee, renamed HMS Belmont. Onboard the Belmont there were three Frenchmen among the crew: Able torpedo man Powell, gunnery rating Fred Grey, and another gunnery rating whose name I cannot remember. I got to know my new shipmates, particularly one senior torpedo man called Randall with whom I shared lookout duty throughout the trip to Halifax. In addition to our military crew there were a number of children and civilians who had been evacuated from London. Once at sea our few days in the Atlantic fell into a typical naval routine: detailed for look out, clean the ship, and hours playing poker.

Rene Dassac (in collaboration with Patrick K. Robbins)

CHAPTER FIVE:
FIRST COMMISSION UNDER THE WHITE ENSIGN

When we reached Halifax, the British sailors who made up part of the crew of the seven destroyers were marched off to a Canadian barracks. There we were separated, in some cases reassigned, and to form the companies of the seven British ships: HMS Belmont, Broadway, Beverly, Churchill etc...

The next day we boarded our ship, occupied the mess to which we had been detailed and started to organize ourselves. I was detailed to the after mess deck with the rest of the torpedo men, some gunnery ratings and a handful of ordinary seamen. This mess was short of bunk space, short by about a third. The ships had been built for peacetime crew levels but there were more of us in wartime. This meant some had to sling their hammocks while others took over the bunks. I was allocated a bunk, which at first glance, may appear to the uninitiated to be a better choice but once we got out to sea in rough weather it was a different story.

A team of American officers and petty officers came onboard to explain to the ship's company how to use the armament. Our ship was fitted with four triple torpedo tubes two on each side. When the American petty officer in charge of the torpedoes talked to me he noticed my strong French accent and asked me where I came from. For a split second I froze. Everything that raced through my mind on that day when Dassac became Powell began to race through my mind again. I looked at him carefully and quickly concluded that the American was an ally. "I come from France."

The American laughed and then continued, speaking to me in French! His French was good so I didn't have to struggle to understand him. How had he learned French? The best way possible: he was married to a French girl he had met in Villefranche sur mer and he missed her. After a while I got tired of hearing about his wife and I asked him,

"Are you guys going to enter the war?" The American answered, "Yes." The way he replied left no doubt in my mind. America was coming into the war; it was just a matter of time. He went on to explain, "So far America has no intention of entering the war, but sooner or later, we will have to join in because Japan will force us into it."

I must have looked somewhat puzzled. At the time I could not make the connection between America's entrance into the war on our side and war breaking out between Japan and the United States. From where we were in Europe we didn't know much, if anything, about the political tension between Japan and America. A year later when Japan attacked America in Pearl Harbor I wondered how a petty officer of the U.S. Navy could have been so sure of himself, so sure of his forecast. Anyway, what he said didn't rattle me because already the British government was saying that it had the willpower and stamina to stand up to the Germans and struggle for fifty years if necessary. Frankly, I thought the "fifty years" bit was normal war time propaganda but, nonetheless, it unsettled me to think I might be an old man and still fighting. That is, if I lived. A lot of men were dying and a destroyer was always in the thick of the action. .

We spent a couple of weeks in port. Sometimes we left for short sea trials so we could familiarize ourselves with our American equipment. Much of it was similar to ours but some of it was new. Necessity is the mother of invention. We managed to turn the ice cream machine into a good washing machine.

When the newness of the equipment had begun to wear off we went to sea for engine room drills, depth charge and torpedo exercises. The first exercises with live ammunition were real eye-openers. Much to our frustration we found that some of the depth charges did not explode. To make matters worse, the only torpedo we fired went mad and started to circle our ship. That scared the crew. Even the captain said, "If we have to use these, we've got to run out of the drop spot fast and hope for the best."

Down in the engine room there were problems that we did not need. When pushed to maximum speed, the steam pipes sprang leaks. One of the engine room crew said the place looked like a shower stall for midgets with all those little steam jets squirting all over the place.

Rene Dassac (in collaboration with Patrick K. Robbins)

The first officer down in the engine room muttered to no one in particular but everyone within earshot, "God only knows how this ship will behave in rough weather." No, the ship was far from perfect but who were we to be choosy? Britain did what had to be done and I don't think the Americans sold us bad ships on purpose. They just didn't work the way they were supposed to. Anyway, we had become pretty good at fixing things that weren't supposed to break.

Onshore was not our idea of a hot town. In fact, Halifax was a strange town: there were no pubs. This meant we had to buy our drinks in the shops and then go outside and drink in the street. By the way, Halifax is not known for good weather so we wound up standing in doorways, huddling under ponchos, drinking and cursing. Finally, after too long, the day came to sail. There were no tears among the crew when we put "merry" Halifax behind us. We sailed to Saint John in Newfoundland, another dry hole but we had no shore leave because we only refueled and headed out into the Atlantic bound for the U.K. via Belfast.

In case you had forgotten: we were onboard a destroyer. In American navy terms a destroyer is called a 'tin can' for several reasons but there is only reason that makes any sense, especially if you are a crew member. A destroyer acts like a tin can because when you throw a tin can into a pond to watch it float, the least breeze or the tiniest ripple makes the can pitch and roll. So does a destroyer! Regardless of whose navy, that ship is a guarantee for one of the roughest rides at sea imaginable. For the first two days the sea was calm but I wasn't doing too well. My stomach was holding up. Seasickness wasn't the problem. My problem was psychological: I was lonely and loneliness began working on my morale. For the first time in ages, I started to feel a painful sadness. The ship was too small and I needed space. I couldn't speak English that well. This meant I couldn't join in with the rest of the mess. They played cards, joked, told stories, but I sat like a lump because I couldn't understand enough, or speak well enough, to keep up.

In those days I was definitely deadweight and it got through to me. But, in a way, my handicap actually started to work for me instead of against me. My mates were good men and they went out of their way to help me understand and speak English. My messmates were all

Welshmen. What happened to my English when I finally got around to speaking and joining in with them? I began to speak with a strong Welsh accent with a lot of bloodying and f…..g between words. How was I supposed to know it wasn't the King's English that I was speaking? After all, others were using it so why shouldn't I?

My action station was at one of the torpedo tubes. During that early period when I was really struggling with the language the captain told me that he would give me my orders in French until I understood English properly. What a man! I started to climb out of the language hole slowly. When my vocabulary improved I integrated with the rest of the mess but my vocabulary definitely did not contain the niceties that would have welcomed me at a Halifax church social.

The good weather began to deteriorate when we got far out to sea. We passed close to a huge iceberg. This was the first time most of the crew, myself included, had ever seen an iceberg. When we came around the 'berg we ran head-on into gale force weather and our ship bucked and rolled, shimmied and shook. It was no longer a vessel; it had become a monster: part wild horse and part jackhammer. Crunching white waves pounded our tin can. When icy seawater started leaking through the portholes into the mess deck we had to cope with several inches of icy water on the deck. All the gear we could not stow off the deck got wet. There was no way to dry out. As we approached Greenland the temperature started dropping. Cold strong winds howling from every point on the compass blasted our little tin can.

We were wet and cold all the way through to the marrow in our bones. There was no escaping. But, I was lucky because 'Help' came from a most unexpected source. When we were in exciting Halifax we went to a civic social center. A French Canadian schoolteacher gave me a parcel containing some warm woolen pullovers she had knitted and a pair of thick woolen pants. I don't know why she chose me but I suspect that someone might have let slip there was a French rating onboard. She singled me out and I couldn't have wished for a more perfect gift. Even wet, the wool helped fight the elements.

I had never been so thoroughly cold in my life. The sea was rough and icy waves shot high over the bow. I calculated that we rolled at least twenty-five degrees, and sometimes even up to thirty degrees. To no one's surprise, our tin can was twisting, pitching, rolling and bucking. It was during one of those awful nights in the middle watch when we lost a signalman overboard. We'll never know how he was lost. Did he fall, trip on something, or was he swept overboard? Blasting alarm horns brought us to our stations. Our searchlights swept the sea. Finally, after many fruitless hours, the captain called off the search. We resumed course. Abandoning a man at sea, a shipmate, is an awful moment.

Onboard a small ship like a destroyer everyone knows everyone else. We couldn't help talking and imagining what his final moments must have been like. With the freezing cold he didn't stand a chance. If there was any mercy in drowning in the icy Atlantic it was this: because of the extremer cold he would have lost consciousness within seconds. Or at least that is what we kept telling ourselves. We were bitter about losing him and bitter that we could not retrieve his body and give him a decent burial. After his accident we were ordered to rig a number of lifelines along the most dangerous part of the deck. One of those lines saved my life.

I was leaving the mess to go on watch at midnight and the ship was rolling heavily. I waited until my side of the ship was up and then I hooked my belt to the lifeline and jumped back on deck. Suddenly, the ship rolled sharply and plunged into a deep trough. I lost my footing! In a flash I found myself hanging over the side of the ship up to my neck in the freezing ocean! It all happened so fast that I didn't have time to shout. In fact, I didn't know what had happened until I was soaked. Luckily, I was not alone. My mate, Randall saw what happened. Somehow he managed to grab hold of me just when another wave washed me back on deck. He yanked me to safety and managed a laugh, "John, I thought you were gone for good." I was shivering uncontrollably partly because of my arctic bath and partly because I had survived a near encounter with My Maker. As if to console me, he assured me, "this is a story to tell your children." He jerked his head toward the aft. Over the roar of the wind I heard him say, "go in the engine room and dry your clothes. I will take your watch until you come back." What a great friend. I was drenched through my oilskins, right through to my skin. I managed to dry-out enough to take my watch against the fourth funnel that kept me warm while watching the 180° horizon on the port side. I guess everything is relative because even though it was dangerous to be above deck, the howling sea air was fresh. This meant it was better than being down below.

Conditions in the mess deck were bloody awful. Seawater slopped on the deck and picked up all sorts of rubbish that had been jarred loose. With the ship pitching and rolling so violently sludge sloshed half way up to our knees. It stank in the mess deck, a foul acrid stench that seemed to freeze onto our clothes and into our heads. All access to the deck was closed; we couldn't get any ventilation. Only after we got through the storm and into calmer waters were we allowed to open the portholes and top bulk doors to let the place air out and dry out.

The forward mess deck directly under the fore deck was drier because it was higher and therefore above sea level. Being dry didn't mean you were better off than the rest of the ship. Up front, anyone with the slightest inclination to seasickness was in trouble. Somehow you felt the ship's pitch and roll more when you were up front. When the ship plunged twelve or fifteen feet there was no way your stomach could take the constant pounding and wrenching.

We had an American journalist onboard; we never saw him once we reached the high seas. He got so seasick his face turned green, as if he was wearing some kind of camouflage appropriate for a jungle raid. But we were in the North Atlantic. When we finally reached Belfast he surfaced, a gray-green ghost none too steady on his feet. The last thing I heard him say was, "I'll never travel by sea again." I wish I could have read what he had to say about our crossing.

When we reached Belfast representatives from the admiralty inspected the ship. Their report must have been damning because we were immediately sent to Falmouth to be made sea worthy. We couldn't get berthed in a larger port. They were filled with ships that had been towed in for quick repairs. At least we made it across the ocean but there was no overlooking the fact that we were not ready to go into active duty. A lot of work had to be carried out on our ship. So much, in fact, that it couldn't be completed while the crew remained onboard.

Talk about getting a good break every now and then, this was one time that the navy really looked out for us. We were lodged in a small hotel that had been requisitioned by the navy. That part of the story is not very exciting. The navy requisitions billeting all the time. What made our billet different was the hotel management: lovely WRENS were in charge. One of those beauties became a friend. Remember, just a few months earlier, I couldn't speak English but by the time we got to Falmouth, I was doing quite well and stories began to circulate speculating about my ability to chat up the young lovelies. I actually volunteered to help with the evening dishes so that I could walk her home. I had other ideas than dishes but dishes and walks were as far as I got. She was living with an aunt, or so she said, but at least I got close enough to start to dream the kind of dreams guys have at times like that. Unfortunately, I was not sure she had an aunt.

In dry dock they fitted our ship with the ASDIC, now called Sonar (anti submarine detector) and a couple of depth charge throwers. They must have had some doubts about the ship's design and seaworthiness. The after mast which was making the ship top heavy was removed, all the portholes were made watertight, we replaced all our American depth charges with British charges, and a lot of repairs were made in the engine room. New equipment meant new men. We got a number of ratings and a petty officer to take over our newly installed ASDIC.

When all this work was completed we received a signal ordering us to proceed to Milford Haven to refuel and then sail to Scapa Flow. Sailors come and sailors go and finally it was time for me to say good-bye to my girlfriend in the kitchen. I kissed her and she looked so surprised but the other WRENS cheered us. We went through the Irish channel without incident, refueled in Milford Haven from a tanker and then continued on our way to Scapa. After passing the Mull, the sea was a bit rough. The sky was overcast with dark storm clouds but the visibility was good considering that it was early December.

We were detailed to Scapa in order to receive further training. The question was not whether we were a good or bad crew. We had not been on our ship long enough to hone our performance and become an effective fighting team. Admiralty's standards were exacting and our performance, although well intentioned, was unacceptable. The commodore in charge of our program told us that he would release us from training only when we met admiralty standards and proved to him that we could maintain them when on station. He left no doubt that he expected nothing but the best. There was no time to waste; we got to work.

In the meantime the Christmas season came and went. For the first time, but not for the last time, Christmas and New Year's were spent either at sea or anchored in the Flow. Despite the weather and cramped conditions it wasn't too bad. Our officers allowed some beer to be brought onto the lower deck and we had a pretty good time considering the pounding the Allies were taking in every theatre.

At Scapa we moored alongside a V and W class destroyer. In the evening, after we had returned from sea exercises, we often played bingo aboard the other destroyer to pass the time. Mess chatter is a valuable source of information. The destroyer's crew told us the hell we could expect to go through. We were at the mercy of our new commodore. In no time we found out they were right except on most counts except one: the training we completed was actually worse and more demanding than any of us thought possible.

December 1940 was indeed very cold. Ice formed on deck and I don't think I'm exaggerating when I say there wasn't one day when the sea was anything but rough and nasty. There was no let up. All the exercises were exhausting. To get an idea of what was going on, try and imagine anti submarine exercises that were carried out with a small charge secured to the end of a long steel line which was dropped over the side above the spot where the ASDIC thought there was a submarine. Once over the side, we had to haul it back onboard. The steel cable was ice cold, our gloves got soaked and then started to freeze. We couldn't work our fingers fast enough to keep our circulation going and we slipped and bumped into each other. By the time the exercise was over we had a hard time closing our hands merely in order to massage them and warm up our fingers.

Night gunnery exercises were the worst because there was no let up and they involved the entire ship's company. We were called to 'action stations' and held our positions until the firing stopped. Most nights when we had gunnery practice the firing went on for hours.

Rene Dassac (in collaboration with Patrick K. Robbins)

When we returned to port we were partly deaf and thoroughly frozen. To the best of his ability, the commodore tried his damndest to replicate the combat conditions we were about to face. Short of suffering incoming enemy rounds or dodging live torpedoes, our training was brutally realistic.

Everyone agreed the commodore was a bastard, but, we also knew he was doing his job. By being exacting, by demanding better and better performance he was also improving our chances of surviving the war. After three weeks living with his hell, he inspected our ship. We all hoped for a let up; enough was enough. After combing the ship he told us he wasn't satisfied. Our performance had to improve. He didn't call us mediocre because he didn't deal with nuances. Mediocre is a debatable notch somewhere between good and bad. "You can be better and you must be better," he rasped. That's it, I thought. We're here forever. Before I could wallow in self-pity and drown out his voice he continued and then he really got my attention. "Furthermore gentlemen, the Germans are fully trained and fine seamen." Just what we wanted to hear, I thought with a twinge of sarcasm. He hammered home his point. "If you do not want to be their victim you will have to be quicker than they are. Destroy them or they will destroy you."

We were big boys now and he was telling us we'd play cat-and-mouse on the high seas. Who is the cat and who is the mouse, I thought? I thought this was his way for preparing us for another long training stint so I was surprised when he said, "I wish I could keep you here a bit longer, but you are sorely needed in the Atlantic and in the home waters. The threat of invasion is still possible." Thank you Lord for little favors. We were shipping out, at least that was something to be happy about. To a man, we probably knew we weren't in top fighting shape but we were better than when we pulled into our mooring a few weeks ago. Steam rose from around his duffel coat as he raised his arm to salute. "I wish you all good hunting and good luck!" That was it. We were officially in the war. No bands, no fanfares, no waving farewell, just a heartfelt wish. There was no doubt that we had acquired new skills. The commodore saw to that. Now we needed luck and guts every day until we won the war, I kept repeating to myself.

Taulus

We left Scapa, sailing past big and famous ships that were anchored in the ways: the Hood, the Rodney, several cruisers, and destroyers like ours. In Scapa, at least for a few weeks, we felt safe. We went out to play at war, finish the games, and come home to our berth. Tied-up somehow helped us push the war out of our immediate attention onto a horizon beyond our ship. If we weren't firing or getting fired at or stalked by a submarine, we felt secure because many other warships surrounded us.

Signals lamps blinked as we headed down the Flow and out to sea. When night fell we were on our own, doing our part in the huge effort that would become known as The Battle of the Atlantic. We were sailing to meet a returning convoy that was several days ahead of us, far out in the Atlantic. Like all young seamen those days, we were absolutely convinced of our immortality. That rock solid conviction was really a game we played with ourselves, a game that stopped us from coping with the reality of our frail little ship. One good hit, and our destroyer would explode and sink with all hands onboard. You can't live with that reality day-in-day-out, so when you make yourself immortal your ship doesn't matter.

The weather was cold, colder even than in Scapa. The winter winds beat the sea into a bowl of towering white caps. There was no way we could slice through the waves and avoid the worst of the weather. No, our ship pitched and rolled. Smashing towers of ice water broke across the fore deck until it was submerged. When the bow was under water the stern was out of water. Above the howling wind we could hear the screws thrashing in thin air threatening to rip off their shafts. I was convinced that we couldn't take too much of our stern being out of water before our ship began to fly apart. Steel made by man is breakable; nature is unforgiving. I don't know what was worse, the fear of the ship capsizing or the fear that the propeller shafts would snap and leave us adrift with no power. We'd die, there was no doubt in my mind. Each time I heard the screws scream I knew they were still turning. But, for how long?

We rendezvoused with the convoy. Fortunately, it had not suffered any losses and we reached Liverpool without any alerts. Liverpool meant shore leave, but not for everyone. Half the crew got leave. The other half, I was in that half, stayed onboard to refuel and load additional munitions. A few hours later we sailed to begin another escort duty. A routine began and we adapted to it because Liverpool wasn't too bad a station. Sometimes we escorted an outward-bound convoy, and then sometimes after the drop off point, we sailed to rendezvous and escort an incoming convoy. This was a fairly nice duty because we usually stopped at Londonderry to refuel and buy fresh food from the Irish who came from southern Ireland to sell eggs, bacon, butter etc ... to us before we reached Liverpool. At the end of one of our escort assignments we were ordered into dock to have our boilers cleaned; this meant there was a possibility of a few days shore leave.

As good as the thought of shore leave sounded, I had a problem because I didn't have any family to visit in England, so I thought of staying onboard to catch up on some sleep and spend a few days visiting Liverpool and the surrounding country side. My messmates had other ideas; several offered to take me home with them. All of a sudden, I was the hottest game below decks. I had more offers than I could handle. I knew, that if I accepted one, I would wind up irritating someone because I hadn't gone home with him. To help me out of this predicament, they decided to have a lottery. Each of my mates who had invited me put his name on a piece of paper in a cap. I picked out one of the papers. And, that's how I first saw Wolverhampton and began a sad saga in my personal life.

Major Randall was my host, a good fellow, but a little too rough on his mother for my liking. Sometimes I thought he was insulting. I kept coming up with excuses for his mother, by telling her, we had just come through a very hard time at sea and that had affected almost everyone. Sweet lady, she said, "John, I know him and his bad language, it's kind of you to find excuses for him." I felt so sorry for her and at the same time I felt uncomfortable. I couldn't interfere and I could never figure out why he was so harsh with her.

*****

One day while we were on leave Randall introduced me to a certain Jack Rowan, whom he had known before the war. Morton was in the company of a charming young lady, apparently his secretary. She and I got talking. She was easy to talk to and I told her that I was lonely.

We all know how conversations evolve, one topic flip-flopping onto another, with no real direction, just a pleasant exchange. Strangely, my conversation with the pleasant young woman took off in a totally unexpected direction. Not only did I get a proposal to spend my next leave at Morton's home, his young lady proposed to correspond with me. Her name was Edith Hart. Unfortunately, we met at the end of my leave. We exchanged addresses. From the look in her eyes I think she wanted more, or at least I like to think she did.

I needed female affection and she fascinated me. Apparently, she was quite interested in me. Why? Today after more than sixty years to reflect on that question, I really don't know the answer. Maybe part of the answer has to include at least two factors. Wolverhampton was an inland town and sailors were rarely seen. For the locals, we were curiosities. Probably the other factor playing in my favor was my true nationality. There weren't too many Frenchmen who managed to visit Wolverhampton. Back then at that stage in our two nation's histories, Frenchmen were liked by most of the British.

If you take those two factors: being a sailor and being French, couple them with a chance meeting, a fluke of fate occurred creating an emotional bond that became the basis for our relationship for many years. Had we become infatuated with each other or, for her, was I an exotic and handsome young man she could look at, pretend to play with, and walk away from? In a zoo, children stare at bear cubs and want to play with them despite the known dangers. I asked myself, was I the cub and she the child? Would I ever get an answer? In the end, what I did not know hurt me deeply and created one of the darkest, and most painful, periods of my life. But, that was much later. Starting with our first meeting, continuing for years, I couldn't get her out of my mind.

I thought a lot about her during the train ride back to Liverpool. She was a good-looking young woman, probably three or four years older than me, about the same height and well spoken. I had trouble figuring out her accent. There were just enough hints in the way she pronounced words to make me think that she might come from an upper middle class family. Something about the accent was definitely different than anything I heard in Wolverhampton and I couldn't place it.

Rene Dassac (in collaboration with Patrick K. Robbins)

By the time we met, I had a pretty good command of the English language and I knew enough about accents to be able to tell where someone had been raised. That knowledge was important below decks because a lot of the constant joshing and kidding centered on a man's origin. Scots, Cockneys and Welsh, looked at the world through different prisms. Keeping emotions under control in our mess required being able to recognize accents and build relationships. Her accent was different and I couldn't figure it out.

Edith was adopted when she was very young. Her features, auburn hair, a fascination with things Irish, would later lead me to believe that she may have been born Irish out of wedlock. In all likelihood she was put up for adoption in one of the Irish schools for unwed mothers. We never talked, in depth, about her origins but I believe there was something she was trying to hide. Later I met her family. Her father, Gunter, was a simple man, a day laborer, and a good honest man. I would have expected her dress to reflect her humble family but she dressed well, as if she belonged to another social circle. What she wore was not flash but it was class. When she walked into a room, men's heads turned to admire her.

Randall and I returned to Liverpool. With the rest of the ship's company, we started preparing our ship for more convoy escorts. We had been at sea long enough to know we were well trained and we had the stamina to deal with the hell of war. Our bodies could stand long stints at sea and our minds knew how to cope with cadavers floating beside survivors. We knew how to care for survivors, bring them back to life in our crowded mess. When we were in port we also knew how to switch off and drink and sing, while German bombs shook the pub's floor and walls.

Air raids were taking place almost every night, particularly over industrial towns and ports. Actually, one night something happened to me that was funny then and just as funny now many years later. I was on my way back to the ship. We were berthed in Gladstone dock. Fred Grey, Randall, and I decided to have a last drink in a pub down on the riverside. The pub was full of seamen of different nationalities. A piano was playing and people were singing, when all of a sudden for some stupid reason, a fight broke out. Bottles and chairs started flying all over the place. I probably hadn't needed that last drink - I was very sleepy. The police were called and to keep out of harm's way I slipped down behind the piano and fell into a deep sleep. The pub closed. No one bothered to look for me behind the piano.

The police cleared the pub but I went undetected because I was out like a light. The next morning, the charwoman who came to clean the pub, found me and shook me saying, "Come on Jack wake up, you are going to be late." I sat up and asked, "What time is it?" She had a gentle face and acted as if she really was concerned. "It's nine o'clock lad. You'd better clean up a bit, run back to your ship and think of a good excuse for being late." She was right, very right. I was in trouble.

As soon as I came on board I was brought to the first lieutenant who gave me a good run down and put me on the captain's report. At 1100 hrs, request men and defaulters were called to fall in on the quarterdeck for the captain's report. When my turn came the situation was both pathetic and laughable. After having read the charges the captain looked at me. He was stern but the corners of his mouth were fighting hard not to break into a laugh. "Well Powell, what have you got to say for yourself?" I know I must have looked scared. This was the first time I had been called to report to a senior officer. Sure, there had been little brushes with the law but this time it was serious. I was standing in front of the captain so I looked him straight in the face and gave a true and detailed explanation of how I managed to spend last night sleeping behind a piano in the pub. My explanation was given in a mixed French - Welsh accent. My story telling did it! Neither officer was able to keep a straight face. Only super human discipline prevented them from bursting out laughing.

I wasn't off the hook but at least I wasn't going to get a court martial. The captain thanked me for my honesty and then gave a good run down saying, "This could have been a very grave punishment if the ship had sailed without you. If that had happened, you could have been charged with desertion." He stared a hole into me big enough to see through. "Do you understand?" That thought never had crossed my mind. "Yes sir," I stammered. He gave me my punishment: "Fourteen days number 11 and stoppage of rum." Somewhere in the back I heard an order, "On cap, about turn, quick march." As soon as

I got into my mess the cock swain told me, "You are lucky my lad. We are sailing this afternoon. You're not going to have to do your punishment." I don't know if the captain, in his wisdom, had decided to scare me and allow his fellow officers to watch the comedy, but it worked. Apparently I was so convincing and pitiful that even the cock swain said he was beginning to feel sorry for me.

We set sail again for another convoy. This time we went far to the west, close to Greenland, to find our convoy. They had changed course several times to slip by a line of U boats that stretched along the northwest to the southwest. The convoy had already been attacked several times and lost a few cargo ships. We made the rendezvous and began a nightmare convoy!

It was slow sailing. We sailed at barely seven knots. Even at that speed many old rusty boats in the convoy had a hell of a job to keep in line. To crown it all, the weather was rough. We had to counter many dusk and night attacks, so many attacks, that we nearly ran short of depth charges and shells. The admiralty knew this was going to be a rough assignment because they included a trawler to pick up survivors. Fortunately, we were spared this nasty job. We got our convoy ships safely into British waters but it was exhausting work. It was as if we were shielding ducklings from big pike. Putting our ship in between where we thought the subs might be was a guessing game and on that convoy we guessed well. Most of our ships made it.

When we reached the U.K. we were sent to berth in Cardiff where a pile of ammunition was waiting for us on the jetty. We were not allowed ashore that night because we had to start stowing it. We worked feverishly because we knew that at some point the Germans would show up and try and bomb us into oblivion. Sure enough, about 10 p.m. the air raid sirens started hooting. Moments later their fat bombers thundered, coming in waves, across the night sky. The first lot dropped incendiary bombs to light up target zones and begin fires. Some of those bombs fell awfully close to the ammo stacked on the jetty.

When bombs are falling on top of you there is no time to think and plan and act rationally. Sometimes we picked up unexploded shells and threw them into the water before they could explode. We wouldn't find out until after the war but many of those bombs had been sabotaged and couldn't explode. Deportee forced laborers in German camps made them. At the risk of their lives, their skilled hands made sure precision millings and fittings were every so slightly imperfect. Good enough to pass inspection, the flawed pieces failed to detonate. Those that did explode did what they were intended to do: fires started all over town.

Wave after wave, their droning was so loud we heard it even over the ack-ack fire. Each wave seemed to have more planes than the previous wave. One wave carried heavy bombs and mines. Some of those bombs fell close to us. One of the hands on deck was looking at a parachute coming down with something hanging under it. He thought the hanging object was a man. The bloody fool ran toward the parachute that was drifting in the direction of the gas works. We just had time to call him back saying, "It's a mine you cunt, come back." We stopped him just in time to see a huge explosion close to the gas work.

We worked all night to store all the ammunition because we knew this raid would very likely continue for several more nights and we sure as hell didn't want to be tied up at dock to have a ring side seat to the Luftwaffe's night show. The raid continued until daybreak. After dawn broke, and the all-clear siren sounded, we were allowed to stand down and have a well-deserved breakfast and get a couple hours rest before continuing to store the ammunition.

Our captain did not want to stay in Cardiff longer than necessary. As soon as we were ready we sailed for Gladstone dock in Liverpool with other escort vessels to wait for the order to go out to meet or form another convoy. After securing in Liverpool, the quartermaster piped, "hands to make and mend clothes," which in royal navy language means, "you get the afternoon off." Even if it meant a couple of hours off the ship, we used it because we needed to gather our strength before we set sail again. Within twelve hours we were headed out to pick up another convoy that was about to be formed off the Mull.

We sailed alone; the weather was good with visibility about two miles. It was, for once, good sailing weather to enjoy. Suddenly, at midnight something strange happened just when everybody was up to change watches. We collided with an Irish cargo ship sailing with all his navigation lights switched on. It was a bad collision. We lost a petty officer chief torpedo instructor who was in the fore mess when we hit. All the fore part of the messes and stores were crunched up against the bulkhead of number one boiler room. All things considered we were lucky because the cargo's stern passed only a few feet from our port side. Our torpedo tubes and torpedoes were stored on the port side. If we had been hit on the port side the exploding torpedoes would have sunk the ship and killed many people.

No one could figure out why we collided. Strangely, our captain was from Northern Ireland. The other ship was from neutral southern Ireland. Furthermore, the collision took place just at the time when there was hardly anybody forward. A clear night and we hit a ship running with all its navigation lights switched on! The loss of the chief petty officer hurt me personally because I liked him. We worked well together. He was a good man who did his best to teach me the rudiments of torpedo and ship electricity. When we finally got into the site that was damaged by the collision we realized that our petty officer must have been reduced to mincemeat and had sunk to the bottom of the sea.

Our ship was too badly damaged to continue. Admiralty ordered us back to Gladstone docks. At four knots an hour our stern barely made white water as we backed our way into port. We had to back because the entire section below the foredeck was gone. Sailing forward meant running the risk of crushing the steel bulkhead of the number one boiler room. During the next twelve hours the electricians and I worked to repair the degaussing cables that were cut in three different places. Our ship was a slow moving target for U boats. Without shielded cables we risked attracting magnetic mines that the German heavy bombers dropped into the sea-lanes. These mines could be kept from a ship like ours provided the degaussing cables worked. Ours had been cut. This meant that we were at a double disadvantage. We were slow moving and therefore we became an easy target for any U boat skipper with one fish left in his tubes.

We worked non-stop to repair the degaussing cable just enough so that it 'worked' well enough to get us back to port safely. Backing into the Mersey approach was not exactly one of the prouder moments in the history of the Royal Navy but the collision was already behind us. We got all the help we needed and the specialist repair crews came onboard minutes after we moored. Working around the clock, we repaired the degaussing cable within forty-eight hours.

When we got into Liverpool the port authority directed us to moor at Birkenhead because we had to get rid of all our ammunition before going into dry dock for repairs. We reached our assigned mooring at 1500 hours, secured the ship, and started unloading immediately. We were not allowed ashore because the ship was due to go into dry dock on the Mersey side the next morning. One experience loading ammunition during an air raid wasn't the only time we had to work through hell. Luck ran out for us that night in Liverpool because we had to repeat the same terrible experience we went through in Cardiff when we had our ammunition stacked up on deck and on the jetty. This time there was a full-scale blitz over Birkenhead.

Come to think of it, maybe our luck did hold out, this had to be a modern day miracle, because we off-loaded the ammunition without being hit. We weren't the most relaxed crew handling all that ammunition; we were scared nearly out of our minds. The punishing slow entrance to Mersey was harrowing, repairing the degaussing cable took every bit of skill and ingenuity we could muster, and we had been struggling with very little sleep during the last three days. Yes, we were trained and, yes we had stamina. But, we had to admit, we were beginning to push our limits.

Early the next morning we were towed away from Birkenhead to dry dock on the Mersey side. It took the whole day to get both ships secured and then to pump the water out of the dock. As the water level fell, we saw the full extent of our damage. It was worse than anyone could imagine. We stared at our ship. The bow was nearly blown off! An entire section, stretching from the bow to the first water proof bulkhead, had been torn off as neatly as if it had been a sheet of protective foil around come crisps. It was pure luck that we only lost one man.

We were ordered into that jungle of twisted and mangled metal to recover a box containing the depth charges fuses. Miraculously they were still intact wedged behind a thicket of jagged iron. This was a dangerous job, because, to reach the box we had to use a blowtorch to cut away pieces of steel surrounding the box. One false move

…..Boom .. We were history, mincemeat like my friend the petty officer.

At the end of the day we got shore leave and three of us, Fred Grey, Randall and I went ashore for a few drinks and to see what Lime Street looked like since our last visit. Unlike other coastal towns in the south, Liverpool had not yet suffered air raids. It was in better shape than, for example, Portsmouth so we had a good time talking and drinking with some girls in the Spanish bar. It felt good to be off the ship, felt good to stand and drink, felt good to have solid ground under our feet. But, good things often come to a quick end, especially in war.

At about 2100 air raid warning sirens started and they were immediately followed by a terrific anti aircraft gun barrage. Then we heard it, the unmistakable heavy drone of bomber piston engines and their throaty full roar. The Germans began attacking Mersey side in large numbers. At first the bombs dropped mainly on the riverside because, we guessed, they were targeting the docks. We were in the thick of it but it didn't stop us from drinking and singing to drown out the noise of the guns and bombs.

Sometimes a bomb would drop close to our pub, shaking the building. We took turns going out to have a look to see where it hit. Once the damage was identified we would come back and shout, "It's alright, we can live with a near miss!" We stayed in the pub until closing time and then went to the Y.M.C.A. for a little sleep. There was no way we could get across town in that air raid. It was hard to sleep because we could see the flash of dropping bombs from our bedroom windows. Many fires raged along the riverside; we felt helpless while the Germans did their best to kill us.

The raid ended at daybreak. After the 'all clear' sirens stopped we rushed back to our ship. We were in another world; the night before we marveled at how Liverpool had been spared. "Keep the memory," I kept saying to myself while we zigzagged back to the ship. We couldn't take the shortest route because the riverside had been badly hit. There was destruction everywhere and the NFS were still at work trying to stop the fires spreading. Even getting onboard was dangerous. We were not allowed to go near the ship because a time bomb was wedged between the quayside and the ship's side. The gate of the dry dock had taken a direct hit. Both the cargo ship behind our ship and ours were lying on their sides while water seeped into the dock. An officer directed us to a hut where we found our officers and the rest of the ship's company. The hut was intact. It became our living quarters until we were allowed to go back aboard. Someday, when our ship was refloated and secure, we knew we would be allowed to go onboard and recover our personal effects. In the meantime, we were detailed to work with the NFS.

The Germans kept up the raids for an entire week. Every night, like clockwork, waves of about two hundred bombers thundered overhead. Gradually the circle of destruction grew larger. Some of the most badly hit parts of town were civilian housing areas that had no military value. At night Randall and I were detailed to help the Civil Defense personnel remove dead bodies from the rubble and put them into lorries. The drivers could have been shuttling broken timbers but in the back, stacked three and four deep were men, women, and children. Old and young, big and small, all the passengers were dead: maimed, crushed, or blown to pieces. Yes, I knew I was a sailor and I was supposed to have a stomach for what I was doing, but I could not stop myself from reeling under the impact of my profound sadness and frustration. I tried to rationalize what was happening to me, what had happened to them, and I couldn't find anything to hang my emotions onto. Many of the victims I unearthed were old women, some children were killed, but many were also badly wounded.

I snapped a couple of times. Normally, I am a very cool and steady person. I look at what's happening, try to understand, and get on with whatever I have to do. Not then. I started yelling and shouting filth into the sky. Over and over again I kept telling those pilots: one day they would pay heavily for these murderous raids. We worked until we couldn't work any longer, caught some sleep, and went back out into the rubble.

One day as we returned to the hut for lunch I heard some sort of a cry coming from under the rubble on the side of the road. Was it my ears, my imagination, a slipping girder scraping against stone? No, damnit, I heard a voice. I turned to my mate, "There's someone underneath." We dropped to our knees and began digging, first furiously, then more slowly, cursing and sweating, we peeled back layers of rubble, broken brick, chunks of plaster until, ever so gently, we touched hair, human hair. We yelled and heard a rescue team running to where we were crouched. No one could believe that someone could still be alive. But, it was true. We found, and helped remove, two women. Emergency personnel took over and the last I saw of them, both quite bewildered, made me think they might make it. Or, so I hoped. They were taken to a hospital and to this day I don't know if they survived.

These Brits are brave, I told myself. There was no other way to look at this hell and make sense of it, sense that could keep me going. I dug, I hoped, I hurt, and I realized that I had become very close to all these brave people. Funny for me, a little Frenchman, I felt as if these Brits were part of my own family. In a way in those days, horrible days, we really were one family. Together we suffered, cried, played, laughed and fought. When I dug out strangers, living or dead, they weren't totally unknown to me because they were my family. Forget that I am adopted. Now I am British I told myself and I was burying my family. Over half a century later, I still feel that way about my British family. They were fine people then and they are fine people now. It was hard enough on my emotions when I helped burying them. Even worse, it was sheer hell picking up their pieces.

We lost track of time but finally Randall and I were given a week's leave. We went to Wolverhampton. Randall went home to his mother's house and I accepted the offer of the Rowan's and went to their home. All of a sudden I started to live a life that was something other than war. I saw Edith Hart every day and pretty quickly, at least on my side, I knew I was in love. I tried to pry her feelings out of her but she was not forthcoming. Maybe I should have learned from that setback but I was persistent and wanted to give myself more time to see if I could get her to admit she was more than infatuated with me. As for me, there was no doubt about it; I'd fallen in love.

I tried hard to have sex with her but I didn't score. My testosterone count was at an all time high because I hadn't had a woman since I left Toulon and that was at least a couple of years. Not that I wasn't amorous, I tried hard, but women with a liberal attitude to pre-marital sex were rarities in those days. They maintained different standards. In England in the early 1940's a majority of the women practiced, or at least it seemed to me, a form of Puritanism to protect them from succumbing to temptation. Edith was Puritanical and I used every trick in my book to tempt her into a happy sexual relationship. Remember, we met in the beginning of the war and the country hadn't yet gone through the full transition to a wartime economy when women served in the forces and worked in factories. Once that happened, Puritan practices were on their way to becoming history. In the meantime, I found behaving like a respectable young man was a painful experience. Eighteen months later was a different story but what I wanted then, in a very bad way, was for Edith to jettison her Puritanical policy.

I left Wolverhampton at the end of my leave with mixed feelings. I really couldn't figure out Edith. On the one hand she kissed me passionately, even let me caress her, but on the other hand, when I wanted to nest, she stopped me. Nothing doing! She even said she would write me every week, and she was the first girl who told me, "I love you." That made me feel good because I could look forward to something but what I really wanted right-then-and-there was something she was not going to give me. Was it her Puritan streak or was there something else? How could I answer that huge question? I was in another world too busy building a fantasy relationship with a pretty woman. In the state I was in, there was no way to recognize that I was playing with fire. The truth of the matter was simple: I hadn't made much progress in building a relationship with her. Too obstinate for my own good, I was blind to the fact that our relationship was lop-sided. I was doing all the work and she was, at best, a pleasant partner.

When I got on the train to go back to my barracks I was forlorn and frustrated. My leave had gone too fast. We parted not knowing that it would be a very long time before we saw each other again. That is, if we lived long enough. The war was taking a bad turn particularly for the Navy. It was stretched to serve all over the face of the globe because there was a serious shortage of ships. England was still fighting alone.

Almost immediately after I returned onboard we were told to get ready to leave our ship to commission HMS Vimy, an old V&W class destroyer built in 1917 that had just been refitted to escort convoys over long distances. In spite of her age she was fast and that really appealed to us. The V&W class destroyers were well respected by sailors: strongly built, they were reliable and handled well in heavy seas. And, there was an added attraction: the Vimy was also equipped to fight U-boats for several days if necessary.

Sadly, the Belmont that I left did not survive the war. She was torpedoed and sunk in January 1942 while escorting a Canadian troop convoy to the United Kingdom. For the U-boat skipper it meant another kill flag on his conning tower. Our loss was awful; all hands went down with the Belmont.

We took the train to Portsmouth, transferred to Victory Barracks, and marched up to the Vimy in the dockyard where she was berthed. Before crossing the gangway, I stepped aside and took a long time and scanning my new ship. By then I had acquired enough sea knowledge to know what to look for. My eyes roamed her full length from bow to stern and from the top of her masts to the waterline. Yes, she looked as solid as her reputation but many vital details bothered me. Her torpedo tubes had been removed and the first funnel was gone. Then, a mate told me the number one boiler had been replaced by a large fuel tank to improve her cruising range. Refueling at sea was dangerous; no one liked being a sitting duck. For a German U-boat commander, two ships for the price of one torpedo were the kind of targets he probably dreamed about every night.

It must have been a difficult decision for the naval planners because what the Vimy gained in cruising range, it lost in speed. Her top speed dropped from thirty two knots to twenty five and that made a lot of difference when we were either chasing or being chased. Despite my misgivings, I finally admitted she was well armed to fight submarines. She was fitted with six depth charge throwers plus the two normal racks astern. This meant she could fire a pattern of fourteen charges at a time. Fitted with new radar, from a distance of between twenty and twenty five miles she could detect a submarine on the surface without being seen.

Any advantage for our side had to help us win this war, I concluded. I kept repeating that to myself as I was directed to my mess deck. It was forward and below the main deck. The mess was divided in two. The port side was allotted to the torpedo men and the starboard side was allotted to the "A" and "B" gun crews. Frankly, I was unhappy because in case of a collision I knew I had very little chance of surviving if I happened to be in the mess when we hit. There was even less of a chance of surviving if the ship were torpedoed or hit a mine. In an emergency there was only two exits, one was through the large porthole situated on each side of the ship. Getting through portholes was possible provided the guy struggling to get out was as skinny as me and there weren't very many of us. The other exit was through the hatch, a round opening four feet in diameter leading to the main deck by a ladder.

Take a minute and try to imagine what was going through my mind. I knew exactly what would happen if we were hit. There would be chaos in the crowded mess, panic stricken men would all start pushing and shoving, trying to get through the hatch. These thoughts weren't a fantasy dreamed up merely to keep my mind active. No, all you need to start thinking the way I was thinking was to have seen a ship sinking. Watching it go down you had a pretty fair idea of what hell was happening below the water line: desperate men scrambling to save their lives. How would I act if I were caught below when we got hit?

Once we had settled into our routine I was finally able to crack a joke with one of my mess mate who was very fat and nicknamed "Tubby." I looked him straight in the face and had a hard time to keep from laughing, "Please Tubby swear to all your mess mates that if we get hit by a torpedo or mine, you will be the last to get through the hatch. Just in case you get stuck in it, we will then pull you out!" There were more grunts than laughs because we all knew what it would be like.

There were two Frenchmen onboard, Fred Grey who was already on the Belmont. He was in the forward mess deck with me but on the starboard side. The other was a petty officer, engine room artificer named L. Power.

The ship was almost ready to sail but we still spent a lot of time cleaning, loading provisions, building up our ammunition stock, going through all the time consuming steps that must be completed before setting sail. Once we were ready we had Division on the quarterdeck. The entire ship's company was assembled and our captain, Lieutenant Commander De Chair, inspected us. He was followed by the first Lieutenant who was intensely disliked by most

Rene Dassac (in collaboration with Patrick K. Robbins)

of the crew, if not all of us. He was an arrogant man; perhaps that was the reason he was disliked. Fortunately, the captain was well liked.

After the inspection he gave us a rough explanation of what our assignments were during the next few weeks. It sounded a lot like what we had already been doing: convoy escort and submarine hunting but I soon found out that I was mistaken. We were going to be part of another operation, something much bigger than we had ever experienced. Before he got to the part of his message that interested all of us, he reminded us that we were a new crew and therefore he emphasized the importance of teamwork. "Get to know each other. That's the only way you can trust each other and work together as a team," his voice boomed. That much was obvious but he said it anyway just to drive home his point. Only a one hundred percent effective team in battle, when the 'action stations' alarm was sounded, had a chance of surviving the war. Finally, he told us we were going to Scotland where we would begin a series of exercises to make sure we were fit for sea. After that, our assignment would be to join the fleet involved in the Battle of the Atlantic. He gave our assignment a grand title and to me it sounded like a lot more than convoy escort and chasing German submarines.

Late in the evening the ship's company was piped, "Hands fall in for leaving harbor, special sea duty men close up." The night was pitch black, no moon, and no stars. There was only a thick cloud cover. We sailed out of the dockyard slowly as if to hide our departure and then we entered the harbor between the Isle of Wight and Gosport. From the harbor we steered west, slowly increasing speed until we reached the open sea. At sea we were called to 'defense station.' That meant each watch kept four on and four off. In the area that we were crossing we had to remain at defense stations because E Boats and U Boats prowled at night looking for prey. Every man on watch had his binoculars glued to his eyes while scanning the horizon in slow sweeps.

The sea changed to choppy and the Vimy began to buck and roll. Suddenly, minutes after leaving harbor we were called to 'action station'. We stood at our stations waiting for orders. After 15 minutes exchanging signals, we learned the other ship that we had mistaken for a U-boat, was actually an allied ship. It was a Free French Aviso of the Commandant Duboc type. Apparently he was aware of us but we didn't know who he was. At night, an unknown ship could easily be mistaken for a U-boat. It was a first for us but the captain of the French boat was used to being challenged. He signaled us, with typical Gallic flair, that we were not the first allied ship to challenge him! He wished us safe passage. Without that exchange of signals we might have begun firing. That close call was a good reminder that we were heading into a zone where we would either kill or be killed.

As the French ship slipped astern we resumed our routine watch stations. It was my first night on watch and I was on the bridge. When 'action station' was called I went to the quarterdeck where I manned one of the depth charge throwers. If we weren't attacking or under attack, I formed part of the damage control party. This meant that we waited in the flat above the engine room. Waiting, especially when we were under attack from the air, was hard on our nerves. We could hear what was happening outside but we couldn't see what was going on. The noise outside was often deafening and it played on our fears. Not knowing what was going on, waiting to be called into action after we were hit, played havoc with our minds. It may be difficult to imagine, but each of us knew it was better to be in the thick of it than standing behind a thin steel bulkhead waiting for our ship to take a hit so we could spring into action.

On the way up to Scapa the skipper kept us on our toes. He sounded 'action station' several times, sometimes twice during the same watch. He included gunnery exercises and anti submarine exercises. Just to make sure we could handle it, he put us through the fire station drill and the abandon ship station drill. By the time we reached Scapa we were very tired. The skipper wasn't demanding outstanding performance for the fun of it. There was meaning behind going through all those drills. He knew a lot about what the next phase of our training was going to be like. We were going to be assigned to the command of a legendary commodore known throughout the Navy as, "the bastard." Ice water ran through his veins and his stamina was legendary. Rumors circulated saying he laughed once but that story could have been an intentional slight on the image of a stern and unrelenting master of the seas.

As soon as we reached Scapa, even before we secured, the demon commodore boarded the ship without warning. Surprisingly agile for his age, he made a rapid inspection of the ship with the captain and the first lieutenant. After completing his inspection we knew why he had his famous reputation. He missed nothing. The ship's company was assembled on the quarterdeck where the commodore lectured us on the exercises he had planned for us. In case he wasn't clear enough the first time, he said each exercise would be repeated until it was satisfactorily executed. There was no room for 'almost good enough.' He wasn't kidding!

We went through utter hell for the next three weeks. Nothing fazed him and nothing tired him. He drove himself harder than he drove us and he was pitiless with us. He made us repeat drills until we were exhausted and then he accelerated the pace. Hour after hour, it got worse but we didn't grumble because we knew the brutal drills were intended for our own good. Over and over again, he repeated that we had to understand that we depended on one another, that we had to work as a team, that we had to know our mate's jobs as well as our own, and the sooner we passed the tests satisfactorily, the sooner we would leave Scapa.

We were anchored in the middle of nowhere in the harbor and we felt that the Commodore was looking at us from his office window. One night, a night when the weather was particularly nasty, he even tried to board the ship to see if the duty officer and the quartermaster would challenge him. He stopped at nothing. Either he got his way, which meant perfection, or we knew our ship would not leave his training program.

After going through every exercise he could conceive of for close to three weeks, night and day, the commodore came on board and gave us the results. Were we going to be 'freed' of "the bastard" or were we going to be held back for more work? That question played on everyone's minds the night before he was piped aboard. Down in our mess we thought we were performing at 100%. Obviously, what we thought of ourselves and what he thought of us were miles apart.

He lit into us. Within seconds after opening his mouth there was no doubt about what he thought of our performance. He bellowed: our gunnery exercises were slow and we couldn't hit our targets. Those two were among the gentler of his opening comments before he gave us a solid salvo. His words slammed into us, detailed verbal shrapnel that cut us to shreds. Every action station onboard the Vimy took hits. No one, neither ratings nor officers, was spared. Taking his barrage was painful because everything he identified wrong with our ship and with us, was spot-on accurate. He wasn't petty; he was brutally thorough. I had visions of spending a year with him but he surprised us. He ended his "comments" with, "I cannot keep you any longer because you are badly needed at sea. But, I am sure you will be able to execute your captain's orders. Good luck to you all!"

We made it! I almost jumped and hollered for joy. The prospect of going into combat was a lot more appealing than spending more time under him. That he was a cranky old bastard was an obvious conclusion. To his credit, and it hurt to admit, we all knew he was right. He carried on an ancient tradition among mariners, the need to train men to survive combat at sea. Whether it was sailing ships and Nelson's time, or Roman galleys slamming into each other, the message was always the same: once at sea and engaged in battle, our lives depended on peak performance every day until we returned to port. That is, assuming we were lucky enough to return.

Vimy was declared fit and entered service. Soon we were sailing to Plymouth where we would receive our next orders. Morale was high. Three weeks in Scapa under the commodore was no fun under an officer no longer refereed to as "the bastard" because we knew it had been time well spent. We didn't look back because we were eager to put to sea. On our way down south, we picked up two submarines, one Dutch and one British. We escorted them to the open ocean because we were sailing through the Irish Channel and it was possible to mistake them for U-boats lying in wait for either incoming convoys or patrol vessels.

We had a bit of trouble when we arrived off the coast of Milford Haven because we ran into a thick fog. Visibility dropped to 100 yards, sometimes even less. We barely moved. Around us we heard a number of ships horns and whistles blasting through the heavy fog.

Rene Dassac (in collaboration with Patrick K. Robbins)

Those were sounds we didn't want to hear because it meant we were in the same path as vessels of an incoming convoy. Straining to see them was like trying to stare a hole through a heavy gray curtain. Judging from the sounds, it was obvious that the ships around us were very close to our three ship convoy. Training that we once thought a massive pain in the backside now became a life-or-death reality. The entire ship's company was ordered on deck with life jackets to be ready in the event of a collision. We inched forward. Suddenly, we heard the roar of tanks being blown and our two subs dove to safety. We never saw them again together but a couple of months later in Gibraltar we met up with the Dutch sub and learned, much to everyone's admiration, that she had sunk a U-boat that was cruising on the surface. The U-boat thought that the Dutch sub was German but the Dutch fired first.

While we were shivering in the cold staring into the soup, a large cargo vessel passed within a few yards and nearly rammed us. Listening for more incoming ships proved fruitless. The skipper decided to drop anchor until the fog lifted. We were on edge because we weren't sure about our location. As long as we couldn't see two feet in front of us we had to stop but we weren't sure we were anchored out of harms way. During the night we heard the sea breaking on rocks that sounded as if they were dangerously near our anchorage. Just because we were stopped that didn't mean we were out of harm's way; we might have been rammed and pushed onto the rocks. Daybreak couldn't come soon enough; when it broke the fog lifted. We left our dangerous anchorage and began steaming at high speed to Plymouth. The sea was calm and the visibility was good. In a matter of hours the weather had turned from being our enemy to our friend.

We were detailed to berth at Devon Port where we immediately filled up our fuel tanks and replaced all the ammunition we used during our trials in Scapa. We worked hard that day because we were told that we would be sailing for Gibraltar the next day escorting four harbor defense motor launches. These small boats could not reach Gibraltar without escort assistance. This meant we had to take them in tow for most of the way and release them when they were close enough to Gibraltar to make the final stretch on their own. The trip plan was simple. Enroute, if there were a call for action station we would release them from tow, coordinate on how we were going to handle the problem, and then regroup once the problem had been solved. Towing assignments were not popular because every surface ship was a sitting duck for the U-boat hunter packs that were prowling for us between Devon Port and Gibraltar.

We were given shore leave. Grey, McLean and I went to Plymouth touring the pubs searching for a couple of girls who were known to be 'friends' of our Scottish mate who was appropriately named Jock. Luck was with us because we eventually found one girl late in the evening. Arrangements were made. After the pubs closed at 2300 we went back to her small flat. We tossed a coin to find out who would be the first to have a go at her. Fred Grey was the winner. Mac and I got comfortable in the living room. We had had quite a bit to drink that night so we stretched out on an empty bed in the corner of the room. At about midnight the air raid warning siren went off and a terrific anti aircraft barrage erupted. The Germans must have been coming in low. Every once in awhile we heard their engines and I tried to imagine what was going through the crew's minds as they began their bombing runs. They had to know that many of the targets were civilian non-combatants but that didn't matter. They were British and therefore they were the enemy.

The girl's flat was in the basement so we didn't bother to go to nearest air raid shelter. The level of the road was half the height of the window that opened out onto the footpath. Listening to the droning bombers cleared the cobwebs out of my head. In a flash I was wide-awake, suddenly sober and conscious of the danger we were in. "Maybe it wasn't such a good idea to stay here," I said to myself, because the bombs had begun to land quite close to her house. As if the German bombardiers had read my thoughts, we heard a high-pitched whistle, a different sound than the thud-boom created by bombs exploding elsewhere in the city. That stick was coming right at us. "This is it", I said, "This is it. This one's for us. Our number's are up." The lights went out and at the same time there was a terrific explosion. Even in gunnery practice, I had never heard a noise like that.

The wall facing the street, and part of the street, came into the room as if pushed by an unseen hand. Bricks, stone, and God knows what else, fell onto the bed that collapsed under the weight. Of course, with all the lights out I was staring into total darkness. I could hardly move but my head was still free from rubble. Instinctively, I had thrown my arms up and crossed them over my head to protect it from blocks and bricks that I could still hear falling. Then it was silent. Nothing moved. From far away, I couldn't tell from which direction, I heard voices. There was a smell, a strong smell of powder or something like it. It burned my nose and hurt my lungs. All this had happened so fast that it took me a few seconds before I realized what a mess I was in. My ears were ringing but, somehow, I could still think clearly. I began to call my mate Jock who was either still sound asleep or unconscious. "Jock, Jock, for fuck sake, answer me."

I wanted to shake him but I had to claw away rubble to get to where I thought his head should be. It was pitch black and then I realized that Jock had been buried by rubble that had blown in from the window. I couldn't get to Jock fast enough. I started yelling to Fred to come out and give me a hand. Fred was deaf and in another world; he was lost to blind lust. He was too busy having a good time with our lady friend but finally he paused, and in that split second, he realized what had happened. "Fred, come over quick," I yelled. From the direction of the bedroom I heard Fred answer, "It's alright the bomb must have fallen in the street. Only the cupboard fell on the bed but I'll put it back up again." Fred had other things on his mind. I yelled into the darkness. "No, Fred you don't understand. I can't move. Jock doesn't answer me when I call him." The wall's fallen on us." Fred tried opening the bedroom door into the passageway leading to the front door and the living room. After heaving and shoving, it finally dawned on him that a bomb had hit the house. Later we learned that the bomb had gone through the roof killing a Free French sailor on the first floor, careened out through the wall and exploded in the center of the street in front of our window. It took Fred a few minutes to climb over the rubble and claw his way into the living room.

While he was groping in the dark the girl fumbled around and brought matches from the kitchen and lighted a candle. Fred started to remove the bricks covering the bed where Jock and I were pinned. Except for some small superficial wounds, I was okay but Jock was a bloody mess. His face was badly lacerated; he didn't recognize us. We helped him to his feet and steadied him. Slowly, we managed to pick our way through the rubble into the kitchen where we started to clean his face. As we were dabbing at the wounds trying to figure out if he was seriously wounded or just bloodied, something happened that was funny, sad, and very human.

The girl, whose body and flat we were using, became hysterical and burst in tears. "I lost everything in London and now here. What am I going to do now?" Suddenly, she dropped to her haunches and peed on the floor right there in front of us. "What am I going to do," she sobbed to herself and to us. I suppose, if the situation hadn't been so awful, we would have managed to have a laugh but we were too shaken to see the funny side, if there had been one. Jock began to shake. Maybe it was the cold; maybe it was the shock effect of knowing that he had nearly been blown to pieces. The girl took pity on him and (God bless her) she wrapped her ratty looking fur coat around him. The four of us made it out onto the street. The raid was still on but we wanted to make it up the street to take shelter in a front door that was still intact. A voice boomed out of the dark shouting at us, "Get out of here. There is a time bomb right where you are standing." We ran like we were being chased toward the air raid warden of the street. He looked at Jock and said, "Wait here a few minutes," he ordered, "and I will call a cab to take him to hospital." The cab came and took Jock to the hospital. We never saw him again.

I was intact but I had lost my shoes so it was quite a job to walk across town. Despite the pain of trying to pick my way through the rubble and sharp stones, we walked / ran away from the area toward the Park on the top of a nearby hill over looking Plymouth harbor. As we ran, I heard the shrapnel from the A.A. guns falling all around us. We saw a park bench and crawled under it and stretched out in order to make ourselves as flat as possible. We lay glued to the ground for hours until the raid was over shortly before dawn. We couldn't get a lift to the dockyard in Devon Port because all the taxis had been mobilized to carry the wounded to the hospitals so we hobbled back to the dockyard.

When we reached dock gates the duty policeman looked at the state we were in and said, "It looks like you had a rough time?" Was it a question or a statement of fact? We sort of looked at each other and then Fred explained. "Yes we had. We've been bombed out of a house!" "Sorry," the policeman replied. "From here it looked as if the center and the eastern side of the town have been hit." Fred blurted, "One of our mates has been taken to hospital, and we're supposed to sail today. I don't think we will see him again." The cop nodded gravely. "Well, so long sir. Good luck to you," Fred said. As an afterthought he said, "It looks as if they will come back again for more runs at us just as they've done in the raids on Liverpool." The policeman nodded gravely and we walked back to the Vimy.

We reported to the duty Officer and told him that Jock would not be back because he was taken to hospital in very bad shape. We went down to our mess, showered, changed to our working clothes, had breakfast and listened to all the other mate's stories. There was no time to moan. It was back to work; we had to prepare the ship for sea. We left later that day and sailed far out of sight from the coast. Our four motor launches were lined up like ducklings behind mother duck Vimy all the way to Gibraltar.

Our escort convoy was not an easy job for the captain. We weren't designed to tow but the job had to be done. We had no prior experience in towing so we created our own tow design. This meant we had to start from scratch and learn from trial and error. The responsibility for finding a solution fell to the boson's mate and the special sea duty men. In the first couple of days the steel towlines separated. During one of those breakdowns the boson's mate got his leg trapped in a loop formed by one of the lines. One of the lads managed to loosen the line before it dug too deep into his flesh and completely smashed his leg. They got him untangled in time but he was badly hurt and stayed in the sick bay until we reached Gibraltar where he was transferred to the navy hospital. Either it was a stroke of luck or a stroke of genius, his accident was the only incident on the trip. With a start like that, no one was upset that the rest of the trip was almost boring. We released the four MTB just after we passed Cape Saint Vincent. They plowed their way through light swells toward Gibraltar.

We waited outside Gibraltar until berthing arrangements were sorted out. At last we were ordered to berth along side HMS Firedrake, Foresight, Vidette, Wild Swan in addition to HMS Ark Royal,

Renown, Manchester, and two or three Tribal class destroyers. We refueled and got a couple of days rest before we went out on short patrols, usually only about a day long. Once we got on station we began listening with our asdic to see if we could detect subs trying to sneak into the Med.

During one of our shore leaves we met three Frenchmen who were on HMS Manchester. They told us something big was coming but, as usual, they did not know what it was. By the time we met them I was sufficiently grounded in the ways of the navy not to dismiss rumors out of hand. Experience taught me to respect rumors because they were often the first sign that something was going to happen. There was a crazy logic living with rumors and it went something like this: it's a fact that rumors are facts. Everything is a rumor until it becomes a fact. There was no doubt in our minds that we were in another guessing game. No one was too worked up about it because we understood that we could not be informed about something important until the last minute. Enemy spies were everywhere. The adage about, 'Loose lips sink ships', was true. Nevertheless, we played the guessing game. We guessed we were going to escort a convoy to Malta. For once, our guess was right.

A few days later our ship, together with the other destroyers moored at Gibraltar, went out into the Atlantic to meet a fast convoy escorted by the Nelson. There were also two cruisers and a score of destroyers. We relieved one of the destroyers. They refueled and we helped escort the convoy make a night passage through the straits of Gibraltar. The straits were covered by dozens of Spanish fishing boats. It didn't take a leaping genius to assume that they were in the way in order to make a nuisance of themselves. There was no way we could allow them to disrupt our convoy so we undertook to disperse them. Vimy and two other destroyers went well ahead of the convoy, entering the straits at full speed. Sometimes we came very close to the Spanish boats. Close enough, in fact, that we heard the crews shouting insults at us. Since none of us could speak Spanish, we assumed that what we heard were insults and not compliments about our fine seamanship. Maybe it was stubbornness, or maybe they thought we were bluffing, but they did not seem too upset about us bearing down on them.

Rene Dassac (in collaboration with Patrick K. Robbins)

Perhaps our first passes were too subtle for them to appreciate. Without ramming their boats we wanted to convey a clear message: leave our convoy alone. Obviously, they were slow learners. None of their skippers appeared to have got the message: get out of our way. We turned back on top of them and pretended to search for subs. When we began dropping depth charges, a few close enough to make them understand that we meant business, the shock of the explosions helped to change their minds. The depth charges did the trick: they got the message and beat a hasty retreat towards Algeciras and La Linea. In order to give the impression that we really were chasing submarines we continued depth charging for a couple of hours. After midnight the convoy came through. There was no sign of the Spanish fishermen; they must have gone home to dry their nets.

After a day with the convoy, Vimy left convoy duty and continued another patrol pattern between the West African coast in the south and the Spanish coast in the north. We continued zigzagging right up to Gibraltar where we refueled and were ordered to stand at the first degree of readiness. The harbor was almost empty because all the big ships had gone to join the convoy. We were not allowed ashore. We did not know if the convoy had already attacked because the BBC made no mention of this convoy. Out of earshot, we knew something was happening. The signal tower was unusually active transmitting and receiving. We got the signal to sail at full speed towards the Cape Bon off Tunisia to escort the cruiser Manchester. She had been torpedoed but was still making her way back at 15 knots with a list of 20° to port.

As soon as we found her we made a wide sweep at slow speed to make sure she was not being shadowed by U-boats. After the sweep, we took our position on her port side and exchanged signals. From the signals blinked across the water we learned that there were 60 killed in the attack. All those killed were soldiers she was taking to Malta to reinforce their AA defenses. In order to keep clear of the ship's gun crews during action station, the troops were quartered in the wardroom aft just where the torpedo hit the ship. This explained the large number of casualties.

During the following afternoon the Manchester put all the bodies on deck. They were lined up side-by-side, tied in their hammocks ready for burial at sea after a short religious service. It struck us that we were only a couple of days from Gibraltar. Burying our shipmates at sea was probably done in order to hide the burial from the Spaniards working in Gibraltar. Without a doubt, our mate's bodies would have been seen by German Intelligence and probably used as propaganda. It was well known that La Linea and Algeciras were infested with German and Italian spies.

At Gibraltar the Manchester was immediately put into dry dock for repairs. A couple of days later we were walking past the Manchester and we saw the three sailors we had already met and we arranged to meet them ashore that evening. Over beers they gave us a detailed description of the battle their convoy went through. We thought about what we had seen and felt sad and ashamed that the French Navy was completely absent from the war at sea. The Vichy nazi navy was broadcasting nasty messages against Frenchmen who continued to fight on the side of our allies. We also heard strange stories about shipmates who were sent to disciplinary camps in Morocco just because they had talked about the Free French Forces.

Another story made the rounds. This time, it was the story about a Vichy destroyer that was passing through the straits close to a British destroyer that was patrolling nearby. A French seaman jumped overboard and swam toward the British destroyer. Both ships launched lighters to fetch the poor devil. The British got there first and brought the seaman aboard their boat. The first request he made was to ask the deck officer who he had to see to get permission to be sent to the nearest Free French recruiting office. This story, true or false, gives you an idea of what morale must have been like onboard Vichy ships.

Gradually, the escort ships protecting the convoy sent to Malta, known as Operation Substance, returned to Gibraltar. By the looks of it they must have gone through hell. The streets of Gibraltar were filled with sailors heading to the nearest pub to have a good time and forget the convoy. In those days, there were no women to be seen apart from married women who were residents of Gibraltar. However, every day a number of Spanish dancing girls were allowed to perform in some of the pubs such as the Trocadero. That pub was full of sailors with their tongues and eyes hanging out of their heads watching the dancing girls. We were watching the stage close to the door when I said, "Look at this big ginger head bloke. I bet you he's going to grab one of the girls off the floor." No sooner had I said that, when we heard him shout, "Come here you bitch." He grabbed her and all hell broke loose. In a matter of minutes mayhem spilled out onto the street. Chairs and bottles, anything that could be thrown, started flying.

This sudden madness spread to other pubs up and down Main Street. Violence was breading more violence. Something had to be done to stop the mayhem before the situation degenerated even further. A call went out to the naval patrol. Marines were called up to help the military police who had to use their truncheons and even their bayonets. Because we were in front of the door we managed to get out quickly and get away from the scene before the military police arrived. We reached our ship without having to have our heads seen to by the ship's surgeon.

God what a night! That was something the people of Gibraltar would not forget for many years. Can you imagine, 30,000 to 40,000 young men aged between 18 to 35 trapped within the boundaries of the Rock risking their lives every time they left the harbor and headed east toward Malta? Once out of the shadow of the Rock, they faced dive-bombers, U-boats, E boats, mines, and some times the Italian fleet. And, if they weren't headed into hell in the east, their ships turned west and sailed out into the Atlantic to battle large U-boat wolf packs. Each convoy lost an average of five to ten ships and with each ship lost there was the inevitable horrible sight of charred and burned bodies floating in the stench of oil fuel.

These experiences remained engraved in the minds of those young men who craved sex or only a little flirt with females who they had not seen for months! If there is no sex, there is drink and that is why the captain's only wise course of action was to close their eyes in port when their crews returned to ship plastered. The captains knew their crews were made up of brave and courageous young men who deserved a little leniency. In fact, there was a sort of grudging understanding between the navy and the people of Gibraltar, and even in particular, the people of Malta. Without the navy and the inevitable sacrifices, both Malta and Gibraltar would have fallen into enemy hands. The Maltese went through hell during 1940 to 1943. They were raided almost every day. Despite the raids, convoys managed to get through. It was rowdy young sailors who helped them live.

Back onboard we were reminded that the war was still going on, barroom brawls not withstanding. It was not long before we were again sent out to help a convoy that was under heavy U-boat attacks. This time we had to sail at high speed for three days before reaching the convoy. On the second day we ran into a heavy sea that damaged the ship. The sea pounded our foredeck and tore loose stanchions. The force was so intense that it also damaged the steel protection shields of the foredeck guns. Under those conditions there was no way the Vimy could reach the convoy on time because the captain had to reduce speed to ten knots. The mess decks were a shambles of broken mugs, and plates. Stinking sludge and equipment slopped from one side of the ship to the other with each roll and pitch. In spite of all the pounding Mother Nature gave us, we managed to repair the damage and prepare the ship for action. We had to get there as soon as possible. Alarming signals from the convoy told us that it was being badly mauled by a pack of U boats.

When we closed to within radar contact with the convoy we began making large zigzags hoping to catch one of the U. boats on our radar screen or on our asdic set. The weather was so bad that to see one of them on the surface would have been pure luck. However long after dark, we got a possible contact on the radar screen and we increased speed to reach the sub's estimated position. The Vimy reared back and plunged into the troughs. Huge waves broke over the foredeck and our propellers whirled helplessly in the fury of the wind and rain.

We could hear explosions coming from the convoy. Finally, we got a good ping on our asdic set. We began our attack by dropping large patterns of depth charges. After many hours hunting there was a strong smell of fuel. It certainly wasn't ours. The captain ordered us to take a sample of the fuel oil that was on the surface of the raging sea. Our chief engineer declared the sample to be fuel used by U-boats! That was encouraging but we weren't sure whether we had scored a hit or the U boat captain was trying to bluff us. We needed proof of wreckage so we continued our search. When dawn came the captain called off the search. We had failed to find any pieces of wreckage. What we needed was a solid piece of enemy boat.

We were disappointed but we also had to admit that what happened was typical of what happens when you are hunting for U-boats. Hunts could last for days without getting a confirmed hit. Enemy skippers were clever and cunning. We knew from other ships that the U boat captains would sometimes release enough oil mixed with rubbish to make the hunter feel he had gotten a hit. Once the allied skipper had something solid he sailed away thinking he had destroyed his enemy. What he could not know was embarrassing: the piece of furniture that constituted his evidence had, in fact, been broken into pieces and released through a torpedo tube in order to lure the hunter away. Without proof of substantial wreckage the admiralty would not accept a claim of a sinking. Their Lordships demanded: give us proof and we'll allow the kill! At least that's the way they looked at it. We didn't buy that line or argument. The way we saw it was different: the fuel we collected was proof of our kill.

After our last run we lost all contact with the sub. Even if he had dived deeply and stayed silent it's doubtful that he could have remained silent for very long. If he was trying to outwait us he had a determined adversary because we were also playing his game. Our skipper had stopped all engines to trick the U-boat commander into believing we had gone. But, unless we had more proof of kill, all we could do was engage in wishful thinking.

We remained with the convoy a few more days and helped keep the U-boats at bay. But, despite our presence, the convoy continued to suffer a couple more losses. We were running low on fuel but the weather was too rough to refuel from the standby tanker. For a time we thought that we may have had to continue on to the U.K., but we were ordered to return to Gibraltar at the most economic speed. We left the convoy. Returning to Gib meant we missed the chance to spend a few days home. The trip back was punctuated by many false alarms.

Just before reaching Cape Saint Vincent we were so short of fuel that we reduced speed again to four knots. In order to gain a few more knots we hoisted the fore deck horning to the mast and rigged a sail. Maybe we even gained a knot or two because the wind was behind us.

Taulus

If a German saw us through his periscope he might have thought we were mad or else that we were a trap. To be on the safe side, we had our asdic pinging in all directions. Before entering the straits of Gibraltar we took our sail down in order to look decent when the Vimy finally managed to enter harbor. Our fuel was almost completely gone. We took our old mooring position, refueled, replaced ammunition, took on fresh food and general stores and were ready for our next assignment.

We got shore leave and for the next few days when we weren't cleaning and repairing the ship, we enjoyed what little of the good life that Gib had to offer. We were tied up to what was then called "the coal wharf". There we managed to attract a large number of cockroaches and rats. Why did they choose our ship, why they wanted to go to sea with us? Certainly, we did not want them and we weren't a dirty tub that would attract vermin. We knew they had come onboard, that's one of the unpleasant aspects of being ashore. What we didn't realize was that they would multiply quickly, in fact so quickly, they made life unbearable for us.

After a few days in Gibraltar we received our new assignment: Freetown, Sierra Leone. With Freetown as a base we were ordered to escort convoys between the Canary Islands, Cape Verde, and as far south as Ascension and St Helena islands. The Germans were sending their U boats and armed merchant ships into this part of the south Atlantic. There had been reports that some German raiders were operating in the South Atlantic but now we had confirmation that their strategy had changed and they were tightening their noose on the allies.

My God it was depressing because you couldn't escape the fact that whatever we did, no matter where we sailed, the enemy was already there! On bad days we sometimes even wondered if God was against us. But, I have to admit that as black as the situation had become, we never lost our trust and faith in the Royal Navy. We didn't know how and we certainly couldn't even begin to think of 'when', but we knew that when the war was over, the Royal Navy would be on the winning side. Faith in the navy and grim determination was the only way we knew how to get through each hour of each day.

Rene Dassac (in collaboration with Patrick K. Robbins)

The eastern Mediterranean fleet under the command of Admiral Cunningham brought us some victories over the Italian fleet at Taranto where many of their heavy cruisers and a battleship were sunk or badly damaged. Later, at the battle of Matapan, the Italians were led into a trap and quickly dispatched. Those victories, those little bits of sunshine, renewed our confidence in the might of our fleet.

Cautious optimism, an unshakeable commitment to seeing the war through until we won, this was the state of our mind as we sailed for Freetown. Getting to a city that was still acting as if there were no war, a city in 'peacetime' was going to be tough but we kept thinking about the bright side: we would be getting away from the hardships of nighttime bombing raids, rationing, everything we had come to accept as our way of life. We met a convoy far out south west of the Canary's, the weather was good and the trip was uneventful. We left the convoy when we were about parallel with Dakar, the French Vichy port, and went to Bathurst in Gambia to refuel. Pulling into Bathurst was also intended to show the Vichy in the surrounding territory that the Royal Navy was still patrolling the area.

We anchored in their little harbor and enjoyed the bananas and African oranges that the natives were exchanging for cigarettes, clothes or almost anything else including money. This was our first call in Africa and for the first time in 30 months we felt as if we were in peacetime. Everything was so quiet. In the afternoon we were given shore leave. The three Frenchmen, Powell, Power and Grey, went out to visit the capital city of Gambia, which was really nothing more than an over-sized village in those days.

During our search for a pub or something looking like a bar we came across a building that was actually a ramshackle grocery-variety goods shop. It was closed; I forgot to tell you, it was Sunday. We heard French music coming from a gramophone through the open window above the C.F.A.O. shop. With nothing better to do, we sat on the front steps of the shop and talked loudly to attract attention from the people living in the flat above. We guessed, we hoped, they were French. Sure enough, after a minute or two we heard a voice above our heads saying, "Venez voir, il y a trois ros bifs assis devant le magasin." (Come and have a look. There are three 'Roast Beef' -

English sailors - seated in front of the shop). We replied, "No we are French and we are looking for a pub." The voice answered, "You will not find a pub here but come up and have a drink with us."

We raced upstairs. They were just as glad to see us as we were glad to meet them. They got fresh news from us and we found out what was happening in this part of Africa from them. Believe it or not, they were the only three Frenchmen in Gambia! Two of them were employed by CFAO and the third was a radio-telegraph man of the French navy who had escaped from Dakar. He was offered the job of repairing the old radio station and getting it to operate for the Governor. He had a good job which I suppose he kept until the Vichy navy in Dakar decided to join the rest of the allies in order to deliver France and the rest of Europe from the Germans.

We learned from him that in Dakar, and on all French units of the navy, it was strictly forbidden to speak about the Free French navy or the Royal Navy. As the afternoon wore on it was obvious that they were more concerned about a possible landing of the British than an infiltration of the Germans in Senegal. When we heard what was happening to the French navy, even old news that had managed to dribble into this remote and small country in West Africa, we were furious. Once again, we felt bitter about high-ranking officers who were betraying their motherland and the men they were commanding.

We had begun to hate those men, fellow citizens who turned their backs the very moment when the nation was crying out for leaders. It is hard for me to write this, and I am taking the position of John Powell, not Rene Dassac, because I cannot talk about those French admirals with any feeling of admiration or sympathy. They had no excuse whatsoever for allowing their morals to sink so low. How did they become admirals? They were scooped from the cream of the French military establishment. They were men for whom honor was a near sacred value, men destined to be great patriots. Instead, they became petty little men who betrayed their country. They were too blind and certainly cowardly, to realize the enormous consequences of the world war that was consuming our lives.

It was only a matter of time before America would enter the war on the side of the Allies. When that happened, wouldn't the tides of war change in our favor? Thinking of them made me furious and I simply could not understand how they allowed their pride and morals to sink so low in these times of great peril? I kept asking myself why' but I couldn't find any answers that made sense.

How could a man born in a democracy, educated in state schools, steeped in tradition, turn his back on his heritage and walk off the world stage in order to sit out the peril in the shadow of the wings while his fellow countrymen fought and died on his behalf? I couldn't answer my own questions but there was no doubt that I loathed those men as much as the enemy.

Those were my emotions then; let's get back to our friends in Bathurst. Having spent an hour or so with them we left and we had our picture taken with a young African lad. Looking at it today, I laugh at how funny we looked wearing our colonial helmets. We went back onboard because there was nothing else to do in this village that was trying to become a town. Vimy only stayed a couple of days at anchor and then we left for Freetown in Sierra Leone.

There were a lot of ships, two V&W class destroyers, the Wild Swan and the Vidette, the light cruiser Vindictive that acted as repair ship, the depot ship Edinburgh Castle, the Free French sub hunter Cdt. Duboc and a few merchant ships. We learned that sometimes a plane came over from Dakar to see if we were getting ready to invade Senegal! One of their planes was brought down by anti aircraft guns. The two man crew was captured and held as bona fide prisoners-of-war onboard HMS Vindictive. It was the commanding officer's call on how to treat the prisoners. If it had been my responsibility I would have sent them off to join the German P.O.Ws. Just like what the Vichy Navy did with the three French ratings of HMS Manchester when she was sunk off the Cape Bon. The crew was interned in Tunisia. Somehow the Vichy guards found out that there were three French ratings amongst the survivors. They separated them from their shipmates and sent them via Italy to Marseille where they were handed over to two German sailors who escorted them to a POW camp in Germany. The German's escort was friendlier than the Vichy Navy bastards. One of the French sailors managed to jump of the train during the trip to Germany and join the resistance in the south west of France.

Taulus

In the beginning our stay in Free Town was peaceful and uneventful. But that wonderful short burst of serenity didn't last long. Our uninvited passengers, the cockroaches and rats that had boarded in Gibraltar, had taken advantage of the fresh sea air on the run down the coast to recharge their sex batteries and reproduce at an astonishing rate. Their invasion was making our lives very uncomfortable indeed. War is bad enough and you learn to put up with a lot of nasty little things in order to survive. Those vermin were different. They were everywhere. They got into our clothing, the mess, into our food; they crawled across the railings and up the bulkheads. If they'd had a commander they might have been able to take over the ship and put us to work! There was no escaping them. Something had to be done.

Our skipper wanted the ship to be fumigated as soon as possible but the war planners had another assignment for us. We had to wait a couple of weeks while we went out on convoy duty. We met two convoys; one came from the north and the other from the south. The two convoys then sailed north to meet a larger convoy at a meeting point south west of the Canary Islands. As soon as we saw what we were joining a guessing game began.

We guessed the convoy was probably going to the Middle East. In the middle of the convoy there was a troop ship with mounds of war material lashed onto her decks. Given the number of ships that were committed to the convoy, a heavy cruiser with three destroyers and two corvettes, in addition to other escort craft, we knew that we were part of a big operation. As usual, we did our job but we were kept in the dark. All the operational details concerning the real purpose and destination of the convoy were highly confidential. If our ship had been torpedoed and some of the crew captured and interrogated the Germans would have gained a huge strategic advantage. Hence, except for a handful of officers, the crew was kept in the dark about the impending operation. We were given simple instructions: make sure the Germans didn't penetrate our defense perimeter. We were successful because when we reached a point close to Free Town the escorts left the convoy two at a time to refuel and then return to the convoy to let the next batch of escort to go and refuel. We stayed with the convoy to a point close to Saint Helena and then we returned to Free Town together with the destroyer Wild Swan. On the way back our captains made us conduct anti submarine exercises.

The U-boat captains stayed away from our convoy. Maybe they knew that, given a bit more time, our vermin passengers were a greater threat to our safety than their torpedoes. Given a chance, they could easily have taken over our ship. The beasts became more aggressive; they acted as if they owned our ship and we were unwelcome company. A rat bit one of the petty officers on his big toe while he was asleep in his bunk. They were everywhere. No one was spared a visit. I found a small cockroach in my jug of tea. I nearly swallowed it but I managed to spit it out thinking that it was a tealeaf. Then we hit a patch of rough weather between the Canary Islands and Cape Verde. Bad weather compounded our woes. Water sloshed back and forth on the mess deck. We had to keep the sea hatches shut to keep from flooding. Battening them turned the mess into a large stinking humid steel box with slimy walls, rats and what could have been the fastest cockroaches in the world. As long as we went through the bad weather zone, we were trapped inside our stinking can. No, we didn't fight the enemy on this convoy but when we finally dropped anchor in Free Town morale had hit a record low. A lot of us were fed up with our fate.

The commander-in-chief of the South Atlantic fleet came to inspect the ship. I know it was my imagination playing tricks but I could have almost sworn that, in addition to the usual complement of sailors lined up at the top of the gangplank to greet them, there were several detachments of cockroaches and rats in full battle gear. A quick tour through the ship confirmed his worst assessment. He announced that arrangements had been made for us to leave the ship for two days in order to fumigate the ship. From the way he described the operation it sounded like a simple and effective procedure that would finally take care of our awful problem.

The next day we removed all our kits, closed all the portholes and hatches and left for a small hotel that someone said had once been a brothel. At last! The navy got part of it right. The lodgings were a lot better than our mess but everyone wondered why the navy couldn't have arranged to keep the girls? After all, we could easily have managed to sleep two to a bed! Unfortunately the ladies had been taken somewhere else. Despite determined search parties from our side, they remained out-of-sight for the two or three days we were ashore. Our stay was short and unpleasant. The nights were hot and sticky and there were lots of mosquitoes. We slapped, tossed and turned and cursed. Even though it was uncomfortable, our bordello was nice compared to the conditions we left onboard.

Because all good things have to come to an end, we were ordered back onboard three days later. We were glad to return, open the hatches and let the fresh sea breezes blow through the entire length and width of the ship. Within minutes after stowing our kit we realized that there was an awful, unnatural, stench everywhere. Certainly, the fumigators had done a good job killing all the vermin. From the overpowering smell, slightly sweet and faintly reminiscent of rancid cooking oil, we knew the spirits of the 'dead' rats were fighting another round in their battle to take over the ship. All the rats were dead physically. But, instead of scurrying down the hawsers to the dock where they were supposed to die en masse onshore, they turned tail and scurried into the most inaccessible reaches of the ship to breathe their last. From their hiding spots, they were still 'alive.'

They were in the airshafts, crankshafts, under the galley stoves, in the captain's quarters, in the head, anywhere and everywhere that was hard to get to, there were dead rats. Decomposing rats reek. The stench was powerful enough to make you want to vomit. Freetown's heat and humidity accentuated the bio-chemical warfare the rats were waging. Much to our disgust, the only way to get rid of the stench was to get rid of their rotting bodies. We began dismantling many parts of the ship. We scraped them into buckets and dumped them into the bay. At least the fish, someone said he saw sharks, got their fill. When we removed the last rat and flicked off the last cockroach we were given buckets of foul smelling disinfectant to disinfect the entire ship. There was only one consolation: the strong disinfectant smelled just a bit better than the rotting rats. It took at least another two days with all the hatches open for the ship to smell 'right' again.

Our shipmate L. Power was transferred to the repair ship, HMS Vindictive. He got a first hand look at the so called 'bona fide prisoners of war', the two Vichy French aviators I just mentioned, and the crew that was downed over the harbor a couple of months earlier.

Rene Dassac (in collaboration with Patrick K. Robbins)

Rotten bastards! For us as Frenchmen, as far as we were concerned those two were living representatives of a treacherous government called Vichy, the only European government that openly collaborated with the enemy. Slime, they were not worth talking to and the best way to handle them was to ignore them.

After a few days rest we were called for an emergency patrol off the coast of Benin. British pilots reported hearing what they presumed to be the presence of a submarine. The pings were feint but there were enough to warrant sending us out. We automatically assumed that it was a German sub. After three days searching we got a strong asdic contact and attacked several times until we lost all contact. During one of the attack runs one of our depth charges exploded close to our stern and damaged the ship's side under the bilges. An alarming amount of seawater burst through the hull. Our evacuation pumps were activated and we began pumping to prevent further flooding. The captain set course for the nearest dry dock, a couple of days away in Lagos, Nigeria,

The skipper sent a signal to Lagos asking them to prepare the floating dry dock for us. They replied, "Why can't you have your repairs done in Free Town? Lagos is very quiet

for the moment and we cannot take the risk of having drunken sailors disturbing the peace in town." Our captain flew into a rage. "We are within twenty hours of sinking, our repairs can only be done in a dry dock and there are none in Free Town. Therefore, we are coming in and, if necessary, we will take the dry dock by force." We had a good skipper! Of course, we did not have to take the dry dock by force but the governor still was not happy about having a lot of sailors trying to drink his town dry. From the wisdom of the governor's mansion, he decided to avert trouble.

He arranged for the civil servants of Lagos to invite members of the ship's company to go ashore and stay with the civil servants. He probably thought that if the ship's company was made to stay with his trusted minions the sailors would avoid having harmful contact with the natives. Fine in theory, his grand scheme of social order didn't work. After a couple of days the system broke down and the crew wandered around town without having to be chaperoned by a civil servant. We were disgusted at the colonial civil servants who appeared to be obsessed with not having any outsiders upset their comfortable little nest. They were blind to the fact that a terrible war was being fought just over the horizon. It was coming closer and closer to them with each passing day.

Our skipper took advantage of the dry dock to have the ship plates scraped and repainted. Half naked native women carried out most of the work at the bottom of the ship down near the keel. Who said dry docks were bad news? We couldn't keep our eyes off them and we almost drove the petty officers nuts. Even pleading with us and asking the obvious question, "Come on lads get back to work, haven't you seen tits before?" failed to break the spell cast by the native women.

After a couple of weeks in the heat and stink of Lagos, and after repairs to the bottom were completed, we sailed to our temporary homeport of Freetown. Long before we docked we had made plans on how we were going to spend our shore leave. Pooling our information we developed a battle plan for pleasure: where to go for a drink and even where to go for a quick screw with some of the best looking half colored girls any of us had ever seen. Great plans, but we weren't in port long enough to enjoy putting them into action. After only three days we sailed in search of U-boats or German cargo ships disguised as neutral flag carriers.

This time we were detailed to meet the light cruiser HMS Dunedin off the Cape Verde islands to coordinate our hunting with her for the U-boats that were supposed to be in the area. Intelligence reports indicated they were trying to refuel from another large sub or a disguised cargo boat. We never met the Dunedin because as we learned a few days after we had put to sea, a U-boat sank her. A Portuguese ship rescued a few survivors. The rest of the crew probably went down with her.

We continued our search. Early in the morning we would start at high speed close to the rocky shores in the hopes we'd catch a U-boat ready to leave a refueling area. We didn't have any luck. After three or four days we left the area to refuel at Bathurst in Gambia. Refueling completed, we got a signal from Free Town to sail to a point close to the Canary Islands to pick up a fast convoy and to escort it as far as Saint Helena Island then return to Free Town.

During all this time we only had one or two possible asdic contacts. We dropped a few depth charges without any results. Back in Free Town we barely had time to refuel and replenish with fresh stores. There was not even enough time for a quick shore leave; we left for another hunt.

This time we heard a number of signals from various sources. One came from a Vichy French cruiser giving details to Dakar about a number of casualties they were taking to Dakar and to prepare ambulances etc. Because I spoke French, the captain called me to his cabin to look at a signal and ask me what I thought of it. I read it a couple of times and then told him that it looked as if a ship had been sunk somewhere. It seemed to me that a Vichy navy boat had been sent to bring survivors to Dakar. The rescue ship was reporting the number and condition of the survivors in order to organize stretchers and alert the receiving medical staff of the type of wounds they had to treat. The captain thanked me. He spoke quite good French but he wanted an interpretation from a native French speaker. As far as I was concerned, there was no need to read something into the signal that wasn't there. The way I read it, the message was clear and straight forward.

Later we found out what had happened. The story was both heroic and poignant. A German sub sank a cargo ship carrying a number of civilian men and women in addition to many Italian prisoners of war. He stayed around to make sure the ship was sinking. Through his periscope he watched the lifeboats being lowered into the sea. Something was wrong. The survivors were mostly women and children and prisoners of war. In an act that was both noble and dangerous, he transmitted a signal in the clear telling anyone monitoring his particular wavelength that he would not attack any ship coming in to rescue the survivors. In the meantime he surfaced and began picking up survivors who crowded onto his deck. From a humanitarian point of view, he acted correctly. Unfortunately, signals got mixed. A patrol aircraft picked up the signal and swung over the U boat and began a bombing run. When the bombing began the German captain quickly put the survivors back in their lifeboats and flooded his tanks. A French cruiser from Dakar later picked up the survivors.

We resumed our search for U-boats, looking for an easy prey, but we didn't get lucky. Finally we rendezvoused with our convoy. They were happy to report they had not suffered any losses - so far. Good news. We took up our station on the forward part of the convoy and began to carry out a zigzagging maneuver only a few miles in front of the convoy's lead ship. The sea was calm with hardly a ripple.

On nights like that I loved being on the bridge looking at the millions of stars. It was quiet and serene for a warship and I used those quiet hours on watch to recharge my soul. I am not sure where it came from or what caused it to happen but somehow I managed to go off duty with a unique feeling of freedom and strength. When I really worked at it I would go below feeling supremely confident that nothing could possibly touch us. After all, we had our asdic and radar scanning the surface of the ocean and the depth of the sea in front, under and around us. Of course now I know that I was playing games with my mind but I was also forcing myself to admit that I would survive the war. Any games other than cowardice that could get me through alive and intact were worth playing.

I wasn't slacking when I was on night watch; I was still alert. But the human mind can concentrate for relatively short periods before it needs a break and when my mind drifted I let it go down private lanes that I shared with no one. I made plans for a future leave with Edith. Okay, I admit, I was falling in love with her and I accepted that I knew very little about her. If I had to be honest with myself, I knew I was playing with fire because I was willing myself to fall in love. I'm a stubborn and determined guy and when I want something, nothing stands in my way. That's a good characteristic to have but it needs to harnessed and managed.

No one was in a position to tell me the truth: I was too young and too inexperienced with women to understand that sometimes it is good to step back and listen to one's own little voices that don't always agree with intuition, and emotion. I accepted that Edith was my only link with the civilian world, the only person with whom I could correspond and enjoy a little tenderness. It's strange to look back and see how my mind was tricking me into believing a person I knew so little about was really in love with me. In fact, if I had thought seriously about her, I would have forced myself to admit to a truth: I was her boy toy she could play with and never get involved. After all, I was always far away. She was safe. Our only contacts were scribbled onto a piece of paper and squeezed into an envelope. I needed someone; she did not need me. Our little love game was, in reality, nothing more than me suffering a bad case of puppy love. She played along for the price of penny postage.

We left the convoy to refuel, made a quick run into Freetown, and raced back at high speed to resume our escort duty until we got close to Saint Helena. As soon as we got to Saint Helena we turned back to Freetown for a couple of days rest before leaving for another sea duty. By then we had given up hope of ever putting our Freetown Pleasure Battle Plan to the full test. The situation at sea was too dangerous to give us anything but the shortest of shore leaves. Beyond our horizons more nations were at war. In the case of Britain, this was a time when misery loved company. Early in December 1941, the United States entered the war.

Japan attacked the United States on 7 December 1941. President Roosevelt called that day, "The Day of Infamy." Call it what you like, America was now openly fighting on our side. The Lend-Lease program had provided Britain with valuable materiel and logistical support but that barely kept us in the war. We needed troops, coordination, and the might of the American military machine. No one expected the war to turn in our favor any time in the near future. In fact, all we could see was more fighting, perhaps for years.

With America in the war we were convinced we would be able to beat the formidable German military machine. No one liked to admit it but the facts were hard to deny. Germany had an extraordinary military machine. It was well oiled, well trained, and well led. Bringing the Germans to their knees would take time. There would be more setbacks. These had to be expected. Winning was not going to be easy just because the Americans suddenly became active combatants. It would take time to bring their military machine up to full speed but once the Yanks and the rest of the allies started to roll, Germany was doomed. Finally, the chances of winning were rolling in our favor. We were not alone.

During the build-up phase American planes were flown across the Atlantic to Kano, Nigeria on their way to Cairo. These long flights were difficult. Sometimes one of the planes would be forced to ditch in the Atlantic and we would be called to rescue the crew. One day we received an emergency call. We left our anchorage at high speed to search the area where those poor fellows ditched. It was a race against time because we knew the odds weren't in their favor. They were battling, burning sun, no drinking water and sharks, lots of sharks. That crew was lucky because we found them before Nature took its toll.

When we reached them sharks had begun to circle their life raft and bump it. With no protection from the sun they were suffering from severe sunburn to their faces arms and backs and they were nearly delirious from thirst. They had spent three long days and nights waiting to be picked up. Somehow they managed to survive by sharing a few biscuits and a few pints of drinking water. Talk about discipline! They were weak and had to be helped up the pilot's ladder that had been dropped over the side. A sentry squeezed off a few shots to keep the sharks from coming too close to the ship's side. The yanks looked like hell but they were smiling, glad to be alive. A lot of men complain about British cooking but judging from the way they tore into their first warm meals in days, they weren't picky. By the time we reached Freetown they were fit to fly again.

Another time, this was before America declared war on Germany, we were called to pick up survivors from an American cargo ship that had been sunk by a U boat despite the fact the cargo had an American flag painted on the ship's side to show she was a neutral ship. Like the downed aircrew, they were also a sorry sight, sort of naïve, bewildered at having been torpedoed. Why us, they seemed to ask no one in particular? Because you are caught up in a war I wanted to answer, but I couldn't say that to a bunch of wet and terrified survivors. Still innocent and in the early stages of the war they had not yet realized that Germany's view of the war had changed. The Germans were waging a total war; anyone in their way became a fair target. Could the Americans know that within a few months, their country would also be engaged in what would become a world war and that it would be fought on three oceans, the Atlantic, the Pacific and the Indian Ocean?

As far as we were concerned, there was too much to protect and we were too few to be effective. There were only two destroyers and a corvette to carry out the many duties for which the navy in Freetown had responsibility. Our mission was easy to define on paper and almost impossible to put into practice. With inadequate resources, we were charged with protecting allied shipping off the coast of West Africa. Now and then other warships would stop to refuel. When we were lucky, they might be ordered to join us protecting convoys passing through the Freetown zone headed either north or south. Getting additional help didn't happen often enough and we became resigned, one destroyer, to doing the job of at least three ships. By then we were facing up to a nasty reality: there were simply not enough ships to adequately protect the allied effort.

It's hard to imagine the difficult decisions the Admiralty had to take every day of the war. The situation was so bad that almost any vessel that floated and could be armed was put into sea service. Sometimes we relieved an old weather beaten destroyer off the Canary Islands, a tub that maybe only a few weeks ago plowed through heavy seas on a murderous convoy to Murmansk in northern Russia. Conditions were atrocious on that run. Ice formed on the superstructures and made some ships dangerously top heavy. They wallowed through mountainous seas laden with vital war materiel. With their hatches battened and bitter cold outside and inside, no wonder the Navy had the highest tuberculosis rate in all the armed services. Many sailors probably lost their lives to vermin and disease. U boats weren't the only killers during that awful winter of 1940 – 1941.

Our depth charges were good, we were good, but it seemed like heaven had turned upside down and our crews, all of us, were living in a hell without end. The enemy shot holes in us and we fought back with everything we had. Behind every round we fired there was still an enormous reserve of grit and pride but it was increasingly clear: the grind was beginning to wear us down. No one talked of quitting but our tempers were short and we were barely able to hold them in check. It was a bad time to be a sailor in the Royal Navy but it was also a time when we knew Britain and the free world depended on us.

At the end of the summer of 1941 we were called back to Gibraltar. We sailed up with the Wild Swan, a destroyer of the same class as our ship plus five other escort ships. We were protecting a convoy bound for the U.K. When we reached Gibraltar we were given twenty-four hours to refuel and re-provision before sailing into the Atlantic to protect more convoys. Intelligence was getting better but it didn't make our job any safer. We were told the Germans were concentrating a large number of U boats in a fairly tight area around the Azores and off Portugal.

We began our sweeps, back and forth, back and forth, back and forth. One of my mates compared us to a high street tram shuttling back and forth between two watery end stations. It wasn't a bad comparison and I rather liked the idea of imaging what a tram would look like when it was equipped with depth charge racks! Until the end of October we sailed up and down 'our line' and depth charged many subs. We must have hit one and damaged it because we saw a large patch of oil ooze to the surface where we had dropped a pattern of ten depth charges. As far as we were concerned that oil meant we had a confirmed kill but Admiralty didn't agree. Not enough evidence, they said so we couldn't paint a sub on our bridge. Once again, had the wily German skipper released oil to take us off his tail and allow him to ease away into the sea, far beyond our reach? We'll never know but we were encouraged. We had hurt him; maybe we destroyed him.

It seemed as if we had standing orders: Off one station, and race to another. There was a convoy far to the west of the Azores that was under heavy U boat attack. We left Gibraltar at 25 knots. As soon as we cleared the straits we smashed into a ferocious sea. Only the Atlantic, at least as far as we knew, could whip up force eight winds. Our ship was hammered. The ship wase thrown high up in the air and then we'd pause for a split second before we'd knife deep into a trough, wallow or shudder, float to another crest and pound through it. The skipper was a fine seaman. He kept us afloat while managing to maintain a punishing speed. It was madness but we knew that every minute we lost meant one more minute when our convoy was exposed to the U boats. God, they needed our help.

The cracking speed took its toll. The sea hit our ship with explosive force and the upper deck structure couldn't withstand the pounding. The skipper ordered the engine room to reduce speed to 12 knots. By then the forward mess was awash. The violent wind had driven seawater through the closed and secured hatches. Our mess deck turned into a watering trough. We turned on pumps to pump the deck dry but as soon as we stopped pumping the deck was awash within seconds. The storm lasted four days, perhaps a few hours more. After that long, who cared? We'd given up counting hours.

Maybe that was one day in Hell; it felt like an eternity. We were locked into a tin. If someone had filled the clothes washer with stones and spanners, there would have been no difference in sounds compared to what we were going through. Pounding, shuddering, tossing and crashing, there was no way to escape the sea. We were numb but not so numb that we were incapable of pushing our bodies to react on a second's notice. Finally, after four days, the weather eased a bit.

Our convoy was out there somewhere. The Vimy had sliced through raging seas in record time and we knew we were close. I was on watch. Where were they? Guiding our binoculars in slow sweeps, we strained to pick them up on the horizon.

Suddenly at dusk we got a radar echo. Action stations squawked and we raced to our positions. There was no mistaking what the echo meant. We had picked up a sub on the surface! The captain ordered 'full speed'. Vimy lunged forward. Spray pushed high over our bow. We closed and trained our binoculars in the direction of the echo. We saw her; her silhouette left no doubt. It was a sub lying low in the water waiting for darkness to fall before commencing its attack runs. I guessed he was an experienced hunter because he was taking his time to prepare for his kills. Like a lion laying in the veldt stalking gazelle he watched his prey, patiently and out of sight. Night was his ally; he was in no hurry. He was preparing for a classic kill: under the cover of night, move into position, aim, fire, and steal away.

Night was also our ally. Carefully, the skipper maneuvered Vimy into position behind the sub. All our running lights were turned off. All hatches were locked shut. Only the sea made any noise splashing out from our hull as we inched into position. Slowly, slowly, we closed from behind. I couldn't make out anyone on the sub's bridge. The conning tower and part of the deck bobbed in front of us. Unless we were hallucinating, the sub was dead in the water. We were almost on top of her and she still hadn't seen us. Finally, was this our time to turn lucky? The skipper ordered full ahead. Vimy almost shot out of the water. He had decided to ram the sub at full speed. At the last moment we received orders to commence firing with all our guns.

If I had been a German standing watch and turned to see the Vimy bearing down, I'd have known that I was going to be killed, shredded beyond recognition. A bright red and orange sheet of molten metal, a sheet wider than the sub was long, was heading my way. No one could have survived the first few seconds. Anyone on the bridge would have been blown apart. We were almost on top of him and still he didn't try to dive or move out of our way. I wasn't surprised that they had not tried to return fire. There was no way to protect a gun crew from our attack. Then the sub blew its tanks and started sinking.

He was too late! The Vimy rammed the sub and ground across her as the U boat slipped under the surface. We heard massive crunching and tearing noises. Our ship shuddered as she scraped her keel across the width of the sub. They had been damaged, perhaps fatally, but we had not got off lightly. The captain ordered damage control reports. Only the chief engineer reported and it was bad news. The collision had knocked out our asdic and we'd lost a screw. There was no sign of the sub. Our skipper changed course and we started moving toward the convoy with one screw.

Suddenly, from somewhere out in the black ocean, we heard voices. Someone was shouting for help. The captain ordered the searchlights to be turned on. Our dark ship was now ablaze with light, a sitting duck for any U boat captain who was after an easy kill. The big lights probed the surface, quickly sweeping an area several hundred meters from our ship. The lights picked up sailors, men in life jackets, just like us. Some were bobbing in loose clusters, apparently trying to stay together for safety's sake, more than any other reason. Others began swimming toward our ship. The scrambling net was lowered and we reached over the side to help our first bunch of prisoners reach the safety of our deck!

I thought, is the world screwed up, or am I going nuts? Just a few minutes earlier they were trying to kill us and we were trying to kill them. Now, without even a second thought, we were bending over into the night to help the enemy come onboard. I grabbed a man's arm so that he wouldn't drown. I wasn't in a kill-or-be-killed mode.

Rene Dassac (in collaboration with Patrick K. Robbins)

I was a sailor doing what sailors have done since man first went to sea: Give help to anyone shipwrecked. Strange, I thought briefly, it was my ship that tried to kill him. He was the enemy, and, here I was helping him to stay alive. Help him live? Come on, this is war and we are meant to be killing each other! My mind raced.

Most of the Germans were young and exhausted. They must have been in the water a long time because their boat was damaged and had begun to sink before we happened on the scene. Someone else on our side got there first and damaged the U boat but, for some reason we'll never know, our side didn't finish them off. There was nothing else left for them to do but sit in the water waiting to be destroyed. The younger sailors were sarcastic and cocky. Their older shipmates, more experienced and reasonable, barked at them and brought the youngsters under control. It was obvious the older men were grateful to be in the hands of mature seamen like themselves.

We took the prisoners in turns to the showers and gave them blankets to wrap up in while their clothes dried near the engine room. After they put their uniforms back on we separated the ratings from the officers. The ratings were taken to the forward mess decks. Some of us were detailed to guard them. I didn't like guarding them because my patience and tolerance had vanished hours, perhaps days, ago. We sailed through hell to get to our convoy. None of us had been able to sleep. The galley did their best to feed us but they couldn't prepare warm meals in those violent conditions. Exhausted and hungry, I guess all of us were short of patience and I wasn't feeling particularly charitable toward Germans.

Maybe it's easier to kill someone when you don't have to stare him in the face. When we bore down on their sub I was wild with the thought that, at last, we were going to get a confirmed kill! That they would lose their lives was part of the war equation: Some live and some die. I wanted them to die so that I would live. Now, I was about to go on guard duty. The enemy looked a lot like us. A few days before they tried to sink ships in the convoy we were ordered to protect. I'd had it. If they moved, they were dead. I reassured myself that I wouldn't get put on report if I shot one.

We ordered them to line up against the bulkheads so we could distribute hot tea and biscuits. The German officers seemed like fairly normal men. They were locked in the captain's quarters with a single petty officer armed with a pistol posted outside their door. Somehow I got the feeling that these men, officers and ratings, would not try something foolish. At least, that's how I was trying to convince myself to think.

I looked at our prisoners. They were all young men were very much like us. The older ones seemed to be glad it was all over for them. They were quiet compared to the younger mates. The youngsters seemed to be laughing at us. Arrogant bastards! I don't speak German, but, every now and then I could tell from the tone of their voices that the older seamen had heard enough and they were warning the kids to pipe down. They were our prisoners and we could shoot them if we were forced to and we knew they had some advantages that we didn't want to spend too much time thinking about. Apparently the entire crew had survived. That meant they had an advantage of numbers and language.

I don't think any of us on guard duty spoke German. We didn't know what they were talking about. Rush us, kill us, mock us? Who knew what was swirling around inside their heads? They were kept in the various mess decks. Only one sentry guarded each group of prisoners. For those of us going on guard duty we realized that if our prisoners were stupid enough to try and rush the sentry and lose some of their own, they could try to break out. They wouldn't get very far because we could overpower them but the battle would be bloody.

It was my turn to mount guard. When I walked in to take over my group they all went very quiet. No mistaking it, there was fear in their eyes. I couldn't figure it out. I wasn't exactly a two-meter tall giant carrying a submachine gun. The senior petty officer on duty came by. He spoke French and I asked him in French, "What's with these guys? I walked in and they all stopped talking." He told me that my reputation had preceded me. One of my mates who stood watch before me managed to tell his prisoners that they had better behave because the next guard was a Frenchman who didn't like Germans. That revelation got the prisoner's attention. Being captured by the British was one problem but being held captive by a Frenchman whose country Germany was occupying was something they hadn't counted on.

I was irritated that my real identity had been revealed to the prisoners. Why had a fellow sailor done something so stupid? Hadn't I worked hard enough to create a new identity? Sure, my accent was a dead giveaway but I could have been called a French Canadian instead of a Frenchman. Anyway, the damage was done and I had more important problems to handle: a room full of prisoners who were staring at me, waiting for the worst to happen. Maybe my mate got tired of the young prisoners laughing at him and he told them something to scare them and shut them up. He did a good job on them. Now it was my turn to laugh. I reassured the petty officer that I was a seaman no different that my prisoners. "I'm not going to open fire unless I have to and then I will without thinking twice." The prisoners looked at us as if they were mutes. Did any of them speak French? I never found out.

What the prisoners would learn to appreciate in captivity was the fact that sailors in the Royal Navy had not been trained by a bunch of Nazis. Our values were better than theirs. They looked at me almost with unblinking eyes. I was on duty, we had our confrontation, they remained quiet and I got through my watch with no problems. In fact, it was almost pleasant.

After a few days with the convoy we transferred our prisoners to a colonial class light cruiser, the Curacoa, and continued our trip. We eventually left the convoy to proceed to our port division Portsmouth for repairs. We were given two weeks leave, so, I hurried to Wolverhampton and stayed with Jack Rowan and his wife.

*****

Talk about being blind and dumb in love! You have to forgive me, but I was so green that I couldn't see through the ruse Jack and Edith were playing right in front of me. It was obvious to everyone except Jack's wife and me. Jack was Edith's lover. The "smart" little Frenchman was a handy screen. Edith played me like a virtuoso piano player while Jack turned her pages. Did I actually see through them but didn't want to admit what I saw? That's a question I've asked myself thousands of times. I still don't know the answer even today.

Their screen should have been obvious to me but I was a greenhorn in love and I was so damned randy I ran like a mad dog to meet her. She was working as an executive secretary for Jack. Our time together was limited to meeting during her lunch break or after work in the evening. In conditions like that it was impossible for me to screw her at my leisure. Or, for that matter, screw her at all. Could I get her excited? Yes! Would she allow me the most intimate caresses? Yes! Would she go any further? No! This unreal relationship started to wear me down. When I'd walk back to the Rowan's after an evening with her my ardor was so aroused that putting one unhappy foot in front of the other was painful. Looking back at myself, I almost chuckle at my immaturity.

It's well known that sea duty takes a toll on the human body, especially when you are young, when you're in that age when you tend to have more testosterone than good sense. When we were at war we lived in a strange and violent world. At an age when Mother Nature made our bodies ready for procreation, or going through the motions, we were out to sea. During that period in our lives, we spent more time in our hammocks dreaming of sex than onshore with the opposite sex. Call us randy or bawdy, the label didn't matter because what we were trying to do was live every minute without any regrets. When we went back to our ships we entered another world. On every one of our tours we watched young seamen like us being blown to peaces or dying of exposure from having spent too many days on a raft hoping for the one ship that never came to pick them up. During my leave I did my best to break down Edith's defenses but she repelled my boarding forays.

My leave came to an end. It had been bittersweet. There were many good memories and some I wished I hadn't had, but I kissed her goodbye and returned to my real family and home, my shipmates and my ship. I didn't know it but Fate stepped in. I think I needed a helping hand.

Once onboard the captain called me and said that I was posted to go to HMS Vernon for a course to make me a Leading Torpedo Operator. It was with mixed feelings that I had to accept his order. I asked the Captain, "May I return to this ship after completing the course, sir?" His reply was a blow. "I doubt it. You see, the admiralty needs people like you because you have gained a lot of experience in how to commission new ships. The navy will have lots of new recruits who will have to be taught all the things you have yourself learned." He continued, almost fatherly, but he was a skipper who was close to his men so I wasn't surprised. "I know how hard it is to leave a ship and your shipmates, but, on the other hand, you cannot remain an able seaman for the rest of your life. No doubt you will find, and get to know, new and good shipmates on your new ship." He stepped back and snapped me a salute. "Alright Powell, good-bye and good luck to you." I returned his salute and went below deck and began collecting my gear.

When I had packed my gear and taken one last look around I made my way to the gangway where my mates had gathered to wish me farewell. I was given a week's leave and went straight to Wolverhampton to see Edith. I loved her. At least, that's what I kept telling myself. What I didn't tell myself was that I needed to open my eyes and see the situation for what it really was. I knew that our relationship was lop-sided. I loved her more than she loved me. That much was obvious. But, I kept hoping that she'd come around and even out the relationship with me.

I could not bring myself to accept that a love triangle existed. Jack and Edith were the two long sides and I was the short skinny side. Jack needed me to be his foil; Edith needed me to draw attention away from Jack and her. I needed Edith because I was convinced that I was in love with her. Damned if I wasn't blind to reality. Even Randal pulled me aside and told me to wake up. "You silly cunt, leave her be. She's Jack's mistress. If you ever get her into bed, all she'll do is screw Jack through you." I didn't want to hear that so I didn't believe him. Damn, I was really stupid! Thankful for what I got, I enjoyed my leave just the same even if all she gave me were kisses and caresses but no screwing!

As soon as my leave was up I made straight to HMS Vernon in Portsmouth. I had to wait for a couple of weeks before I was transferred to a girl's college near Brighton which had been requisitioned by the Navy. While I was in Portsmouth I made the mistake of going on shore leave without knowing that I was actually on damage control duty. As it happened, there was an air raid while I was ashore. When I came back the next morning I was given a week of scaling and painting one of the walls on a building, along with four Wrens. We painted and scraped, joked and engaged in friendly banter. I actually got friendly with one girl. I helped her when we were high up on scaffolding attached to one of the walls. She was terrified of heights so I told her not to look down. "Only face the wall." She obeyed me as if I were a drill instructor. Then I taught her how to descend the scaffolding. That was more difficult because when she moved she had to grab hold of my arm. Shaking like a leaf, she moved slowly while I steadied from one level to the next.

She was sort of cute. Maybe she was a year or so younger than me. She was grateful for my helping hand. We worked together for the entire week. I was her guide and she kept me supplied with cigarettes as a way of thanks. We became good mates but unfortunately I could not even go ashore with her because on the day that I finished my punishment I was sent to Brighton and I never saw her again.

Brighton wasn't a bad posting. In fact, I was fairly happy. I used to go ashore with another Frenchman who was on a similar course. He was a good violin player and he even composed music. Sometimes he used to leave the lecture in a hurry saying he had to go to the toilet. As soon as he got in the stall he would grab a bit of toilet tissue and write a few of the notes he had dreamed of while the teacher droned on in his lecture which was about a distinctly non-musical topic. If I had stayed longer with him I probably would have learned to play the violin.

One day a German pilot roared over. He was returning to his base, probably in France, and he took an unnecessary shot at a Wren who happened to be on the open ground when he flew over. He had to know his target was a woman because he was flying very low and no one was firing at him because the air raid warning had not been given. Bastard, I hoped somebody would give him the same treatment some day.

My course finally ended and I was promoted LTO and sent to Greenock, with many others, to board the Queen Mary bound for New York to commission the first lot of American build LST's. This was September 1942. We had no idea what these boats looked like but we didn't care because we were glad to go to the USA, the Land of

Plenty where people lived as if the world was at peace. Most of us had forgotten what life was like in 'the other world' before the war. After a few days easy sailing at a speed over 25 knots we reached New York.

Lorries were waiting at the dock to take us to a naval barracks where they had prepared a huge lunch for us. In front of us there was more food, even delicacies, than we had seen in years. There was rationing on our side of the pond in Europe where people were dying. As a service man I ate managed to eat well because the military looked after its soldiers and sailors but what we ate every day was nothing like the spread the Americans laid on. There was turkey, ham, chicken, bread, glistening steaming mounds of white potatoes, gravy tubs bigger than tin wash-up basins, pitchers of thick creamy milk, butter tubs and enough pies and cakes to make us think we'd been invited to judge a baking contest. We ate until it hurt and then they herded us out of the mess hall. Everything was organized like clockwork. Immediately after lunch we loaded into busses and were taken to Asbury Park, about 60 miles from New York, where we were billeted in two great hotels.

There were already some British sailors who were waiting for their ship to be repaired so it could return to sea duty. Our stay in Asbury Park was very much appreciated because it was a step back into peacetime. No black-outs or restrictions of any sort, the food was fantastic; we ate as much as we wanted. Very often American families would call for two or three sailors to have dinner with them at their home. Their kindness was touching.

However, a bizarre incident occurred that is worth mentioning because it showed that, even at this stage of the war when America was actively engaged, there were still a number of Americans who were very pro German. I'd even go as far as to say, some of them were definitely pro Nazi.

One night some of the boys went to a bar that was a bit outside town where most of the customers were of German extraction. There was even a picture of Hitler on the wall, the swastika and all sorts of Nazi slogans tacked onto the walls. To no one's surprise, our boys were not made to feel welcome. They went in anyway and made their way to the bar. Within minutes someone said something, insults were traded and then words gave way to fists. Our lads were drawn into a huge fight but unfortunately the British were outnumbered. They beat an honest retreat carrying their wounded with them: bleeding noses, a broken arm and a broken leg. A fight like that didn't go unnoticed. The commanding officer was informed of the incident. After hearing the British side of the story he was satisfied that his men had not picked the fight. Furthermore, given the circumstances, "You were right to treat them as enemy," he said. That's all we needed to hear.

The following night a group of our boys went back to the "German's bar", started a brawl, and for good measure they set the pub on fire. The American authorities were informed of the circumstances surrounding the incident. It was never mentioned in the press. Perhaps one of the reasons the press did not report the fights and the fire was because there was a lot of sabotage going on in American factories and dockyards. Something was brewing. We heard the FBI was getting ready to make a nationwide raid on all Nazi organizations. A few weeks after our incident the raids took place throughout the United States. Again, rumors turned out to be facts.

One evening I went on leave and stopped at a bar called the "Jungle Bar." It was almost empty except for a girl sitting at the bar. I sat down near her, but not next to her, but the barman began making signs as if he wanted to prompt me to start talking to her. One look was enough to tell me she was not the happiest woman I'd ever seen. Her face was drawn and she had tears in her eyes. I started talking and asked her why she was so sad. She replied that her boyfriend was in the Marines and at Guadalcanal where a terrible battle was raging. Apart from press reports, she had no news about what was going on and whether he was dead or alive. I understood how she felt and I told her that I was without news from my own family since 1940.

Somehow I found enough courage to tell her that she wasn't doing herself any good worrying so much. I used simple logic because I had been in battles. I told her that, of course, there are losses but the majority of the fighting troops come through in good shape. We continued our conversation for a while and then she asked me what I was doing that evening. I replied that I had no particular plans. She brightened up and suggested that I go to New York with her. That was a great idea but, I confessed, I only had a few dollars. She laughed, "Don't worry. You're my date." She looked around the bar. Two customers didn't exactly fill up the place. "This place is so damn dead. Let's go to Times Square and have fun." She looked at me, "OK?" As if I would say no! "Come on let's go."

We took the train into New York and made straight for Times Square where we had a few drinks at the Jack Dempsey bar and afterwards we went to a cinema. When we came out it was late and we decided to go to a hotel to finish the night. We asked to be called at 6 o'clock so I could catch the train back to Asbury Park and be back at the barracks by eight o'clock for the morning call. What began as a quiet evening became an evening in Paradise. My night with her was every sailor's dream: I screwed her until I was drained. I didn't have to tell her I didn't know when I'd have another chance, if ever. She was just as pleased as I was. When we reached Asbury Park we kissed goodbye. We never saw each other again.

As soon as I reached the barracks I was directed to join up with the future crew of LST 407. They gave me a couple of minutes to ready my kit and board the train to Baltimore where we were to take over our new ship. During the trip down the coast we got to know each other. I met the able seaman torpedo rating assigned to work with me. He was a nice enough kid but I soon realized that I would have to teach him everything because he had been called up before having completed his apprenticeship.

There were also five massive lads from Newfoundland among the crew. All of them were ex-fishermen, good seamen and very sturdy characters. These guys were big but they didn't use their bulk to be imposing. Almost like a pack of Newfoundlander pups, you couldn't help but like them. I got on well with all of them.

When we reached Baltimore the U.S. Navy billeted us in a hotel down near the docks. After a light lunch we were marched off to see the state of our ship. Talk about shock! We stared at the superstructure and, to a man, damn near passed out. About a third of the ship had not even been started! The ship didn't look like a ship. It looked like a human anthill because it was swarming with welders, men and women, who were working non-stop, day and night. The only time they weren't working was when they walked on or off the site, ate a meal or went to the toilet.

Taulus

One of the American duty officers accompanying us realized we were in a state of shock. He explained how the ships were built, how tight schedules were always met, how every man and woman we were staring at wanted to build the best ship possible in the shortest possible time. "Don't be surprised, but," pausing to make sure he had our fullest attention, "I think you'll take over this ship in four or five days." He absolutely exuded confidence. We were British seamen who had been taught to respect, and sometimes even tolerate, our officers. It would have been poor form to laugh in his face but everyone thought his confident explanation was just another case of American bullshit. Give us our due, we had not been in the States long enough to appreciate how well organized the nation was behind their war effort. Time would prove him right or wrong, we thought as we marched back from the dockyards. That afternoon, if a poll had been taken of the crew, none of us would have given him our vote of confidence. From the looks of her, it was unthinkable that we'd board any time in the near future.

Sure enough, four days later we boarded our ship. The human anthill that had been crawling across our ship had been moved out of our way. They were already working on another ship next to us. I recognized a couple of the women in their overhauls and tin hats cradling their rivet guns on scaffolding that seemed to stretch into the grey sky. Only a few engineers, still finishing and testing various pieces of equipment, were left onboard our ship. We didn't have time to act surprised. There was too much to do and I took advantage of the fact there were still engineers around who could answer my questions. The American engineers were patient and helpful. They listened to my questions and then showed me everything I wanted to know. Within a couple of days I understood how all the equipment worked for which I was responsible, how to trouble shoot it, and what kind of performance to expect. One man was particularly kind and thorough. What he taught me in Baltimore was a great help during the remainder of the war.

I became very friendly with the leading radioman, a chap by the name of Reiner. He had already served on a motor torpedo boat in the Free French Navy. We used to go ashore together and he told me he had an affair with the daughter of an American politician in Boston; he was even thinking of getting married to her before leaving the U.S.

Everything on our ship was electrical except for the diesel engines. Much was new to me and therefore I had a lot of learning to achieve in a very short period of time. I could not rely on the seaman who was supposed to be my mate because he had no practical experience. The two of us learned together because I took him along with me and got him involved with everything I was learning instead of giving him a less complicated job to do alone. We began to bond; he was a quick learner. After a few days the ship was ready for testing. In record time, perhaps at a pace dictated by the Americans for whom time was a critical element in constant short supply, we carried out all the work-up exercises necessary to handle the LST. We even amazed ourselves. Barely a couple of weeks earlier none of us knew anything about the type of ship we were now beginning to call our own.

We liked our ship but we disliked our captain. He was an RNR Lieutenant Commander who had a knack for rubbing everyone the wrong way, including his officers. Fortunately, our first lieutenant was also RNR and he was a gentleman who was well liked. The chief engineer was a kind man, ex merchant navy and RNR. Two RNVR lieutenants completed the officer staff. In civilian life one was a lawyer and the other a bank employee. The last two had practically no sea experience but they seemed to enjoy the privilege of being officers on a HM ship!

We laughed at them two characters, just waiting to see how they would react when we hit really heavy seas. Our clumsy fat ship was built to roll and pitch. Maybe it wasn't designed that way but that's how she handled. There was no way she would slice through the water like a destroyer. No, she wallowed and bobbed, a clumsy vessel except when tied-up to a dock. After completing all our working up exercises to the satisfaction of the American hand-over staff, we were detailed to proceed to New York to take on a cargo of high-octane gasoline.

That news was an eye opener! It was about the worst cargo we could think of but then one of the Newfoundlanders said he knew of something that was even worse. They could stack some ordinance on deck! Gallows humor helped but there was no hiding the risk we were ordered to take. If we were torpedoed or bombed, our ship would burn like a torch with all of us in it. We knew there was no way to abandon ship and not get caught in floating flaming fuel. Some of our religious mates went to sleep that night with a new prayer: Please Lord, get us to wherever we're going safely. May God have mercy on our souls!

In New York we received a huge LCT that occupied the whole length and sides of the deck above the tanks and vehicles space. We had the American crew of the LCT bunking with us. They were all Texans and we got on well with them. At this stage two things happened within our crew that rattled us. We had already spent enough time working together and enjoying shore leave to begin to feel like a family. Slowly, conversations led into the murky world of our private lives and the man behind the name began to emerge from most of us.

Remember our five Newfoundlanders, the men-puppy giants? As I said, most of them were former fishermen with limited educations. Like nearly everyone else, I was probably the only exception because mine were dead; they were lucky because they received letters from their mothers and grandmothers. Getting a letter was nice but since their letters were in French, a language they could not read or write, I became their loved one's voice and the men's letter writer. It didn't take long before I became their closest friend. I probably knew more private details about them than anybody onboard. This is how I learned that one of them had already been sunk four times.

In the eyes of the other four, the survivor was bad luck. They pulled him aside and told him bluntly: either he left the ship before it sailed from New York or, if he refused, they'd push him overboard at the first opportunity. Hearing that kind of talk rattled the poor kid. He began to believe he was going to get sunk for the fifth time and he also believed the burly Newfoundlander's threat. He deserted the day before we left harbor. The navy has a lot of superstitions and many, such as a jinxed crewmember drawing bad luck, are believed. That's perhaps why no one was in a hurry to report the missing seaman to the shore authority.

The other test of 'family ties' concerned my mate Reiner, who decided to go to Boston to get married before we left. He asked me to cover for him until he came back which I did quite successfully until the day before sailing when the first lieutenant called for him. I had to tell him the truth: "Reiner's gone to get married." For a minute I thought he was going to explode but he held himself in check. I don't know what made me do it but I looked him straight in the eye and promised him that Reiner would be back onboard before we left. I held my breath because his reaction could have gone either way. Fortunately the number one was a nice man. After giving me a good reading of the regulations, he reminded me that I would also be punished if Reiner did not come back in time. Cripes! I was in it up to my eyeballs and Reiner was out of sight, maybe for good. Reiner kept his word and the first lieutenant kept his mouth shut. As far as he was concerned, the captain thought he had a full complement. I shuddered to think of what might have happened if the captain had got involved. There was no way of avoiding the truth. The captain was a hard man. In fact, we thought he was one of those awful people who are born nasty and only get worse with age. Without him, we would have had an extremely harmonious crew.

LST's were not popular ships. Because they were not the most sought after ship they generated a lot of rumors. Some said they were built to do one job; they were never built to face rough weather, that we would be very lucky to survive crossing the Atlantic, never mind surviving more than one landing. That kind of talk could have gotten through to us if we had spare time on our hands but we were so busy doing our jobs that we didn't believe a word of that bullshit. The same could be said about the Victory Ships, built in record time to fill the gaps left by the loss of merchant ships that were being sunk by U-boats almost faster than they could be built. Twenty years later I saw Victory ships in many of the ports we entered.

Finally we received our orders to sail. All we knew was that we were to head out and join a convoy somewhere far out off the coast and then sail toward Bermuda. We got to Bermuda and stayed there a couple of days and got some shore leave. I went ashore with my mate. We weren't going to let slip any opportunity to have a good time. Starting with this trip and lasting for God-only-knew how long, we were in for some tough trips. More than once the thought crossed our minds that we might not make it. If that was a possibility, and hopefully not likelihood, we decided not to leave anything to chance. Without any fanfare or signed documents, we made a pact to enjoy life to the hilt in every port we hit. First on the list: get screwed in every port! That was a fine idea. We were proud of our genius at coming up with such a wholesome commitment to life. So proud, that we decided to have another round before inaugurating our pact.

Outside the pub we had to admit we had a problem trying to execute our plan. No matter how hard we looked, we couldn't find any birds. That was impossible. It didn't make sense. We were in a port and all ports have the kind of women we needed. There had to be a solution!

We flagged down a cabbie and asked the driver where the birds were hiding. He laughed and gave us a long story about Bermuda. He was a Negro, probably of African origin. He described the white people of Bermuda (a lot of aristocrats) who did not mix either with the blacks or working class blokes like us. We replied that we didn't mind because we were color blind. Forget color. All we wanted was to have a good time before we got blown to bits. He looked at us half smiling and said, "OK, I'll find you one but you will have to do it in the open air on the grass because here blacks and whites don't mix." We agreed. We were healthy young men; we liked fresh air and he drove away. In the meantime our imaginations ran riot. We shared images of beautiful mulatto girls with long legs and wavy hair tied up in colorful scarves, sensuous creatures quivering with boundless passion.

The driver wasn't gone long. We stared into the back of his cab. Was this guy playing some kind of a joke? By god, she was ugly! She was big, she was black, her hair was frizzed up in little spikes and when she smiled half her front teeth were missing. She heaved open the door and lumbered toward us. We glanced at each other and laughed nervously. The woman bearing down on us had to be the ugliest female either of us had ever seen. My mate may have had more to drink than I had so I let him have the first go. The more I looked at her the more I knew there was no way I was going to get anywhere near her. Even my carrot was cowering. He finished and we paid her off: one try for the price of two. I think if she had asked for more we'd either have paid willingly or we'd have taken off through the field running for our lives. Back at the ship I let my mate know that he had one up on me. At the next port I promised to even the score.

Finally we received word that the convoy we were to join was passing close to the island. Once we caught up with it we were assigned a position at the tail end probably because the convoy commandant knew we were carrying a dangerous cargo. As far as our crew was concerned, being assigned tail end was a bad omen. There was some dark talk in the mess about us not making it to the other side but I fobbed it off as just another round of superstitious seamen jabbering away the time.

After two days the weather changed. In the space of a couple of hours we went from pleasant cruise ship sailing and plunged into a vicious storm. The ship started to pitch and make loud cracking noises that couldn't be ignored. We'd hit a trough and CRAAACK …SNAP….CRAAACK … POP would rip through the mess. We looked around fully expecting to see something hanging by a wire or a bulkhead loose and ready to fall on us. Critics from the honorable members of the mess deck were convinced the ship was going to fly apart. It was only a matter of time. "This f….g ship will break her back before we get to the other side. If this keeps up we'll have to dump the LCT up on deck." This got a big laugh from the LCT's American crew. Most of them had never been on a ship before. They were seasick and frightened. In their minds the ship was going to fall apart; it certainly sounded like it was breaking up, piece by piece. If jettisoning the LCT meant improving their chances of surviving the trip, they were more than willing to help us cut the lashings.

My troubles started just about the time when the storm was really raging. At the end of the afternoon the captain called me to the bridge. "The steering gear isn't responding correctly. Find out what's wrong." My, the old man was certainly chipper. Must have missed his tea, I thought. When I got down below to the steering gear I smelled an odor telling me something had burned. It didn't take long to find the problem. The coil controlling the brake that stopped or released the rudder had burned out. I clambered back up to report to the bridge and explained that I would have to stop the steering gear to change the broken coil. The captain must have had his tea because he was almost cordial. "Quick as you can Powell, let me know when you are ready so I can stop the ship." Great! That was really what nobody wanted: alone, dead in the water and our convoy steaming out of sight.

Our breakdown created considerable tension; no one wanted to stop. When you are in a convoy there is safety in numbers. No matter how bad the situation, you want to keep going and not be left behind and risk being picked off. The captain had no other choice. He went on the PA to explain why he was stopping the ship to carry out emergency repairs. Bucking and wallowing, we were a U boat captain's dream. Imagine how the footage would have looked on Nazi propaganda newsreels: an allied ship on fire, sailors floundering in the burning water and plumes of black smoke billowing into the sky, another allied funeral pyre.

I went below with my toolbox, a seaman electrician, and began the repair work. I was lying down with my lighted pipe in my mouth and the seaman was lying just over my head holding a nut with a spanner while I was unscrewing to release the coil. Because we were not underway the round-bottomed ship was pitching and rolling. Unfortunately, soon after I began working the wind picked up and white caps began forming. We wallowed into deep woozy swells. Time was running out. I focused on the job at hand. I knew that working as fast as I could in cramped quarters, the last thing I was going to do was to take valuable time and look around to see what else might have gone without me knowing. I was working on the principle: "If it ain't broke, don't fix it." If I had taken a split second to look up I'd have seen that my seaman's face had changed color from a ruddy tan into a pasty green. His eyes were glazed and his Adam's apple raced up and down his neck.

He wasn't talking but he made funny little noises, almost mewing, from between his pursed lips. He vomited on me in one powerful geyser, covering my head and chest. He was a large lad and he had managed to stow a lot of food into his belly. Possibly several meals trickled off me down onto the deck. I was furious and yelled at him. "Fuck off. I'll finish the job by myself." He hauled up the ladder and I went back to work slipping through his slime that was coating the deck. It only took a few more minutes to complete and I reported my adventure to the bridge.

Everyone was laughing. It takes so little to make people happy, I thought. The captain decided to rib me, an experienced seaman. "For a moment I thought it was you who had been seasick." I didn't say anything but the look on my face told him he'd gone far enough. "Thank you, sir," I replied dryly. He waved me away. "Alright go below and take a shower. You stink." He ordered 'full steam ahead'. In less than an hour we caught up our position at the rear of the convoy.

Fixing the steering gear made me the hero of the day but no one wanted to sit next to me at mess until they were sure my shower really had washed away the remnants of my adventure below deck. Unfortunately the steering gear gave us trouble two more times before we reached Oran, Algeria. After the second time I repaired it, alone, I had figured out what was causing the coil to break. The coil was too weak to handle the constant stress produced by the steering gear. Knowing what the problem was didn't help me. I couldn't come up with a solution because we didn't have the equipment onboard to machine a new part. Before reaching port I arranged with the chief engineer to have the coil modified in Oran.

Nearing the Straits of Gibraltar the weather deteriorated. We had to fill the ballast because with the LCT on deck the ship was top heavy. Just another storm we thought so we didn't give it too much attention. On the way over to Gibraltar we encountered some fairly heavy weather but in the approach to the Straits the ship began rolling like never before. Her rolls and bucks prompted everyone to vent his frustration and give his opinion about our ship's sea worthiness. No bets were placed but if money could have been placed on whether or not she would break in two, the odds would have been 2-to-1 that she'd break in two. Betting against your own ship brought bad luck so we didn't put our money where our mouths were. I was too busy keeping her running to speculate on what else might happen.

The ship was fitted with three powerful diesel-generating sets that had to be transferred from one set to the other every day. I spent a lot of time in the engine room and got caught in a quarrel that started between the chief engineer and the first lieutenant. The chief engineer wanted me to be part of the engine room rating but the first lieutenant would not agree. He was a stickler for playing by the rules. According to regulations, the torpedo branch in the Royal Navy was part of the deck staff. Fortunately, the first lieutenant, of course, won and I remained a deck hand.

Taulus

I had two duties onboard the LST that were quite different from each other. The ship had two smoke floats forward close to the two 20 mm AA guns and two aft under the 12 Pd gun. My action station was to make smoke at night when we anchored off a landing beach. In theory, billowing smoke hid the convoy under a curtain of thick fog. Lack of visibility made it difficult for enemy airmen who were trying to bomb us out of the water. When we were at sea my job was damage control. This job allowed me to stand by on the bridge with the lookout and the duty officer, signalman, and the quartermaster on the wheel.

Up to now I haven't said much about our captain, lieutenant commander RNR Harris except to say that he was thoroughly disliked. There were probably as many reasons as there were men onboard but there were two recurrent complaints: he was a heavy drinker and he was always critical of someone. It was impossible to get it right with him. After a few weeks his nastiness permeated the ship like a bad smell. Not quite as bad as the dead rats, but bad enough to almost affect morale. Compared to him, the rest of the officers were kind and polite. They never swore at us although we provided them with numerous opportunities to lose their tempers. Their restraint and commitment to simple principles of leadership were appreciated. Below deck, especially the lower deck and engine room crew, conversations that didn't contain foul language were so few that I can't remember any!

Sometimes I wondered about the American crew of the LCT; they stuck together in a world that was only open to them. It was hard to communicate with them because they were not very talkative. Had they been ordered not to associate with us because they knew an operational secret that could not be shared? We never found out. It was as if the ship housed two camps who were afraid to talk to each other. Perhaps the way the British crew acted was one of the reasons we remained apart. From their perspective we must have sounded like a wild lot. On those rare occasions when we did sit and swap stories, ours were often so wild and exaggerated that they placed us in a category all by ourselves. For the Americans, we were indeed strange shipmates.

Outside Oran our ship, and a couple of others, were ordered out of the convoy and into port. We tied-up at a special wharf where there was a huge crane that lifted the LCT to the dockside. From the way the operator swung his hoists into action you'd have thought he was loading cotton bales instead of a huge ungainly landing craft. The Yanks formed up and marched down the gangplank. Some were smiling and waved back at us but a lot of them were grim. I kept thinking that they knew something we didn't and that thought haunted me. We gave them a good send-off, a hearty British cheer, and "Good luck to you all." In the end I think they probably came to the conclusion that we weren't as bad as we talked. Of course, I could have been fooling myself. One way or another, it was either that or else they were great at hiding their relief at being able to distance themselves from a bunch of Limeys, some of whom acted and talked like pirates.

We remained in Oran for a couple of days to refuel and go through the routine re-supply steps. On the first day we were granted shore leave until 11 PM. I planned to go ashore with my mate Doug Reiner, "Doug of Bermuda and the Beast fame". Our objective was to reactivate the pact and have a well-deserved screw before being blown to bits. I know this sounds melodramatic but we couldn't escape persistent rumors concerning our cargo of 'mystery' barrels. The juiciest and most alarming rumor held my attention. We weren't transporting gasoline but another liquid that was more dangerous and even sinister. I had a mate in signals and he told me that most of the signals or orders we received concerned the 'gasoline' barrels. For example, after having got rid of the LCT why did the port authorities order us to be moored at an isolated side of the port, a part of the port that had nothing to do with a ship carrying a cargo of gasoline cargo. Ostensibly it was to allow the crane to be used by another ship but no one believed that was the real reason. It turned out that we were carrying gasoline and it was destined for the RAF base at Alexandria, Egypt. Knowing what was in the drums and barrels didn't reassure us because it would only take one hit to turn us into fish food.

In the afternoon we went ashore and had a look at the town, walked through the brothel area and started to have second thoughts about implementing the Algerian phase of our Bermuda pact. I had never seen anything like it. In front of each brothel there was a queue of

American soldiers and other servicemen extending several yards back up the narrow smelly streets. Doug and I decided that, in view of the numbers, we had lots of times to look for something else to do so we went to have a drink at one of the big pubs with a large terrace outside. We sat with two other shipmates who were already there. Beer was served in glasses cut from the bottom part of a wine bottle. The cut-off bottle/glass wasn't a tourist gimmick. Glasses, and just about everything you associate with civilian life, were in short supply. The cut-offs showed us how badly the locals were suffering!

A French navy surgeon was seated a few feet away from us. He kept staring at me and I suspected he was probably asking himself, "Where have I seen this guy before?" Maybe he started to put two and two together. Could he have been asking himself, "Isn't that young man the boy cadet in Brest I once treated for mumps?" Remember, I was in Royal Navy uniform, talking and laughing with my mates. By then my English was good and I fitted in with my RN mates. The fact that I spoke English probably confused him. Certainly, the changes in my physique and face hadn't been that great since I was a cadet. Who is he? Trying to identify me must have driven him nuts.

I didn't have his problem because I've got a good memory. I recognized him immediately but my guard was up and I wasn't about to lower it. Why should I trust him? How could I handle his reaction when he learned of my identity change from Dassac to Powell? Face it, I told myself, in the eyes of the French navy I'm a deserter a lowly seaman, the type of little 'mec' French officers disliked and mistrusted. Darlan had been assassinated a few weeks before. The Free French had not been fully integrated into the allied command structure. There was confusion and just because he was wearing a French officer's uniform there was no guarantee where his true loyalties were placed. For some men, a uniform is a disguise hiding the real man. I wanted to talk to him but something held me back. Was it training or was it my instinct for survival. Where were his real loyalties?

We glanced at each other again but nothing happened. I felt pretty good about myself because I recognized that I was disciplined enough to resist the temptation to reach out to a near stranger and re-connect with my past. What went through his mind when I sat down? To be fair, each of us knew that we had met. Maybe the details were fuzzy for him but they were as clear as a bell to me. As far as I was concerned, we could not talk; it was too risky.

However, the civilians I met were not at all hostile to us. On the contrary, shortly after Darlan's assassination, my mate and I were invited for dinner with a French family. They were nice people but just the same I kept up my guard. I did not tell them I was French. There were too many true stories of good people being reported to the police as anti Vichy terrorists. I preferred to be cautious, maintain friendly contact until I knew more about what was going on. I gave them a tin of 50 cigarettes that I had taken with me to use as barter.

The next morning I asked the first lieutenant for permission to take the motorboat to go to the submarine center located on the other side of the docks to get some distilled water for my batteries. Our supplies were low and I did not have enough to service all the batteries on the ship. Actually, that was only part of the reason I wanted the boat. What I really wanted to do was use the trip to the sub center to see how the French navy would react to my request. Permission granted! I left with a small crew and empty containers.

After we secured the boat on the quay I looked around and saw a French seaman. I recognized straight away. He stared at me in disbelief. His name was Boué. Three years earlier we were in the same company together at the torpedo school in Toulon. I jumped onto the quay and walked toward him and said, "The way you looked at me I guess you recognize me." Before he could reply, I continued, "I recognized you straight away." I told him I was glad to see him and we shook hands warmly, not the usual greeting grip, but a genuine clasping of hands by two young men who once shared the same mess. "May I have some distilled water," I asked. "Of course, but before I give you the water I want you to come onboard my sub and have a beer with me."

I went onboard without any problems. We found a quiet corner in the mess and began talking, trying to span the years since we had last seen each other. He said that he knew I was in England because one of my previous shipmates, a sailor who had returned to France in June 1940, had met him. It was a chance encounter. My name was mentioned as one of the old mates who had stayed behind in Britain.

In the mess where we were sitting there was a picture of Marshal Petain. I asked him "why" since now "his" French navy was on our side. He burst out laughing, "We don't even know who our President is yet. It's been chaotic as hell around here since the Brits and the Yanks landed. I guess someone just forgot to take him down." He was right laughing about it. The French were busy reorganizing themselves. Petain's portrait was the least of their worries. Anyway, I was really happy to see that the Navy was glad to be back where they should always have been, and I said to him, "with their allies".

It would not be the same with a few stubborn officers, as we shall learn later. The French Army had already sent troops to help the American army on the Tunisian front. Germans had already infiltrated the territory by air and by sea. As usual the German army wasted little time building a good line of defense. But, one must admit, the Americans fought well, in spite of their lack of experience. In parallel to this conflict the British Eight army under General Montgomery was preparing a vast offensive against the Germans led by Rommel.

Once the re-supply operations were completed we were given instructions to prepare the ship to leave Oran for a port called Bougie where we could hide until Tunisia was completely freed and the passage between Bizerte and Sicily was secured. The Luftwaffe had been weakened but they were still around and still strong enough to wreak havoc when they got through our land and sea defenses. It was obvious that we needed to reverse the situation. Airpower was critical to the war effort.

From talking to other crews I gathered they were carrying aircraft parts and other materiel. After awhile we finally concluded that our cargo really was high-octane gasoline. Knowing we could go up at any moment didn't make our ship any safer. We sailed early the next morning and kept close to the coast. We arrived late in the afternoon. The ship entered a narrow strait bordered on both sides by mountains making it an ideal place to hide when the mooring area was covered by a smoke screen. We secured alongside the only jetty; we were the only ship.

We were told that all the other landing craft were concentrated in Dedjeli, a small port a few miles further down the coast near the

Rene Dassac (in collaboration with Patrick K. Robbins)

Tunisian border. The Germans were watching the build-up of allied ships in the port and they carried out raids almost every night. There was a raid on the night we arrived so we were ordered to make a smoke screen. The sea breeze carried our smoke into the battle zone. We were close enough to the action to hear AA gunfire and exploding bombs. We knew from earlier reports that a fierce battle was raging in Tunisia. Montgomery's 8th Army was closing in to the south of Tunisia and they were pushing out some of the remnants of the Africa Corps and some retreating Italians.

Bougie was peaceful; it was as if the war had swung around the little city. When we weren't on duty we went ashore to enjoy beer and a badly needed visit to the one and only well run brothel. I think the whole ship's company had a go at it in that brothel! In the beginning we were the only service men there but as the allied armies progressed we had more and more British soldiers to compete with. We took the competition with good humor but we still felt they were pushing their limits by using BOTH our pub and brothel.

The German air raids ceased when the army finally gained control of Tunisia. This didn't mean fighting stopped. Fighting continued but we turned on each other. Instead of attacking the enemy on the battlefields, the allied troops and sailors started barroom brawls. The allied command allowed the local pubs and cafes to remain open until 11 p.m. Every pub was full of rowdy, boisterous drunken service men. Inevitably, fights broke out and inevitably the army sent in their red cap MPs. Army versus navy, we had to send our own shore patrols because our seamen refused to receive orders from the MPs.

Every night we mounted our own patrol consisting of four able seamen with a leading seaman in charge. Our naval unit patrolled the streets. When eleven o'clock approached they asked our boys to leave the pubs. With a bit of friendly persuasion and diplomacy, our lads usually left quietly and went back onboard. Finally, it was my turn to lead the shore patrol. I didn't mind the duty but the timing could have been better. A new battalion of the 8th Army had arrived with their tanks and support vehicles. The soldiers had been in the desert for a long time and they were determined to have a good time in Bougie. One look at them told you that they had been through hell. From the way they walked and talked, it was obvious that they were not going to be pushed around by any MP or anyone else.

Eleven o'clock came and all was not well. Our lads and the new soldiers were singing, making a lot of noise, but not harming anyone. The Red Caps showed up. Instead of using a bit of Royal Navy diplomacy, instead of asking everyone to leave, instead of using an easy approach backed up with just a hint of persuasion, they burst into the pub and started shouting and throwing their weight around. To make their point they bellowed, "Get out", and then they brought out their truncheons as if to drive home the message. It was obvious the MP's meant business and expected the revelers to obey them immediately. 'Now', a ruddy-faced MP Sergeant barked and flexed his shoulders as if he was about to raise his baton.

The pub exploded. It was easy to understand why Monty's boys couldn't be pushed around. Many had been in the desert for three or four years. Some had lost their mates and all been to hell and back. There was no way were they going to be told by a bunch of MPs to stop drinking and leave the pub as if it were an ordinary night in peacetime England. Insults and bottles flew as soon as one of the MPs grabbed a soldier by the shoulder to move him out. Fortunately, we had better control over our men.

We knew them and that made it easier for us to "ask" to them to leave before real trouble started. Our lads followed my request. As they started to move out an MP shoved one of our hard case boys. He was a bad lad to shove because he was a strong Newfoundlander about as tall as the MP. Our lad, by the name of Doyle, flexed his huge fisherman's hands and landed a punch in the MP's face, knocking him out cold. That crunching punch started the brawl. The three standing MP's struck out blindly with their truncheons at anyone within reach.

The soldiers, no boy scouts, rushed the MPs who retreated down the street away from the pub with Monty's boys in hot pursuit. The MPs jumped in their jeep but the soldiers kept following them throwing bottles and yelling. The MPs drove into a dead end street, hit a civilian and broke his leg. That accident stirred up a bunch of Algerians who went berserk. The situation was spiraling out of control. Somehow we got a call out to the army and within minutes they roared onto the scene. Order was quickly restored when we saw the army meant business: troopers approached the milling soldiers with fixed bayonets.

My patrol was getting jittery. The situation was calm but we knew there would be an enquiry after such a serious brawl. We cleared out of there fast, grabbing any of our stragglers as we rushed back onboard. I reported the matter to the duty officer who thought that our ship would get dragged into the enquiry because the Military Police would certainly mention that the first aggressor was one of our seamen. Doyle was a good bloke and we didn't want his heavy hands landing all of us in hot water. I went below and told my shipmates that we all had to use the same story if we got involved in an enquiry.

Our story line was simple so that even the thickest guy could repeat it: "we only heard about the trouble when we got back onboard." At first they didn't want to go along but my arguments prevailed. In addition to an enquiry, the last thing we wanted was to provoke the skipper. He was bad enough without giving him added incentives to make our lives miserable. Once I got them calmed down I took my patrol back into town. We made another sweep through the port area, checked the local brothel to make sure we hadn't left anyone behind, and made it back onboard.

We weren't surprised when the next day we were told that all shore leaves were cancelled until further order. This lasted for a few days. Staying onboard was a pain but it was easier to take that reprimand than to have to go through an enquiry. In the meantime we were told that the narrows were now safe. This meant that we would sail to our final destination to get rid of, at last, our horrible cargo of high-octane gasoline. We sailed for Alexandria at full speed and kept close to the coastline. It was a nerve-wracking run because we were fully exposed to enemy air attacks. Britain had established an almost complete control of the air but there were still reports of enemy aircraft attacking troop columns and ships.

We had come a long way with our nasty cargo and we hoped that Lady Luck would keep on looking after us for just a few more miles. We remained at our battle stations in the first degree of readiness. It was a short trip but it took too long. Time passes slowly when you're waiting to get blown up. The entrance to the port area kept stretching ahead of us. We passed one of our patrol boats and started to breathe easier. At last, Luck was indeed a Lady; we had beaten the odds. Dirty old Alex rose from the sea and dirty old Alex never looked so good.

Alexandria lived up to its reputation. It's amazing how Alex survived the various phases of the war in the Middle East. It was as if this ancient city was a mute with a body and soul. If she could talk she would have told tales, the tales of a spectator, witness to all the awful events that had unfolded in and around her in the past and that were now, in the twentieth century, unfolding around her. So much was happening but Alex seemed to shrug off the war as if it were just another series of jolts in its ancient life. Armies had trooped down its streets for thousands of years and navies docked under its walls for as long as man roamed the Med. She had witnessed horror then and now in modern times she heard familiar cries of sorrow and despair.

If Alex held the promise of some respite from the war, we could not forget that at sea we were still losing ships to the Germans. The Barham was blown up and over eight hundred officers and men were killed. Losses of that magnitude couldn't be shrugged off. They weighed on our minds because we were in a phase of the war when it seemed that everything we did was doomed to become a disaster.

When I stopped and thought seriously about the war and our losses, I caught my morale slipping edging toward despair. I had to fight not to show what I thought at times because it was no good for anyone, including myself, to think about our setbacks. "We have to be strong," I kept telling myself. To get encouragement, all I had to do was look around me. In spite of almost daily setbacks, the navy and all the armed forces went on with their missions as if they knew that in the end, luck would swing to our side. Despite fleeting misgivings, I had always felt sure that we would win this damned war but when my resolve showed signs of strain, doubt crept into my thinking but didn't stay too long.

All I had to do was look at the Brits. Call them what you want, there are two words that keep coming to my mind to describe them when I think of the Brits in those war years: guts and courageous. Maybe they mean the same thing to you. To me guts meant hanging on with physical resolve and courageous meant hanging on with spiritual resolve. The Brits had both and most of the time it was almost as if you could reach out and feel their determination. Some say war brings out the best and worst in people. From what I experienced, the Brits were truly magnificent in those years when England was alone facing the Nazis.

The emotional turmoil I was going through was similar to what hundreds of thousands of other service men and women were experiencing. It was an awful period but I was proud then, and I am proud now, to have shared those years with the British, to have felt their suffering and to have been strengthened by their resolve. Sorry, about this diversion and sharing my feelings at this point in my story, but after sixty years tears still come to my eyes when I think too deeply about these years. The British will always remain very close to my heart.

North Africa was clear of the enemy. Alexandria was safe. Egyptian dockworkers came aboard under the supervision of military officers and nco's to remove the gasoline barrels. Most of the dockworkers were fairly small, almost as scrawny as me, but they were as strong as donkeys. They shoved and pushed the barrels into the loading nets without a lot of grunting and groaning. Their guards kept a close eye on them and made sure they didn't stray from the deck to inside the ship because we had heard some hair-raising stories about their cunning.

Given a chance, they would steal anything they could lay their hands on. As if to prove a point, one of the sentries stopped a dockworker and ordered him to lift his long shirt-like robe. The worker began to complain and jabber in Arabic. The sentry used sign language and got his way. Slowly the robe was raised. To no one's amazement the dockworker just happened to have a dozen forks and spoons tied up around his legs.

Carrying out our duties was the order of the day and we pitched in with considerable enthusiasm. Shore leave was promised only after the cargo had been off-loaded and the tank space had been cleaned and hosed. We worked through our chores in record time. Three of my shipmates and I made straight for the fleet club, one of the best places in Alex, with lots of shops, a great bar with all the drinks you could ever hope to want. We even made bets to see if we could manage to down one glass of everything the club offered.

In the center of the fleet club there was a stage with an orchestra where some hostesses were singing. Tables and chairs had been spread out for a bingo game. From the looks of it, the game was popular because we had difficulty finding seats. The contest began at 2100 hours. The club director announced the evening jackpot: £100, not much by today's standards but sixty years ago that was a lot of money. I looked around and saw many civilians crowded around the tables. They were mostly ship pilots and employees of the Suez Canal Company and their families.

We ordered lots of beer and some sandwiches. It was a great crowd. Everybody was singing along with a female vocalist up on the stage. She warbled, "Lilly Marlene, I dream of you each night." From out of nowhere I was hit with a huge dollop of nostalgia. My thoughts raced to Wolverhampton and to Edith. I tried to push her out of my mind but she kept coming back the more I pushed. I wanted to be away from the war, I wanted peace and quiet, and I wanted to talk to the woman who I was desperately trying to make love me. It was all I could do to keep a cap on my emotions and channel my despair away from thinking about her and come back to the drinks and laughter swirling around me. I went up to the bar and ordered more beer. By the time I came back to the table I had gotten a grip on myself and could join in laughing and joking with my shipmates.

The singer we'd been ogling left the stage and started walking around the tables asking for somebody to come back up on stage to sing with her. My shipmates, who had been kidding me for the past hour, lifted me out of my chair. "Take this little fellow. He's got a big voice." Little guys with big voices, someone called out, "Put Sinatra up there." As I began backing away, she grabbed me and dragged me up onto the stage. I tried to hold back, complaining that I did not know any English songs. Or, at least, English songs that could be sung before a mixed crowd weren't in my repertoire.

I told her that I only knew one song and that was a French song. My honest admission was a colossal mistake! She said that everybody in Alexandria understood French and in any case, she promised to help me. She asked me what I wanted to sing and I told her, "J'attendrais".

Rene Dassac (in collaboration with Patrick K. Robbins)

In the middle of the applause the musicians started playing a familiar bar and I let go and began to sing. In all seriousness, I wasn't all that bad. If you take into account all the drinks I'd managed to consume, the fact that the air was so blue with cigarette smoke that you couldn't see across the room, my voice carried and the room almost got quiet. I was even surprised at myself, surprised at the great applause and thankful for all the rounds of beer that were sent to our table when I sat down.

Later in the evening during the bingo game one of our mates won the snowball of £90. The money was given to us onboard ship the next day because the club said that it was too dangerous to carry that amount of money, especially at night, because there had been cases of winners being attacked by thieves.

What a wonderful evening. Outside the club we hired a horse and carriage to take us to the dockyard gate. Life was easy for the next few days. We kept the ship in good working order because we knew that we'd be sailing soon for another operation. The rumor mill was in full swing but one destination kept cropping up so we figured there had to be some truth to it. The next time around we were going to be landing troops on enemy beaches. Victory in North Africa was too important for the allies to give the enemy time to rest and digest their first defeat.

The British weren't the only allied ships in port. In 1939 The French Eastern Med fleet had been ordered to operate with the British fleet under the command of Admiral A. Cunningham. In July 1940 the Admiralty decided to immobilize all French warships in order to prevent them from falling into enemy hands. The French admiral in Alexandria was not as stupid as his counterpart in Mers el Kebir. When the British told him he had three options he took his time weighing each one. While he was thinking his way through each option his ship's guns were trained on the British. In turn, the British warships trained their 14", 8", and 6" guns on the French ships. In the end, the French admiral reached a face-saving compromise. The futility of blasting each other out of the water, the horrible bloodshed, would have been written forever in the history of modern naval warfare. No one in his right mind wanted that to happen.

Disarmed, the French fleet was anchored in the harbor. As long as they did not pose a military threat they were effectively bottled up. The French command didn't know which way to turn. Were they going to ride out the war or were they going to join the Free French Fleet? Looking at their ships I realized that there was a lot of firepower that could be brought into the war on our side: one battleship, three heavy cruisers, four destroyers and two submarines. Something must have shaken them out of their stupor because before we left Alex they were starting to rearm and prepare to sail for the U.S. to undergo a complete refit and modernization. Later, ships of this fleet took part in the Normandy invasion and in the landings in the south of France.

It set my guts on fire to look at those ships and watch their officers and crew strut about in their pretty uniforms. They disgusted me and made me ashamed to have been born a Frenchman. I steered clear of them when I was on liberty. Those pompous bastards spent three years idling in port while the British fought off the most ferocious attacks the Royal Navy had ever known. Somehow the Royal Navy managed to survive but not without a tremendous loss of ships and many brave young men. And those bastards staring back at me from across the water did absolutely nothing except eat less to keep their weight down. I couldn't stomach them. Look at us. We were beginning preparations for what had to be the hardest part of the war that was still ahead of us: Landing in enemy territory. Let them rot, I thought.

Alex was a great two-week break but it was time to sail for Tripoli, Libya. No one knew why we were going to Tripoli. All we knew was that the town had been the scene of many bloody battles between the 8th Army and the Africa Korps a few weeks earlier. We sailed along the coast passing Tobruq and Benghazi. Both had been taken and lost several times in the past three years. Entering Tripoli was like sailing through an obstacle course. There were numerous shipwrecks in the entrance to the harbor and all the way to our mooring.

*****

Rene Dassac (in collaboration with Patrick K. Robbins)

We berthed close to a destroyed building that still had the remnants of a tall tower poking from the top floor. In peacetime the view from the building must have been spectacular because from it you could see all the approaches to Tripoli. The Germans immediately recognized its strategic importance and installed an anti aircraft battery. When we arrived, all that remained were some destroyed guns and an awful stench that convinced us came from the gun crew's splattered remains. The hot and humid summer air held the stench firmly in place like an invisible shroud the wind blew into our faces.

We coughed and gagged and almost got down on our knees to beg the army port authorities to do something. They sent us an officer to follow-up our complaint. He agreed with us that it stank. But the problem wasn't that easy to solve. We needed a long ladder that would reach up into the tower and the army didn't have one! After a short discussion with his superiors the port authorities authorized us to move to another mooring. Their decision helped us but it didn't solve the problem because the ship stank from bow to stern. For security reasons we were expected to tie-up with the ramp locked in vertical position. The army bent the rules and told us we could open the ramp to create a draft strong enough to air out the ship.

That solved our problem but the army was left with the knowledge that one berth could not be used until the top of the tower had been cleared of all human remains. To thank the army for giving us another berth we lent them half a dozen of our best seamen to rig a rope ladder so they could climb up and remove the decaying body. The boys did a good job and removed the German. But, we still could not get rid of the stench. Finally, we were left with no other alternative, short of burning the ship, than to keep the ramp open and turn all the extractor fans on full speed. That worked but there are days, even now, when I think about our berth in Tripoli and I think I can still smell the dead German. All it takes for me is to smell something awful and my mind flips back to where I wish it wouldn't go any more.

Soon after we got rid of the smell we were told that we were going to sail for a large-scale operation. We began boarding a large number of soldiers with their half-tracks, tanks, lorries filled with ammunition and infantry men. I couldn't believe my eyes or ears. We heard them before we saw them marching toward the gangplank led by a piper. The Scots Black Watch regiment was about to board. What an honor! These troops weren't ordinary soldiers. They were hardened men with a fine fighting record. Some of them had been in the desert for two to three years. When they got settled and stowed their equipment properly, we organized a party in our mess. Many Scottish lads accepted our invitation and almost felt at home because we had a young Scot in our mess.

By God, we enjoyed that evening, helped along with healthy sips from our stashed rum rations. In the Royal Navy it was customary to be given a tot of rum every day before lunch. And, it was also customary to keep a small amount of rum aside in a special bottle that we would take with us in case we had to abandon ship. Who knows? Maybe this custom saved some seamen in the north Atlantic when they were riding out a gale. We were happy to share our survival tots with the Black Watch.

We drank and talked. No one knew what we were headed into but everyone knew it was going to be big. All the soldiers knew was that we were going to land somewhere in enemy territory but no one knew where. Next morning we formed a convoy with some merchant ships and left Tripoli. Two days later we joined another large convoy with a heavy escort. There were some cruisers, one monitor, other LSTs, LTCs, LCIs, etc. In our guts we knew this was not going to be a picnic.

*****

Soon after we took up our position in the convoy, our first lieutenant ordered us into the mess deck. Normally we were a pretty rowdy lot but that afternoon we were unusually quiet as he began to speak. He was not an inspiring speaker but he was good with words. It was obvious he had rehearsed his presentation because it was crisp and flowed easily. We listened carefully to the details of the landing operation, code named "Husky", that involved us.

Husky was a combined operation involving a night drop of airborne units inland while commando units would be landed by LCT and LCI at 0400 hours. We were to land in Sicily on a beach call Avola, close to the road to Syracuse, Augusta, and Catania. Our ship was to anchor fairly close to the beach and wait until the area was sufficiently safe to bring our troops and their equipment ashore. He answered the question on everyone's lips, "What about resistance?" Matter-of-factly, he told us to expect resistance. In particular, air attacks.

The Luftwaffe had not been defeated. We could expect heavy bombardment from experienced enemy aircrews. Unfortunately, allied air support had to come from Malta. Given the distance this meant that we would have limited fighter protection flying allied cover over the landing beaches. For a moment all I could think of was the crazy phrase, "a sitting duck." If the Luftwaffe had their way, we stood a good chance of being blasted out of the water. Was my number up on this operation? I didn't want to think about it and I managed to turn my thoughts to something positive. We had armament and we were probably pretty good at using it but we hadn't been put to the test. As if the lieutenant had been reading my mind, he reminded us that this was our first landing operation under fire.

Everything we did had to be carried out with precision because our lives depended on every man performing to the best of his ability. "You've been preparing for this for months. The time has come when you will see why all the training was necessary," the first lieutenant intoned. He was the kind of officer who got the attention of his men. He paused, looked at us almost pensively, and said, "I have no doubt, none whatsoever, that you will perform well as individuals. And, I am confident that all of us are going to execute well!" So, there it was. Success, and perhaps even our survival, depended on each of us as individuals and on how well we fought together. We had to perform as a tightly knit fighting unit. Whether or not you liked someone was no longer an issue. What really counted was whether he could do his job. And I caught myself thinking, how am I going to hold up under fire?

Each of us in his own quiet way was running a cinema in his mind. We were trying to imagine what was going to happen to us, what it would be like to get shot at by soldiers? Up to now all the action we had been involved in was fighting an enemy we could not see. I knew what survivors from sea conflicts looked like. We rescued enough in the past to harden me but I couldn't imagine what it would be like to receive men who had been chewed up on land. Somewhere a voice started talking to me. I heard my father's voice telling me about the Great War, the thousands of bodies and the wounded crying for help and for their mothers. Oh God, is it going to be like that, I thought? The voice was gone and I heard my own voice telling me, "Well, it won't be long now."

*****

At 0300 hours the "Action Station" call sounded. We dropped anchor two or three miles from the beach. Some of the damage control party and I helped the commando group get ready in their assault barges. Quickly and silently we lowered them into the water. We were waiting for the order to push them off because they were going in under a terrific gun barrage that would be carried out by the cruisers, destroyers and the monitor with its twin 14" guns. It was still dark apart from the moonlight that would soon disappear.

We didn't say much but I think we were all wrestling in our minds with the same question: What in God's name was going to happen when they pushed off from the relative safety of our ship and started toward the shore with nothing to stop the German bullets from ripping them to shreds? I couldn't stay focused on that question because it was too awful to think about and it took up too much of my brain. I needed to focus on my job, on what I was trained to do.

The captain arranged for a jar of rum to be given to the commandos but they refused. They needed to have their brains clear to do the job they knew in detail that they had to do. To no one's surprise, the rum did not return to the spirit room! We made sure it was detoured to another safe storage area. Soon, the ship's company would share it.

We heard waves of aircraft flying low over the convoy. They were RAF transport planes carrying paratroops that were to be dropped just a few miles behind our landing area. We were nervous but nobody broke. If anything, the waiting to go into action was the worse part because we wanted to get stuck into the fight, get on with it and finish it whatever the cost. Of course the firing hadn't started and we were

Rene Dassac (in collaboration with Patrick K. Robbins)

incapable of imagining the awful cost in human lives that would be made to gain a foothold on a well defended beach.

It was quiet, very quiet, nothing was happening. Surely, someone on the beach must have heard the ships offshore dropping their anchors, heard the clatter and banging as anti-aircraft crews swirled their guns and leveled their sites? Noise travels quickly over the water and there were a lot of ships trying to be quiet. No shots had been fired from the shore. Was silence from the shore an encouraging sign? We were scared enough to clutch at any hopeful sign.

At 0400 hours a terrific gun barrage started. That was the signal the commandos were waiting for. They loosened their tie lines with a 'splash', about the only noise that came from our ship. The barges began moving slowly toward the sandy beach that was now suddenly lighted by flares, bright lights arcing into the night sky. The sky was sometimes white and hundreds of eyes on our side were searching for bunkers or some sort of defensive action. But everything was so quiet, so unnaturally quiet.

For a few unreal moments we thought we'd caught the enemy sleeping. What a story to tell: the landing was going to be a simple romp through the sand. Wishful thinking! While the assault barges plowed toward the shore, the gun barrage stopped. After the roar and crash of the heavy guns silence fell again, a silence punctuated only by the barge diesels droning toward the shore, quietly, as if to land a search party on a distant island somewhere in the world where it was peaceful. As soon as the barges hit the beaches we heard machine gun fire. It wasn't ours. The 'sleeping Germans' were awake and firing on the commandos as they struggled through the sand and water to reach cover beyond the shore line.

With dawn's first light we could begin to see what was happening. We watched men who'd been in our mess a few days before firing their weapons, running, jumping and sometimes falling in mid-stride. We could barely make out a German gun but every now and then we'd glimpse an artillery piece; was it a tank camouflaged in the brush and trees? Whoever was firing wasn't moving. It began firing on the ships anchored in front of them. What a dumb move! The German managed to squeeze off a few rounds before we got him spotted and radioed in his coordinates. I don't know who got him; it may have been several ships almost at once, but he was quickly blown out of action. Around one o'clock in the afternoon the beaches were secured. Halftracks and lorries started to move inland. We began preparing to offload our Sherman tanks. All we were waiting for was for the beach master to give us the green light to begin.

Our bad luck! Just as we started to open the door and lower the ramp the Luftwaffe showed up. The ramp was too far open to shut. Anyway, we had begun the landing. A LCT with a Sherman tank and landing troops was already a few yards off our starboard side. I was on my beaching station aft with my headphone switched on waiting for the order to let go the stern anchor. Before moving aft I put the three generator sets on in parallel and switched on all the extractor fans to clear the tank space of the fumes made by the dozen or so tanks and lorries that were revving up before racing down the ramp. Their roaring engines created a lot of noise that masked the whistle of the dive-bomber's bombs. Some bombs exploded in the sea; others blew huge holes on the landing beach. From my vantage point I could only see the open sea. We were moving at a speed of 5 knots when, all of a sudden, there was a huge explosion and I saw pieces of steel fly past close to were I was standing. I ducked and moved closer to the starboard side. I was horrified at what I saw.

On our starboard side a fully loaded LCT was heading toward the beach when it took a direct hit. Body pieces hung over the guardrails; bright orange flames roasted those who had the misfortune to be still alive. They were screaming and I began to shake. My mind switched into another mode and I thought of my mother and talked to her and asked her to look after me from were she was. It was just as I used to do as a kid when danger was getting close and all I had to rely on were my wits and hopes that some unseen hand would shield me from harm. That pause, a quick switch from reality to fantasy, might have lasted a second, no more than two or three, but suddenly my mind switched back to reality and my adrenalin kicked in. I knew what I had to do.

First, I asked myself, why haven't I received an order from the bridge to let go the stern anchor? We were still going at high speed. The beach was coming up on us fast while precious seconds slipped away. I called the gun's crew who were just above me and asked them what was happening on the bridge. "All dead." Their response thundered through the din again, "All dead!" Sub lieutenant Higgins, our former lawyer from Toronto, screamed at me, "For God's sake let go the stern anchor!" He was as white as a handkerchief and trembling just as much as I was. I let go the anchor and told him, "Sir, you better go and order the engine room to go full astern." He looked at me as if he didn't understand what was going on. "At this speed," I continued in a calm and matter-of-fact tone, "The stern anchor will tear the capstan out of the deck." Then, as if to make my point, I felt the deck tremble. "Look sir, the deck is moving." Without waiting for his order I relieved the tension on the cable before the cable snapped or the electric motor of the capstan burned-out. I swung around to see where the sub was. He had disappeared and at that precise moment our ship smashed into the beach at 11 knots and came to a shuddering, screaming, screeching halt.

The shock nearly knocked me down. I immediately dropped my headphone and jumped over wreckage strewn in my way and made it to the bridge to see what had happened. The bridge was a mess. There was blood everywhere. The captain was lying on the deck half conscious. His white shirt was blood soaked and I could see blood oozing from his chest. The leading signalman screamed at me. "Look at my back, look at my back," he shrieked. He turned so I could see his back and couldn't believe my eyes. His back was full of steel and wood splinters. They stuck through his life vest; they looked as if an insane costume designer had glued them in place. I reacted as if I had done what he wanted every day of my life: I began pulling out pieces and letting them drop to the deck. A sickbay attendant bent down to take care of the captain who was more badly wounded than two other lads who were on the bridge when bomb shrapnel sprayed them.

Coming in at eleven knots, and the way we hit, there was no doubt that our ship was secured on the beach. Just as I had been taught to do during action station training, I left the leading signalman and took up my job on the damage control team. On the bridge, apart from small holes in the bulkheads, the navigation and communication equipment appeared to be intact. Working my way around the wreckage I found the first lieutenant and reported to him the extent of our damage. He was in the front of the ship where he was engaged in a heated discussion with the Beach Master and the C.O. in charge of the army detachment on the beach.

On my way forward I noticed a few holes on the ship's side. I didn't take the time to inspect the damage but it looked like we had been badly peppered with bomb shrapnel but none of the holes looked big enough to sink us. That is, if we ever got afloat. The din was so loud that it was difficult to talk. All our A.A. guns where firing like mad at the German dive-bombers.

I saw Jimmy, the first lieutenant, and told him what I had seen. He said he knew something had happened but did not know exactly what. From where he was in the tank space he couldn't tell what was going on elsewhere in the ship except there was a lot of noise. I told him what had happened to the captain. For a split second he stood thunderstruck and then he swirled and ran to the bridge. He was now in command. At that point we didn't know if the captain was dead or alive but one thing was certain, if he was still alive he was in no position to stay in command. I stood on the ramp and tried to understand what I was looking at.

Most of the tanks had clanged ashore; the halftracks and lorries were moving out. In spite of the damage to the ship our cargo had survived. Not only did it look like it was intact, our troops and their equipment were moving off the beach to engage the enemy. A cameraman was knocked off his feet when he was filming the offloading. A bomb landed close to us in a nearby vineyard. The impact concussion knocked over a lorry loaded with ammunition but the bomb didn't explode. A tank came and pushed the wreckage out of the way. Soldiers grabbed the ammunition boxes and dragged them away before another round set them off. I came back to my senses again when I realized that the cameraman was intact. Thankfully, the bomb was a dud and it didn't do any real damage other than scare the wits out of the cameraman. He sat in the sand shaking his head staring at the crater the bomb made. The bomb should have either blown him to bits or crushed him. Dazed, he staggered to his feet not quite knowing what to make of his close call.

A number of corpses were lined up on one side of the vineyard. I left this scene and went up on the upper deck where the soldiers manning the remaining halftrack and lorry were getting nervous. This is

Rene Dassac (in collaboration with Patrick K. Robbins)

something I had noticed during the whole campaign: soldiers don't feel safe on a ship and it is just the opposite with seamen. I asked one of them why he was so jumpy and he told me that it was because he couldn't dig a hole on the deck and lie down in it!

The RAF chased most of the Luftwaffe raiders from the landing zone. At least we didn't have them to deal with all the time but we still had a lot to do. We managed to get rid of the huge RAF radar that was secured on the lift. It was an important piece of equipment because it would eventually be used as soon as we took the first enemy airfield that was located somewhere near Augusta. While we were lifting the radar onto waiting trucks the rest of the vehicles on the upper deck rolled off.

All the time while equipment and men were being shunted off the ship, a separate operation was already underway to transfer our wounded to the hospital ship that was anchored about 10 miles off the landing beach. Our captain and five other people, including two soldiers, had been taken to the hospital ship by one of our assault barges. For the captain, at least, it was not an easy passage.

Someone told me that able seaman Doyle of barroom brawl fame had not been very gentle with the captain whom he did not like. Doyle wasn't upset by the severity of the captain's chest wound. What really had him upset was the fact that the captain had singled him out for petty reprimands with little or no justification. As far as he was concerned, the captain 'had it out' for him. In his eyes it was always a case of being caught by the captain for a petty infraction of the rules. Once he had Doyle on something, the captain let rip. Doyle was convinced: he had become the captain's whipping boy. Now after the raid, it was Doyle's chance to get even.

The lad was huge and strong as an ox. Because of his size he was detailed to help lift the wounded men and strap them into hammock style bags that made it easier to handle them. The wounded were lying on the deck waiting to be lifted, one at a time, above the guardrails and then lowered into the assault barge. As Doyle picked up the captain he squeezed him hard around his chest wound and this made him cry out in pain. That episode didn't go unnoticed.

The story went around that Doyle squeezed the captain on purpose in order to take revenge for all the punishment the captain had meted out. Admittedly, the captain was disliked by all of us. But, there has to be a limit on what you do to people. I told Doyle that I didn't think the captain deserved to be treated that way. Most of the lads agreed with me. We didn't get into an argument; we were too tired to waste time over that issue, but Doyle knew how we felt. Once the wounded had been prepared for transfer they were shipped off but their ordeal was not over.

No sooner had they reached the hospital ship than a dive-bomber that managed to slip through the RAF cover attacked it. The hospital ship was heavily damaged; it had to leave the area to be repaired. Our wounded were taken to a destroyer. Their ship's surgeon did his best to stabilize them before they were transferred to the hospital in Malta.

We had done our job. Men and materiel were landed successfully but now we had to dislodge our LST from the beach. That was easier said than done. A standard dislodging procedure was ordered. Both engines roared full astern. My stern anchor winch smoked as it strained against the anchor. Nothing worked. We were dug into the sand and she wouldn't budge even one inch. We even tried to ease her loose thinking that a slow and steady reverse action might do the trick. Our ship wouldn't budge. In the meantime signals received a warning that more dive-bombers were sighted heading in our direction. Stuck on the beach, our LST was an easy target. The landing area was full of ships and the law of averages said someone was going to get hit. A Liberty ship carrying ammunition for the army beached about five hundred yards on our port side. Army landing crews swarmed over her like ants, working feverishly to offload explosives and vehicles before the German pilots returned.

They managed to get a lot of ammunition ashore before the Luftwaffe roared in to give us another plastering. Right in front of our eyes we watched the Germans begin their run. The Liberty ship exploded with a huge roar. The explosion was so powerful that it blew a lorry wheel across our ship where it landed off our stern. Bodies flew through the air as if they had been shot from the mouth of a circus cannon. What happened to one poor bastard remains in my memory. The percussion of the explosions flattened him against the bridge with his arms wide open like he had been strung out on a cross. We had to look at him for several days. Why? Maybe there was too much else to do stay alive and fighting. Why waste time scraping up a body? He wasn't going anywhere.

The enemy pilots didn't linger to admire their work. They undoubtedly concluded our fighters were on their way back from Malta. The invasion still had not secured an airfield. Until air cover operations could be provided from Italy we were not fully protected from the Luftwaffe.

Before nightfall all those who were not manning A.A. guns or doing essential services were sent to gather bodies floating close to the ship's side. We fished them out and laid them in temporary graves. We buried them because keeping them uncovered was bad for morale. As soon as it was dark, dinner was piped. We sat down but no one was very hungry. Instead of eating, gathering in the mess gave each of us an opportunity to talk and share what we had just gone through. It was almost like a confessional; talking probably did more for us than a warm meal.

At about 2200 hours an air raid warning screeched. Our AA gun crews raced to their stations and readied their guns. I was ordered to make smoke so I ran up to the smoke floats forward and aft. As usual the startup resulted in the smokers belching sparks that could have given away our position but, fortunately, we had not yet sighted any enemy planes. I had to stop all the fans to avoid filling the mess decks with smoke. We waited at our stations. Every pair of eyes strained to spot the planes that wanted to kill us. At first it was feint, then the roar of their motors became louder and louder. They growled and prowled across the night sky trying to pick out targets that were hidden under a smoke screen cloud. They dropped flares onto the target zone.

A light breeze began blowing and the smoke began dispersing. They began a bombing run on the far side of the anchorage but they flew into a terrific AA barrage. Their bombs fell short on that run but there were other runs and we knew we had been targeted. They were on top of us! Our AA guns fired non-stop into the night sky. To the best of our knowledge, we didn't down any enemy aircraft but it is difficult to imagine how any plane was able to fly unscathed through the sheets of steel our gunners pounded into the sky. There was so much metal going up that we actually heard our own shrapnel falling on our deck. Our hammering must have unnerved the pilots because all their bombs fell well away from the vineyard across the beach where we had men and equipment.

The next morning we saw more reinforcements pouring onto the landing zone. During the day some of our lads went into the vineyard to pick up some grapes that were ripe. To keep us from getting blown to bits the army cordoned off a passage that they had cleared of anti personal mines. A young Italian boy shouted at them and made a sign, gesturing as if he wanted them to come up the hill towards the farmhouse. They started up the hill but a sniper opened up and wounded one of the army chaps. The army reacted quickly and fired a few rounds in the direction of where the sniper seemed to be hiding. One of our AA gunners happened to be working forward near his 20mm Oerlikon gun. He saw where the German sniper fire was coming from. He opened fire on a big tree the sniper was using for cover. The sniper was shredded. No one moved but the soldiers heard a child's voice, and another voice that we thought could have been his mother's.

At first it was hard to make sense out of the voices but when they started yelling we recognized screams of terror sweeping down the vineyard. An army patrol went up to where the screams were coming from. They didn't speak Italian so it took them a few minutes to understand what the woman and child were trying to say. Sign language got their message across. We were in the middle of a zone that had been mined and booby-trapped by the Germans. The Germans had strapped traps to the tree branches at head height. Anyone reaching into trees or poking into the vineyards would set off an explosive device. Even though we wanted grapes we weren't willing to let the Germans turn us into grape jelly. It was hard to stomach, but that little kid was actually trying to lure our soldiers into the sniper's field. Why? The objective of war is to kill the enemy. How you fulfill your objective is a question of technique. A cunning enemy used the kid; their ruse failed.

Our position on the beach was more of a nuisance than anything else. The beach commander requested the help of the monitor Arabus to get a cable to our stern and pull us out. We opened our engines full astern and began pulling on our stern anchor. Surely that would get us off this damned beach! No luck; nothing doing. We were stuck fast. Gallows humor started and someone wondered whether we would ride out the campaign as a great big target wedged on an Italian beach.

The beach master, at least, saw the benefits of having us so close by. He and his staff moved all their equipment off the beach so they could set up a base of operations onboard our ship. Not a silly move. It was a much better way to sleep and cook than sleeping on the beach in a tent. Not only did he appreciate our hospitality, he even asked us to help him with some jobs on land. He was short of men and we didn't have too much to do. Of course, our captain agreed but instead of detailing us he asked for volunteers. I volunteered along with some other lads. We reported to an army officer who marched us down the road going towards Augusta, shouldering our picks and shovels as if they were rifles.

Sometime during the previous frantic days I forgot to tell you that our first lieutenant was promoted to Lieutenant Commander RNR. Mr. Carling was our new captain of LST 407. He was a real gentleman, very religious, and some said he was a "blue blood." He did his best to keep us cheerful. Let's face it, for us as seamen, we weren't very happy. We were stuck in the sand on the beach and there was no prospect of us getting off. The longer we sat, the more the odds ran against our not taking a direct hit. There were heavy air raids every night.

One day, the army officer to whom we were reporting, took us to bury German soldiers. He told us to either take a gas mask or make some kind of a mask, preferably dampened with after shave or camphor from the ship's medical stores because many of the body's were in a state of advanced putrefaction. Off we went on our morbid journey; this time no one was laughing. Stinking work was also dangerous work. Before we could take the body's identity tags we had to stand back a few yards. Someone would loop a rope and hook it around a limb. Once the looped tightened he'd shake the body just to make sure one of his mates hadn't left a booby trap underneath him. We worked our way across a field strewn with bodies. No one talked. The stench and the tension were awful.

Late that afternoon we came across a big German soldier. He stank, we smelled him before we saw him and when we saw him we disturbed hundreds of blue shit house flies feasting on his bloated corpse. Fortunately he was lying on his side on the edge of the dirt road so we dug a hole next to him. When we finished we pushed him into the hole with our boots. As he rolled, he landed hard on his belly. There was a horrible rumble from his innards and he let a huge final fart. It scared the hell out of us. There we were, working under a hot Sicilian sun and all of a sudden, the German let rip. We all jumped and looked around. When I realized what had happened I said, "This fucking bastard gave us the wind up to the very last minute!" That night when we told our story to our shipmates we became the laughing stock of the ship's company, including the officers. We weren't laughing at the soldier. Even though he was an enemy he deserved to be treated with the respect that is due the dead. If it had been one of us in that hole, we'd have wanted to be treated with respect.

By now battles raged throughout Sicily. Montgomery's 8th Army was racing towards Catania which was defended by the famous SS Hermann Goering regiment. They slowed our advance a little but the issue was sealed in only a matter of days. With the Germany army getting pounded the Luftwaffe intensified their raids to try and slow down, or even stop, allied reinforcements from reaching the beach. In one of those raids the Germans did our LST a great favor.

Every night German dive-bombers roared in to try and take out the radar unit at Augusta. The radar crew would send us advance warning so we had time to light our smoke floats and cover our area with a thick smoke screen. As a result, their bombs tore up a lot of soil but they didn't do any significant damage to the Allied ships. We were determined to get off that beach. No one had any new ideas and as a result we settled into a routine. Every morning after the Luftwaffe had gone and we were given our 'all clear', we fired up the engines and made 'slow astern' while pulling with our stern anchor to see if we could move the ship. Morning after morning it was the same old story. We were stuck.

Rene Dassac (in collaboration with Patrick K. Robbins)

One night, no different than all the other nights, the air raid warning was given too late to light the smoke flares. The Germans were circling right above our heads. By then we knew enough about their tactics to know that when they circled they were actually forming up to begin a bombing run. The raid was particularly fierce. Our AA guns fired almost non-stop. A long line of lads raced between the 20mm shell magazine and the batteries in order to keep the gunners supplied with fresh ammunition. I heard the captain yelling, "Powell hurry up and make smoke!" I felt like telling him to shut up and look up. I could hear the planes circling above us and I was torn between obeying his order and asking him to think again. Didn't he realize that if I started the smoke floats the Germans would see the sparks and dive straight for us? But, my naval education told me to obey with neither hesitation nor murmur.

I was on the quarterdeck. Shrapnel was falling around me and on me. Except when it hit my life vest making a dull thudding sound - like being hit by a whole branch of wind driven acorns - the falling shrapnel made a sharp clinking and pinging noise on the steel deck. Above the din I heard the captain bellowing, "Powell, for God's sake, make smoke." There was so much lead falling from the sky that I was afraid our shrapnel would tear up my shoulders or arms. I ran forward trying to think myself 'thin.' It was a situation of mind-over-matter. I managed to convince myself, that if I thought 'thin', I actually shrank my body so small that it fit inside the rim of my tin hat. If I got that small, I would minimize the chances of getting hurt. In my mind's eye, I was no bigger than a cricket bat handle propped up inside a tin hat. That stick was me. And, if that's the way I saw myself that's how small I must have become. All in my own mind, of course.

Some of my mates didn't see the thin-man me. When I got to the floats one of the gunners mistook me for an ammunition runner and he shouted at me to get him some more ammunition. "I can't load," I yelled over the din of the guns. "I've got to light the smoke flares." He glared at me and began screaming so loud I was sure the captain must have heard him. "If you light these floats I'll fucking shoot you." He wasn't kidding but I knew he could not shoot me because he couldn't depress his gun low enough to get me in his sights. Anyway, what happened next was to be expected. When I lighted the floats sparks shot up from our deck as if we were having our own Guy Fawkes fireworks party.

Sure enough, our sparks were what the Germans were looking for. We heard the dive-bombers screaming towards our ship and then the whistle of a stick of bombs heading straight for us. I dropped to the deck and flattened my skinny frame as thin as I could make it. I lay waiting and listening. I don't know what I was waiting for but I certainly didn't think I was going to be killed that night. I knew I could get killed but I kept reassuring myself, "Tonight's not my night." Somehow I convinced myself none of the bombs had my name scrawled on it. All those thoughts raced through my mind in a matter of only a few seconds. But, sixty years later as I write, I can still hear those bombs screaming through the night sky.

Four or five bombs exploded in the sand a few yards in front of the ship. They shot huge amounts of sand and stone high up into the air. From my position lying on the deck I could feel the reverberations of each impact. Was it my imagination or did I feel the ship lifting slightly off the beach? I didn't have time to ponder the physics of what was happening. Shrapnel tore into my back. I lay for a few seconds trying to talk myself out of the hot stabbing that was searing my back. I told myself, "This is it. Shrapnel has got me. I'm wounded. My fucking back feels like a pepper pot." A medical corpsman's observation came out of nowhere and gnawed at me. I remember him saying, "At first you don't feel any pain but then it comes later."

I got up on my hands and knees and crawled to the mess deck where my mates were greasing shells and filling the magazines for the AA guns. I must have been whiter than a sheet and I was shaking. They looked at me strangely and asked, "What's the matter John?" I stammered, "I got a packet." "Where?" I shook my head and nodded in the direction of my back. One of my mates stopped loading a magazine. "Let me have a look." He lifted my shirt and the bastard began laughing. "All you got is a lot of shit and sand." Suddenly, the pain vanished. I felt like a new man and went back up on deck. It was a bad raid that went on for hours, almost until daybreak. We were exhausted and the situation was still tense. We didn't know if they were going to try a daylight raid so we stretched out and slept at our stations until a well-deserved breakfast was piped.

At 0800 hours we were called to gather astern like every morning. I began to close up on the stern anchor; the engine started slowly astern. I started pulling on the anchor not really expecting anything to happen when, all of a sudden, the anchor began to pull. Much to our delight and surprise, the ship started moving gently off the beach with the whole ship's company yelling, "Hurry!"

The beach Commander kept us standing by until they were transferred to Catania. We stayed there until the end of the Sicilian campaign. This first landing on enemy territory appeared easy at first but the allies paid a heavy price for their mistakes most of which were due to a lack of coordination between the two armies. We all hoped they would learn from their mistakes because we knew more landings were being planned.

We were transferred to Bizerte, Tunisia, for repairs and to service our diesel engines and generating sets. Amazingly, in view of the amount of ordinance that fell around us, there were only a few holes and they weren't serious. We came through the landing with very little real damage.

Bizerte was completely flattened. The main military harbor was cluttered with a lot of wrecks. Ferryville lake, where we were anchored, was a staging area for all kinds of ships: LST, LCT, LCI. We were assembled to load troops and equipment for the next landing. But, where were we headed? No one knew except maybe the officers and they weren't talking. The lifetime of a rumor was measured in hours: the morning's hot 'fact' was stone dead by evening.

Before we began loading operations we were given shore leave into Ferryville, a small military garrison inhabited by French families. British engineers were repairing the dry dock. A couple of divers worked on wrecks that blocked access to the docks. Ferryville was a civilized place. Although it was small it had what we needed: a couple of pubs and a nice brothel. Unfortunately, the brothel was 'out of bounds for Brits and Yanks.' Just our luck! Can you imagine hundreds of young men, most of whom have just had a close brush with death, wandering around town hornier than hell, with the only brothel in town deemed foreign territory? Only French sailors were allowed in. The army had the bright idea to block the entrance of the street where the brothel was located with a mixed patrol of British red caps and American M.Ps. The military police were a formidable, but not insurmountable, barrier to our ingenuity.

We met some French sailors who told us that one of their French naval doctors responsible for assuring that a visit to the girls was 'risk free' was a regular visitor to the brothel. If they were safe enough for him, an officer, weren't they safe enough for us? Certainly they were. Unless we missed something in our training, there was no rank when it came to getting a horn on. The situation was definitely looking up. Trust Jack to find a way to get in no matter how many police stood in the way! French sailors and British sailors wore the same battle dress. We discussed our problem with our new friends. One of them came up with a brilliant idea: change hats with them. We'd give them our British hats and they'd give us their pompons. That was a stroke of sheer brilliance. There was no way the MP's would know we were British, especially if I was speaking French when we walked through their cordon.

Off we went, confident that we would succeed in getting into the brothel without being caught. With our French berets, red pompons, and my loud French, who would know the difference? Reiner, the radioman and I began our mission with great determination. We joined the queue with a bunch of joking Frenchmen. Then it was our turn to pass in front of the MP's. They looked us up and down. I didn't care how carefully they looked at us; we acted like genuine French sailors. I was relaxed, speaking my best French, rather loud I might add, and joking as if I were telling a funny story. We walked past them and pretended not to notice them.

The front door of the brothel was only about one hundred yards from the cordon. It was all we could do to force ourselves to saunter, not be in too much of a hurry but move just fast enough to make sure that one of the MP's hadn't started to chase us. Slowly, slowly, barely daring to breathe and afraid to look over our shoulder for fear we'd give ourselves away, we walked inside as nonchalantly as if we had a right to be there. It would have been easy to let rip with a nervous laugh but we controlled ourselves. In the reception room the madam motioned us take a seat and served us with a beer. She peered at both of us and then turned to me. Pointing to Rainer she said, "Your friend is not French!" I was almost speechless. Damn! I managed to blurt, "How do you know?" The madam pointed to his bare arm. "Look at his tattoo." Blue, red and green, his tattoo was distinctly British. She began wailing. "If the MP's saw it and think about it, they'll be here in minutes." I tried to argue but she managed to convince us that the MP's, unfortunately, were not as dumb as they looked.

No sooner had she stopped than one of the girls near the door said, "I think they are coming here." The madam looked at us and looked back at the entrance. "Quick, follow me." We scurried upstairs behind her wide backside and followed her into a second floor room. "Just be quiet." She motioned to a roof trap above a little table in the middle of the room. "If you hear them coming, go up onto the roof." For a big woman she moved quickly. We heard her thunder down the corridor before the MP's arrived. A huge argument had broken out downstairs. I didn't like the sound of the way it was going so I told Rainer that we had best get up on the roof and drop down on the other side where we could run through the vegetable gardens to safety. The idea was a stroke of genius but executing it was a problem There was no way could we drop down onto the street. Sure as the day is long, the MP's would be waiting for us. Rather quickly, I had to accept they weren't as dumb as I'd hoped. I hoisted him up through the trap and he pulled me up. We eased the door shut and stared at each other.

Theoretically, we were better off than being on the other side of the trap door taking our chances with the MP's. When we put the trap door back in place it didn't take long for us to get our bearings. We were stuck. The roof was so slippery that we were scared to move a muscle. One false step and we could either fall and break something or land intact and be carted off to the brig. We were stuck, glued to the roof like a couple of human insects on a roll of flypaper. The only thing we could do was wait out those bastards until they decided to fuck off. It was a long wait. They finally finished drinking and left well after nightfall. On the way out they told the madam that they still didn't believe her. I heard one of them say, "We're going to stick around the house just to be sure those guys aren't in here somewhere." Just what we wanted to hear! Our muscles had begun to cramp but we didn't want to risk moving, especially in the dark.

Below, we heard noise in the room. It didn't sound like a customer being serviced. Through the closed trap door one of the girls whispered, "You can come down now, but don't make noise. They're not far away. You can jump from one of the windows in the back of the house and run away across the back gardens of the other houses." She continued, "After you're through the gardens head for the center of town and you'll be okay." Her assurance sounded good almost too good to be true. We reversed the process, lowering ourselves back into room. She led us down the creaking corridor to an empty back room overlooking the gardens. We shinnied down the back of the house and took off running as fast as we could. Our racketing caused pandemonium among the chickens and ducks that didn't like us barreling through their sleeping quarters. We made so much noise that the neighborhood dogs began to bark and growl. Above us we heard shutters banging open. Alarmed voices began crying out into the shadows. All the mayhem we were creating in our wake was too much for a neighborhood that had gone to bed.

We ran full tilt, like madmen, right into a chicken wire fence. It tore crosshatch marks on my face but at that point I was beyond pain. Our shoes were covered with mud and chicken shit from the hen houses. Don't ask how, but, we finally made it out of the gardens and found our way to the center of town. Eventually we got back out to our ship. The duty officer stood at the top of the gangplank. We summoned our last strength in order not to stumble onboard and be forced to answer his questions. Saluting briskly we walked by but he looked us up and down before we made our way, as discreetly as possible, to the showers. The next morning we had a good laugh about our nighttime adventures when we retold the story to our shipmates about our rooftop sentry duty above the brothel.

*****

The build-up for the next operation began slowly but the pace picked up once the first ships had loaded. All the loading and maneuvering was organized and supervised by the American Army. When it came to organization, they were tops. They mastered thousands of details,

Rene Dassac (in collaboration with Patrick K. Robbins)

calculating everything in order to complete the operation without wasting any time. As soon as the last man or vehicle was onboard his ship it was sent to the staging area to wait before it joined a convoy. The amount of time the dockside moorings were empty between ship's departure and arrival was measured in minutes. Once it started the huge war machine could not be stopped.

Our turn came. We went to our point of embarkation where troops allocated to us waited with their half-tracks, tanks, lorries, etc. The loading procedure was pure perfection. The half-tracks and vehicles with machine guns moved in first. They parked on the upper deck so they could provide additional firepower against aircraft during the landing. Hats off, somebody in their organization had put a lot of thought into the deployment. For once, the planners earned our respect. The rest of the moving equipment was parked in the tank space. The lorries carried everything you could think of: big jute bags of sugar, boxes of individual field rations, even blankets which, in Italy, were greatly coveted by the destitute civilian population. There was also a fair amount of cigarettes and soap. Those were two items that were actively traded on the black market.

The troops were billeted in the passageway under the main deck and on each side of the tank space. They were grateful because they slept in bunks near the showers and toilets. For most of them, this was a luxury they hadn't known for a long time. For many months they were sleeping in tents or out in the open. We shared our galley to give them a chance to cook three proper meals a day.

All our troops were Americans. It was fun to listen to their different accents and watch them settle in. They were great lads but they were green. I was stupefied by the way they talked and thought about the war. For most of them our landing, wherever that was, would be their first time under fire and from the way they talked and acted, you would have thought they were headed out for a Sunday picnic. I managed to keep quiet and keep my thoughts to myself because I didn't want to pop their bubble. They were fine young men and we got to know each other because we were locked onboard for nearly two weeks with no possibility to go ashore.

We were sent back to our old anchorage to wait for our convoy to form. We devised all sorts of ways to kill time. I knew my mind would swing between two moods: Stifling boredom before operations began that was quickly replaced by fear when we were getting shot at and bombed. We came up with all kinds of ways to make time fly. A request for permission to go swimming was bucked up to the captain and then into harbor command. It seemed like a logical thing to do. The brass didn't approve but they gave a good reason. Enemy frogmen were trying to penetrate our defenses and mine the ship's. Day and night a small patrol boat zigzagged around the lake dropping small demolition charges to keep frogmen out of our staging zone. For a time, watching the patrol boat was our only excitement.

One day my mate and I sat on the open ramp of the ship with some American soldiers. Someone came up with the astute observation that, about sixty yards away, there was a grocer's shop with some wine containers stacked up outside. Slowly the conversation began to drift toward wine, the patrol boat, and whether we could swim over to the shop without attracting the attention of the patrol boat. Despite the zigzags, we noticed that the boat always sailed, more-or-less on the same course. Creative minds started to speculate on how long it took the boat to go from its farthest point and back. The time it would take it to come back would be the operating time we had to reach the beach, get the wine, and make it back to our ship undetected. Of course, we had to pull this off at night.

The ink black North African night became our willing ally but logistics were difficult to sort out. We had to keep the operation simple and doable. In a nutshell, we needed to swim ashore, buy some wine, and swim back without getting caught. A lot of creative thought went into planning each step. During the first phase, in order not to attract the attention of the deck sentries, we encouraged some of our mates - the guys with really bad voices - to sing loudly and drown out any splashing sounds made by the swimmers. That part was easy.

The second phase required even more thought because it was the most critical. How could we get the wine back? That was a difficult question. There was no way our guys could slip into the water with an empty water jerry can. Finally, after numerous non-starter ideas, we came up with a solution. It wasn't perfect, but it was practical. We calculated, four of us who were good swimmers, could strap on four army canteens each. Sixteen canteens were enough for the first raid. That meant, provided we made it back, we'd have at least eight liters to pass around. Keeping the money dry wasn't a problem. All the currency was paper so we crammed the cash into condoms fastened shut by a string tied around our necks. Planning reached an almost feverish pitch. We chose three swimmers whose names were drawn from pieces of paper thrown into a hat. Naturally, I was one of the team because I spoke French.

After we agreed on the plan, we spent an entire day making sure that every phase had been well thought out. Talk about geniuses! We were positively brilliant. The plan was checked, double checked, and revised, checked again and finally accepted. The following night was chosen for the four swimmers to slip over the side at 2000 hours. By then it would be dark and our officers would be in their wardrooms after making the night rounds. Everything was stored in my workshop because my door was close to the ramp in the tank space.

At last our 'D Day' arrived. A dozen wretched voices, a sound somewhat akin to parched animals braying before an empty water trough, shattered the night. The mess deck and quarter deck bulkheads vibrated. Underneath and out of sight, we waited for the patrol boat to pass. When we were pretty sure it was out of our zone, we slid into the water, quietly, ever so quietly, and began paddling toward our goal. Allied commandoes and frogmen would have been proud of us. Fish made 'noise' compared to us. Slowly we glided toward the beach until we were crouching with only our eyes barely above water. Hardy breathing, we scanned the beach, scanned behind us, and slid out of the water. We crept single file down the beach and headed toward the little ramshackle shop near the water's edge that had been under surveillance by our 'invasion planners'.

The storekeeper sat in front of his shop enjoying the cool night air. A small paraffin globe lamp cast a pale yellow cone of light. The night was calm and he seemed to be at peace with his world. We approached him from his blind side; he didn't hear us coming. I coughed to get his attention and he jumped straight out of his chair. A rocket up his backside couldn't have been more effective. He started babbling and I assumed from his accent that he was Tunisian and not some French émigré of dubious loyalty who had been forgotten by the war.

It was hard to tell which gave off more light: his little paraffin lamp or the whites of his eyes. I quickly explained to him what we were after. He stopped trembling and burst out laughing, "You sailors will never change!" Looking at us, he admonished, "I suppose you know that what you are doing is very dangerous." At least, we knew he wasn't going to panic and start screaming for the shore patrol. We weren't there to discuss the merits of our adventure so I agreed with him. After all, I didn't want to debate the obvious so I told him that wartime meant we had to take chances. Does anyone know what's going to happen tomorrow? For that matter, I added, do we know what might happen on the way back to the ship? That was heavy philosophy, the kind of topic you bring up late at night when you're tired of discussing women and pubs. We probably could have continued until dawn.

He was harmless but he was a shopkeeper. It wasn't every evening when foreign customers arrived eager to be served. He filled our canteens. When we unwound the condoms from our necks he began chuckling as we piled the cash into his hands. We said good night and shook his hand. I stood in the doorway and looked sternly at him. "Promise me you will not tell anyone about our visit." He wailed something in Arabic and gave me his word and waved me out the door. I believed him because I knew it was little guys like him, honest and simple people who will never make news, who keep their word. Single file, walking as if we were creeping through a hen house, we slinked back to the beach and lay in the grass waiting for the right time to start the swim back to our ship. The coast was clear. A breeze had come up and it was almost chilly when we slid back into the water. On the return trip, instead of condoms around our necks we carried the world's most eagerly awaited wine.

Not too far from shore we heard our mates who were still braying; our ship sounded as if it was full of army transport donkeys. We made it back undetected. Never, even in later years when I could afford good wine, did a wine taste as good as what we brought back that night. What a great night! But, with the advantage of hindsight and looking back on that escapade, I think we took insane risks. Were we nuts?

Maybe? Let's face it: we were also at an age when we took big risks because we were convinced that we were invincible and invulnerable. From their point of view, the Yanks probably thought we were slightly nuts. Sanity or not, putting that question aside we learned something very important. That escapade was one of those wartime episodes that taught us, Brits and Yanks, how much alike we were. Forget accents and nationalities. Underneath we were all alike: Young men with a zest for living, young men who managed to have great fun together, young men caught up in war.

Time dragged. We ached to sail, anywhere, but just sail and get out of the lake. By now we were convinced the enemy knew we were assembling a considerable force waiting to be thrown at them. But, where were we headed? Spies were watching our every move. As time dragged rumors about where we were headed spread like the plague. Every conversation seemed to turn around the "Where" question. Even when the topic involved women someone was bound to ask, "Where are the brothels?" The 'where' guessing game involved hours of speculation, the strangest sites were suggested, but no one got it right but we kept on guessing.

*****

September 1943. Operation Avalanche. After nearly three weeks of preparation and mind splitting boredom, we were ordered to weigh anchor. Our cargo of American troops lined the rails to get a last glimpse of a coastline at peace. Ships began leaving the harbor in batches, four or five at a time. We regrouped to form a huge convoy that was accompanied by many escort vessels. Their main job at this juncture of the operation was to chase the convoy vessels into their positions in the convoy. Watching them reminded me of sheep dogs harrying a flock into a huge pen. Darting here and there, I found myself admiring those beautiful destroyers and wished I had been on one of them instead of on a waddling flat bottom landing ship. To be frank, I was a bit jealous but I told myself, "this is life and in wartime it's better not to tempt fate. Just accept whatever is given to me in order not to have any regrets later." Maybe I was becoming a philosopher or maybe I had learned to accept the realities of war.

We waited. No matter in which direction I looked, all I could sea were ships and more ships. All of a sudden, with no forewarning, we began to move out early one morning at daybreak. We still didn't know where we were headed but by then we quit wasting time speculating about the "what if's" of the war. There were more important matters to be addressed. The ship's company was called to the first degree of readiness. There was always the danger of an air attack even though, by now, the allies had more control of the skies than a few months earlier. At least, we felt safer and it was almost reassuring to be able to look up into the night sky and know that whoever was flying above us was probably not going to turn and make a bombing run. That contrived sense of security didn't give us complete protection but we convinced ourselves that we were pretty much out of harm's way. Unfortunately, that feeling of "security" from enemy fighter planes wasn't shared when it came to feeling secure from the threat we knew was lurking below the surface of the Mediterranean.

Enemy submarines were a constant threat. As long as they were able to sink us, life at sea was very dangerous. There was always the possibility that one or two enemy subs were patrolling the area through which our convoy was moving. We knew their tactics: They would stay below the surface and run silently when they heard us coming. If our side was lucky our destroyers and mine chasers would pick them up on their Asdic. But luck wasn't always on our side. German submariners, known as the elite of the German navy, were well trained and motivated. They could not be underestimated. Professionals to a man, we knew they were capable of sending a full salvo of torpedoes into the convoy at any time of day or night. Our minds weren't playing games with us by exaggerating the enemy's competence. Being realistic, we accepted that our convoy was made of many ships and many opportunities. Strewn across the sea, we were the targets every U boat captain dreamed of attacking. Fat troop transport ships, heavy fuel tankers, and freighters loaded with ammunition and ordinance, a well aimed fish would almost certainly blow its target sky high.

By mid morning the convoy formed and we sailed at twelve knots. During the following night the convoy split into two battle groups.

Rene Dassac (in collaboration with Patrick K. Robbins)

Our group was ordered to slow down to allow the first batch to go ahead with the American rangers (commandos). We watched the American heavy cruisers kick up impressive stern wakes as they raced through the invasion fleet. The British battleship Warspite maneuvered into position as her huge cannons swiveled toward shore. A number of French fast light cruisers began moving faster to provide cover for the assault boats. Despite all this activity we still didn't know the exact location of where we were going to land our troops. The rumor mill had ground to a halt hours ago; that was normal. Heading into battle we were simple too busy to waste time speculating about something we couldn't control. In due course we'd be told but in the meantime all we knew was that we were sailing towards Sardinia and Italy. Beyond that, the answer to the 'where' question still hadn't been revealed.

On 9 September 1943 at 0330 hours, the first assault craft landed on the beach at Paestum near Salerno. All hell broke loose. The enemy was waiting for us. Our assault troops ran into heavy fire. Word came back from the beaches that they were having a hard time gaining a foothold. The first news was bad news but it was news we had to hear. At the same time, it was news we didn't want to hear. Every possible thought was racing through our minds when we thought about our troops getting torn up. Sometimes I'd catch myself thinking about the good times I'd had in Tunisia. In a flash, something would snap me out of that and I'd remember the hell of what happened in Sicily.

I wasn't the only one trying to keep myself focused. All my shipmates felt the same way. Tempers were fraying, some guys were quieter than usual, while others shouted and cursed. At times like this the ship was either too small or too big. Depending on where your mind was you either wanted a way to crawl into your own private time and space or to get away from everything or you needed to get right in the middle of the entire crew and pretend that, because you were surrounded by your mates, you were secure. At some point I'd stop swirling and tell myself two simple truths: I was alive and I wasn't wounded. Each man, in his own way, was preparing himself for the worst.

During the next few hours events unfolded that outstripped our worst and most private thoughts. For those who survived the Salerno landing, we'd remember Sicily as a cakewalk compared to what we were about to go through. But, we couldn't know that. Our clumsy looking ship rolled and pitched, creaked and groaned while we stared at the horizon where the fighting was raging with ferocious intensity.

We could see funnel smoke and big white-blue clouds belched by the ship's big guns. And we also saw enemy dive-bomber runs on our troops who were exposed on a narrow long stretch of beach. They had no shelter and the enemy was picking them off. Right or wrong, we had the impression the enemy had been waiting for them right at this very spot. Maybe it was an ambush or maybe it was just coincidence or the enemy's good luck, who knows? There was no escaping what was unfolding in front of us: our guys were getting pounded. Bombs exploded and shot sand columns high into the sky. Dark chunks flying into the sun were bits of men and equipment and not only rock.

During the day we heard that Italy had signed an armistice. As far as we could tell nobody had got the word to the Italian troops who were pounding the shit out of us. Our troops had been on the beach for more than twelve hours. From what we could see of the battle, superior forces pinned down our guys because they couldn't break out. To make matters worse, we were told to keep clear of the landing area. We had to keep moving because if we anchored we were sitting ducks for the dive-bombers. Unlike in the Sicily landings, this time the Luftwaffe was using radio control flying bombs.

Deadly accurate, a flying bomb scored a direct hit into the funnel of HMS Warspite. What a horrible loss! A great ship, she had been causing severe damage to the enemy's heavy artillery that was dug in far up on the hills overlooking the landing area. She was badly hit. I could see fires breaking out and as a damage control man I could imagine the hell her damage control teams were fighting. She continued to cover our men on the beach. Huge clouds of cannon smoke roared from her big guns.

My god she was a heroic sight. It was hard for me to imagine how she kept going but she even managed to provide effective artillery barrages with her secondary armament after most of her main armament had been knocked out. Talk about the British fighting spirit, we were watching it! Despite enormous damage and loss of life, Warspite never let up.

Fighting continued throughout the night. The night sky was alive with cannon fire and tracers. Every now and then flares turned darkness into daylight. By daybreak it was obvious that we had taken considerable casualties. In fact, we started getting casualty reports that were worse than first estimates. Despite the awful loss of men and materiel, we still had not broken the enemy and forced him to retreat from his well-defended positions. In fact, after twenty-four hours we hadn't moved very far inland. Many landing craft were destroyed on the beach. Some of them carried ammunition. They exploded when they were hit. Their crews never had a chance to know what hit them. An almighty roar blasted across the water. Men became statistics, 'killed in action'.

Two U.S. cruisers collided. They had been zigzagging at high speed to avoid the dive-bombers. In the hell of battle, accidents happen. They limped off station to be repaired. Without them it meant we had a gap in our defenses, a critical gap. Their firing had been accurate and steady, a great support for our men trapped on the beach. But, no sooner were they ordered out of the line when two more ships slid into to plug the gap. The A.A cruiser HMS Dido and a light cruiser of the Arethusa class swung into position.

The situation continued to deteriorate on the beach. It was so bad that we were ordered to stand-by because there was a strong possibility that we would receive orders to assist in an evacuation of the landing operation. After a few more hours, sometime during the morning, orders were given and the Hampshire regiment landed. Their landing began turning the battle in favor of the allies. At the cost of many casualties and dead, the allies broke through the enemy lines. Finally, secure forward points off the beach were established. From these positions the Hampshire soldiers fanned out and moved up the hills to clean out enemy bunkers and artillery emplacements. At last, the situation was changing to our advantage.

The beach-landing officer still had not ordered us in to disembark our troops. We had to wait a few more hours before we landed our

Yanks. Waiting to go ashore was hard on them. They were kitted up and ready to go but we couldn't land them. Instead of landing and fighting they were forced to watch the battle raging on land and at sea. All around us ships were being blown up. Smoke billowed above the shore and over burning ships sending greasy fat black and orange fireballs bubbling into the sky. The Yanks morale started sagging. All they could do was watch, worry, and try to keep from snapping. I've often wondered since that day which is harder: fighting or waiting? For our men from the Fifth Army, at that particular moment, waiting was probably worse than fighting. Finally we got the order to advance into a landing slot. Minutes after beaching the first men streamed down the ramp. Soon a long line of men, half-tracks, trucks and Sherman tanks wound its way out of sight. A few soldiers turned and waved. They were good blokes. I've often wondered, how many survived the war?

We received fresh orders: Head for Bizerte with casualties. Litters were lined up in long rows waiting to be brought onboard. I had never seen so many wounded in my life. Every possible wound imaginable was on litters stretching for more yards than I wanted to count. Corpsmen moved between the litters, sometimes stopping to adjust a dressing, sometimes stopping to lift a blanket to cover a man's face. Less than an hour before, fresh American soldiers had marched down our ramp. Now we loaded men who were mangled or limping, living or soon to die. No one needed to tell us about what kind of resistance the first wave of troops had run into. Our cargo of human wreckage told the story.

Heavy firing was still coming from enemy positions. Water geysers marched across the sea; shrapnel peppered our deck. The sight of those poor lads brought back bad memories of our landing in Sicily. The shelling we received was bad but it was nothing compared to what we had just gone through during the previous forty-eight hours when the shelling and bombing had turned the beachhead and the sea into a raging hell.

Even though we were sitting ducks and wanted to get out of there, we knew that we had to stay until we loaded as many of the casualties as we could carry. At last we were ordered to leave the beach area and join a convoy bound for Bizerte. We weren't meant to be a hospital ship and we weren't flying a Red Cross but, from what it looked like below decks, we could have been a hospital ship. Hundreds of wounded and dying soldiers were stacked throughout the ship. Every inch of deck space was taken up. Amazingly, no one from our crew had been wounded. Other than basic first aid training, none of us knew how to take care of our wounded passengers. Compassion replaced medical skills and we did the craziest things to make the wounded boys comfortable. We even shared with them some of the wine we still had left after our foolish swim ashore on the lake Ferryville. It was a difficult trip, we did our best, but some soldiers died of their wounds before we got to Bizerte.

By the time we reached Bizerte we heard that Monty's 8th Army had linked up with the U.S 5th Army off Salerno. That was good news but the war was not over, far from it! We disembarked our wounded. Army ambulances took them to military hospitals that had sprung up around Bizerte to handle the hundreds of men who had survived the landing. Watching them leave I knew that many would never fight again. Certainly, more would die from their wounds. What an awful and pitiful sight to see those men hobbling down the ramp. Some managed to lean on their mates, some staggered on their own, but many were carried on litters. They looked like hell. Their bloody and dirty field dressings were matted into their uniforms but their spirits were high.

Within a couple of hours we were reloaded with British troops with their halftracks and lorries. They were Guardsmen and we got along well. There was one in particular, a wiry little cockney, who kept us laughing with his stories about peacetime in London. But his laughter masked a darker side. He told us how, in Sicily, he killed his first German. He didn't boast, he didn't laugh, and his admission came from somewhere deep inside him because it was obvious that he was struggling to tell his story. It was also obvious that he talked as if he regretted pulling the trigger. "It was night," he began and told how their officer led him and three of his mates on a silent patrol. They knew that they were in the midst of Germans, and their patrols were probably closer to them than they realized. In a low voice, the officer said, "You two lay down here and don't move." As if it was a second thought, he continued, "At least one of you must keep watch if you want to be still alive when I come back." The officer left with the other two blokes to position them further away.

They lay quietly, weapons cocked, ears straining for any sound that would warn them of someone approaching. Maybe it was half an hour later they heard somebody coming toward them. The chap on watch fired a shot in the direction of the approaching steps. Out of the thicket a loud voice burst out swearing, "You fucking idiots I did not tell you to shoot at me!" The bullet missed but there was no doubt the officer was furious. "Why don't you use your brains? You knew bloody well I would be coming back this way?" He calmed down and cautioned them. "Now be careful because anyone coming this way will be either Italian or German." Fair enough. They had almost killed one of their own and now they knew that the next person on the path would be an enemy.

Much later during the night they heard somebody walking slowly and whispering into the dark, "Hasler?" Obviously, the man was lost. From the way he whispered the name two or three times they could tell from his voice that he was German. One of the Guardsmen was so scared that he could not move. His rifle was a couple feet from him. Shaking with almost uncontrollable fear he managed to inch forward, grab his rifle and wiggle into a firing position. Sensing danger, his mate was now awake. The German was now very close to him, walking slowly and carefully so as not to make any noise. He was still whispering words the Guardsman could not understand. From the sound of his voice it was obvious the German was just as scared as the Guardsmen. The German was so close to the Cockney that he almost walked on him. "So I shot him and he fell next to me. He was dying slowly and I kept saying to him, "Sorry, sorry, sorry, until my mates told me to shut up because Hasler was probably not very far away." He stared straight ahead. That was the end of his story and I couldn't really understand how he felt because I thought, in war you had to kill or be killed.

We ferried more troops to Salerno. The front was now moving north probably toward Naples because it appeared that the allies now had a number of airfields. Monty's 8th Army had captured the port of Bari on the Adriatic and they too were moving north. For the time being enemy air activity was non-existent over Salerno. Once we had

Rene Dassac (in collaboration with Patrick K. Robbins)

landed our troops we sailed to Palermo in Sicily where again we collected fresh troops. We had been at sea for a long time without a break and in Palermo we were allowed a short run ashore. It was my first contact with Italian civilians. It was hard to figure them out because it was my first time 'in Italy' but they seemed glad to be free in spite of the shortages of food and utilities. But, what really amazed me on this run ashore was the black market. What an eye opener! There was a fantastic black market. The soldiers we met were eager to tell us what the market would bear and which were the most profitable articles to trade. American army blankets were in great demand and the Sicilian women were actually making dresses out of them! Cigarettes were also in great demand. What the soldiers got in return was anybody's guess but everything was up for barter, even women.

We loaded American troops and their armament and sailed to Sorento, close to Naples. Sorento was not yet secure; we were directed to Amalfi where we dropped anchor off a lovely sandy beach. Behind the beach there were cliffs, high white cliffs similar to those one can see near the Dover coast. It didn't take too long before a group of young girls appeared on the beach and started to giggle, making all sorts of signs that, at first, we interpreted to be suggestive. Or, at least, we hoped that's what they meant but we were too far away to communicate. Suddenly, we realised that their sign making was actually an attempt to warn us. On the cliff towering above our ship, a cliff probably 120 feet high, there was a group of Germans with a small gun. We were so close to each other that we were at a stand-off. They couldn't depress their gun sufficiently, even if they wanted to, and we could not elevate our guns enough to harm them. The Captain ordered the ship to move further offshore and by the time we were in a position to fire the Germans had disappeared. The allied armies were now moving so fast that these Germans had probably become separated from their main unit, were lost, and certainly did not want to attract any attention. They were outgunned and they chose, quite wisely, to disappear rather than start a firefight they would certainly lose.

Castellamare was now freed and we were directed to land our troops there. We reached our destination without any trouble and landed our troops without a problem. Once in awhile Lady Luck smiled on us.

Castellamare was a lucky landing. Considering the fierce battle that had been fought in the area, at least from what we could see, the town was not too badly damaged. All we could do was stare at the town because we were not allowed ashore. As usual onboard, the rumor mill was in full operation. The most persistent rumor was that the Fifth Army was entering Naples and that the city was in a very bad state. Thousands of people were dying of typhus, cholera and other highly contagious diseases. This meant that the town would be out of bound to troops until these diseases were brought under control.

Then we heard news that everyone was waiting for: Italy had signed a ceasefire, the Corsicans had liberated themselves, the Italian occupation army was gone, and Sardinia was free. Things were moving fast. We received orders to go to Cagliari, south of Sardegnia, to receive a battalion of Italian prisoners with all their armament and to take them to Palermo. I had seen P.O.W's before but never this many and they did not look like heroic losers. They were sad, tired, and dirty. From the way they looked and the way they smelled, they hadn't had a wash in days, if not weeks. They came aboard with their mules, old fashion gun carts and old fashion rifles. Some carried hay bales to use as mattresses. Enemy or not, they were pitiful wretches. We showed them where they could shower and we even made room on bunks so they could stretch out and have a decent sleep.

Maybe it was a language problem, maybe it was battle fatigue, but for reasons we could not understand, most of them preferred to sleep on deck without having a good wash. Or, maybe they were so tired that the only thing they wanted to do was to sleep. I could understand their sadness. They did not know what was going to happen to them but their C.O. knew. Once at sea, in the evening, they began to sing sad songs, calling out to 'mama'. Someone had saved his mandolin. He plunked along with the singers, sometimes leading and sometimes following their sad voices.

At first they did not want to fraternize with us. Perhaps they had received orders not to mix with their captors but it must have dawned on more than one of them that we were not savages. It didn't take too long until we started noticing little signs indicating they wanted to communicate. Once the ice was broken they talked to us in a mixture of Italian, English and French. They were our prisoners but we also recognized they were human beings just like us. Only they had lost the war and we were convinced we would win it.

When we docked in Palermo they stumbled down the ramp and assembled on the jetty. Once the last prisoner had left the tank space we went below to have a look at how filthy they had left their detention area. Our captain ordered their C.O. to clean the tank space and leave it as clean as they found it when they came aboard. It was awful below decks. There was such a strong smell of urine and excrement that I had to start the extractor fans to get rid of it. Even after they cleaned the tank space, it still smelled strange. It should have smelled of lorries, fuel, heavy equipment, rubber, but there was an almost sticky rotten stench left by broken, filthy men. This time we were lucky and we stayed for a couple of days. We were allowed a quick run ashore for a few hours and then we loaded another batch of troops.

We took a full cargo of U.S. Air Force personnel and their equipment to prepare an air base in Corsica. Enroute to Ajaccio we stopped at Castellamare to pick up some more air force personnel. We left after sunset and arrived at Ajaccio forty eight hours later, early in the morning. I was excited. This was going to be my first visit to France since 1940 and I was very impatient to set foot on French soil. I wondered how they had fared during the occupation. It was well known that they had mounted a good resistance against the occupation in Corisca and they had actually liberated themselves with the help of French troops from Algeria. But, my wonder turned to amazement because I was not expecting to see what we saw when we sailed into port.

There was no way I could have expected the welcome that was waiting for us. A huge crowd had assembled and from within their midst men were happily firing off rounds into the air. If we had been under enemy fire, we'd have taken cover. No, this was a traditional welcome, from the heart and wild with joy. No one seemed to worry about the fact that the Germans had not completely evacuated Bastia which was only one hundred and fifty kilometers from Ajaccio. Somehow amidst this explosion of joy, clapping, and shouting, nobody thought twice about a U.S. LST that was lying in the harbor, badly damaged after a dive bombing raid. Her crumpled superstructure was a mute reminder to the fact that we were still at war. As we slid into our mooring next to her it didn't take a genius to draw the obvious conclusion: It could have been the other way around. Our ship could have been hit and theirs could have been sliding alongside.

Relief is always temporary in war. We were exposed and in a dangerous situation. No one was completely convinced the port area was fully secure and a lot of civilians were exposed. An American officer grabbed a megaphone and tried to reason with the crowd and tried to get them to disperse. His French was pretty good, I guess he was understood, but no one cared. The crowd continued singing but there was less firing and more much hugging. When the troops disembarked with their vehicles people climbed onto anything with wheels or treads, trucks, tanks, halftracks, and began kissing and hugging them. It's another world when kisses can stop a mighty military machine. But that's what happened. It was an insane outpouring of gratitude that made driving all but impossible. From the way I saw it, some of the girls were good looking enough to stop for a very long time. It was fantastic; it was raw joy in a war full of raw cruelty.

I could barely contain my excitement and I was given permission to leave the ship and go down to the jetty to talk to some of them. A young lad stepped out of the crowd and invited me to have dinner at his home with his family. Of course I accepted but I told him to wait for me because I had to change and ask permission to go ashore. The Captain granted my request because he knew what it meant to me. The boy and I walked across the town and up a small hill to his house. His parents were waiting for us in front of the house and they grabbed me, a total stranger, and started kissing me as if I were one of their family. The warmth of their welcome hit and I felt like I was home again. They spoke the local dialect between themselves and I, more or less, understood what they were saying. They were trying to figure out what they could organize for dinner. I asked the lad what they lacked the most and he replied, "Soap, coffee, sugar, butter, cigarettes." The list was long, more proof of the difficulties they had endured under occupation. "Okay," I said, "grab a bag and follow me." I followed him back down to the docks and he followed me onboard. I filled his bag with all kinds of soaps, butter, coffee and K Rations. I had hidden my loot in the workshop, building a stash to barter when we returned to Italy where I could trade in the black market.

We trudged up the hill to his parent's house, the lad leading while I shouldered my bulging sea bag. When we returned to their house they were, of course, quite embarrassed. They wanted to pay me and I refused. "But, why not," they questioned and then I told them that my own family was in Lyon and they were probably suffering just like them and by being able to give this little family something, maybe, just maybe, in a round about way, I was helping them. We spent the evening talking about everything that had happened during all the years of occupation.

It didn't take long for me to realize that I had become a stranger in my own country. Looking at the situation in another way, I was an outsider 'observing' a country and a culture that was no longer really mine. After years away, years immersed in another society and another language, I was a stranger in my own land and I caught myself, much to their amusement, searching for correct words in French because I had been mixing English with my French and they got lost trying to follow me.

We stayed in Ajaccio for a couple of days and enjoyed the kindness of the Corsican people. Certainly there were other pleasures and Reiner, two other shipmates, and I paid a visit to the local brothel that was like a well kept cabaret compared with what we had seen up to now. It was really nice to be back 'home'.

After a few days we sailed for Castellamare and then into Naples. During the past few weeks the engineers had de-mined the port and made some basic repairs. The situation was safe enough for us to land some army medical specialists who set to work spraying the local population with DDT in order to prevent typhus and cholera spreading. I didn't see it but we were told by reliable witnesses that the situation was so bad in parts of the city that they had seen families piling their dead into wheelbarrows before carting them off to the open pits in the public cemeteries. It sounded like something out of the middle Ages, the Great Plague: little lines of black clad mourners shuffled through the rubble to dump their loved ones. When we arrived in Naples we were not even allowed to enter the port so we anchored outside near an old fort.

A rowboat invasion began soon after the anchors dropped. The rowers had girls onboard. The men begged for cigarettes and tried to make us understand that they were prepared to pay for cigarettes with a commodity wanted and needed by every man onboard. We hung over the side yelling and laughing while the girls in the bobbing boats lifted their skirts to wiggle their bottoms and spread their legs so wide they should have split. What a lovely sight! Our captain, a very religious man and perhaps the only man onboard who did not share our ardor, ordered us to use the fire hoses to get rid of them. In the end, he was right.

Later we found out how depraved the Neapolitans had become. Venereal disease was rampant in Naples and allied troops had suffered from this silent enemy. The Germans pinned down the northern defense at Monte Casino. That was a bona fide military problem but VD had infected the equivalent of ten allied divisions! This silent enemy had to be fought as well. Eventually, we were allowed to enter the port and tie-up but only to disembark our medic specialists and then to speed back to Palermo where we loaded a US regiment with a large number of lorries full of food supplies, drinks, and army blankets that would soon be transformed into a civilian two-piece suit for the black market.

Our US soldiers were a raucous lot, happy-go-lucky, real specialists in trading on the black market. They gave us important tips on how to deal and what to look for and what to avoid. My workshop was an ideal place to stock stuff for our future commerce. For security reasons the door to the tank space was always locked and I was the only person who could unlock it. The overhead hatch could easily be locked from the inside and I made a bell warning system to warn me of unwanted visitors! My American supplier gave me two rolls of army blankets, two big bags of sugar and some K rations against some rum and wine I still had in stock. We already knew how much a blanket was sold for in Palermo and in Naples and the Yanks assured us that it was a seller's market and the prices would rise even further. What a lovely prospect! Between Reiner and me we had long conversations on how rich we would soon become. Fantasy, perhaps it was but fantasy was one way to stay sane, one way to make life bearable in the middle of a world full of misery everywhere we looked.

Off we sailed to Naples, two great merchants about to deal in fortunes. Our heads were full of the good time we 'knew' we were going to have. With all our money, nothing, absolutely nothing we wanted was out of reach. Money meant pleasure and we had our own very clearly defined ideas of how much fun we were going to have.

By now Naples had become a huge transit place for the allied armies. Instead of order there was chaos; instead of a return to civilian life crime and prostitution was rampant. On every corner, in every door, someone was selling his or her body, adults and even children. It was sickening. Via Roma, the main street was choked with troops of all nationalities strolling up and down looking for God knows what. The small streets feeding into Via Roma were indescribably filthy. This wasn't filth you'd expect to find in a twentieth century city in Europe. This was filthy living that you'd expect to find in the middle Ages. For example, people opened their windows and dumped garbage out as if they were living on the edge of a cliff. Didn't they care? Didn't it dawn on them that every time they went outside they had to step through their own filth? Toilet waste trickled down the middle of the streets, chickens scavenged, and little kids wandered barefoot through the muck, dragging their feet through the brown water as if they were out on a beach dragging their toes through the sand at the water's edge. But it wasn't sand and it wasn't water they were playing in. It was accumulated filth of years and the stench seemed to shoot from the walls, an invisible vapor that seared our nostrils and made our eyes water.

When Reiner and I went ashore, like everyone else, we went up the main street and found a huge canteen that was only open to servicemen. An orchestra, the musicians were Italian, played all sorts of tunes on request. We were close enough to the bandstand to hear what the musicians said. They were getting paid to do a job, and they played, but it seemed like every second request was for Glenn Miller's, "In the Mood." The request would come and they would grind it out, "It's In the Mood again," their voices filled with disgust and boredom. I could understand just enough Italian so I said, "How about playing, 'O Sole Mio'?" They really ripped into it. They were smiling and obviously enjoying playing a tune that meant something to them. Reiner and I offered them drinks and then they really loosened up. Quietly, I asked the band leader, "Do you know of someone who wants to buy army blankets?" Without batting an eye, he replied, "Don't tell anybody. I'll buy anything you want to sell." Motioning for us to be quiet he told us where to meet the next day. He was a good businessman, reliable and full of good tips. He even told us to avoid screwing girls off the street. "They're rotten." We must have looked crestfallen but he said, "If you want to get laid I'll take you to a safe place." He kept his word and for the two of us, our first few days in Naples were good in spite of the misery everywhere.

*****

We ferried troops between Sicily, Castellamare and Naples. The front was bogged down in front of Monte Casino and the weather was rotten. Shades of the First World War; our soldiers sank in mud. Above them, high in the mountains, some of Hitler's best troops rained murderous fire on the soaked allies. A combination of rain, heavy resistance, and no forward movement began to affect their morale. These troops weren't expecting the Germans to put up such heavy resistance. Bad climatic conditions and difficult terrain combined with a well dug-in enemy meant that it was going to be very difficult to dislodge the enemy and gain the high ground.

The French army started to arrive from Algeria. Among them there was a large contingent of fierce looking Moroccan mountain troops with their mules, donkeys, and modern arms that had been supplied by the Americans. These rough men were to prove themselves later in breaking through the famous Gustav line. For anyone who took the time to look around, it was obvious that something was brewing. We did not know what was going to happen but another big operation was building up. There was too much going on and we were in the middle of it. We were sent back to Castellammare where British and American troops had been assembled. They were armed with heavy assault weapons and that fact alone made us think that our hunches were right. Something big was about to happen.

Rene Dassac (in collaboration with Patrick K. Robbins)

We took British troops onboard with lots of halftracks, tanks and lorries. Once all secured onboard, we received orders to leave the port and anchor outside where we waited for orders. When they came we sailed with a strong escort including several cruisers, two Dido class AA Cruisers, and a number of destroyers. Now we knew what was up because we were bound for a landing further north. The British were landing at Anzio and the Americans were going in at Nettuno. It was a perfect landing at both sites. The few Germans our troops encountered were still in bed and were captured without firing a shot. In fact, the Americans had such a nice and easy landing that the American general in charge of the landing managed to fuck it up. It was so easy he thought it was a trap. Instead of advancing fast with tanks and artillery to secure a protective line up in the hills overlooking the bay of Nettuno and holding the main road from Rome to the Gustav line, he dug in on a fifteen mile perimeter. Only infantry held the line and he left his tanks and heavy artillery on the LST's. German field intelligence immediately caught onto his decision and turned his error to their advantage. The result was catastrophic for the American troops.

The Germans did not waste any time. They opened up with heavy guns hidden in railway tunnels. Mortars crunched into the American lines and well trained SS paratroopers attacked with a ferocity none of the Americans had ever seen. Afterward, our troops told us they experienced what their father's had gone through thirty years earlier in the First World War in the trenches in France. They were dug into hostile rocky terrain and once they were in position the sky opened up with a massive downpour that lasted for hours. Soon they were up to their hips in water, sloshing in their trenches. The Germans opened up with a savage salvo: rockets, grenades, mortars and artillery shells of every caliber fell on and around them.

We were riding offshore; there was no way to help them. Visibility was bad. Allied air power couldn't duck through the clouds to find and attack the German positions. In the meantime, their heavy guns pounded the beaches and the ships anchored offshore waiting for God knows what! We were up against a professional enemy who knew exactly what he was doing. A lot of thought had gone into their defenses. As soon as our bombers were spotted they withdrew their guns back into the mountain tunnels. Both allied navies suffered losses. One landing craft loaded with ammunition was blown up. Under cover of darkness we beached our ship and released our troops who were not happy with the fuck up that general Lucas had made of this operation.

Immediately after we disembarked our troops and their materiel, we steamed away from that bloody hell at full speed to reload with fresh troops. Then we began a milk run back and forth between the landing beaches and Naples. From Naples we ferried fresh troops and lorries filled up with ammunition to Nettuno. It was during one of those trips to Nettuno that I saw something truly remarkable happen. We were unloading vehicles and I looked out on the jetty. To my astonishment there were two of the greatest generals in the allied armies standing talking as casually as if they'd bumped into each other on a high street somewhere in England. The American Mark Clark and the British General Alexander acted as if they were totally unaware of the shells landing around them in the unloading zone. A couple of rounds came too close and I took cover inside the relative safety of our ship. Was it bravado, heroism, a way of bolstering our morale, or was it simply a statement by them that they had business to discuss and, the 'enemy be damned'?

On the return trip to Naples we carried wounded soldiers and empty lorries. Every time we came back to Anzio, there was shelling; we could hear the shells whooshing past and falling into the sea. To a man, we had the feeling that one day one of them would hit us and that would be the end of all of us. No matter how many times you're exposed to enemy fire, no matter how many times you escape, you come out the other side and you're still afraid because fear is something that you can't get rid of no matter how hard you try. It's hiding somewhere inside you and all it takes is the sound of a screeching shell or a bursting bomb, or even the likelihood that you're going to hear it again, and fear crawls out from deep inside. You can't get rid of fear until you die.

Ferrying the wounded was hard work. None of us was a medic but we spent as much time as possible talking with them and comforting them. A majority of the soldiers were out of danger because they had received enough field treatment to allow them to travel by ship to Naples but some were very weak and remained on their stretchers. It helped them to talk. They were hesitant at first to open up. Once they started it spilled out and became a torrent of criticism wrapped in bitter curses. The war wasn't the object of their fury. It was the way the fighting had been planned and executed. Listening to the survivors of the first landing wave it was obvious they could not accept why so many of their mates had been killed or wounded. Somebody had screwed up and they were incredibly bitter at having paid the price for so many lost opportunities. Later historians would write about our landing and agree with the troops but that was comfort after the fact. I believe that the commanding general Lucas must have gone mad when he realized his errors because he later committed suicide. In the meantime, we listened to them and did the best we could to help them through their ordeal.

By 27 February 1944 the beachhead was secured to a depth of maybe five or six miles inland and about twenty-five miles on a north-south line. Three British cruisers, the HMS Penelope, Orion and Spartan, returned to Naples to take on more fuel and ammunition. While on station they caused considerable damage to the enemy surrounding the beachhead. We didn't want them to go; we still needed them. The enemy was far from beaten. They had been weakened but they were still dug in well enough to inflict horrible casualties on their attackers.

Before reaching Anzio we saw a Liberty ship that had been sunk by mines only a few hours before we got there. She was close to the coast; her superstructure stuck out of the water. That ship could have been ours. Right after we got to our usual anchorage the Germans greeted us with a rainstorm of shells that landed in the sea. Fortunately, none of the ships in our anchorage zone was hit. They had been raided several times by radio-controlled flying bombs and some of them scored hits and caused heavy damage. Enemy spotters zeroed in on us and we started to draw fire. Working like demons we got rid of our human and material cargo in record time but heavy artillery fire kept coming from a hill twenty miles away. Enemy shells whistled overhead and splashed into the ocean. It was terrifying but somehow, in the midst of this terrible attack and the set backs we were suffering on land, we were still confident of our invulnerability.

Taulus

We returned to Puzzoli, a small port close to Naples that served as the army's assembly and transit base. While we were enjoying the calm of this quiet port we were informed that HMS Penelope had been torpedoed and sunk in the Anzio area. That loss struck home because for days we had grown accustomed to her protection. It was sobering to lose HMS Penelope because she had a glorious past. She was knick named, "Pepper Pot Penelope", because she had been subjected to heavy dive-bombing raids during the famous Malta convoys. A combination of luck and ferocious fighting power enabled her to survive but her sides were full of holes. Unfortunately, her luck had run out. Now, we began wondering, when is it going to be our turn? Sometime, who knew when, an enemy shell had our number on it. We lived with that certainty; it was inevitable.

How could we drown our fears? Find lots of Italian wine and women! We didn't have trouble finding wine that we could trust but finding women we could trust was another matter. The risks of getting a case of VD was always in the back of our minds but, thanks to a good stock of condoms, most of us enjoyed our adventures with the willing young women.

Ferrying up and down between Naples and Anzio was beginning to have an effect on our morale. It started to dawn on us that no matter how we approached Anzio, no matter how we tried to break out, the Germans always had the upper hand. We couldn't shake admitting for the time being, we were fighting a battle in which the other side was still strong enough to hurt us. We'd seen Penelope in action. The next week, she was sunk. The haunting outlines of Liberty ships with their funnels barely poking out of the water did nothing to reassure us. All these thoughts were going through our minds as we set off, once again, into that hated place called Anzio.

To make things worse, once again the weather turned nasty. Our ship rolled dangerously from side to side in the high seas. As I explained earlier, an LST was a smooth ride if it was in a pond with no waves or, even better, if it was moored securely in an inner harbor. Because of its wide beam and shallow draft, the ship picked up every ripple and magnified it as we hammered and rolled up the coast. One night, when it was pitch black and I was on duty in the wheelhouse, the ship dropped shuddering into a trough pitching me into the captain. He was a rather righteous person who never swore but the shock was so violent he blurted, "I wish this bitch would stop rolling for a few minutes."

In the early hours of the morning, when the sun had not yet started to rise above the horizon, we saw other ships anchored near us. Among them was the silhouette of the HMS Spartan that had been brought back to the Anzio theatre. She was a brand new A.A. cruiser very much like the Dido. As we came in closer to our anchorage it was eerily quiet. Our air force patrolled, searching for the flash of the big guns hidden in the hills. We dropped anchor and carried on the usual daily routine after breakfast: half the ship's company on first degree of readiness defense station. It was 29 January 1944. During the day we were subjected to the sporadic shelling from enemy guns. The shelling caused no damage but it did crank up our anxiety level. Everyone was afraid.

Just after sunset a sneak air raid began. Before we had time to call for full action station we witnessed an apocalyptic sight. A radio-guided bomb struck HMS Spartan, a beautiful cruiser. She went up with a whoosh and a roar. One of her main ammunition magazines must have been hit. My eyes were glued to the smoke and flames. Fear and anger, not cold, made me shake like a leaf. Briefly I caught myself asking questions which will never be answered, "Why was she anchored so close to the mole?" But before I could carry on with my silent dialogue, another radio-guided bomb hit a Liberty ship carrying ammunition. She was a US merchant ship and luckier than the Spartan. The next day they managed to tow her out to open sea before she blew up.

I was still swearing with all the best of my British Navy foul word vocabulary when it was our turn to be attacked. All our AA guns and the 20mm guns on the armored cars started firing. Even the soldiers on deck put up a terrifying steel umbrella trying to protect us and shoot down anything the Germans threw at us. It was a formidable defense and it almost worked. Through our sheet of hot steel a dive-bomber got lucky. He launched a small bomb that hit us right forward. It exploded under the ramp and doors blowing a huge hole in the ship's hull.

In my capacity as damage control I went forward to try and see how bad the damage was so I could get enough information to be able to report back to the bridge. As I clawed my way through the wreckage I was afraid that the Oerlikon gunners had taken the brunt of the explosion. "Are these guys wounded or killed," I kept wondering? When I got closer to their battle station my doubts vanished. Our brave Newfoundlanders were still firing ferociously. What a relief. Ships can be repaired and returned to life but you can't bring back the dead and our Newfoundlanders were incredibly brave and good men.

Damage on the upper deck was nothing compared to what I figured I'd find below deck. Once below I quickly went over to the tank space to see what could be done. The front of the tank space was a mass of twisted iron. A fire was spreading, possibly out of control, and I immediately called the chief engineer and the first lieutenant on the phone. At least, for the time being, our internal communications were still working. "Powell here. There is a fire on the tank space. We can't fight it, maybe we can contain it but not for long. I need help ... it's spreading towards the paint store." The image of the fire creeping into the paint store galvanized them into action. They raced down with some stokers who started the water pumps.

It was too late. Flames arched and snapped at the bulkheads. Suddenly, as if on cue, the fire began racing toward the first row of lorries that were fueled ready for disembarkation. The captain ordered the soldiers into the six assault barges and ordered them to head for the shore. That was good thinking. They were in our way, kitted up to land and they couldn't do much to help us. In fact, they were in our way and if the fire did get to the lorries, especially those filled with ammunition, the explosions would shred and burn them like paper dolls thrown onto a bonfire. I left the fire fighters to start the three generating sets but only after I isolated all the circuits feeding the forehead equipment. I had to prevent the possibility of short causing even more trouble.

When I got to the engine room the three stokers on duty grabbed me and pumped me. "What's happening," they kept asking? It was easy to understand their fear. I knew there exists in every man a fine line that separates fear from panic. They could easily slip out of control because they were stuck below decks, below water, in a ship laden with fuel and ammunition, a ship that had been hit, a ship that was on fire. I explained, as calmly as I could, what had happened and as I talked I could feel them regaining their self-control. I knew how they felt. During action down in the engine room you can hear and feel vibrations from the exploding shells and bombs. It sounds as if somebody is banging on the ship's sides with a big sledge-hammer. The noise is so loud you think your eardrums are going to explode. You can't leave even if you wanted to because all the hatches and watertight doors are secured shut.

Your mind plays games, bad dark games. Your imagination goes wild. Locked below water you're almost alone. Terror keeps you company. You can't swallow but you can taste fear. "What if the escape hatches warp and can't open? How will anybody know we are locked up here?" When you start to lose control your mind starts slipping its hold on reason. You're a human being and if you are lucky in that kind of a situation, somehow, someway, you don't crack. Some pray; that is what I did. My prayer was simple: "I have always respected everybody; I haven't harmed anyone, so please help me get out of this once again." It must have worked. I am still here and fit.

I did all I could to allay their fears. I promised them that they wouldn't be left below. Either the chief engineer or I would come and get them. My commitment helped them and they calmed down, as much as anyone could stoking boilers in Hell. I felt glad to be on deck and out of the terrible heat and noise coming from the three generating sets. I climbed up to the bridge and reported to the captain who put his hand on my shoulder and said, "Thank you Powell." He looked sad. His face was ashen. Smoke from the deck billowed into the wheelhouse. His eyes were watering and bloodshot. One look at him told me the situation was bad. A lot must have happened fast while I was down in the engine room.

I stood glued to the deck waiting for orders, a dumb man listening, while the captain spoke into the phone. "All right, number one. We are going to sink her near these rocks over there." He motioned off in the dark somewhere. I smelled the flames, burning paint and cordite. "It will be shallow enough to drown the fire. The vehicles on deck will be recovered later on." He was calm and almost matter-of-fact. He took the loudhailer. "All hands prepare for leaving harbor." He then rang the engine room, "stand by" and shouted with the loudhailer, "Let go the chain anchor and let me know when it's cleared," he thundered. He ordered the chief to fill the ballast to make sure that the water level in the tank space would be high enough to drown the fire when we hit the rocks. At that level it would make her sink faster. The order to sink his ship only took a few seconds. We stood gaping at each other, sad and numb, oblivious to the air raid exploding around us.

I looked at the Captain waiting for his next order. In the middle of Hell, he was haggard but he radiated a powerful and reassuring calm. I was going to live. He broke the spell, speaking clearly with conviction and compassion. His courage generated confidence and for a few seconds my fear was replaced with a profound admiration for this remarkable man. Maybe I've got it wrong. This time I am going to die, I thought, but that didn't make sense because my inner voice told me that my captain was going to get all of us out of this mess. He gave another order, quite matter-of-fact like an usher showing you to your seat, 'please sit down'. "Abandon ship. Swim to the beach. Find cover and we'll assemble and start calling out to see who is missing." From the way he sounded, so calm and inviting, I'd have sworn that if we weren't getting shot at his order sounded like he was issuing an invitation to an evening's outing on the beach. Did we hear him correctly? No one had begun to move. Abruptly, in a louder and firmer tone he ordered: "Come on now, every man for himself. God bless you all." I shook the cobwebs out of my head and ran to the radio room looking for my mate Reiner. I found out later that about the same time as I headed up to the radio room the chief engineer was heading down below and led the stokers up on deck.

Reiner sat in his chair staring straight ahead. His eyes were wide open, his mouth was moving and trying to talk but he didn't make sense. He was in shock. "Come on mate. We've got to leave the ship now!" I was yelling at him, mad as hell that he was just sitting there when the ship was sinking. He shook my hand off his arm and said, "John, look at my neck." In the dim light I peered at his neck and saw a small piece of steel sticking out. Neither he nor I will ever know how he got hit. A razor sharp piece of shrapnel had shot through two or three steel bulkheads. There was hardly any blood coming out of the wound. My mind was racing a thousand miles an hour. "I don't think it's that deep." I'm not sure he understood because he looked at me as if I had just told him he was going to be late for mess. "Brace yourself because I'm going to pull it out gently." His eyes caught mine. I began pulling slowly, making sure that I pulled straight back so I wouldn't widen the wound. There was no blood and I felt my first reaction was probably right: it wasn't deep. He was in shock but he managed to get to his feet once I got out the shrapnel splinter. There was no medical kit so I told him to tie his handkerchief around his neck. I grabbed him and shoved him toward the door. He looked at me as if he wasn't sure what to do. I made the decision for both of us: "We're jumping overboard." I think it finally dawned on him that there was no other alternative other than staying and dying. He nodded when I said, "I'll wait for you," and then we groped our way to the edge of the ship.

I was in such a state that I am not sure I can remember how I felt. All I knew was that I was in a hurry to jump overboard. I had completely forgotten that the raid was still on. Shells were still falling around us, not a continuous barrage, but just enough from time to time to make you wince and duck. We both jumped overboard into the water that was only two or three feet from the deck where the vehicles were still piled. Some of our shipmates were still in the water paddling away from the ship as best they could. I was a fast swimmer and I am sure I broke all the speed records even though I still had my shoes on. Maybe my trousers and shirt slowed me down a bit but I moved through the water at a cracking speed.

Half way to the beach I stopped to look around for Reiner to see how he was faring. While I was looking around I remembered that the raid was still on and that realization frightened me right down to my bones. I realized that if a bomb or a shell fell close to us it would be the end. With all the power left in me I shouted to my mate, "Come on, come on! For fuck's sake, get a move on." I turned back toward the beach and managed to stagger ashore and collapsed onto the sand gasping to catch my breath. I rolled over so I could see the others making it through the waves. They were a pitiful sight! Some were bleeding, some had bandages tied around their arms or heads, some wore their life vests; others were clinging to pieces of life buoys or clinging to each other. Some floated into the beach the whites of their eyes probing the sky, others paddled like tired children left too long at the sea's edge.

I tried to stand up but terror had turned the muscles of my legs into wood. I lurched but they were too stiff with fear and fatigue to hold me. Actually, that was lucky. Some soldiers had dug in on the beach where they were manning a 40mm AA gun. They yelled at me and made signs that I understood were meant to keep all of us lying flat, as low a profile as possible. Shells were falling all around us. Man after man, in ones and twos, the rest of the crew made it ashore. They staggered or crawled a few feet onto the sand before collapsing. All we had to do was barely raise our heads to see the sky erupt. We felt the earth shake and shudder every time a shell or bomb landed. Later we learned that we were not the only target the Germans were firing at but with all that was happening, we felt we were their only targets.

I don't know how long we stayed flattened on the sand but it seemed a long time until calm was restored. We didn't budge from our little burrows. As silly as it sounds, we believed the shallow grooves we scooped out of the beach would protect us if a bomb fell in our midst. I don't remember how long it took before we dared look up; we started to move our legs and arms. Slowly, from a crouch to a stoop, we stood up and staggered away from the water's edge. Some soldiers directed us toward a tent that turned out to be a field hospital. But, we weren't allowed to enter. We stood in front of the tent, quite bewildered, waiting for something to happen. A couple of American nurses came out of one of the tents followed by someone we assumed was a doctor. First they talked to our captain who, by now, looked more like a drenched beachcomber than our ship's senior officer.

We were called into an inspection tent in groups of four. The head nurse ordered us to undress so we could be cleaned up by them and, at the same time, given a good look over by the doctor. I'll leave it to your imagination what kind of racy comments our mates came up with as the nurses began cleaning away the oil patches that had collected below our belt lines. The nurses had a good sense of humor. Also, they were armed with alcohol swabs they used to remove the oil. "Now, you behave or this wet swab just might have to take some oil off your little friend." Despite our exhaustion we fell into line and behaved. There are some things even a strong guy can't stand. The doctor did not waste time. When he saw that we were coming back to life he sent us to another tent to be issued dry tunics. We were given G.I. uniforms and transferred to an army staging area to wait for a ship to take us back to Naples.

Our officers began counting us. They moved through the tents and stopped to confer. , Our five brave Newfoundland seamen were missing! "Has anyone seen them?" one officer yelled above our din. Thunderstruck, we looked at each other in total disbelief. Everyone swore they saw them. Weren't they bunched together just before we jumped off the ship? We knew they were good swimmers; they couldn't have drowned. Slowly it began to dawn on us that our valiant Newfoundlanders weren't dead but they were up to something. What? That was a good question and no one had a plausible answer. They hadn't washed up onshore unnoticed and they hadn't gone for a stroll down the beach.

The next day the first officer ordered four of us back aboard. We took one of the assault boats that the army used when our captain ordered them off after we were hit. Trying to think like Newfoundlanders, we went straight to the bridge and the wheelhouse. It was dry up there. The door to the captain's sea cabin was ajar. From the tilting deck we had a good view of what was going on in the landing zone. A groan from inside the cabin cut short our 'sight-seeing'. We opened the door carefully to allow in more light. A heavy roaring snore followed another groan. There was just enough light let in to help us find our 'lost' Newfoundlanders; they were stretched out on deck, blind drunk!

Sobering them up was another matter that required some careful thought. In view of their size and the condition they were in, we knew it was not going to be either easy or free of risk. We yelled at them and then we prodded their ribs with the toes of our boots, making sure to stay well out of reach in case they suddenly roared to life. The smallest Newfoundlander was bigger than the biggest man in our party and we knew what havoc they could wreak with their fists. Slowly, with much cursing, farting, moaning and belching, they began coming around. We stayed well out of their reach because they weren't at all happy about being 'saved.' One of them began talking, more like rambling, while the others joined in to piece together a story that was a tribute to their ingenuity in the face of overwhelming odds.

Only man's imagination limits his ability to turn adversity into opportunity. Our big grumpy Newfoundlanders were geniuses.

They were at different battle stations when the order to abandon ship was given. Keeping a promise they made to each other when they first shipped out together, they regrouped and began to leave the ship together. One of them, we never figured out who the ringleader was, pulled them back into the shadows. They watched us jump overboard. There was so much confusion on the beach they concluded that no one would notice their absence for quite a long time. They had seen and felt the ship grinding into the beach and concluded that it was not going to sink. Another shell might hit it. But, the guys on the beach might get shelled too and this led them to conclude that they were about as safe onboard as they would be stretched out on the beach. With no one else onboard and in no danger of sinking they resolved to rescue the rum stock from a horrible fate: someone else might find it.

Even today, with vivid and painful memories of having been sunk and forced to abandon ship, I cannot help laughing every time I think of these lads. All the rum jars were locked in the spirit room that was located below sea level and flooded. Good seamen, they improvised diving gear out of gas masks left on board. They dove, broke off the lock to the spirit room, and took some rum jars back up to the surface, plus some tinned food and then they treated themselves to a marvelous feast while we lay shivering in the sand. When we stopped laughing we realized we couldn't stay onboard until they were sober enough to be seen by the officers. They could stand, they could talk, but they couldn't walk a straight line and they reeked of rum and sardines. In the end, we got them to cooperate and follow us onboard the assault boat.

An officer was waiting for us on the beach and we followed him into the transit tent. Our captain was waiting for them and he was genuinely relieved to know they were safe but I am sure he did not want to believe what he heard. After he heard them out he gave them a serious dressing down. He had to take a hard line merely in order to maintain discipline but I suspected he was just as amazed at their exploit as we were. Being a good Christian, he kept the story to himself.

Rene Dassac (in collaboration with Patrick K. Robbins)

We waited in the holding area and finally we found out that another LST, an American ship, would take us back to Naples. I forgot its number because my head was spinning. I was glad and sad at the same time. Glad, of course, to get out of the dangerous theatre but at the same time very sad to lose our ship. If I had been offered a choice, I think I would have preferred to stay in the fighting area, on our ship and with our shipmates, instead of returning to the safety of Naples and an uncertain future. Onboard our ship we were close friends and my mates had become a family for want of a better way to describe our relationship. Going back to Naples, leaving our sunken ship, meant that we would be split up. It was clear to all of us what we had lost and it was also clear that no one could foresee how tomorrow, or the next day, or the next, would turn out. Uncertainty and being reassigned to other ships were two big teeth gnawing into our morale while we waited for our ship to fetch us.

We sailed into Naples and we were assigned billets in an old fort, Forto del Ovo. Morale was at rock bottom. All our officers had been sent somewhere else. We were under the command of men we did not know and to whom we were complete strangers. We were forbidden to go ashore and that meant we were cooped up when what we needed was freedom to get out and move around. We were shoved into a big room filled with dozens of wood bunks that looked as if they had been taken out of a warehouse somewhere in pieces and hastily reassembled for us. The bunks were dirty and rickety. Even by standards in our mess, we were too crowded. Only a couple of electric lights had been strung from the ceiling. Whoever was responsible for the lighting never checked his work because our new 'barracks' were in semi-darkness even with the lights turned on. The situation was grim.

We were alone because our officers were assigned to a separate billet. Unlike 1940 when the Belmont's officers had a choice to remain with their crew or leave, this time our officers weren't given a choice. Loyalty was not an issue; it was a matter of organization. We remained, temporarily, under the same command but in separate barracks. I don't know what kind of billet they were assigned to, but ours was awful. Our bunks were infested with thousands of bugs and lice. No sooner would you stretch out than the little bastards would start crawling across your feet and up your pant legs, onto your balls, up your chest, over your hands, onto your face, through your hair and into your ears. They smelled, they bit, and when you killed one, by the time you threw him to the floor another took his place. Sleeping was impossible. We gave up and spent most of the time on the roof. Compared to down below, the roof was paradise because it was like a large terrace overlooking the whole bay of Naples and the crowded city right up to Mount Vesuvius.

One of those nights while we were on the roof scratching and cursing we witnessed a particularly fierce air raid or at least that is what it looked like to us. The cruiser Dido was moored at the foot of the fort and she was firing her five twin barrel 6 inch guns like mad. Some of her shells passed so close to our 'observation deck' that we could feel the whoosh made by shells passing overhead. From the way the battle was going it looked as if our old fort wasn't a target. The enemy could have hit us if they wanted to. But, why waste a bomb? The Germans had spies everywhere. It was pretty safe to assume that one of their operatives had told them that the bugs below were doing more damage to us than their bombs could ever hope to achieve.

Our morale had sunk to a dangerously low level. Some of the guys had managed to get shore leave and had found willing women who sent them back to barracks with good stories but nasty cases of a particularly bad kind of gonorrhea. As soon as they got their first symptom they went on sick call and they came back grim and unsmiling. They were told that their cases were very difficult to cure with regular medicine. Penicillin, the new miracle drug, could not be used because their medical condition was classified as a 'self inflicted wound.' Furthermore, penicillin was in short supply and therefore it was only to be used to treat battlefield casualties. Fair enough, that was something nobody could really argue with but what really got us down was for gonorrhea to be classified as a 'self inflicted wound'. Having VD was awful, but when your medical record showed that you had inflicted a wound on yourself, a true sign of cowardice, that was unfair.

How did the military come up with such a stupid idea? Probably, but this is merely a guess because we'll never know, some soldiers couldn't take any more combat. In order to get sent back from the front lines they made sure they got a case of gonorrhea when they were on R&R. Once their officers found out what the game was, they changed the rules. Maybe the rules were appropriate for the foot soldiers but they shouldn't have been applied to us. What really got us was the way the military wouldn't take our special situation into consideration. No authority seemed to want to acknowledge that we had been blown apart, our ship was sunk, we had managed to survive and we were in limbo waiting for reassignment. We weren't cowards and we didn't deserve to be treated that way.

By now we were truly FED UP and the situation was getting uglier by the day. Tempers were short but we managed to channel our frustration into doing whatever was necessary to get through the day. All we could think of was to find ways to spring us from our army hellhole back to the real world of the Royal Navy in Malta. Most of us had bed bug sores all over our bodies that easily became infected. Some sores were small, but others were large and oozed pus onto our sheets and uniforms. Trying to sleep at night was a nightmare.

We lay sweating in our bunks while our sores oozed. The more they oozed the more the bugs crept out of nowhere to feed and eat away at our bodies. Finally, probably because the situation had become so bad not even the officers in whose temporary custody we were held could deny the fact that we had problems; the medical officer in charge ordered the removal of all our gear to be disinfected. On arrival at the fort we had been issued new Royal Navy uniforms and Royal Navy blankets that were white. Later, we got back our uniforms and blankets but they had turned yellow as if they had been heated over a slow fire, not quite burned but singed yellow, and then returned to us.

Our tempers were short. Despite our self-control frustration started to turn into blind anger. Nasty belligerence was barely kept in check. Definitely a 'them' versus 'us' confrontation was building to a violent explosion point. We had been through too much hell to put up with the kind of treatment we were getting. The medical officer intervened and ordered us to show-up for a general medical check up. Our health was one issue but I think the real issue he had to deal with was how to defuse a situation that was waiting to explode. Anything might have set us off. Right when I thought the whole place was going to blow the wheels of military administration began to turn.

Taulus

Some of our boys were sent to various ships bound for Malta like my shipmate Reiner whom I saw again in Malta a month later. But, coming back to me, when it was my turn for a check-up I got a surprise. The medical officer checked me over, and despite the fact that I was still skinny, I was in pretty good nick for a kid who'd survived what I had gone through. He looked at me and I could tell there was something wrong. "Have you always been stuttering," he asked? You could have knocked me down with a cotton swab. I looked at him surprised and replied, "I ... I ... I have never been tut, stut, stut, stuttering b....b...before, sir." He peered at me, probably to see if I would flinch and not stare back. Our gazes remained locked until he reached over and grabbed a piece of paper and began writing. When he finished he handed it to me. "I think you need a little rest. I'm going to send you to Capri, across the Gulf of Naples, where we have a rest house. You'll be there for a week and then I'm ordering you to be shipped to Malta along with the other men. You'll board a troopship and it will take you back to the Royal Navy." Before I could say anything he called an attendant who told me where to go and how to take the boat to Capri.

I guess we were about a dozen onboard the boat to Capri and I was the only sailor. The rest were soldiers and some of them were in really bad shape. A couple of guys sat staring at the water with unblinking eyes locked wide open in fear. Compared to them, I was in very good shape and I wondered why the doctor had sent me. The thought occurred to me that maybe I looked a bit shell shocked but I wasn't acting goofy and then I started to laugh to myself but quickly stopped when I thought the attendants, big guys who didn't smile, might think I had gone off the deep end and was really quite mad. Somehow I managed to get myself under control but when I thought about it I really wanted to sit down and howl with laughter.

When we got to the rest house an English sister welcomed us. There was no doubt who was in charge; she instructed us on how she wanted us to behave. The house rules and regulations were simple and strict. Inside there was to be a minimum amount of noise, we must not talk loudly, really no noise of any sort, just maintain calm so we could rest. Above all, do nothing to upset the other patients.

We were shown to different rooms. In my room there were a dozen beds. My bed was between a young Polish commando (4th battalion) and a corporal of the Welsh Fusilier regiment. The Pole was nineteen years old. He had managed to leave Warsaw a couple of years before. Despite the fact that Poland was completely overrun by Nazis who held the country in an iron grip occupation, he managed to cross a large part of occupied Eastern Europe on foot. His saga was an extraordinary epic as he wound his way slowly to Palestine where he joined the Free Polish Army. He had been wounded on the Casino front and something snapped, not a muscle, not an organ, but something in his brain went.

He and his group were out on patrol and they ambushed a small group of Germans. He was shot twice on the thigh. Somehow, he never told me how, he managed to grab a German soldier and attack him with his trench knife and he began stabbing and shredding his enemy. His mates heard him screaming Polish names but the names didn't mean anything to them. Who knows, maybe they were names of friends and family who were victims of the Nazis? By the time they got to him he had finished off the German. In another world the Pole could have been on a picnic. He sat on the German's body calmly using it as a bloody cushion. He was eating an apple and humming. Obviously, he needed time to recover and that is why they sent him to Capri. From what I later heard, he actually did recover and returned to his unit.

The Welshman was another story. He was a shell shock case; the least sudden noise, a door slamming for instance, made him jump with fear. He was genuine but I had my doubts about another case, a soldier who I think was pretending to be mad in order to be sent back home. Every morning a duty sister would come and give each of us a few sweets. This guy was very quiet and calm. He took the sweet from the paper, set the sweet aside, and then ate the paper!

Admittedly, I had my problems but I was completely lost in this ward. Not only was I the only seaman there, the mental conditions of the others were having an adverse effect on me. Instead of healing, I thought I was really slipping off the deep end. Finally, I was able to see the attending doctor and I told him that if I stayed there any longer I was going to sink into a deep depression. My problem was minor compared to the big problems the other guys had. My argument must have worked because two days later I was on my way back to Naples. I can't remember when I stopped stuttering.

I was sent back to the old fort where some of my shipmates were still waiting to be shipped to Malta. After what I had seen on Capri, the fort didn't look too bad! During the period I spent waiting for my ship I went to see a couple of our mates who were in a field hospital outside Naples. They could walk so we went to the cemetery. Our mates showed us some open graves. According to the cemetery attendant, Germans had visited these graves and had taken all the gold teeth, rings or any jewelry left with the bodies. And it wasn't only Germans pillaging graves. I had heard of similar cases of vandalism in Sicily where the robbers, certainly only Sicilians because they were so dirt poor, even stole the boots off the German's soldiers and left their bare feet sticking out of their temporary graves. Naples and Sicily weren't any different in my mind. Only the robbers changed names and motives.

Our mates were in fair shape but as soon as we got there we started hearing rumbling noises. Was it coming from heavy guns on the front? We started looking around for some kind of shelter. In the center of the cemetery there was a church and every time the locals thought the Germans had broken through the front they went into the church to sleep and wait for further instructions. The rumbling got louder. From the sound of it we should have been moving because the 'artillery' was heavy. We decided to head back to the comparative safety of the fort.

On our way out to the coast we found out what was causing the rumbling. Hundreds of people with all sorts of transport were streaming past going in the opposite direction of where we were headed. Some led donkeys; others rode their poor skinny beasts to safety. The refugees fled as if a Panzer column was closing fast. We couldn't speak Italian and they couldn't speak French but through sign language we managed to ask one question they understood. "What's all the panic about," we signed. "Vesuvius, Vesuvius," they shouted and waved frantically in the air. From where we were standing we could not see smoke coming out of the mouth of the volcano. None of us spoke Italian. How could we understand why they were so upset?

Heading back to Naples we saw what a disaster the eruption caused not only for the inhabitants of the affected area but also for the city. Naples had enough problems. Now, with panic-stricken refugees streaming into the city it was almost too much for the military and civilian authorities to handle. A wind blew thick ash laden clouds over the city and out to Capri. For a moment I thought of those poor blokes in the rest home and wondered what was going through their tortured minds?

In Naples I met a French military police sergeant. He was part of a motorcycle unit. The Americans had given him a great big beautiful Harley Davidson motorcycle and he was proud of his machine. It was sort of funny when you stop to think about it. Here we were in the middle of a war and this guy was putting around on his machine as if he was the Lord of the Manor. He didn't have a fat head but he had an interesting story. He was an Alsatian and after the fall of France Alsace was annexed to Germany. As a consequence, he was forced to serve in the German army. In his mind he was French but in uniform, after the annexation, he was a German soldier, and as it turned out, one of the few to have survived the eastern front in Russia. His stories about life on the front in the winter were horrible and it was easy to understand how happy he was when his regiment was transferred to the Italian front.

As soon as he got to Italy he realized that he was 'close to home.' He began scheming of ways he could desert and join the French army. He had to act quickly and carefully because he could be shot either by his German mates or by the Allies who would certainly consider him to be, at least at first sight, another German soldier.

Finally, he got a break. His unit was moved to the Monte Casino front where he was put in charge of a ten-man section. Their task was to move as close to the enemy lines as possible and probe their perimeter defenses in order to pass fresh field intelligence back to the German army intelligence units. They moved carefully because they knew there were allied troops ahead of them. Suddenly they heard voices but they were too far away to know whether they were Polish or French. He knew he had to act, to move forward but not draw fire either from the allies or the men in his unit. He chose a spot where his men could hide without being seen and he ordered them to remain quiet no matter what happened. The lines were fluid; they could easily draw fire from friend or foe. Whoever it was, they'd shoot to kill. "I'm going ahead to scout out who these guys are." Someone whispered, "Who do you think they are?" The Alsatian shrugged, "Either French or Poles and we need to know."

Moving slowly through the underbrush he crept from rock to rock, rock to tree, using every bit of natural cover he could find. He managed to creep close to a position where he could listen but not be seen. His heart jumped, "They're French." He continued to listen to make sure his mind wasn't playing tricks. No, they were French, no doubt about it! He heard different accents and knew there was no way this allied unit was a trap. They were his countrymen. To stand-up and call out to them was to invite instant death. If the French weren't forewarned they'd shoot him. After all, he was in German uniform, carrying a German weapon, in a place where the allies knew the Germans were probing. Each of his few options was risky but he began yelling.

First in a low anxious voice, then louder and more determined, pitching his voice so the French soldiers would listen and maybe, if he was lucky decide not to shoot first and ask questions later. "Don't shoot me, I am French," he began and then he said, "Je suis alsacien, malgres moi incorporé de force dans l'armée Allemande." No one moved on the other side. His plea was met by silence from the other side of the bushes. He heard his blood thundering in his ears. A voice replied from somewhere he could not see. "Come forward with your hands up." As if to make sure there was no misunderstanding the voice continued. "Come alone or else we'll shoot every one of you." He dropped his weapon and rose slowly to his feet. He stretched his arms stretched high over his head so that whoever had him in his sights could see that he was unarmed.

An allied soldier in French army uniform stepped from behind a tree, eyed him carefully, and stuck out his hand. Other French soldiers slipped into the little clearing and again he shook hands, this time with every man in the unit. "Are you alone," their leader asked? The Alsatian steadied his voice and replied. "No, I've got ten men

Rene Dassac (in collaboration with Patrick K. Robbins)

stashed in the bush behind me. I've left them in a safe place and they're waiting for me to come back." Rapidly he told the French unit leader what they were doing. "I've left them in a safe place and if we swing behind their position we can take them without firing a shot."

At first he thought he wasn't making sense so he continued. "They've gone through Russia together, they don't want to fight, they're good guys, and they sure don't want to die." And then he remembered telling the small French unit, "I can't stab them in the back. You've got to trust me. We can take them prisoner." The French shrugged. War is unpredictable. Who knows, could this be a trap. The French sergeant weighted what the Alsatian was saying. It sounded reasonable but was he taking his men into a trap? For what seemed like an eternity to the Alsatian the sergeant thought about his alternatives. There was something genuine and convincing about the French speaking German soldier who pleaded for his men. "D'accord," the sergeant snapped.

Spread out to avoid a possible ambush, they followed the unarmed 'German soldier' back to where his men were hiding. Before the Germans knew what was happening they were surrounded and taken prisoner. No shots were fired. The French force acted firmly and fairly and were compassionate toward the German soldiers who a few moments ago were prepared to kill them.

Hands behind their heads, the German POW's marched off to another future than the one they might have thought of that morning when they set off on their patrol. The war was over for them. In the meantime, their Alsatian sergeant was taken to an intelligence unit for debriefing. After being debriefed he was reintegrated into the French army. Listening to his story, and in view of what I had been through, I couldn't help but realize how lucky I had been compared to him.

It was early May 1944 and we were getting tired of waiting in Naples. At last the long waited for troop ship arrived. It was a French ferry liner called 'Ville D'Oran'. Before the war she was on the Marseille - Algiers run. We assembled on the dock, a few remaining hands from our ship and seamen from other ships. We left with mixed feelings. On the one hand we were relieved to be out of Naples and going somewhere and on the other, every man was anxious about the future.

Taulus

It is hard to say whether I was war-weary or merely fed up. I was coping reasonably well with the destruction around me and I was grateful to still be in one piece but I was tired of not belonging somewhere. My ship and my mates were history and except for knowing I was going to Malta, I didn't have the vaguest idea what was in store for me. Of course, I wasn't the only bloke who felt this way. There must have been thousands who were thinking exactly like me.

Nature has a strange way of not letting you wallow in self-pity. As soon as we cleared harbor the captain opened up the engines and we sped ahead at over 25 knots. When we reached the open sea between Sicily and Sardinia we ran into very strong winds and had a rough sea that lasted all the way to Malta. She may have been a liner but in that sea she was just another bucking boat. Even among the ship's crew there was a lot of sea sickness. By the time we sailed into the calm waters of Valetta harbor most worries about what the future might bring had vanished. All we wanted to do was get off that ship and enjoy the strange sensation of being able to walk without having to hold onto a railing or a guy rope.

At disembarkation all the Royal Navy personnel were sent to St. Angelo which was the local transit barracks. It was like coming home, wherever that might be. Immediately I felt as if I had always been there. The navy routine, our life, took over. I felt better because I was back in a world I knew. Another medical check up, revaccinated for the third time in six months, they gave us brand new uniforms and then some of us were drafted to a unit called a NAN. I don't think we were told what the letters meant, or if we were, I forgot but what was important was the likelihood that we were going to be sent to Italy again, this time on the east coast near Bari.

All those included in the NAN were called to report to the parade ground. I had never seen any of the other members of the NAN unit. One of the officers explained that we were going to begin a course of commando style close combat! I couldn't believe it. I was a sailor, not some fancy army guy running around with camouflage netting, stealing through the night to slit a sentry's throat. I asked one of the P.O. torpedo men like me, "What the fucking hell are we doing in this lot?" He shrugged, "I wish I knew," he replied. He was of no use but he continued, "from the buzz I've heard, we are going to follow the Eighth Army along the coast and work with the army engineers to repair ports so that cargo ships can land." And I had to be a commando for this? At times, the military doesn't make sense, I thought.

After suffering through bloody hell in their commando course, with every bone and muscle in my body either aching or bruised, so damned tired it hurt to breathe, we were told that NAN was disbanded! From spooking around the training area, climbing cliffs and learning how to fight with our hands, elbows, heads, knees, anything that could be turned into a weapon, we returned to a routine that was as comforting as it was boring: peeling potatoes and onions, cleaning anything that was either dirty or thought to be dirty, scrubbing down the walls and floors of an old stone fort that had probably been a barracks for the Crusaders!

From what I saw of buildings in Malta, I realized why the Maltese had not really suffered too much during the blitz. Every building was made of hard stone and it had been designed to last centuries. German bombs managed to damage some buildings but few were completely destroyed. In addition to the buildings and stone outcroppings, the contours of the land flowed into natural defense positions and trenches. Combined, these were formidable obstacles for any enemy who decided to land troops and fight to take control of the island.

Most of us were waiting to be repatriated to the U.K. We'd been away from home for more than two years and that meant we qualified for home leave. In addition, we'd been sunk which was also in our favor because we moved to the top of the rotation list. But Lady Luck was not shining on me. It was June 1944 and the second front had begun in Normandy. All shipping into and out of the United Kingdom was temporarily cancelled. I understood the logic but nevertheless, I wanted to go home. I'd seen enough to know that no one had a guarantee that he would make it through the war alive or, for that matter, in one piece.

I saw Reiner before he was transferred to Algiers. He survived his shrapnel wound and he even laughed about it but we didn't waste time talking about the past because we didn't have time to waste. All we had was time to say goodbye and wish each other good luck. We had been mates for a long time; when he left it was like losing someone in my family. When he walked away he waved and my spirits sagged. Good friends are hard to make and he was a good friend, someone I could talk to, someone who could share shore leaves and laugh.

I went ashore with some of the lads who had been with me in the NAN. They were good guys. We used to drink a lot and spend a lot of time in the Maltese cabarets. In one cabaret there were two homosexuals with a drag act. They wore women's evening dresses and were always good for laughs. One was called Bobbie and the other Sugar. Someone told me that Bobbie was originally from Gibraltar and had actually been a boxer! They were so well dressed and made up that they could easily be mistaken for women, and rather good looking too! Although my shipmates and I did not have any appetite for that kind of 'woman' we used to talk with them because they were so funny. But there was a fine line between being friendly and being familiar. Usually, they were easy and not pushy but, sometimes, they would mistake our friendly attitude for a proposition. We didn't want sex; all we wanted to do was joke and talk to them. Once 'the girls' understood our sexual orientation we got along famously.

One evening one of them, either Bobbie or Sugar, I can't remember which, was dancing with a drunken stoker. They lurched around the floor when, for some unknown reason, the stoker gave his 'woman' a hearty slap on 'her' bare back and raised red welts. The poor 'woman' broke down and began to cry, sobbing like a girl who had been hit and humiliated. It was pitiful to watch. My mate and I called 'her' over and tried to comfort 'her'. I still can't remember whether it was Bobbie or Sugar who got hit but Bobbie never forgot my mate's kindness. After that, when we went to their cabaret, 'she' always made sure to come over and greet us and offer us a drink.

One night, we had really overspent. We paid our bar bill but when we got down to the jetty no one had any money to pay for a rowboat to take us to St. Angelo. A long, loud, and quite drunken discussion ensued. In the end we resigned ourselves to going back to the cabaret and asking Bobbie to loan us ten shillings. She was playing the piano, surrounded by cigarette smoke, laughter and joking sailors. Not missing a beat, she looked up and said, "Certainly dearies but on one condition." The music stopped and everyone could hear her voice. Puckering her heavily rouged lips she murmured, "Ten shillings and a little kiss from each of you, you sassy young devils." Much to our disgust, she got her kiss, the place roared with laughter and we tottered back to the quay. True to our word, the next day Bobbie got her ten shillings.

Lots of new personnel were arriving from the U.K. so we thought that it would not be too much longer before we were rotated on home leave. I was almost running out of luck. The end of our unpleasant surprises was not on the cards. Three of us were called to the drafting office. I showed up with a petty officer engine room artificer and a radio rating. All of us had been overseas well over two years and two of us had been sunk. We stepped into the office in high spirits because we obviously thought that we were being called to board a ship due to go home. Again, no lucky draw was waiting for us. We were told to report to HM submarine Sickle. Fortunately the drafting office was in a stone building because we raised merry hell with the drafting officer. He heard us out and told us there was nothing he could do but we could take up our gripe with the drafting skipper.

A lorry was detailed to take us to our submarine. We grabbed our bags and hammocks and set off for the submarine depot. On the way I kept thinking, "For years I've been trying to blow up submarines and now I've got to serve on one!" I was in a foul mood when we reported to the captain. He was fair and heard us out. "Surely, there is a mistake somewhere. We're due to go home." He listened and let us blow off steam. "I understand your feelings and as far as I am concerned you are to stay onboard for only one patrol and when we return I will release you." Fair, but not good enough for us. We kept pleading our case and I think we argued so well that, in the end, he said he could not do anything about our assignment. "I understand your feelings", he concluded. We were dejected. "Now, let me give you some friendly advice." We listened while he suggested that our best course of action was to request permission to see the fleet padre and get him to intervene on our behalf. We saluted and raced across town to see the padre.

He listened to us, asked some good questions, and then told us to wait. He came back smiling. We'll never know whom he saw or what he said but he got results. A few hours later the three of us were back in St. Angelo. He saved our lives. Three weeks after our meeting with the padre I read that HMS Sickles was reported missing. Later I learned that she disappeared in waters off Greece, the Dedocanese. Her last patrol would have been our first and only patrol onboard the HMS Sickles.

At last, after almost giving up hope that it would happen, the day came when a few of us were called to the drafting office. Orders were cut for us to join an armed mine laying cargo bound for the U.K. I had a strange feeling. For the first time in longer than I dared remember I was happy. I caught myself realizing that it was strange to feel happy. It was as if I was looking at myself and wondering, "What the hell is going on?" For years I had known fear, heard guns roar, saw bombs dropping out of the sky and bodies blown to bits, lived in close cramped quarters, made good friends, survived, which is more than a lot of guys could say, and now I was going home and I felt happy. And feeling happy meant feeling strange but it was good to feel that way.

For months Edith and I had been writing about getting married and now I also had that to look forward to in addition to getting off Malta. It was hard to come to grips with the fact that maybe I could start to think about my future once the war was over. No one knew when that day would come but nearly everybody I knew honestly felt the war was somehow drawing to a close. The Germans couldn't hold out forever. On the allied side we had too much weight, men, weapons, and willpower for them to continue to resist us. All in all, I felt great. There was another world out there, a world without war and I was heading into it, still young and fit.

Thinking about France troubled me because I did not think that France would be liberated so quickly, especially after having seen how slowly and painfully we pried Italy loose from the Germans. And, to be honest, I wasn't really too sure what had been happening in the U.K. during the last two years. Yes, I had been in touch with the U.K. via Edith but we were talking about other matters, things that interested young lovers. What was happening out on the high street escaped me; I had no clue what to expect. My thoughts were swirling. It was normal. All I really kept thinking about was the leave I'd get when I finally got back to the U.K. Nothing else really mattered although I did try and follow what was happening now that the Normandy beaches were secure and the allied forces had begun to move inland toward Paris. The ban on convoys bound for the U.K. was probably lifted because the Channel had been secured and we could sail in relative safety.

When we boarded our ship we were told that we were bound for South Shield near Newcastle. I was in a daze. For someone who has a mind for details, I cannot remember the name of the ship and I cannot remember anything about the trip home. I boarded in Malta and disembarked in the U.K. In between, I was a passenger but sort of a working passenger. She flew a white ensign; we were members of the crew. This meant we stood watch and were assigned chores in the daily cleaning routine. But beyond those two recollections, I really can't remember anything until we reached South Shield. Once on land we were sent to our respective port divisions by rail. I took the train to Portsmouth Victory Barracks. After everything I had gone through I was glad to see that the barracks had not changed in the two years that I had been away. The same gray walls, the neat footpaths, the crisply lettered signposts, the uniforms, and the flags were still there. Nothing had changed.

I reported to the duty officer, was given two weeks leave, and left immediately for Wolverhampton where I stayed at the Rowan house. I saw Edith every day and although I wanted more, all I got was kisses. Events in one's life almost look absurd when you have the advantage of hindsight. Looking back, I can't help but realize how bloody stupid and green I was to think that my romance by mail would turn into something physical when I finally got back. Looking at our relationship perhaps from another angle, writing to her and getting her letters were my one link with another world, a saner world and a gentler world that I desperately wanted to be a part of no matter what it took.

Her letters and my dreams were all that linked me to that other world. The dream world she and I created on paper was different than the reality of living together with my shipmates onboard a rolling and pitching LST. As long as we wrote, I lived in a cloud and swallowed everything she said as if it were a bible truth. I can't remember much of those two weeks because I think I had to block them out of my mind. There might have been some pleasant moments but if they happened they happened so long ago that I cannot, and really do not, want to remember.

At the end of two weeks I returned to Portsmouth. While I was in Wolverhampton many Royal Navy Frenchmen had arrived in the barracks. I joined this group and we were told that we would be given forty five days compassionate leave as soon as it could be organized to ensure our safety back in France. It was late August and Paris had been liberated but the Jerries were still putting up bitter resistance in northeast France and parts of Belgium. When we assembled on the parade ground I looked around to see if there was anyone I knew or recognized. It had been a long time since I had been in the company of so many of my fellow countrymen and surely, somewhere in this group, there had to be someone I knew.

We recognized each other at about the same time. I went over and greeted Sargent, a mate I had not seen since 1940. He had been drafted to a cruiser, HMS Bervick, and from the sounds of it, he too had gone through some rough times. Almost as if to get rid of a heavy burden, he told me of another Frenchman with an incredibly sad story. When his ship was sent for a big refit, he was paid off, and put into a pool for reassignment to another ship. He was attached to his ship and he told his mates, but not his skipper, that he did not want to leave. After all, he explained, his ship was his only home and his shipmates were his only family. No one took him seriously. He committed suicide by jumping from the mast into the funnel of the ship. His death shocked everyone, even his captain who was dumfounded when he finally found out why the young man had taken his life. "If only he had come to me, I'd have kept him," he said to a group of seamen after the funeral. "On the contrary, he was a good seaman, really, very well thought of by everyone."

Such a waste and put into context it makes one begin to realize how deeply attached men become to their shipmates and their ship. Hardships and suffering onboard are shared experiences that affect ratings and officers. Take any major event, a storm, an attacking enemy dive bomber, a fire onboard, those are events that don't just happen to one person, they are events that involve everyone. To be cut loose from one's ship, in the case of the young seaman, was to be cut loose from his reason for living. Especially in war, it is not unusual that a man's ship becomes his life.

*****

Waiting dragged on forever but I guess it wasn't too long until the day came when we were called to the drafting office and given orders allowing us to travel to France to see our families.

I found Sargent and he asked me to come with him at least as far as Paris. "I don't know, it's more hope than anything else, but I think I can find my uncle and sister." He shrugged the way people do when they are talking to you but really they are talking to themselves and they aren't sure that what they are saying really makes any sense. "My uncle is a communist, a real hard case, and knowing him, he must have got himself in trouble with the Germans." He sort of laughed and I tried to imagine what the uncle must look like, that is, if he was still alive. Not really listening to him, I began to wonder what I would find once I got 'home'. My sisters and brother, my aunts and uncles, nieces and nephews, where were they and what condition were they in? Did they survive the bombings, the food shortages, the Gestapo? It had been so long. Did I still have a family?

We took the ferry from Newhaven to Dieppe where we transferred to an army lorry that drove us to Paris. Going through the countryside gave us a firsthand glimpse at the extent of the destruction that had taken place since the Allied landing. Whole villages had been reduced to rubble, isolated farm houses, or what was left of them, had been blown apart, ancient oaks uprooted as if they were once child's toys stuck upside down in the mud. No one talked much and as we got closer to Paris I started to get that familiar sensation in the pit of my stomach that told me not to expect too much when we got to Lyon. Fear and sadness welled up inside me and I caught myself saying, "This isn't what I want to see." But as bad as it looked, I also had to admit that the Germans were gone and I was going home. Happiness had been replaced by foreboding. I knew that I had gone through a lot and surely, I kept telling myself, "You can get through this too."

In order to travel we had been given a note to show to the RTO in the railway stations. For me it was just another piece of bloody paper to carry around and I didn't bother to read it and study the details. Whenever someone asked for my note I whipped it out and much to my amazement, I was immediately given a first class ticket.

In Paris we were taken to the Grand Hotel that had been requisitioned as a transit hotel for British armed forces. At the reception we were again given more instructions and recommendations. The receptionist said, "If you have any trouble, all you have to do is call in to the nearest allied centre with this paper." He waved it in our faces as if to make his point that what he was holding was a magic wand that made the difference between comfort and a cold billet somewhere else. Sargent and I were assigned to the same bedroom, a big comfortable room that was a lot better than the B&B's we were used to in the U.K. For the record, the next time you are in Paris go to the center of the city to the Place de l'Opera and you can see the Grand. It hasn't changed too much since we stayed there sixty years ago!

We had a wash and shave and then we went down in the dining hall that was under the supervision of British troops. We didn't let the incongruity of being in a French restaurant under the control of British mess officers bother us at all. When the steward came to our table to take our order he was amazed to see two sailors. "What's the navy doing in Paris? Aren't you a little far from your ship," he asked half jokingly? Looking around, he was right. We were the only sailors in the dining hall and we stood out in a sea of army green uniforms. "We're in transit, or at least I am," I explained. Sargent was staying in Paris and I told him that I was going to Lyon. The waiter frowned. "I know you probably haven't been in touch with your family but they're really short of food down there." I don't recall being shocked but what he told me confirmed some of my private fears. In the coming days I was going to find a Lyon far different from the city I had left before the war. "Let me help you out," he said. "Get a kit bag or a suitcase and meet me in the pantry after the meal and I'll give you whatever foodstuffs I can spare."

After lunch I waited until the hall cleared out. My new friend the waiter scooped up nearly everything edible he could lay his hands on and dropped it into my bag. I lugged the bag back upstairs and stashed it an old armoire and locked it with a huge clumsy key. The lock was impressive and foreboding but a kid could have picked it open with a lollypop stick. There was a fortune 'locked' behind those doors and I felt good knowing that if I did find my family, I would not return to Lyon empty-handed. And, since I didn't know what I was going to find he explained that depending on the outcome, if I needed more help there was an RAF camp at the airport. He told me that I could probably tap into their stores too. There was no way I could thank him enough. A total stranger, he reached out to another, and gave a helping hand by helping himself to the Crown's larder!

The next morning Sargent and I walked to the building in Montmartre where he thought his uncle might still be living. I don't think he was too optimistic and, as we walked up to the four floor building, he grew quieter. He rang the bell. A concierge came to the door. He was an old man whose entire life had probably been spent opening the door, answering questions, and cleaning the building. Sargent introduced himself. "I am looking for my uncle," he said in French. The concierge looked at us in surprise to see two English sailors speaking excellent French. He regained his composure and replied, "He could never keep his mouth shut. One day the Gestapo came and took him away and we never saw him again." He spoke about the event as if it was a daily occurrence, neither significant nor insignificant, just one of those events that happened all the time during the occupation. "And what about my sister," Sargent asked? The old man thought for a moment before replying. "I think, but I am not sure because I have not seen her for a long time, I think she works for a doctor?" "Where?" "Not too far from here," he replied and he gave us an address. We thanked him and walked to the doctor's office that in fact, was not far away.

Sargent rang the bell to the doctor's office and the doctor came to the door. Again Sargent introduced himself and stated his business. The doctor smiled and stepped aside so that we could enter. He led us to a waiting room and called out a woman's name without telling her why she was wanted. "Oui, I'm coming," she replied as she walked into the room where we were standing. She stopped at the door, looked at

Sargent, burst into tears and threw herself into his arms. I was happy for them but felt that my presence really wasn't needed. The doctor patted her on the back as if to calm her. "Now, now, I'm sure you have a lot to tell each other and this is not the place." He told her to take off the rest of the day and he accompanied us to the door.

I started to leave. They were talking faster than I've ever heard two people talk anywhere and in any language. Theirs wasn't really a dialogue. It was more like a torrent of word bursts, laughs and sobs, while they clutched each other.

Before I left I managed to get in a couple of words. "If I don't see you tonight I won't see you until we get back to the U.K." Sargent looked at me. He was smiling, laughing, almost crying. "Tomorrow I am leaving for Lyon." He nodded his head and we shook hands. We really couldn't talk because of the lumps in our throats.

As I walked back to the hotel I kept telling myself that Sargent's finding his sister had to be a good omen. "If he could find his family", and my thoughts started to race toward Lyon, "There's no reason I can't find mine." I was absolutely sure of myself and absolutely convinced that my search would end well.

Before going back to the hotel I walked to the Gare de Lyon station to find out what time a train was leaving for Lyon and whether or not I had to make a reservation. The station was fairly busy and I spent a few minutes looking for the RTO. Two officers were on duty, one British and one American. The British officer looked startled. "Hello, what's the navy doing here?" They were good humored and frankly curious so I told them my story. They listened intently and, sensing my nervousness, they immediately put me at ease. They handed me a special pass and a ticket that allowed me to travel anywhere in first class! I wasn't accustomed to train travel in France because all my travel had been in the U.K so I was amazed when they told me to be sure to come to the station at least three hours before the scheduled departure at 2200. They even told me that an escort would take me to the special allied army carriage. "Why so early," I asked because their instructions didn't make any sense. One of them chuckled and I think this wasn't the first time someone had asked the same question. ""Wait and see. Tomorrow, you'll find out why."

Rene Dassac (in collaboration with Patrick K. Robbins)

Fair enough. I learned an important lesson long ago: in the military it's useless to question instructions that don't make sense. As an afterthought, the duty officer instructed me not to give my seat to anyone as long as the train was in the station. I snapped a crisp Royal Navy salute and turned to leave. The British officer called out after me, "Good luck to you and don't forget that if you have any kind of trouble just report into the nearest allied office or consulate." I couldn't imagine that I'd get into any trouble but, nevertheless, it was good to know that if I did have a problem I knew where I could get help.

I went straight back to the hotel. Winter had officially started and it was cold and windy. Christmas was a few days away and no one was in a festive mood. Too close for comfort, the Germans were dug in just across the border in Belgium and the allied troops were stalled. No matter where I stopped I could hear people, ordinary people who had survived the occupation, talking about another big German offensive. There was even worry that they would break through the allied lines and drive toward Antwerp.

I had completely forgotten about the German threat because I had been locked into another world for a few days. My world was a place where I could start thinking again about my family and what kind of a life I might lead once the war was finally over and we didn't have to worry about bombs and invasions. Suddenly, it dawned on me! If the Jerries swung back through Paris and caught me before I could escape, I'd be in a messy fix. As long as I could pass myself off as a Frenchman I was in fine shape but if somebody decided to turn me into the Germans as a Brit pretending to be French, I was in serious trouble. That realization bothered me as I walked across Paris. I needed company, and fortunately, I found myself in front of a café that was full of civilians and soldiers of all nationalities.

I started talking to a British NCO who, in the course of our conversation, sounded as if he 'knew' what was going on. In retrospect I now understand that all he was doing was passing on well-worn rumors, and probably adding a bit here and there. According to him, the allied front had been weakened because the Americans, mostly Negro troops, had stolen so much petrol to sell on the black market that the allied equipment on the front could not advance. "We're paralyzed," he droned. "It's got so bad that some of the guys they've caught have been court martialed and sentenced to death." I found him hard to believe, it was typical barroom bullshit, but I didn't dismiss him out of hand because I had heard similar harrowing stories since coming to Paris. Lorry fuel tankers were disappearing. It was hard to believe but the facts were there for anyone to see: too many lorries vanished, too often. Somewhere, there was a serious problem.

Listening to him ooze doom-and-gloom wasn't what I needed. I was edgy because I was no longer in my element onboard a ship with my mates and my routine. I was in the middle of Paris, in the middle of a civilian world that was alien to me. While he droned on about the front and the losses the allies were taking, I guess my heart started sinking, because I was not listening to him. Perhaps I had remained quiet for too long because he finally said, "It's bad, but you've got to realize that the allies have stabilized the situation." I looked up at him. Surely, he saw how worried I was. He continued, "We've come too far not to go on and I think we'll start pushing the Germans back in just a few more days." How in the hell would he know, I thought to myself? Certainly, if he was in a position to know what was going on, he was talking too much. Maybe it was the beer, maybe he too needed someone to talk to, but when he said he felt the allies were going to be able to move forward I started to feel better. "Nice talking to you. Good luck," I said and stepped out into the cold afternoon.

No one loitered on the sidewalk. The wind had come up and a wet cold cut through my winter coat. As I walked back to the hotel, hunched against the wind, I kept telling myself over and over, "The bastards are going to lose; the bastards are going to lose." I'd earned the right to talk to myself, to listen to my inner voices and to trust them. No, I was not going to give up hope and give into despair. Germany's defeat had to be sometime soon. The hell of war couldn't go on forever. I had that feeling deep inside, as if another rib was trying to grow through my chest; I called it bloody-minded optimism. "They'll lose, I know they'll lose," I kept telling myself but I also knew that the final stages of the war would not be easy. A lot of hard fighting still lay ahead of us. No matter how optimistic I felt, the reality of more fighting was getting to me, grinding at my optimism when I walked into the lobby of the Grand.

After I made sure that everything I had packed in the armoire was still there, I went downstairs and found the steward who had given me all the food. I needed someone to talk to; he had the time. He gave me a good description of what I was going to see and he reminded me to be vigilant because there were a lot of ex-collaborators who had still not been rounded up. That wasn't any real news because before we left the U.K. we had been briefed thoroughly. Above all, we were told, do not use your French name. "In all circumstances, act as a British service man and continue to play the role you adopted years ago." That was sound advice. The last thing I wanted to do was to get caught in a situation in which I had to justify who I was. For years, I had been John Powell, and that wasn't going to change just because I returned to France.

He had to go back to work but he left me with my head spinning. Things were beginning to move fast now and I was full of questions, questions that weren't necessarily followed by answers. My mind started to play 'what if' tricks and it almost drove me nuts. "What am I going to find?" Many of those questions I had asked earlier but somehow I was able to put them aside. Now they came flooding back. "What if my family had become followers of the Vichy government?" After all, it had happened all the time and why should my family be an exception? I didn't think it was possible, but, it could have happened and I would not have known. The more questions I asked, the more I became convinced that I would not be able to sleep so I went down to the bar and had a few drinks to help me apply brakes to my thoughts. Even after a fair number of drinks questions kept pouring out of dark corners of my mind. Later that evening alcohol took over and I staggered upstairs and fell into bed in a deep sleep.

The next morning I woke up and lay in bed planning my day. My train didn't leave until late in the evening; that meant I had an entire day to spend before going to the station. I began by brushing and cleaning my uniform so that I would be as smart as possible when I traveled. That took a little time and I concentrated on the uniform instead of asking myself questions. I took my kit bag and suitcase down to the luggage room and stepped out into the cold morning air. As I strolled down the boulevards I stopped to examine the buildings and they didn't look as if there had been an occupation. After four months of freedom the municipal authorities had done a lot to clean up this central part of the city. Time dragged and I kept walking to kill time.

I went to the Champs Elysées where I had marched in the 14th of July parade in 1939 just before the war broke out. I stood on the curb and reveled in flashbacks of another time and another world. I could see myself clearly, even when we were in ranks waiting to begin our march down that glorious avenue. The crowd was wildly patriotic and, to a man, we were caught up in their enthusiasm. We were proud to be serving our nation. I even remembered a woman pushed her way out of the crowd lining the curb and gave me a bottle of wine. I am not sure what happened to it but I know it didn't accompany me on parade past the President! Five years later, five short and awful years, and we had begun another era. I wasn't sure I understood what was going on. While I stood staring into my memories lining the Champs Elysees, I realized people were staring at me. I was an unusual sight, a British sailor, and they gawked. No one came up to me. That was fine; I didn't try to talk to anyone. 'Best to keep my distance', I thought. My feet hurt after all the walking and I returned to the hotel for a rest before going to the station.

It felt good to visit Paris but I was tired of the city and I wanted to move on and find my family. I took the metro to go to the train station. As usual, the metro was crowded but with my kit bag on my shoulder and my suitcase I had no difficulty pushing my way into a carriage. And, in order not to raise other passenger's tempers, I laughed and swore in English. The sound of English, my slight stature weighed down with two big bags, must have looked funny because people around me started laughing with me. So far, so good. I felt good because I had actually managed to make them laugh. Later I would find out why they were never smiling. Daily life was very difficult. All food was rationed. Most of the people I saw had to spend hours queuing for food. But if they had money, nearly everything was available on the black market.

Rene Dassac (in collaboration with Patrick K. Robbins)

In the railway station gendarmes were checking suitcases looking for food bought on the black market. Of course, this didn't concern me and I went right through the control and straight to the RTO. There must have been thousands of people waiting to board the trains and now I understood why I was told to come at least three hours before my scheduled departure time of 22:00. Gendarmes and railway staff lined up passengers before they boarded the trains, checked documentation and somehow managed to keep order in a situation that could easily have become unruly. An MP escorted me to my carriage and showed me my seat.

Two American officers were already in my compartment and I saluted. "Better sit down and stay seated otherwise you'll lose your seat," one of them said. Outside in the corridor you could barely move because it had filled up with people sitting on their luggage. My seat was near the door opening onto the corridor. Almost in front of the door there was a big fat woman carrying a child in her arms. She was loud mouthed. "The Germans were better educated than these guys," she said to everyone and no one in particular. "At least they would give up their seats to ladies or old people." She wasn't getting much sympathy and I didn't let on that I could understand every word she said. I had seen gendarmes chasing away people who had slipped in to take unoccupied reserved seats. I sat tight, waited, and came up with a plan as to how to deal with her. I told the two yanks what the woman was saying and they laughed. "Don't waste your breath," one of them replied. "The train's leaving."

As we rattled into the night the passengers out in the corridor started to settle down. They found seats wherever they could. The fat lady stared, trying to drill holes through me with her glaring eyes. I didn't like being insulted, being compared to the Germans, and that burned me into action. I got up and said in my best French, "Now Madame, the gendarmes have gone and I will be glad to share my seat with you." She gasped a big fat gulp of air. "If I had given you my seat in the station the gendarmes would have caught you and they would have taken you off the train. And I am sure they would not have treated you as gently as the Germans you seem to admire." Her face registered shock again and she turned ever so slightly red. "I'm sorry ... I lost my temper," she apologized. I'd made my point or, rather, I had almost made my point. "Forget it. I just wanted you to know that

I don't like being compared to those I have been fighting for so long." She didn't bother to reply. She shifted her gaze away from my face and she remained quiet for the rest of the trip. We switched seats from time-to-time all the way to Lyon.

The train was terribly slow. Many parts of the tracks had been destroyed and were in the process of being repaired. We lurched, stopped, inched forward, and stopped again only to lurch forward again. I began the trip counting how many stops we'd made but I gave up when the number of times got too many to remember. Who would believe me; did it matter? What was important was not the number of stops but the fact we were moving in one direction and not getting shot at. Some of the bridges we crossed were temporary wooden bridges and my mind raced. "How much strain can they take," I asked myself? Finally, I got a grip on myself and started to relax by staring out into the night. No wonder it took us so long to get to Lyon. Sometime during the trip we passed through Pont de Veaux, just before Macon where my first love lived. For a couple of minutes I tried to imagine what it would be like if I hopped off the train and pitched up on her front door? It was a thought, just another like all the others, racketing through my mind during that long trip home. That is, if I even had a home? What if they were dead?

After about ten hours of what I had begun to think of as a never ending trip, a trip that seemed to require stopping in every station of any size, on a train that jerked and never really got up enough speed to lull us into a real sleep, we finally lurched into Lyon just as day was breaking. It was about 0700 and it felt good to stand up and shoulder my bags.

I creaked out of our compartment, murmured a 'goodbye' to the Yanks, and followed the crowd toward the exit. It was slow moving because the gendarmes were stopping passengers and searching them to see if they had any black market goods. They nodded at me and waved me through. I marched down the stairs to where I remembered the trolley station was located and looked for the trolley bus number 13. Unless they had changed the route, it would take me to the Croix Rousse suburb. I felt good about being able to still remember that important detail after so many years away but I wasn't completely sure I was right.

While I was grappling with whether or not I remembered correctly, something struck me. The other people milling around the bus station were silent, almost dead silent. Their silence was a huge difference to what I saw in Paris. Okay, it was early, and maybe they weren't awake, but still, it was eerie and unsettling. Only later would I learn that probably everyone I saw was trudging off to work with a half filled stomach.

Before boarding the bus I asked the controller, "Is this the right bus to the boulevard de la Croix Rousse?" He grunted 'oui' and I stood outside on the back platform. With my kit bag and suitcase I was out of place and people were looking at me probably wandering who I was. For them the war had been over for a few months and certainly, they had never seen a British sailor before. But, my ears were open and I heard a man say, "C'est un anglais," (He's an Englishman) and I was grateful for that because I really didn't want to be talking to anyone.

When the last passenger squeezed on the bus left the terminal and began winding its way through the city. Slowly, I began to recognize parts of the town I had not seen since 1939. I stared hard at each building and I even managed to remember enough to get off at the bus stop that was only a few yards from where I thought my uncle and sisters might still be living.

I stood in front of the block of flats to see if the shutters to their apartment were open but they were closed. Were they still sleeping? I had butterflies in my stomach and I knew I was more nervous than I had been in a very long time. All sorts of questions were going through my mind, "They don't even know whether I am still alive. And on their side, how many of them are still alive? How have they managed to survive, and will they understand why I did not give any signs of life?"

I don't know how I managed but somehow I overrode a rising fear that was so intense it almost squeezed the breath out of me. It was still dark in front of their door. No one was awake; I rang the bell. The dinky little tin bell made a shrill racket somewhere inside the apartment. In less than a minute I began hearing footsteps coming to the door. A hand threw the double lock and slid back the dead bolt. The door opened just a fraction, enough to let an eye peer out onto the landing. Slowly part of a face filled the crack. It was barely visible in the dim light but then I saw two eyes peering at me. I recognized them immediately. They belonged to my uncle and from the way he peered at me it was obvious that he did not recognize me. "Oui," he asked? In a flash I opened my mouth to speak, I started to choke and all I could do was blurt, "Bonjour monsieur." Cautiously, he opened the door a few more centimeters until some of his dim light shone on me. The old man looked at me more closely. "Uncle, don't you recognize me?" I wasn't asking a question. I was calling him back to another time. "It's me, Rene." His head snapped as if an invisible hand had slapped him hard across the face. Then he reached out and took me into his arms and whispered, "Your sisters are still sleeping, don't make a noise." He was stumbling over words, trying to put together sentences, but I knew what he was trying to say. He was trying to find the words to tell me that they had given up on me. What he was trying to say was exactly what I had feared about them: "We thought you were dead."

Someone moved behind my uncle. Paulette, my sister, had heard the doorbell and had heard someone whispering. Something strange was going on at this hour of the morning and she got up to see what was going on. I stood framed in the door with my kit bag and suitcase. A weak hall light shone down on me, just enough light to put me in clear view. Paulette looked at me with eyes wide open. The color drained from her face and she slowly fainted onto my uncle. Gasping, and with great difficulty, my uncle tried to make me understand, as quickly as he could, why she fainted. "We thought you were dead." He almost lost his breath trying to make me understand that they were convinced that if I were alive, somehow they would get news from me before I returned. That made sense but I had learned that in war the unexpected happens more often than the expected and I could understand their bewilderment. By then my other sister, Juliette, had joined us and she managed not to faint. She threw herself into my arms crying, "Oh my god, why didn't you let us know you were coming?" For a second I thought that by turning up on their doorstep unannounced I gave them more pain than the anguish and certainty they had learned to live with: I was dead and life had to continue without me.

Rene Dassac (in collaboration with Patrick K. Robbins)

Before ringing their doorbell I thought I had anticipated every reaction but, of course, I hadn't. I had so much on my mind there was no way I could have begun to answer so many questions. They came at me in salvos and then I realized that it was hard for them to believe that I had actually survived. After all those years, and without admitting it to me, they thought I was dead. Or, and this question gnawed at me, "Were there other reasons?" Paulette came back to life and we started talking, all of us and at the same time. They told me that my cousin Raymond had been a prisoner in Germany since 1940 and since the Germans had been pushed out of France they had received no news. Understandably, my uncle was beside himself with worry. Raymond was his only son. In the First World War he had seen what the 'Boches' could do and he feared the worse.

"Do you have any ration tickets," he asked? "I don't have any idea of who I should see." In a flash he flipped through a gamut of emotions from shock at seeing me standing in the door, speechless with joy, through to the survival instinct. "How are we going to feed you," he almost wailed. "It's not a problem," I said patting my kit bag. He stared at me dumbly. He had no way of knowing what I had carried with me from Paris. "This is full of food." They stared at me not daring to believe their ears. "When we run out of this I can always go to an allied camp to get more food, even chocolate and cigarettes." I'm sure they thought I had lost my mind in one of my battles. To show them I was not kidding, I opened my kit bag and spread out all the tin food on the kitchen table. They could not believe their eyes.

When my uncle saw the big tin of coffee he started to really come alive. "Enfin, enfin, at last I am going to have a real cup of coffee." He was lost in reverie and I brought him down to earth when I told him that I didn't have any sugar. The thought of having a cup of coffee, sugar or not, was almost too much. "But, instead of sugar, I've brought a big tin of golden syrup and we can use that for sugar." His face broke into a huge smile and soon the kitchen was filled with that most delectable of all morning odors, freshly brewed coffee.

I asked about my brother. My sisters told me that he was also in Lyon, married and had a son. "He was arrested by the Gestapo just before Lyon was liberated and was freed by the Americans."

Apparently it was serious because they said that if the Americans had not shown up when they did it would have been all over for him. "All he had was two days at the most." Thank God. He was alive. "When can I see him," I asked? He was working and his shift wasn't over until later in the afternoon. I longed to see his face, meet my new sister-in-law and hold my nephew.

We spent the whole day talking about all the various things that had happened during the terrible years when war had separated us. One of my sisters rummaged around and came out with a box of photos. Some were photos of friends and family members, others were shots of scenery that must have had some meaning for someone but we really couldn't figure out for whom. As they were looking at some of their photographs I picked up one of me taken when I was at the Navy Boys School in Brest. I turned it over and on the back I saw a drawing and verses Juliette had written. This snapshot of me pretty much confirmed what I suspected: My family thought I was dead. I shook my head. "Why hadn't the navy told them what had happened to me after Dunkirk?" My mind was boiling. I remembered the French seaman I met in Oran, the same man who went to torpedo school with me in Toulon just before the war, and I distinctly remember him telling me that he knew I was in England. But, why hadn't word filtered back to my family?

I looked up from one of the snapshots and asked my sisters, "What made you think I had been killed?" "Remember, we were in a convent school. One afternoon we were listening to the radio and the announcer said the Germans had sunk the Savorgnan with all hands." Paulette's face was drawn. "I burst into tears and Juliette fainted." Soon after that episode the teachers forbade the students to listen to the news broadcasts because of the devastating effect it was having on their charges. Funny, I remembered having heard the same broadcast but from my perspective I knew it was pure German propaganda. No one even gave the announcement a second thought; there was so much false news then.

In a life full of uncertainties we had at least one grim comfort. We knew that the Vichy government had condemned us to death as part of their war against collaborators. And, I had to admit, the fact that the French admiralty never mentioned anything to my family did not surprise me. It was what I had come to expect from them. Either they felt the guilt that comes when a coward admits his cowardice or they decided to keep the information about me quiet for security reasons. In the second case I was giving them the benefit of the doubt but emotionally I felt more inclined to believe the first as the most likely reason.

Even after so many years, I was still white hot furious at what I felt was the simple and unquestioned treachery of the admirals. For me, there was no excuse for their cowardice. Decades later as I reflect on the torrent of emotions that I was caught up in that day, I cannot help but feel the same intense hatred for the officers who, in their strutting pride, marched off to ride out the war in safety, leaving us to fight to free them, fight to free France.

We had lunch but how we managed to swallow was difficult because we were all talking. After we finished, late in the afternoon as night fell, we went across town to see my brother who was living in one of the poor quarters of Lyon. On the way there they told me that he was part of the communist resistance party. He had been picked up in a Nazi sweep and caught carrying false identity papers and ration cards. I didn't know what to expect. He opened the door. Strangers but still brothers we stared at each other. In a flash his face opened thousands of little doors and dams in my mind, barriers that I once thought invincible. They started to crumble and sad memories began pouring out.

After our parents died we led a miserable existence. War had not been easy on us. From the way he looked, drawn eyes sunk in pale skin, a skinny scarecrow for a brother, I saw he had gone through hell. I can't remember who moved first but we lunged at each other and I felt could feel his scrawny frame as my arms wrapped around him. We sobbed with an intensity that had built up during years of fear and anguish. Brothers, we were alive, we managed to survive the war. Standing in the doorway, we were overwhelmed with relief and gratitude.

Slowly, laughing and sniffling, we managed to get control of ourselves. "Rene, this is my wife." Rinette entered without me seeing her. She was carrying my first nephew who was just a few months old. All this was new to me; the night before I could not imagine this was how the first day with my family would turn out. My brother worked in a factory manufacturing nylon and from the sound of it, he had a good job. But, the fact he had a good job could not hide the fact that he and his family were hungry. There simply was not enough food to be found. A real meal was an exception and cigarettes were a luxury. I remembered what the waiter in Paris had told me. "Go to the RAF base and get them to let you stock up for your family."

One day when my brother was working the night shift he guided me across town to the RAF base. I was directed to the commissary and asked the officers if I could stock up with some food for my family. They listened to my story but in the end they told me they could not help me. Cigarettes and chocolate were possible but they could not supply me with food, which is what I really wanted. I tried every argument I could think of but I couldn't chink a hole in their defenses. We trudged back across town. I felt like I had let down my family but we did not return empty handed. We had a huge stash of cigarettes and chocolate from RAF canteen. My brother was a heavy smoker and for him, when it was a choice between a meal and a cigarette, depending on how hungry he was at the time, nicotine usually won. I left my brother and promised to come back in a few days time. Meanwhile, another scheme was brewing.

My uncle told me that one of my uncles lived in a small village, Chane, near Macon. He was a wine maker and there was a chance, a pretty good chance, he could probably get us some meat, a foodstuff that was all but impossible to find in Lyon. Imagine, Lyon, the eating capital of France, and no meat. The meat shortage was just another sign, as if I needed another one, to remind me that the civilian population was managing to exist. Living a normal life meant being able to buy whatever food you wanted with no restrictions. From what I saw in Lyon, the days of well-stocked shops would have to wait a few more months.

We hatched a simple plan: I would go to his brother's house in Chane and his brother would go to a farmer he knew, surely he knew someone, and get some meat. I would carry the meat back to Lyon. As an allied serviceman I would not be stopped and searched by the gendarmes. No risk for me, great benefits for my family, I set off with a good stash of tobacco to be used as a convenient and convincing barter tool. On the morning I left, I doubt if any Frenchman in Lyon had as much tobacco on him as I did when I set off for Chane.

I left before dawn to catch an early train. The clock was ticking and I did not want to spend more than a day in Chane. Dressed in uniform, I had no difficulty passing through the police checkpoints. My stay in Chane was a whirlwind but I caught the train back that night. As I approached the police cordon outside the train station I caught the attention of a gendarme. He snapped me a salute and I gave a brisk Royal Navy salute in return. "Monsieur, is American," the gendarme asked. "No," I replied in the thickest British seaman accent I could muster. "Tres bien," and he patted me on the back. I almost fainted.

Did he know he patted a leg of mutton that I managed to get with my Chane uncle's help? Thinking back to that little trip, it now strikes me as quite a humorous episode because I only spent a few hours with my uncle in Chane. Commerce and the prospect of a nice meal, not family ties, drew me to him. He was my godfather and to the best of my recollection, I can never recall him spending one centime on me. He was known in the family as a real tight wad but I couldn't let that memory stand in the way of getting my family something to eat. I told him I was very grateful for his help. And, he was equally grateful for the manner in which we settled our transaction. I paid him with two tins of cigarettes, fifty cigarettes in each tin. Depending on what you wanted 'to buy,' that was a lot of money.

When I got back to Lyon and walked into his apartment with my precious gift and took off my rucksack, my uncle cradled the leg of mutton with great reverence. He held it with tenderness and pride, gazing at it with reverence. Was this the way he looked when he first held his newborn son? The strength of a sentry rippled in his arms. "Did he give you any wine," he asked? "No," I replied and sat down to take off my wet shoes.

The apartment was cold, my feet were cold, and I was tired and I really did not want to get into a long discussion about his brother. Maybe later we could dissect what made his brother so tight, but not now. Uncle Gabriel shook his head. "How can he be so stingy," he muttered? "At least he could have given you two bottles of the best wine he has sleeping down in his cellar." I started to massage my wet feet and smiled at him just to let him know that I felt just as mystified as he did. But, what the hell, he had his wine and we had a leg of mutton. No one on our street in Lyon could make the same claim.

Later that evening I told my uncle and sisters that I wanted to leave for Ales to see my oldest sister. A cousin on my father's side of the family had adopted her. He was a barrister who had four sons. My sisters told me that they knew one of the sons had been deported to a concentration camp in Germany. A Dutchman, who pretended to be an allied airman brought down over the north of France, betrayed him. A local resistance movement picked up the Dutchman. Had everything gone to plan, he would have been transferred via the resistance underground to a group who would have helped him cross the border into Portugal.

In fact, the 'Dutchman' was a Gestapo agent and my cousin was part of the resistance group penetrated by the agent but there was no solid proof. From the Gestapo's point of view he had to be picked up. His house was ransacked but no incriminating papers were found. Because he was a magistrate he had access to the immense law library of the court system and he used the hundreds of meters of bound files and law volumes to hide all his secret papers. Even though the Germans could not find anything to link him to a resistance group he was, nevertheless, arrested. Had they found anything incriminating he would have been shot on the spot because Epernay, where he was caught, was a particularly strict zone. Fortunately the Gestapo stopped with the oldest son. The two other sons were also lawyers in Ales and the fourth was out of danger because he was a catholic missionary in Rangoon.

If I had a bit of luck maybe, and this is just an outside comment that came to me recently, the missionary son might have been able to communicate with my family in France. When I was onboard the HMS Vimy in Freetown I asked my captain if I was allowed to send my cousin a letter. He thought for a moment and replied, "Since he is in the Commonwealth, I think it would be allowed." I sent him a letter and he actually got it but he never contacted my family. I was probably thinking that somehow he could use 'Church mail' to contact a priest in France, someone he trusted, and he in turn could get word to my family. It was a hope and, of course, under Nazi occupation it was high risk. What mattered to me was the fact that I had tried and that was all. No one in occupied France was able to contact me. Maybe it was better that way. If they thought I was dead they didn't have to worry about me but if they knew I was alive they had to worry about whether I was wounded or taken prisoner.

I appreciated knowing what they had gone through because I actually knew very little about my father's side of the family. Therefore, I went with an open mind, but even without knowing them, I admired their courage and I knew that I would receive a warm welcome. Before leaving I went down to the train station and made all the necessary arrangements with the Railway Authority. Thanks to my special pass I was treated as if I was 'Mr. Special'. They told me that I had to change trains in Nimes. A large book full of train schedules lay open in front of the booking clerk. "From what I can put together, I don't think you can get a train out to Ales on the same day. Sorry." Actually, that wasn't a problem because my sisters told me that a close friend of my mother's, Madame Andree, lived in Nimes and that if I couldn't make a connection she might be able to put me up for a night. That was good news because the thought of sleeping rough in the Nimes station did not appeal to me.

It was early February and I left Lyon under dark clouds. A cold mist fell and soaked into every crack, the kind of soaking mist gardener's love if it were springtime and twenty degrees warmer. The train hissed and clattered south and gradually I noticed the temperature began to change the closer we came to Nimes. I had a window seat and as I watched the vegetation changed from the rich lushness of Burgundy to the sparser hills of the South, my mind began playing tricks with me again and the sight of umbrella pines, tall cypress trees, squat farm buildings and the occasional donkey, memories of my childhood began to come alive. For a few fleeting moments, I was a little boy again, with sisters and brothers and a mother and father. I must have had cares then, all little kids have to care about something, but all I could remember was the strange feeling of being happy.

The trip was actually pleasant. The passengers in my compartment were curious and asked me many questions. I enjoyed talking to them in English. In fact, I had to speak English, because if I had begun to speak French I would certainly have wound up in custody. There were still too many enemy agents around, some on the run, some staying behind to make trouble, and if I wasn't what they expected me to be, I would have a lot of explaining to do so I simply played the game. We laughed as they tried out their English on me and with my hidden advantage I helped them get their points across. It was my little joke that I played on myself because I pretended as if I didn't know what they were talking about between themselves!

From what they said it was obvious that they knew little about the suffering Britain had been through. For years they could only listen to the German news reports. Anyone with a radio strong enough to pick up BBC was liable to be arrested, deported, or shot. They were amazed to know that food in England was rationed just like in France and they knew London had been badly damaged by the Luftwaffe. When I told them London had been just one of many targets, that nearly every major city had been attacked, they were awed into silence. By the time we reached Nimes we had formed another set of wartime friendships and it was as if we had known each other for a long time

I had no difficulty finding Madame Andre's flat. I knocked, hoping that my knock sounded friendly to someone who had just stopped living in a world wherein a knock on the door could have meant the Gestapo. She opened the door, looked me up and down, and said matter-of-factly, "I knew you would be coming back." I wasn't expecting that kind of welcome and she continued, "Because your mother was a saint and she was always trying to look after you and ensure your welfare. I kissed her and said, "You haven't changed. Always cheerful." We sat at her kitchen table and laughed, talking about old times and friends, many of whom I could barely remember and some I had completely forgotten.

"And what about your family," I began hesitatingly because I knew there had to be a sad tale. She straightened her apron on her lap. "My son is a prisoner of war in Germany," she began in a quiet voice the way any proud mother would speak of a successful son. He had been shipped off to a farm where he worked as a day laborer for a woman whose husband was on the Russian front. He could actually write letters. Life on the farm was hard but he worked for a good and fair

Rene Dassac (in collaboration with Patrick K. Robbins)

woman. Sometimes she even helped him send food to his mother. News traveled between mother and son fairly often and she was not as worried about him as she could have been had he been sent to one of the camps. But, after the Normandy invasion, there had been no news and she had begun to worry more.

The Germans were beaten. It was only a matter of time until Hitler's regime collapsed but what would happen to the French deportees once the system collapsed? She had begun to wring her hands, but I must have said something comforting because the conversation moved back to old friends. As an anecdote, her son survived his deportation and returned to France when Germany surrendered. He remained on good terms with the farmwoman and when life began to improve in France he arranged to send her food parcels when he found out that life in Germany was very hard. Although this sounds strange, it was not unusual. Many Germans died on the Russian front and left widows and orphans. In fact, there were quite a few cases of POW's employed as farm labor who wound up marrying their former employers after the war.

Throughout the war Mme Andre had been a cunning woman. When France fell and the hardships of occupation made daily life difficult, she made a resolution: I will survive. If necessary, she'd turn the tables on the occupiers. Nothing violent was necessary. Only skill, determination, and a willingness to lead life according to the new realities would get her through, she told herself. There was no question of forsaking her values, her humor, and her independence. No, she would always manage to get food. At night she set traps for the pigeons that came to roost on her window ledge. Fresh pigeon, a handful of peas, maybe even the luxury of a small strip of lard, "why, those made wonderful meals," she told me.

One day while I was still waiting for my train to Ales I smelled a wonderful rich odor from the kitchen. Onions in olive oil, they were easy to recognize but there was something else. Another smell, gamey and almost sweet, was mixed with the onions. We sat down to golden fried onions and a rather long and narrow piece of meat that had no fat. It was tough. My fork tines had trouble holding it to the plate. Fortunately my knife was sharp and I managed to slice off a bit of the end. I pushed it onto the fork and bit in, somewhat hesitantly at first but then with greater determination. The word 'tough' couldn't be used to describe what my jaws and teeth were struggling to pulverize. I bit harder and it fought back, almost kicking. Mme Andre watched me and I could tell from the way her eyes started to bunch up on the sides that she was holding back another good laugh. We had already shared many. "Is this the first time you've eaten donkey?" I gulped and managed to swallow at the same time. And, not even out of politeness, I had to agree with her when she continued, "It really is a nice piece of meat."

She cleaned her plate. "You know, it gives a lot of energy and I need it." She did need help, all the help she could get. Not only was she planning for her daughter's marriage, she worked full time as a house cleaner. In front of me sat an old woman whose body was riddled with rheumatism, whose malformed hips jutted from her waist like bent tree limbs, and yet, she found strength to laugh, work, and live well in spite of what life had thrown at her. She was a genuinely fine person and I like to think there were many like her in France during those horrible years of occupation.

At last! My train to Ales was confirmed and I went into the kitchen to say goodbye. She made me promise to come see her on my return trip. "Please tell me all about your sister," she implored. The trip to Ales only took a couple of hours. Ales was not a particularly pretty town. In fact, it was ugly, what you would expect of a coal mining town: gray, dirty buildings, smoky, sad and very communist. My sister was an operating bloc nurse who worked in one of the better clinics in town. Of course, she was not home when I went to cousin Brun's house. Our cousin, my sister called 'uncle,' was a well known barrister and he had a son Henri who was also a barrister. I knew Henri before my father had died.

He had been a POW but managed to escape a few weeks after his capture when the Germans were still enjoying their victory as if they were having a holiday in France. He told me of the occasional unfair treatment that had been meted out to some of the so called collaborators. Some had been shot without trial. There was a lot of hatred and lies in the aftermath of the German withdrawal and a lot of the accusations often had nothing to do with collaboration. Accusing someone could have been jealousy or a handy way to settle old scores.

Henry took me to the clinic were my sister was working. He dropped me off in front of the gate and then continued on to court to defend one of his clients. When I walked in and saw my sister there was a great uproar. At least she didn't faint but we laughed and cried. Grabbing me by the hand she paraded me through the clinic, showing me to all the doctors and nurses. From the way she spouted off you'd have thought I was a great hero and I finally gave up trying to restrain her excitement and joy. The head of surgery gave her the day off and we went home, talking all the way. On the way she told me that Mme Brun was in a bad state. "It's only a matter of time now," she said with the quiet voice a nurse can muster when she knows that death is inevitable.

It was a fact. Whatever else we wanted to think, her illness had gone too far and Mme Brun would not live. True to my sister's prognosis, Mme Brun died while I was in Ales. Because death had become an inevitable topic, my sister told me about a woman she had consulted a couple of years ago, a woman renowned for communicating with the dead.

She asked the woman to tell her whether I was dead or alive. The seer pondered the question and replied, "He is alive and well but he has trouble with his teeth." I probed a bit because there could be something to this story. I started to piece together enough to put her visit to the seer into a time frame and then I remembered that the date my sister was talking about corresponded with the date when I had a tooth removed in Brighton when I was doing my LTO course in 1942. I distinctly remembered the dental surgeon had to put me asleep because the tooth was lying horizontal to the jaw line. He had no other choice but to open the gum to remove the tooth. Before he put me to sleep he asked me, "Where do you come from; do you still have family in France?" I told him I did. "Alright, think of them while you go off to sleep." I went under and I clearly remember dreaming of my sisters. I don't believe in stories about people who can talk with the dead but in this case, far too many facts lined up and I must admit that the whole episode was 'strange' to say the least.

Mme Brun died three days after my arrival. It was pathetic to watch her slip away. We stood around her bed, looking, waiting, helpless. My sister was the only one in the old lady's room who moved. With great tenderness she plumped the old woman's arms to find a vein in order to administer a dose of something to ease her aunt's pain. Disease and age had taken their toll. A filled syringe, sharp end resting on a piece of cotton wool that had been dabbed with alcohol, lay useless on the bed next to Mme Brun. My sister looked at me and made I sign I knew only too well. "She's dead," my sister's eyes said and then she made a sign to me, a slight downward motion of her hand. Once, twice, and finally on the third time the enormity of the event sunk into her uncle. His wife was dead and he was alone. At first no one moved and no one said anything. Five minutes before she was my aunt, now she was 'our' corpse.

I was surprised at how detached, almost cold, my sister had become in those final moments. Dying patients were part of her daily routine and she went about those final moments without showing what really was going on inside her. She was the total professional, the person attending to a dying patient. The fact that the patient was her aunt was never apparent. A delicate job had been undertaken; she would see it through to its inevitable end. She remained in total control of herself, doing whatever she could to alleviate the old woman's suffering. Her uncle moved forward, as if to say goodbye, and left. My sister, still very much in control, walked with me out of the bedroom into the end of the hall, far away from where her uncle could hear her wrenching sobs. I put my arms around her and held her tight. We'd both seen death far too many times for it to become a casual experience. Each death is different and a death in the family has its own pain.

I stayed until the funeral was over and then I left. My long leave was running out and I still had stops to make in Lyon and Paris before returning to Victory Barracks in Pompey! The return train connection back to Nimes was better than the trip down and I managed to keep my promise and spent a day with Mme Andre. She listened eagerly to all the news about the family. Death was part of life's ritual, the final act, and she appeared to accept the fact that one more person was now gone, someone who had been part of her earlier life.

The Railway Authority assured me a seat back to Paris on the 10:00 train. I had a seat on a special military train powered by a huge diesel locomotive. In a way, I was now glad to leave and start heading 'home'. I had trouble coming to grips with that feeling of happiness because, after all, I was French and I was leaving my family and my country behind. What I felt was not a sense of guilt. After all, I had risked my life for freedom from tyranny for my family and my country. Many others had even made the ultimate sacrifice but I was alive but I also I had a lifetime of memories stored in my head. Images of mangled and bloody corpses, ships on fire, men screaming, it was all there and still is even today. Some things you don't forget. No, I accepted that I had nothing to be ashamed about, but I also had to accept that I had become a stranger in my own land.

The way 'they' lived, the French, had become alien to me. Living conditions were harsher than in England and, certainly, England was no picnic. Something was missing in France and I couldn't really figure out what it was. Maybe it was me who was out of step with the realities of France. That thought began to work its way deeper into my conscience and finally I had to admit that I didn't like being in a country where there was a great feeling of uncertainty, the feeling that something chaotic would happen at any moment, and the feeling that my political beliefs were very much at odds with the communists who were going from strength to strength made me uneasy.

Yes, I had to admit, I wanted out and I wanted to get back to my mates and my life. My trip home was important because it gave me a chance to find my family. We were all alive and I knew that when the war was finally over, we would be able to rebuild our lives. Neither France nor my family would ever be the same but at least we had the chance to build a new future. Maybe it was that thought, moving to something new, that made me want to leave and move on.

When I got to the station I went down the quay until I found my wagon in the train. It was already filled with French air force personnel and I took a seat in front of two airmen. They stared at me the way children would probably stare at a shipwrecked sailor washed up on the beach. Certainly they were wondering, "What's a British sailor doing here?" While we were trying not to stare at each other, something happened that I will never forget. A French army MP, a captain, asked me for my papers. Remaining seated, I handed them to him and continued to look out the window. He shuffled through the documents and then muttered under his breath in a voice loud enough for everyone to hear, "How can he (meaning me) remain seated and still continue to smoke?" I looked up at him and gave him my dumbest and blankest stare. He could have been talking to a statute as far as I was concerned. Of course I knew what he wanted: take my seat and shame me out of the carriage. He probably thought I was a French sailor and from the way he talked and acted, it was pretty obvious that he did not like the navy. From his looks it was clear that he was of the old army school. A big drooping moustache hung across his face. Who knows, maybe General Gireaud was his hero because he seemed to be trying to look like him.

I continued to sit and stare because I wasn't about to enter into an argument with him. My silence won. With a loud 'harrumph,' he gave me back my railway ticket and stalked away, his shiny boots glistened under his big floppy bum. Two airmen seated behind me burst out laughing and hooting. I heard one of them say to the other, "Silly bastard, he couldn't even recognize an Englishman." They guffawed. And in a complaint familiar to anyone who has served in the ranks, one burst out, "How can you be so dumb and be an army captain too?"

The train lurched out of the station and after we had cleared Nimes I told them that I had understood everything 'Hair Face' had said. "I agree with you; he was too dumb to argue with." They laughed and we soon started talking. They were about my age and we talked for most of the trip.

There was a big difference in the way we looked at the world although I wasn't that much older. I completed my training before and during the war and they, draftees, were training with newer equipment and instruments. There was definitely a technology gap but I had the advantage, if you can call wartime experience an advantage, of reality, of how and when to use equipment in actual combat. Somehow I managed to keep them from probing too much about my background and even the question of 'how come you speak French so well' was skirted. "A pretty girl who didn't speak English helped me because I had to learn French to get what I wanted." They laughed and true to the commitment that I gave the intelligence officer before I left for France, I did not reveal my identity. In fact, I did not reveal it until the war was over.

I arrived in Lyon and by then my sisters had returned to their convent to continue their education. I missed them not being there but I went out to their school and it was fun seeing them again. They acted as if they still had not quite got over the fact that I was back in the land of the living. I was still a curiosity for them. Pesky girls, they kept asking me all sorts of questions. I could answer most with out too much difficulty but when they started probing about my love life, our discussions became heated. Paulette kept asking me what I was going to do back in England and I finally told her that I was going to marry an English girl. "Une anglaise, c'est pas possible," she hissed. "There are plenty of French girls who would like to meet you." Before she got too much further and actually tried to introduce me to someone, I had to steer the conversation onto a more reasonable path. "Remember, I haven't had a 'normal' life like most people my age." She nodded in agreement. "After all, I don't have a girl friend from school and the only girl I know is English." Paulette accepted that point and conceded that I didn't fit into the pattern of most French young men. "In England I can talk with people who, like me, have suffered in the war. We have something in common. Here, I have nothing in common except my nationality." I could see that my argument was making sense to her.

When we spoke of the future it became clearer to her that my commitment to England was something about which I had given considerable thought. "I don't know what I am going to do after the war." By now I knew that the war would be over soon. There was no way the Germans could survive the tightening allied noose. "I know more people in England than I do in France and that's important because the people I know will help me find my way." She agreed with me that, aside from our family in France, there was no one who could help me get started in civilian life. By the time we had said what was really in our hearts we had somehow managed to steer the conversation well away from serious confrontation. She knew I loved my family and I knew she would always be the strongest supporter of our family clan.

I didn't have the same problems making myself understood with my brother. He and I talked easily and openly. Once he heard what I was thinking of doing he stopped questioning me about my plans for the future. Even when I mentioned that I wanted to marry a British girl, I did not get the same negative reaction that I got from my sisters. He had married a foreign girl, an Italian, so maybe it was easier for him to understand my decision.

"Here's my address." Now that it was possible to send mail between the two countries we could stay in touch and that made me feel better because I was beginning to have mixed emotions about leaving. Waves of sadness smashed against waves of relief in those last few days. I was sad about not being able to do more to help them. They needed everything I could think of to make daily life bearable. Having access to RAF supplies had helped but once I was gone there was no way they could get the occasional tins of cigarettes, chocolate, coffee, or even basics like sugar and cooking oil. Years of rationing still loomed ahead of them and I could do nothing to help. On the flip side, I felt relieved and glad to be able to return to my navy family and my navy routine. There is comfort in order, especially when the order is one of choice, and I was glad and proud to be a British seaman. I promised to write and then we said good-bye. "Not for years, but for only a few months," my uncle roared above the crowd as the train station left the station.

The return trip to the UK was easier than the outbound trip to France. Six weeks had elapsed and the war front was moving eastward. The allies had begun to enter Germany and the Germans were boxed in. It was only a matter of time until they were defeated. In Paris I stopped at the Grand hotel where the transport authority gave me my permit to take the train back to the UK. This time I returned to Dieppe by train and then took the ferry to Newhaven where the customs guards had already resumed work as usual. They were thorough and went through everything because they were looking for captured German weapons that the boys were taking home as souvenirs. I was clean and they let me off without any further delay.

It was good to be back in barracks. Six weeks is a long time to be away from your mates and everyone had an interesting tale or two to tell. For some, like me, it was a happy homecoming because everyone was alive and accounted for. For others, it was a painful return.

The most pathetic story I recall involved a chap from Lorraine. He was the son of an army colonel. Like me he pitched up at the front door unannounced but he had a horrible shock. His father kicked him out of the house for having deserted the navy in 1940. In his father's eyes his son had committed an unpardonable crime: He had not gone into exile with the rest of the French navy who had chosen to sit out the war instead of fight the Germans as part of the allied war effort! The chap was broken and I don't know what became of him because, within a few days, I was drafted to a huge repair ship that was having a complete refit in readiness for her departure to the Far East.

I stayed on her for about three weeks and then returned to the barracks to wait for God knows what. War is always about waiting. You wait for it to start, you wait to go into action, you wait forever until the action stops and you wait until someone signs a surrender document. We were waiting again, waiting for the war to end. By the time the allies penetrated deep into Germany we were placing bets on 'when' the war would end, not 'if' it would end.

A lot of changes were occurring in the UK and the admiralty was beginning to transfer ships to the Far East theatre to operate with the U.S. navy. At the same time, while ships were leaving the UK, others were returning with survivors of the Japanese prison camps. The horrors they told were, at first, unbelievable but we heard the same stories so many times from so many different sources that in the end we had to accept them. The enemy barbarity stiffened our resolve to get the war over in the Far East as quickly as possible.

*****

In the middle of a world torn apart by war in the West and the East, I asked Edith to marry me. She accepted. I was surprised at her response. I had toyed with an unsettling idea: our 'love' wasn't the real thing. Was I testing my commitment to her or was I merely playing mental games to kill time. I was fairly sure I would have been hurt, but not totally surprised, if when the time came for me to pop the question, she'd quit playing our love game. We were still corresponding and our letters were becoming more and more torrid. I explained to her that it was highly likely that I would be shipped out to the Far East sometime in the near future. My logic centered on the, 'let's get it done now' school of thought. I was a kid and I had got the steps horribly wrong because I was about to take one of the most important decisions in my life and I wasn't even thinking clearly. My thought sequence was disastrous: do first and then think rationally about the merits of what I'd done. Action was supposed to make up for all the shortcomings I should have seen in our relationship.

Now, and only with the advantage of hindsight, I am able to admit: asking Edith to marry me was, without any doubt, the dumbest question I have ever asked. I'll never know why she accepted my proposal. She was no more in love with me than she was with Michelangelo's statue of David. My reasons for getting married really weren't sound at all and I am sure my 'reasoning', if you can call it that, was nothing more than a case of extreme infatuation wrapped in a whirlwind of dreams and fantasies that were nurtured by a love-smitten lad who had spent more time at sea than he had with her. Lust was an important factor because I had several years of blocked ardor. To be truthful, my little head below my waist was definitely influencing the one at the end of my neck. We didn't have a physical relationship and if I had boiled down my thoughts and taken the time to put them in black-and-white and look at them coldly and clinically, the facts surrounding our relationship would have told me not to marry her. Have an affair? Of course, that should have happened but it hadn't and I couldn't see clearly beyond my lust and infatuation.

The way I figured, if I loved Edith, and I was convinced I was deeply in love, Edith had to love me with equal passion and sincerity. My rational argument was totally irrational. Nothing could have been farther from the truth. Admittedly, Edith was elegant and reserved. I rationalized that she was just playing hard to get. I did not want to lose her. My mates had girl friends so why shouldn't I?

There was something fishy about our relationship but I didn't step back two steps and have a long hard think about what I was getting into. Certainly, I was old enough to know better than to go rushing blindly into one of life's most important decisions: the choice of a partner for life. But, because I was hell-bent to get married, I overrode my basic instincts. I never stopped to recognize my emotions for what they were: warning bells ringing furiously to slow down, stop and get serious about what I was doing. Instead, I barreled my way into what became an awful marriage.

If only I had stopped to reflect on the fact that we'd never made love and we'd never played house and shared dreams of what kind of life we could build together. We jumped from passionate letters into tying the knot. As far as I was concerned, our letters were solid "proof" that Edith loved me. The way I saw it, once we slipped on those rings, life would be one great big happy love fest.

My commanding officer granted me a two-week furlough to get married and I left for Wolverhampton with my neatly pressed number one navy uniform. The Rowan's offered me their guest room. Something must have happened and I think I have blocked out what triggered my change of heart. At the very last minute I got cold feet. Something made me come to my senses and I started to seriously rethink my decision to marry Edith. Maybe it was watching Rowan and sensing his relationship with Edith was much, much more than a relationship between a friendly boss and his pretty young secretary. Desperately, I finally realized that I was suffering from something other than a classic case of last minute jitters. I was waking up to the fact that I was about to make a massive mistake. I wanted out. I'm not the kind of person who panics but when I woke up to the mess I'd got myself into, I wanted out. Now! No delay. Stop and walk away. That's what I wanted to do but there was a huge gap between what I wanted to do and what could be done.

Rowan must have heard me shuffling around in my room because he caught me packing my bag. "What are you doing?" I looked at him and told him the truth: "I'm not getting married tomorrow." Before he could reply, I shot back, "I'm taking the train back to barracks." He stood in the door to my room barring my way. "You bloody fool, you can't back out now. You've got to go through with it." I started to argue but he persisted. He explained that once the banns were published we were legally obligated to go through with the marriage. How was I to know whether he was telling me the truth? Admittedly, I knew the Brits were law abiding people with strange customs, and for all I knew I was locked into my decision. Listening to him, once the banns were tacked onto the church notice board, there was no turning back. My head sank and I shut the door on him. My instincts shrieked: "Get the hell out you silly bugger," but reason and a sense of duty overrode them. I had to be a good British citizen and obey the law and make my marriage work.

The ceremony took place on a nice summer day in June 1945 in the All Saints Church. There weren't many people in the church. Her parents and sister attended and the Rowan's, all smiles and full of good cheer, 'represented' my family. After the ceremony the 'happily married couple' went back to her parents for drinks and lunch. None of my mates attended. The war effort needed them. The following day we left for Blackpool for our honeymoon where she had made hotel reservations.

On the first day of our honeymoon I had a shock: we were unable to consummate our marriage. Even if Edith had been in a hurry to get married, was it too much to ask for her to do a bit of pre-wedding personal planning? Much to my disgust, on our first day of married life she told me that she had her period! I felt awful and I simply could not see any sign of her love towards me. It seemed as if she had to strain to touch me and she moved away from me when I caressed her. It's not unusual for honeymoons to be tense and ours was not starting out right. Nature was not an insurmountable barrier. During the night, in spite of everything including her protests, I made love to her. She didn't respond; there was absolutely no sign of any desire or satisfaction from my new bride. This wasn't supposed to happen, I kept telling myself. I thought, aren't "we" supposed to be in love?

Typical honeymooners, we wandered about town looking into shop windows and stopping in a few pubs. She refused to show any signs of affection. On the contrary, it was if I didn't exist and she was walking alone. I started to make excuses. "Maybe she's shy and we are just getting to know each other, maybe all the excitement triggered an early period, maybe, maybe, maybe...." Hours stretched into days and the longer we stayed together the more my mind switched to paths it had been on before we got married.

For starters, my wedding ring still felt funny on my finger. Often, when I looked at it, I remembered Randall telling me when he introduced us that Edith was Jack Rowan's mistress. Who in the hell did I think I was to wedge myself between those two? Why didn't I listen to everyone who tried to warn me away from her? Starting with our grim honeymoon in Blackpool I began a fifteen month journey into a mental hell that I had made for myself; no one else was responsible for the mess that seemed to stretch forever between June 1945 and September 1946.

After more than half a century, that is more than ample time to reflect, I'm not sure I can answer my own questions. Admittedly, on the eve of our marriage I was a very sentimental and sensitive young man who desperately wanted to fall in love and be loved and I know I was prepared to put up with a lot just in order to land her. Probably, and I don't think I'm fooling myself, I heard what Randall was telling me about her but I could not bring myself to believe him. "Not her," I kept telling myself until I finally believed my own self-deception.

Perhaps my idealized vision of marriage was also a normal desire coming from someone who had grown up an orphan and who had spent the previous six years at war. The way I looked at the world, marriage was synonymous with peacetime, a normal world where you could have children, go to the pub, have friends over for dinner, and walk the dog in the evening after work. Any advice that might have popped my illusions (maybe they were delusions, who knows?) was rejected because I had to be right and they had to be wrong. Didn't the fact that we'd been corresponding mean something?

I can't remember how I acted when we returned to Wolverhampton. My memory is a total blank on details but I do recall her adoptive parents Mr. and Mrs. Gunter received us warmly. They were very ordinary people. He was a simple laborer and she was a fine old lady. By most standards they were poor in material things, but, they were very rich in spirit. Without a doubt, they were two of the kindest people you could ever meet. They never interfered with us when we stayed with them. Whenever I was on leave I made it a point to always bring them my ration tickets, cigarettes and whatever food I could collect.

*****

Edith was still distant, present but not quite 'there' when we were together. She wasn't overtly uncivil in public; she was merely that other person in the room. Far too quickly for my own good I started becoming resigned to how our relationship was unfolding. Without making excuses, maybe I had become accustomed to her and decided to let her be. In my mind I was rationalizing away our problems because all I could do was deal with symptoms. My inner voice began to talk to me and I had to admit, not all the time I heard it but every now and then, there was something going on. Even Edith's sister, Emily, was uneasy.

After a couple of weeks as a married couple, and as gently as possible, she cautioned me to be wary about Edith's relations with Rowan. Emily was married to an 8th Army soldier serving in Libya. He was in the thick of it and three times he had been reporting MIA and three times he managed to return. In the end, he actually survived the war but I never got to meet him. Emily was a nice woman with two children. She was concerned about me but she was in a difficult position. How far could she go in trying to get me to wake-up and take charge of my life?

What she had to do was unpleasant, no sane person likes to talk about adultery, especially in her family and to someone who just married her sister, but somehow she had to lift the blinders I had slapped over my eyes and talk common sense to me. Love is deaf and blind, and there's no cure for obstinate romantic love. Delicately, with ever so much care, she cautioned me to be less tolerant about the relationship Edith had with Rowan. I thought about what she said and probably fobbed her off with something ridiculous like, "It's just sisters being nasty to each other. Happens all the time," or something like that. Even the wife of my old shipmate Fred Grey said the same thing, "You need to watch out." I heard them but I was deaf and dumb when it came to Edith. I repeated to myself that I did not and could not begin to have doubts about my wife. My God! The ink on our marriage certificate was barely dry.

My ability to rationalize was almost pathetic. I looked at our relationship and told myself that Edith was my wife and I had married a good woman. As far as I was concerned, she simply wouldn't be unfaithful because good people don't do bad things to the person they love. In view of what was going on between us, my attitude was downright stupid, to say the least. I believed in my intricately woven self-delusion even when she became pregnant but that was months later.

In the meantime I started to unravel. The war was winding down and when it was over I would have to make a go of my life in the new post war civilian world with a new marriage that wasn't working out. I had to get a grip on myself but I couldn't. Events were spiraling outside my control in what should have been the happiest months of my life.

Germany had surrendered. Amidst the excitement I managed to get permission for compassionate leave to go to France to see family members who had returned from German POW and concentration camps. I was given four weeks leave. This time I knew what to expect; my bags were filled to their bursting point with foodstuffs that I knew my family could not get. I told Edith I was leaving and she shrugged nonchalantly. She didn't say anything nice like, 'safe trip' or 'say hello to your family for me.' All I wanted was some recognition, something to let me know that I mattered to her.

*****

When I arrived in Lyon I immediately went to see my cousin Raymond. He was in a sanatorium because he had contracted TB during his four years as a POW. He was in great form and once he found out how well I spoke English he hatched an idea. "Why don't you come back to France and work with me as a comedian." We laughed. It was one of the craziest ideas I'd ever heard. "We'll be a great success," he said with a theatrical wave of his hand. Actually, he was a good actor and he knew what he was talking about.

He studied theatre before the war. In his prison camp he organized a camp comedy troupe that performed with considerable success. But, we hadn't seen each other for years and he couldn't realize that I had evolved and belonged to a different world. Our interests were too far apart to make sense of his project. Anyway, in order not to deceive him I told him to get himself cured first. "Once you are healthy enough to walk on stage we can talk about making plans for the future. In the meantime, I'll think about it and I'll let you know what I want to do after I've been demobbed from the armed forces." It was a fair response. I still had a commitment to the armed forces to think about and he was far from well.

My uncle and I had a long talk about my meeting with Raymond. He was plainly very worried. "He listens to you but he won't listen to me." I nodded in agreement. "He is sicker than he is willing to admit," his voice trailed and I nodded again. "He can't leave the hospital. He has to stay until his treatment has run its course." The old man made sense but I tried to explain to him that I could understand why Raymond wanted out. "Remember, he has been locked up for four years. He wants out of the sanatorium to prove to himself that he really is alive. He's got to do something that won't keep him confined inside four walls." My uncle listened to me carefully. I could tell he appreciated my genuine concern for both of them. He shook his head. That's when I realized I wasn't going to sway him so I agreed to try and persuade Raymond to stay in the sanatorium under medical supervision.

My God, Raymond was stubborn! I used every argument I could think of to convince him to follow his treatment. "With all the new miracle drugs they have now, you'll come out a new man." Raymond laughed and pretended to push me away. In the end, I lost. He refused to take my advice, or anyone else's for that matter, and by refusing advice he hastened his death. Another cousin, Louis Brun, returned from Malthausen. He was a walking skeleton. Even though he had received medical treatment in Switzerland he was still a pitiful sight. His legs were crosshatched with angry red scars, permanent reminders of when the German guard dogs had attacked him.

Their apartment was cramped and the air was stale, definitely not a healthy environment and I was worried about what effect it might have on his sisters. They wanted to help, they wanted to be close, but their health was also at risk. "Keep the rooms open and ventilated," I advised. They were puzzled but I told them that one of the reasons why the navy had such a high percentage of TB among its personnel was the fact that we lived on top of each other and there was not enough fresh air being pumped into the ships. My experience and my logic was something they could not argue with and they followed my advice and took the necessary precautionary steps caring for them.

But my biggest difficulties with my sisters and brother were related to Edith. In their eyes, because I had married an English woman that meant I would not come back and live in France. I guess I started to sound like a broken record because I kept telling them that England was not far away, the war with Japan would soon be over, a new era of modern transport would begin, and we'd still be the same family and we'd still be able to visit each other. They grumbled and scowled and I realized I was not going to win any converts on this trip.

While on leave I took advantage of my time to look around and get a 'feel' of how things were evolving in post war France. Based on my first trip back, I was concerned about the political scene and social stability. I went to Nimes and Lyon to see my sisters. At least my oldest sister's routine had not changed. She was still working and I wondered aloud when she would get married and start a real life for herself? She pretended not to hear me; that was enough of an answer for me not to pursue the topic any more.

Instead of me asking them a lot of questions, they kept pestering me with questions about what I was going to do. Their constant questions got a consistent reply. "I don't know what I'm going to do when I demob, but, I do know there's plenty of work for me in England." That response never sank in because in a matter of a few hours I'd hear, "Rene, have you ever thought about what you are going to ……" Truth said, I felt more at home in England than in France. I had managed to integrate into the English way of life and I felt more at home in England than I felt in France where, by birth at least, I had the right to feel at home. I didn't want to admit to myself that I felt like a stranger in my native land.

Our world, the world of naval seamen, was changing rapidly. The war in the Far East was drawing to a close. The Japanese, like the Germans, were no match for the allies. I met some ex Free French Sailors and we started talking about enlisting in the French navy. One of them laughed as if he had an inside joke. "What's so funny," I asked? His answer shocked me. "From what we've been able to figure out, the French navy doesn't want to ever see us again." "How do you know?" Apparently one of them had been able to get a good look at the registers and saw the names of the French sailors who chose to become Free French. All their names were underlined in red. "We've been red lined." In anybody's book that meant no promotions and rotten assignments. "Do you want to serve with the occupying forces in Germany, or some other hole?" The question hurt but it made sense. "In their eyes we were wrong to have been right in 1940." So, there it was. In a tight little sentence, whatever thoughts I had about joining the French navy were blown away. War wounds are slow to heal.

Maybe being red lined wasn't so bad after all. There was no way I would not get into trouble if I had to take orders from officers whom I considered to be traitors and unworthy of my trust. Admittedly, not all French officers were alike, but I knew enough of what had happened to know that I could bring myself to serve under superiors I did not respect and trust. So many unpardonable things had been done during the war against Frenchmen by Frenchmen.

I remember the story of three French seamen who were on the cruiser Manchester when she was disabled off Cape Bon in Tunisia. The Manchester was scuttled and the entire crew, officers and ratings, were put in a Vichy internment. When the guards discovered that there were three Frenchmen in the crew they separated them and shipped them via Italy to Marseille where a German navy escort took them to a prison camp in Germany. Apparently, even the German naval escort could not understand this level of cruelty from the French Vichy navy authority and with their 'help' one Frenchman managed to 'escape'. I don't know what happened to the Vichy officer responsible for this treachery but I know what I would have done. I wouldn't have thought twice about killing him.

Probably at about this stage, sometime late in the summer of 1945, I made up my mind about what I was going to do with my life. Like many of my shipmates, I decided to stay in the UK and remain a good British citizen. Come what may, my decision was taken and I felt relieved. It was the fourth week of leave and I headed 'home' in Pompey Barracks. I made the rounds and said goodbye to my family. We expected to see each other very soon but little did we know that the next time would be many years into the future.

*****

It was "Reunion Time" back in Pompey barracks. Within a couple of weeks I met many former shipmates I had not seen since July 1940 when we joined up in the Royal Navy. When on duty we worked hard and we played hard when we were on shore leave. In the beginning of the war, after a few tries in other pubs, we finally adopted one and made it "ours." It was the Wheel Barrow in the South End. The publican was a good bloke who had no difficulty with his navies who spoke French and English. Maybe it was because we behaved or, it could have been because he was discreet, he never asked us enough questions to put two-and-two together to make four. I'm sure he had a pretty good idea of who we really were, but he didn't bother us because we always paid our bar bills and we weren't too unruly.

We'd play darts and cards until, "Time, gentlemen," was called and then we lurched our way to a three-story house that we called our "sleeping club." It was a sort of boarding house, not a brothel, run by a wonderful spinster, Miss Vereker. We called her aunty and she spoke to us in French, good French. I've forgotten how she learned it; from the looks of her it wasn't from a French lover.

Aunty made us share rooms. Most of the time we were only RN French seamen but occasionally some Polish sailors were lodged there also, probably attracted by the low room rates. Each bedroom had two or three beds. In the winter, we fed the gas heater pence to try and stay warm. After the war was over we went back to see her. For aunty, seeing some of us again was a great another reunion. Miraculously, her boarding house had survived the German air raids.

Returning to the boarding house produce a happy surprise that managed to put a further strain on my relationship with Edith. To explain what happen I need to back track to the early 1940's. A heavy air raid began one night when we were sleeping off the evening's joy in the pub. Auntie's house was full and some of us were sleeping on the floor. In front of her house there was a big park with anti aircraft guns 'manned' by ATS girls. They were wonderful. Very professional and committed, they fought hard and when the raids were over, they played hard. It was crazy but every time we survived a raid we'd go across to them with pots of tea or coffee. They really enjoyed seeing us coming and it wasn't long before some of us were able to start a little bit of flirting. That happened years ago. In the meantime I was married and shouldn't have been flirting but I was beginning to make all kinds of excuses for the way I was thinking and the way I behaved.

Taulus

When I first went back to auntie's after years of being away I was amazed and happy to discover 'our' girls were still there. I looked around and asked if Maureen was still assigned to the battery and, sure enough, she was. Three years earlier we had a friendly little affair, one of those wartime encounters that turn out well. No sooner had I asked for her and ….. there …. she was. What a smile, what a laugh, her eyes were dancing and she threw her arms around me and gave me a big hug. In fifteen seconds I had more genuine emotion from an old female friend than I had experienced all the time I'd known my wife. Maureen was wild about seeing me and I fell for her again. Yes, I know, I was married and flirting violated the letter and spirit of marriage but, without wailing in public, I was desperately unhappy. My relationship with Edith was not worth the ink scrawled on our marriage license.

Maureen and I met almost every evening when we were off duty. It was paradise but too good to last. After a couple of weeks of this lovely time she was transferred to Brighton so we had to organize meeting on weekends. That was more difficult than either of us had imagined. On one of our wonderful weekends I got her back to barracks after hours. Naturally, she was punished. Over the phone she told me that she was confined to barracks for the coming weekend. I gave that situation a lot of thought. There had to be a way to get together. "Don't worry, I'm going to talk to your commanding officer and get you out." There was a long silence on her end of the line finally broken by a skeptical, "Oh?" I had it all figured out. I'd tell her C.O. that I had been drafted to the Far East and it looked like I wouldn't see her again for at least two years.

The following weekend I showed up in uniform at the duty officer desk at her barracks in Brighton. I saluted and requested permission to speak. "Mam," I began slowly and plaintively, "I have a problem." And then I really spun it! I explained that we were planning to get married but I had been drafted to the naval base at Trincomalee in Ceylon. "We're going to be apart for two years and that's really an awfully (I really dragged so hard on 'awfully' it almost made me wince) long time." She looked me straight in my eyes for a few seconds.

If her eyes had been drills, the back of my head would have had holes in it by the time she blinked and picked up the telephone. "Get me Maureen," she ordered. When Maureen came on the phone the duty officer asked her, "Why have you been confined to barracks?" Maureen gave a straight answer. The duty officer hung up long enough only to make another call, this time to a more senior officer.

I couldn't hear the conversation but I had the feeling that the situation was going in my favor. She put down the phone and riddled me with another piercing stare. I couldn't read her this time but I did manage to tell myself that she was only a couple of years older than me. Finally, after studying my forlorn face, she said, half-smiling, "I'm going to let her out only because her punishment ends on Monday. You must take full responsibility that she will be back in barracks before 2400 hours tonight." I saluted her again. "I will make sure she is back in time." Whew! We were almost there. I stood back from the gate and waited for Maureen.

It wasn't a long wait in time but it was too long to wait in case the duty officer decided to ask more questions. When Maureen arrived I saw the duty officer get up and go over to her. I barked out at her, "Why the bloody hell did you manage to be late last week?" Maureen was startled but she picked up the hint. "I missed the train and don't you yell at me," she shrilled in sudden fury. As we stalked away I saw the duty officer's incredulous face reflected in the window. Once around the corner and out of sight we burst out laughing. I was chuffed when she told me I was a great actor. But, I came down to earth fast when she said, "And, I'll have you know, the D.O. thinks you are bad luck."

We spent a wonderful day together. That happy day is still etched in my memory as one of those times in life when being alive with a woman you care for is exciting, one of those brief interludes when everything is right. To be honest, that day finally managed to prod me toward admitting to myself that I was drifting away from Edith. We hadn't been married six months and I think I knew the gulf between us was too wide to ever be bridged. I should have recognized this conclusion / observation, call it what you want, was an important sign of a failed marriage but it was probably too soon for me to admit my mistake. Maureen was warm and affectionate, the very opposite of Edith.

I was still too blind, perhaps too proud, or too stubborn to accept the truth: my relationship with Edith was doomed from the beginning and I should never have married her. I couldn't be honest with myself and admit time was not going to improve a relationship that was dead in the water. But, even when I knew in my heart that I had made a colossal mistake, I kept telling myself that I was committed to her, "till death us do part."

I was torn between being practical and admitting I had made a horrible mistake in marrying her versus pretending that a miracle would happen and turn our marriage into a happy relationship. "Won't something good happen that will make us go 'click' and suddenly, miraculously, our marriage will work?" I was still a kid trying to dream his way out of a mess. Realistically, every time I compared Maureen to Edith, my wife came up a very distant second. I felt as if I was in a battle and I was too busy trying to stay alive and fight the pain to think about my wound. I worked hard at "willing" the problem to go away but nothing I did stopped my grinding despair. I was in a situation that was getting worse instead of improving. Could it get worse? Yes, it not only could, it did. Edith sent me a letter that floored me. She was pregnant. It must have been sometime late in September or early October.

"What do you want to name it," she wrote? Those were the days before you could find out the baby's sex before it was born. Suddenly, I found myself thinking about a name for my future son or daughter. I hated her question because it confused me even more. I started asking questions that no prospective father should ever have to ask because, at least the way I was brought up to believe, the miracle of child birth was something you wanted, something miraculous and good you shared with your wife. Did I even want a child? Was it right to feel the way I did or was it wrong to feel the way I did? What's going on with my life, I kept asking? I couldn't answer all the questions that popped up my head out of nowhere but I realized that I had to come to grips with the mess I'd made in my personal life.

Her letter arrived when my emotions and loyalties were being torn in opposite directions. There were two worlds: my professional life in the navy and my private life. Each of those worlds, in turn, was crumbling. Did I stay in the navy or did I become a civilian, whatever that meant? Did I stay with Edith, if so, how could we make our marriage work or did I find another woman like Maureen and start all over?

Life in the barracks provided the reassuring comfort of a daily routine. I met the chap who went through the LTO course with me two years earlier. War hadn't changed him too much: he was still playing the violin and writing melodies. But what was important for me was not his music but the fact he had married an English girl from the north of England and his marriage was working. It was obvious that his wife loved him. Together, they managed to create a normal life despite being separated, he in the barracks and she in the north.

He hired a room in the South end so that he would not have to go to a hotel when his wife came down to see him. "Matey, there's another room in the same house. Grab it quick," he said. I went to see the room and immediately hired it before anyone else could get it. Rooming was at a premium; I was very lucky to have a nice room not too far from the barracks. I began to move some of my personal items into the room in the hope that, however small and cramped, Edith and I could start to live like any other normal happy couple waiting for their first child. Again, hope was stronger than reason.

I hoped a change of locale would somehow cement our relationship and we could pick up the pieces and move forward together. If I had been reasonable, I'd have told myself to shove off. She wasn't going to leap into my arms. Sure enough, Edith's reaction or lack of reaction was another warning sign. She remained uncommitted. As far as she was concerned, having a room to be together was neither a good idea nor a bad idea. Having a room so we could live together was a non-event; so what? Her reaction hurt but I didn't say anything. What could I say? Tell her to take our child and get lost? I couldn't bring myself to say something that cruel to her. It even upset me when I found I was talking to myself that way.

My mate began teaching me to play the violin. I wasn't starting completely from scratch. Before the war my uncle bought me a violin but I never had the time to learn it properly. Life as a naval cadet and the war prevented me from continuing so I never did learn to play properly. I sat in my little room that was on the floor directly above my mate's room. From my window I could look down on the backyard of a Wren residence. We'd sit in front of our windows and play, sometimes well, sometimes a little hard on the ears, but what we lacked in skill we made up in vigor. The girls loved it. They would wave to us and shout, "more." While I fiddled and screeched, at least as far as I was concerned, total strangers showed me more affection than my wife. God, I was lonely and lost!

Soon after I moved in a girl who lived on the same floor knocked on my door. I opened it, "Yes," I asked. She introduced herself, "I'm Virginia Ford." "I live down at the end of the corridor." She fidgeted with a tassel on her blouse. "I wonder if you could spare me a couple of matches." She was nice looking; spoke well, probably in her late teens or maybe even about twenty. She was attractive, no raving beauty, just a nice girl who used the excuse of having no matches as a way to meet me. "Here you go," and I handed her some matches. She hesitated. "Sometime when you're free, please come over and have a cup of coffee or tea with me." She laughed. "Actually, that's what I wanted to say. Are you free?"

I followed her to her room that was larger than mine. It had a kitchenette and a small bedroom. "Are you the one who is playing the lovely violin?" I shook my head. "No, it's my friend. I'm the one who makes noise. He makes music." She laughed again, an easy laugh. I looked around her tidy apartment. "Do you do these?" I pointed to partially painted cups, mugs and plates. "Actually, I do." She worked on orders from home for a company. "When the war's over I'm going to Paris to study art." Still sort of a kid, long on dreams, and obviously someone I felt I could enjoy being with.

Our chemistry was right. Beginning with that contrived encounter we started a relationship that meant a lot to me. We used to go dancing in a pub that was not used by my shipmates because I was flirting in earnest. Flirting is one thing but I needed a more physical relationship. Another right strong-willed lass who was determined to let me go only so far and then she made me stop. Our sessions lasted until the very early hours of the morning and you can imagine the kind of shape I was in when I went back to bed aroused but unsatisfied. I was ready to explode but I kept coming back for more. This happy, but frustrating, interlude lasted for quite awhile.

In May 1946 Edith sent me a telegram telling me that Victoria Kathleen had been born and she asked me to come to the hospital. I was given special leave to meet my daughter. Or, at least when I left the barracks I thought she was mine. When I got to the hospital the sister in charge met me. I asked to see Victoria Kathleen. "Who are you," she asked? I was proud, happy, and just a bit cocky. "I'm the father." She scowled menacingly from under her white coif. I could see why she was the head nurse because she was imposing and authoritative, a master sergeant of the syringe brigade. "Impossible," she quipped in a haughty tone of voice that I associated that came from someone who was righteous and powerful.

My head must have snapped. Was this some kind of a joke ward sisters play on first time fathers? If it was a joke, I wasn't laughing. "The father left just a few minutes ago," she harrumphed. Was she trying to play games with me? Then it started to sink in. The awful heavy truth hit me and I could feel myself turning white with rage. The 'father' was none other than Edith's boss and our good friend, Jack Rowan.

I don't know how I managed to remain calm and control myself but I acted like a model sailor. Admittedly, this wasn't combat but I was at war with my emotions. During the shooting war, I learned that when I used my head to survive, I always made it through. I fished into my tunic. "Here's my navy pay book." It had my name. I held it steady with my index finger under the line that had my name: John Powell. She studied the document carefully, looked at me again, and her features seemed to soften ever so slightly. Was it a sign of compassion, her recognition of the truth that had thundered across my life only moments before? "Follow me," she ordered. If she had barked 'Quick march' I would have fallen in smartly.

We walked down a shiny corridor and turned into a ward room with four beds. There were two or three women propped up in their beds. One was feeding her newborn child. She smiled in my direction and then turned back to her baby. Obviously, Victoria Kathleen wasn't the only baby born that week. Edith and I stared at each other. The sister said, in a tone that was part triumphant and part biting, "Your husband has just arrived." The word 'husband' was too articulate and slicing to leave any no doubt in my mind as to what she knew about our relationship.

Edith was tired. There were big dark circles under her eyes; I'd never seen her so unattractive. Her puffy little red-rimmed glassy eyes stared at me. I could have been the local fish-and-chips vendor for all she cared. Would she start crying? I took her hand because I hate to see women cry. I can't remember our conversation but it was probably something fairly common for those circumstances: "how do you feel," and, "the baby is lovely." I think I probably said anything to steer me away from having to deal with an ache inside me that was quickly turning into a wildfire that was spreading to every part of my body. My head ached, my arms ached and my mouth was dry. I wanted to yell as loud as I could but I didn't let on to her that I was close to snapping.

We kept up the charade for the better part of an hour. I think I said something about leaving the navy and looking for a civilian job, but the more I nattered the more I knew that I was beginning to lose my last reserve of self-control. I needed to get out of there. My mouth was saying something but all I kept hearing was not my own voice but what the sister had said. The tension had become too intense and I felt that if I didn't get out of there I might regret it. "I'm out on a special leave and I have to get back to Portsmouth on the next train," I managed to say with as much feeling as I could muster. I kissed her and squeezed her hand. "We'll be in touch." I quickly left the room, a new father who wasn't a father.

Rene Dassac (in collaboration with Patrick K. Robbins)

CHAPTER SIX: DEMOB

The navy was my family. It was warm, stern, and fair most of the time. I always knew where I stood and they looked after me. I remembered what the commodore said when I signed up as a Royal Navy seaman: "If you ever need help or advice, your officers are there to help you." I was lucky to have someone to turn to because, I had to admit, I was one of thousands of young men who were about to take major decisions concerning their futures. Now, for the first time, I thought it would be good for me to start asking for advice because I had to come to grips with some pretty hard facts about my life and I felt lost. I couldn't bring myself to admit that I really didn't know what to do with my life.

Arrangements were underway back at the barracks to organize the demobilization of all the H.O. ratings. I know this probably sounds strange, especially coming from someone who had been through the war at sea, but I started to feel sorry that the war ended so quickly. "At least, they could have waited until I had figured out what I was going to do with my life," I kept thinking. Everyone was talking about where to find jobs, what to do, what life would be like in the civilian world.

Darrey was joining the police force and taking a course at Scotland Yard. Fred Grey was going to join his father-in-law in the Midlands working for a railway company in Birmingham. Boswell had married a Londoner and was going to work in her family's grocery shop. Tyrell was off to Bermuda and my shipmate from the Savorgnan de Brazza had married the widow who looked after him when he had been temporarily discharged because he got frostbite in the feet while surviving ten days on a raft in the north Atlantic in the winter of 1941. He was on his way to London where he had found a job as steward in a well-known London hotel. L. Power was like all the others who married in England. As far as I know, none of them went back to France with their English wives.

To ease our way into the civilian world, the navy issued us with two civilian suits, two white shirts, socks, shoes, and even a nice felt hat. I had managed to save some of my pay and with this I treated myself to a made-to-measure suit from a London tailor located near Victoria Station. My own suit was good for my ego and, I have to say so myself, I looked rather smart. I might have been dressed properly but all the finery and trappings didn't prevent me from comparing my life to my mates, good men looking forward to starting new lives. Life is a two-headed coin. Sometimes when you flip it the Hope head lands face up and sometimes Despair stares at you. They flipped the Hope side of the coin.

They were lucky and I knew it. Their wives loved them and this meant they could build a future in the new post-war world. It wasn't the same for me. My marriage, if I had to use that word, had crumbled beyond repair. It hurt to see my married mates so happy. No matter how hard I looked at my relationship with Edith, there was nothing to build on. Was I doomed to play the fool; did she expect me to love Rowan's daughter?

I finally got the courage up to admit that she was an adulteress. One weekend I went to see Edith but she was not home. Her mother met me at the door. "Didn't Edith get my telegram saying I would be here this weekend?" Her mother gave a weak smile. "Yes, as a matter of fact she did, but she's gone to spend the weekend with the Rowan's." I stormed out of the house barely in control of myself. I let myself into Rowan's house and found them sitting alone in the lounge. Only by practicing enormous self-restraint was I able to restrain myself from doing something to him that would have made me a loser. I acted like a gentleman but I was very close to snapping.

I had absolutely no desire to make love to Edith; she didn't encourage me. "I'm tired," I complained but in order to humor her I said, "My you look nice." Actually she looked nice but she didn't arouse me. One afternoon when we were alone she turned on me. In a voice dripping with mockery she asked, "Could there be someone else in your life, someone else to share your bed?" She was needling me with a bitchy comment that struck me as odd. Who did she think she was accusing me? Or, was she on to me and taunting me? I was furious. "Nonsense," I snarled. "You only sleep with me to favor me and I sleep with you because I'm trying to be a good husband."

Another time I came home and she looked up from some mending and said, quite casually, "Oh, hello. On leave again?" Even after weeks of absence there was no spark. She even told me, "I don't want to have sex with you." What little civil relationship we had began unraveling faster and faster. Not surprisingly, we seemed to be locked into one unending argument after another.

It was nasty; the more we argued the more I started to recall things that happened before the baby was born. Things that had happened should have tipped me off that something was seriously wrong. Once she wrote that she was due for a holiday. "I'm off to Blackpool with some friends," she wrote as if I really did not exist. Her response sort of worked in my favor! I didn't want to be caught with Virginia but at the same time I didn't want her to feel she could fob me off so casually. If she had come to Portsmouth she might have been tipped off to my relationship with Virginia but I decided to play the game and I replied, "The least you can do is come spend your holiday with me." Although I played the game, Edith's response hurt and I told Virginia about it. She became furious at the idea of me sleeping with my wife. If it hadn't been so painful it would have been comical so long as what was happening didn't involve me. But it did and for a few days I managed to juggle the two relationships.

Before she arrived Virginia made me promise that I would see her every day. Her eyes moistened and I finally broke down and let her know what was really in my heart. I admitted what I had known for a long time but could not bring myself to admit to anyone. "Edith and I never loved each other." Almost as an afterthought I continued, "And we will never be able to love each other." I said it, and I meant it. True to my word, I booked a room for Edith in a hotel that was only three or four blocks away from Virginia's little flat.

Coping with Edith wasn't my only problem. Probably as a result of an innocent slip of the tongue during one of their infrequent telephone conversations, Virginia told her parents about us. Her father was furious at our relationship. He sent her a scathing letter that she wouldn't let me read. It must have been brutal because our relationship took a direct hit from his withering broadside. I gathered he used no-nonsense blunt language and gave her a choice: Either she broke off our relationship or he would never see her again. She was shocked and cried a lot and that didn't help things at all. Between sobs and sniffles, she managed to blurt, "Go back to your wife. When you divorce her we can start a new life together." I thought about that. At least I was managing to sort out one of my relationships.

A few days later she went home to her family in Scotland. Instead of making a clean break of it, we agreed to correspond through a friend of hers in Chelsea who agreed to act as a letter box. After more tears and kissing we said our good-byes and each went his and her way to start a new life. As was the case with Maureen, we never saw each other again.

I was beginning to think more clearly. In one last vain attempt to make our marriage work, I decided before doing anything stupid I would go back to Wolverhampton and try to settle things with Edith. One last time, I vowed to myself: try and make the marriage work. I went through London on the way to Wolverhampton and I bought a lot of things for Edith and the baby. Coming laden with gifts made my return a little easier. To her credit, I must admit that she was not as aggressive as I was expecting her to be. Of course, her civility might have been because she wanted to avoid a row in front of her mother, a good plain woman but not stupid. I strongly suspected Mrs. Gunter knew a lot more about her daughter's behavior than she let on but she was not going to get involved. She was happy playing the role of a good doting grandmother who spent a lot of time looking after her grandchild.

During that period when the baby was quite small I came home on most weekends. Our life was almost normal at first. We managed to be civil to each other for a few hours but it didn't take much to start us arguing again. Constant quarreling was too much for me. Day by day, I was turning in on myself. I quit eating properly and I couldn't even get a good night's sleep. All night long I'd toss and turn and try and solve my problems. The more I tried to find a solution the more frustrated I became. I was in a downward spiral but fortunately I still had friends. I was a civilian but I still had my family of navy friends.

Rene Dassac (in collaboration with Patrick K. Robbins)

I went to see my ex shipmate Randall who went with me to Wolverhampton to look for a job. Finding steady employment was not easy. I was a trained mechanic but, in those days after the war, a lot of companies did not want to hire someone with my background because we were 'safety risks'. I didn't understand what they meant but in their mind's it was quite simple: during the war we had been trained to waste no time making repairs. Our priorities were: repair first, safety second. In civilian life that spelled danger and pounding on doors was a frustrating and depressing experience. Randall lost his temper several times but finally I landed a job in a company that made rayon.

I was hired to work on a shift that repaired spinning motors. These motors operated near acid baths. Vapors and spills ate through the electrical insulation. The factory worked on a twenty-four hour shift basis. Our job was to get the motors back into operation as quickly as possible after they shorted out. The work was interesting and I had some good mates. There was a jovial ex 8th army soldier who loved to put money on the horses. I knew nothing about horses. One day he talked me into putting a fiver on a horse, "a sure winner." Would you believe it? The horse won. I was over the moon and glad to share my quite substantial win with him.

One thing led to another. We were beginning to create a friendship. He began telling me about the problems he was having with his wife. Naturally, I told him my own troubles. During the war he had been in Libya for a few years. While he was away his wife took a (wartime) lover. He found out about it and told her he was prepared to forgive her if she quit seeing the other bloke. She agreed but continued the relationship on the sly and he caught her again. She was distraught and told him she wouldn't break-off the relationship. Did that sound familiar to me? At least he had confronted his wife; I hadn't gotten that far with Edith. We agreed that we had tried to put their infidelity behind us but it wasn't working. Each of us was caught in a mental hell. No matter how hard we tried, we could not put our wives and what they had done to us, out of our minds.

One day when I was working the morning shift, he came on the job all smiles, singing and joking. "What'd you do? Win on the horses again," I asked jokingly. He burst out laughing. "No mate, I just strangled my wife this morning." I laughed. What the hell? I was accustomed to rough jokes. A couple of hours later the police came into our workshop and arrested him on suspicion of murder. I was devastated. That senseless crime only added to my feeling of utter hopelessness. He had spun out of control. Could the same thing happen to me?

The following weekend when I saw Edith I told her about what happened and tried to make her understand the suffering this poor chap went through. She was distant and pretended not to hear me. "I can understand how that guy felt," I said hoping to get her into conversation. She didn't even try to respond. She went on with whatever she was doing as if she hadn't even heard me. I wanted to scream at her, "Don't you see? That guy snapped. So can I." But, I didn't; I kept myself in check. To my credit, because I was on the thin edge between violence and deep despair, I hid any outward sign of my hurt and forced my emotions to simmer inside.

I could only hide so much. My health began to deteoriate to a point where even my friends could see the changes in me. Emily, Edith's sister, pulled me aside and again told me to tell Edith to end her relationship with Jack Rowan. Her advice was easier said than done. He existed in her life before I was on the scene, he fathered her child, and he mattered to her. I did not.

My friend Randall rescued me. The military had a social service to help men like me who were having problems making the transition to civilian life. Through him I got an appointment with an understanding military lawyer who advised ex servicemen. He was an officer at the RAF base because there was no naval facility inland at Wolverhampton. Our meeting was both strange and comical. Certainly, my mood was grim and I didn't feel like laughing but the outcome of our meeting almost made me burst out laughing. He looked like a lawyer and acted like a lawyer. I liked him immediately and I thought I might be able to relax with him and tell him my problems.

He asked me to sit down opposite him and then he leaned back from his desk, the picture of "Mr. Relaxed" and asked, "What can I do to help you? Please don't be shy and tell me your problems." My mental floodgates burst open. I spoke quickly, often in great detail.

Once I started I couldn't stop. I gave him all the details of my relationship with Edith from the start right up to that very day when I was sitting in his office pouring out my soul. He listened intently without interrupting. When I finished I felt as if someone had lifted a huge weight off my scrawny back. He rose and extended his hand to me. "What the hell is going on," I thought? In deep and serious tones he said, "Welcome to the club." I didn't know what 'club' I'd joined but we shook hands anyway. "Our members number in the thousands, in the tens of thousands!" So, I wasn't the only one in England with a marriage on the rocks.

His admission that there was a 'Misery Corps' provided me with some comfort but I still had to get out of my mess and get on with my life. Member or not, it was up to me to sort out my problems. "You have an advantage over most of us. You are younger and you can rebuild a new and better life for yourself. My advice to you is to start making the necessary procedures for a divorce." He outlined the procedure. It was simple and it was free. "You have a good record in the Royal Navy. They are short of experienced personnel like you." I had heard something similar but I really hadn't concentrated on it because of my problems with Edith. "In fact, they will pay you a bonus to sign up for an extended four years of service." This was music to my ears. It sounded so good to be needed once again. He agreed to give me a letter that I had to take to my port division in Portsmouth. Once I had signed up and volunteered for overseas service I could start divorce proceedings with the help of a naval lawyer. "Some of the steps are tricky but they work."

In rapid fire I was told to ask Edith to come see the lawyer with me. Once I was back in the navy I would be given married seaman housing onsite when my ship was assigned to a foreign port. For instance, if we were assigned to South Africa she would be invited to join me. If, she turned down three requests, or better still, if she refused to even consider my offers, a legal process was started that she could stop only if she joined me. Refusal to join me constituted "desertion without cause." Once I received three written refusals to join me I was instructed to give the letters to the navy lawyer. From then on, all I had to do was wait out the procedure because divorce proceedings would probably take around three years to complete.

It all sounded so logical and so simple. He asked me to avoid having heated arguments with her. "Tell her that you don't feel happy in civilian life and that you are planning to go back into the navy." His advice made sense. I thanked him profusely. As I started out of his office he said, "Don't forget … no arguments with your wife." It would be hard not to get caught up again in our verbal battles but the outcome he described was too attractive to waste on an argument with her. "Oh, by the way," he called out to me, "tell her that you will keep her informed of all your movements and you will arrange for the navy to send her monthly allocations." I waved thanks and started out the door with the prospect of a new and better life. For the first time in months I began to feel like my old self again.

On 2 September 1946 I signed up for four years extended service. It was a turning point in my life. My "marriage" had lasted fifteen months. I tried to find a reason why my marriage had ever taken place. About all I could manage was to convince myself that Edith and Rowan schemed to have me marry her so that 'our marriage' would provide a convenient screen for them. Marrying me was a way to protect their love affair from his dumb wife who should have been asking for answers to obvious questions. For starters, she might have asked, "What's going on between you two?" During that brief unhappy fifteen month period, I had tried civilian life and that was a failure. For the time being, I did not fit into the post war world as a civilian, as a Mr. Everybody who was happy to work in a factory. My marriage was a crushing failure. Doomed from the start, it only got worse.

All-in-all, my first months in the new post-War era hadn't turned out too well for me. While Europe was trying to dig out of the war's rubble, I had almost collapsed under the weight of two failures. I was bitter but not broken.

Looking back at September 1946, I now realize that I took the first of many steps that would lead me, eventually, to a point where I was controlling my own life. The next transition to a new life had begun. But, it would take a long time to finally land on my feet. And, it would be painful but there was no way I could know that in advance.

*****

Rene Dassac (in collaboration with Patrick K. Robbins)

I followed the lawyer's advice about how to handle my wife. It wasn't easy but Edith wasn't up to another round of bitter arguments. After a few days I left for Portsmouth Victory barracks wearing my old uniform that I had been wise to keep. At the barracks I was presented to my new commanding officer to whom I gave the letter the lawyer had given me. This officer must have seen many similar cases because he was very matter-of-fact in our meeting. He was comfortable walking me through the steps I had to take to get back into the system. Listening to him I kept telling myself, "It all seems so very natural. I belong in the Royal Navy." He continued. "You will be given a new official number because the one you had was for hostilities only." He looked at my papers again. "However, in your case you will have to get yourself naturalized." He gave me the address of a lawyer who would handle the legal side for me. "After that come back to me with the papers he will give you and the rest will be done from this end."

I had wasted months and countless hours boiling in a painful private cauldron of my own making. Now, my life was starting to take a familiar shape. He continued, "I see that you are volunteering for overseas service. We are so short of experience ratings that you will be drafted overseas without any problem." That was good news. He touched on something that was worrying me: what if they don't accept me for an overseas posting? According to him, there was no problem.

He saw me to the door and I can't describe how relieved I felt. Relief really isn't the proper word because what I was experiencing was a feeling of happiness knowing that I belonged somewhere. Once again, I was back in the navy, my real family. I knew I would plunge into the routine as if I had never left the navy. I was so lucky! Even their financial offer was attractive. I got a £50 signing bonus plus another £25 for having signed on for another four years.

I saw the lawyer who made me take the oath of allegiance. With my hand placed firmly on the bible, I swore to be loyal and serve my king, country and the British Empire. He registered me as René Dassac, also known as John Powell. He told me that I would not be able to keep both names. "Sort that out with the navy or the immigration authority. It shouldn't be a problem."

As far as I was concerned choosing a name was a huge issue and he was almost cavalier about it. I was understandably skeptical about the ease of the paperwork because I knew that if the navy had to start wading around in the 'if's and but's' of my life there was a chance something would get screwed up. But, I followed orders. My division officer in the barracks told me to apply for a passport. "At the time of registration, the officer there will tell you what name to take," he told me. That sounded simple enough but I was still skeptical.

I went around to the immigration service. "It's not up to me laddie to choose your name but if were, I'd advise you to keep on with your name of Powell," he told me. As if to mock the system and I know he wasn't trying to, he said, "Because it's so British! Nobody will question your nationality." That was sound advice but what he then said made me think. "You never know what the future may bring. Governments come and go, pleasant and unpleasant, but with such an English name it will be easier for you if you don't have to go into lengthy explanations if we ever get involved in another war." Yes, we had won the war and no, civil society was still afraid another war might break out. "John Powell will do me just fine," I replied. After all, everyone in the navy knew me by that name and my records were all recorded with that name, so it really was an easy move for me to become John Powell, a citizen of the United Kingdom.

Within a couple of weeks I was drafted to HMS Actaeon, a frigate built in the later years of the war. It had just gone through a complete refit. The crew was new. Most were very young called up ratings. Among the lower deck ratings you could count on one hand those who with more than three years service. Because I was one of them I was chosen to be in charge of the starboard forehead mess deck. This class of ship had not been modernized to the point of having fixed bunks; we slept in hammocks whose design hadn't changed for centuries. They may have been uncomfortable but hammocks were a real advantage in bad weather. In a hammock your body swings through the bad weather instead of rolling around in a bunk. For every advantage, there is a disadvantage: you have to sleep on your back. Everyone who snores sleeps on his back. It was noisy down below.

The older sailors stuck together talking about the new navy and sharing war stories. Shipboard life began a familiar routine. We made new friends. My best shipmate was John Knight who had served for a time as radio cipher on a Free French Torpedo boat. He was from Liverpool and he had a signal man mate who also came from Liverpool. I forgot his name, but we used to call him "Scouce", which is local slang for a Liverpudlian. They were both leading seamen; and like me they were in charge of their mess deck. There was a popular gunnery instructor (GI), a real comedian, always good for laughs when we were ashore. There were ten new recruits in my mess who had to be taught everything. They were young, quick learners and pretty easy going which helped to keep the inevitable friction under control.

Commander Cuthbert RN was our captain, a true gentleman who never lost his temper. I served under many captains and I rank him as one of the best. The first lieutenant was lieutenant Hayward-Butt RN, a sad looking chap who never smiled. He appeared to be deeply unhappy but whatever was eating him didn't get in the way of his work because he was efficient. We had two sub lieutenants and a midshipman all RN. A warrant officer was in charge of the armament. He was a very good person and he really knew his job well. He began his career at the bottom of the ladder and worked up the decks to become warrant officer. Petty officer Davidson was in charge of the anti submarine weapons and of the electrical equipment. It took us three weeks to get the ship ready to be commissioned and ready for working up exercises. HMS Actaeon was a good ship with good officers and crew. Everyone was working hard to adapt to the new peacetime navy.

We had our first Sunday division during which the captain told us of the many changes that were going to take place. For example, the torpedo branch was now purely electrical. This change in systems meant new weapons would be commissioned soon and we had a lot to learn. He was obviously proud of his ship and wanted his crew to share in the pride and make HMS Acteon an efficient ship admired throughout the fleet. Good news came last. We were to be stationed in Simon's Town S.A. However, before we put into Simon's Town, we had to spend time in Malta to continue our training.

During all this time I was so busy adapting myself to the new navy and so thoroughly enjoying myself that I found that I had too much to do. I didn't think about Edith and my failed marriage. Following my lawyer's instructions I wrote her and gave her all the details of our sailing to South Africa. Once we had established our port of call, I told her that I would arrange for her to join me. The navy provided housing for married people. She replied that she did not like the idea of going there because all her friends were in England. Chalk up one goal for my side! Her response didn't surprise me but it certainly was taking me one step closer to my divorce. I kept her letter because it contained her first written refusal to join me. I only needed two more until I could start divorce proceedings. All in all, I was happy.

Acteon was ready to sail. The quarter master piped over the loudspeaker, "Special duty seamen close up, hands fallen for leaving harbor." That command struck me hard. I'd heard it before and days later, in waters I'd never sailed, men who I would never see face to face, tried to kill me and I tried to kill them. But this time was different. I had survived and I was alive and this trip was going to be different. As far as I was concerned, we were on a peacetime cruise through the Med and down to South Africa. No one was going to shoot at us. What a strange notion? I was actually curious and caught myself thing, 'What's this peacetime navy all about'?

We left port on a beautiful October morning headed toward our first stop: Gibraltar. As we left Pompey we lined up on deck in our N° 1 uniform, standing to attention when we slid by the signal tower and the other warships tied up to the quay. I took deep breaths to clear my head. I was happy but also sad to leave the Pompey barracks I loved. I remembered all the hard times this town had gone through and the wonderful people I had known there. I could feel the mighty screws thrusting under the deck. The ship was 'right' and I was 'right' but I also felt a twinge of nostalgia. "God knows when I will see Pompey again," I thought. I'd sailed out before, a young inexperienced seaman heading into war. Now, I was a veteran sailor. Many of our younger recruits must have strained to see their families on the mole as we steamed past. It couldn't fight my emotions and I caught myself thinking about my "family." I shook my head as if to tell myself that sad chapter in my life was closing for good. No good would come from dwelling on what life Edith and I might have enjoyed if our "romance" had become the kind of reality shared by all those anonymous families lining the mole. It hurt to admit but I had to face up to the fact that I still had a lot of living to do, a lot of sorting out my life, before I could feel like a normal human being with a family he loved and a family who loved him.

The trip to Gibraltar was, of course, uneventful. There were no U boats, enemy planes or ships to worry about. How utterly novel! If there hadn't been so much to do it might have been boring. We were kept busy teaching routines at sea: how to stand watch, how to clean the mess, and how to live at sea. We went through action station exercises firing our three 4inch guns, 20mm AA guns and anti submarine exercises using our radar and asdic searching for a submarine dispatched from Gibraltar to simulate an attack. Performing that exercise took me some time to adjust to because I couldn't forget the past that easily. But, once I made the transition I couldn't get over the thrill of hunting for the sub and knowing that he was not going to sink us if we didn't sink him first. For an old hand like me, it was almost fun but I could not forget how inefficient my crew mates were compared to the wartime crew I lived with just a couple of years earlier.

If there was no urgency in the crew there was, nevertheless, a real desire to come up to the very high standards the captain had set for us. Maybe we weren't getting shot at but we had to be ready for war in case it broke out. The captain walked around his ship with a critical and constructive eye. He took notes and identified our weaknesses and then we drilled to eliminate them so that we would meet the high standards required by their lordships.

When you are living in cramped quarters for long periods you can't help getting to know each other rather well. There's always friction and there's always the possibility that friction leads to fist throwing but we were lucky because no fights had broken out. I knew fights are most likely to start when ships are in tropical climates and the heat turns the close space of the mess decks into hot and humid hell holes and men's self-control is tested without respite. As far as I was concerned, our run down to Gib was a piece of cake compared to the war years.

Taulus

We arrived in Gibraltar on a fine sunny morning in October 1946. Compared to what it looked like during the war, the harbor was almost empty; it used to be jammed. There were only a couple of subs and a few small ships. After cleaning the ship we were given shore leave. John Knight, the G.I. Mac and I went out together to look for the old dive we used to frequent.

The Trocadero hadn't changed. Maybe the owners should have hung a plaque on the wall telling all the newcomers that it was in the "Troc" where the biggest fight Gibraltar had ever seen broke out. We were there when history was made but that was another era; some events are best forgotten. Now, Gib was strangely quiet. The excitement and sense of doom had vanished. A few things hadn't changed: The drinks were still plentiful, and the food was still good. Only the faces were different. There were no laughing men with haunted eyes. They were history, men from another time, my time. In 1946 we were not dying and we were no longer living each wartime day to its fullest because we never knew what was going to happen in the next minute.

We only stayed in Gib for a week. We went through a couple of sea exercise, drank too much on shore leave, and then we weighed anchor without having left our mark on the Rock. We were on our way to Malta in a moderate sea with easy swells. The scene was almost photo perfect. There was a deep blue sky with only a few scattered white clouds to form a canopy over our ship. As we cruised along the North African coast I could not help but think about the number of ships that lay at the bottom, especially as we got nearer to the Cape Bon off Bizerte. The loud speaker crackled and it was the captain. "We are now over one of the deepest points of the Med. And for those of you who are geography students, the deepest point is just south of Malta." We were wondering why we had stopped. "Anyone who wants to have a swim in the deepest point of the Med can have a go. We'll be here for ten minutes." A few went over the side and I went too but I must say I did not stay in more than a couple of minutes. I just didn't feel that good swimming over a hole in the sea floor. What if I sank and went straight to the bottom? There were thousands of feet between the seabed and me but at least I had something to tell my grandchildren. It felt good to clamber back onboard.

As we neared Malta we began to get news of the dire situation in Palestine that was unfolding. Thousands of Jewish refuges were fleeing to Palestine from all over Europe. They were crammed into leaky old cargo boats. From what we heard, very few were seaworthy. The Royal Navy set up a blockade to prevent them from coming to Palestine which was a British protectorate. It was obvious that if a massive arrival of Jews were allowed chaos and bloodshed would follow. A blind man could see that. What with the open dislike and hatred between Arabs and Jews, an invasion of Jewish Europeans would tip the situation into chaos.

Because we were sailors we were meant to be neutral but that didn't mean we couldn't have our own opinions. Already, voices throughout the world were accusing Britain of being heartless and unthinking by refusing to allow the Jewish refuges to flood into Palestine. Some of these voices came from the same forces that were trying to break up all the colonial empires. Even the French and the Belgian empires were included. Was it right to break up these empires only a couple of years after the war ended? No one had an answer but discussions on the mess deck were heated. If our future was a hot topic down below, I assumed it was equally hot in the wardroom. Sooner or later we would have to stop one of those overcrowded rusty floating wrecks and tell passengers who were fleeing from hell to go back to where they came from. It was more than any of us could stomach. Fortunately, we weren't forced into the type of confrontation none of us wanted. We stayed on patrol but we did not stop any blockade breakers.

Until we got a permanent base, Malta became our temporary home port and our stay there was pleasant. Drinks and food were plentiful but we had frequent brushes with the Maltese police. For no reason whatsoever, and that's the truth, the police chased a couple of shipmates and me. They caught us and frisked us, and let us go. "Why," we asked. "Because there's fighting everywhere in Valetta and we saw you." Underlying the obvious tension was a new reality. The Maltese were beginning to talk about independence and the relationship they had with Britain during the war was long forgotten.

Our scuffles, their mistrust, this was only the beginning of the unwinding process of the British Empire.

Three days before the Christmas and New Year holiday period began we were at sea doing exercises with a sub. It was tedious; the drill was dragging on longer than any of us wanted it to. Finally, at the end of the afternoon, before we returned to our berth in Valetta harbor, the Captain called for the crew to 'fall in' on the quarterdeck. We knew what was coming: We'd hear from him and his senior officers who had been supervising the exercises from the beginning, what we had done correctly and what needed to be improved.

The ship was moving slowly and the sea was just heavy enough to give her a slight roll. One of the ratings that belonged to my mess was perched on the middle steel cable of the guardrail on the starboard side. Like everyone, he should have been standing but he was trying to sneak a rest on the guardrail. Suddenly, a wave bigger than previous ones, hit the side of the ship and she gave a sharp sudden roll. Our mate was thrown off balance and he pitched overboard. "Man overboard," sirens screamed and we began executing the rescue mission we knew by heart. It was something we never wanted to do but if it had to be done, we were prepared. A life ring sailed through the evening dusk in his direction but it landed too far. He saw it and began swimming. It was heavy work and he was weighted down. Sea boots, oilskins, winter gear, the weight was too much and he began to bob, flailing at the water, and then he disappeared from sight.

A lighter crisscrossed where we thought he must still be. Every man onboard was willing for that poor bloke to be found alive floating far from harm. We searched for four hours after sunset. Searchlights poked through the night flooding the black sea. They swept in every direction. The sea won; we lost. When the captain called off the search we went below. When I stepped through the hatch way I gave the water another look, one last desperate hope to see him and bring him onboard.

The despair we felt was so real, so palpable that you wanted to reach out and sweep it away but we couldn't. It was everywhere, an invisible layer of grief, frustration and stupefaction. "He was there next to me and now he's gone," one bloke said to no one in particular.

Without saying it, each of us knew that it could have been one of us who were swept over instead of him. At times like that there is no logic and no justification for what happened. No, he shouldn't have been perching and yes, his number was up. He was a good mate. It always happens that way.

He was jolly when we knew he wasn't really in the mood but he knew his laughter was contagious. Mates like that are rare. "What about his family," someone asked? We shared information about what we knew of his background and managed to piece together a picture of how his family would feel when they got the bad news. Here it is Christmas, and their present is a dead son. The navy was sensitive and they withheld news of his death until after Christmas but they finally had to inform his mother a couple of days before New Year's. We passed a hat around and collected a tidy sum. We sent the money and letters from his shipmates and the captain to his mum. We'd lost a member of our family and she had lost a son. What a way to start the holiday period! Life must go on. I still remember him when Christmas rolls around. Life must go on!

*****

Admiralty finally ended our stay in Malta and we began sailing to South Africa. Once again we passed through the Straits and stopped briefly in Gib to refuel. When we started through I had pulled watch up on the bridge. Not a bad assignment. But, it was unnerving because I could not help remembering how many times we had sailed up and down the same coast listening with our asdic trying to find U boats before they got us. One part of my brain was telling me to relax, "It's peacetime," and another part was screaming, "Keep your eyes open. The bastard's out there somewhere." Maybe the landscape was peaceful but I was having a lot of difficulty adapting to the peaceful scenery as we slid by. Even the weather was nice and I actually found myself enjoying the setting sun. It was cool but there was a hint of warmth. I caught myself chuckling, "Why we can even keep the portholes open." During the war, we were locked up inside our ship hoping we wouldn't get blown out of it. Life was beginning to be good, even comfortable.

I spent a great deal of time reading medical books that I had bought in Portsmouth before leaving. In the back of my mind an idea had been growing and I wanted to encourage it. "Someday, when the opportunity is there, maybe I can study medicine." It wasn't a silly thought. The war was over and I had a right to dream and plan a future. And, reading medical texts was an excellent chance to improve my vocabulary and learn some words that I could use in polite society. As for my foul language vocabulary, I was amazed at how foul I could be. Now, if only I can balance that a bit, I thought to myself, I will sound like a rather fine fellow. It wasn't a question of putting on airs; I merely wanted to improve myself.

Approaching Freetown, where we had to stop to refuel, we knew we were getting closer because we could smell the port before we could see it. A heavy odor of rotting fish hung over the sea. In fact, it was so far out to see that we smelled Freetown before the naked eye could pick up the low coastline. My mind started playing up again and I wandered back to the dark years of 1941 when I was stationed there with HMS Vimy. Memories began pouring out from dark recesses in my mind that I thought were firmly shut. I kept forcing myself to look at the harbor as it was instead of how I remembered it. There were very few ships compared to what it used to be like during the war when I wondered whether there were more ships than water to float them in. But, some things don't change. We still had to refuel along side an old tanker at anchor. The quay still needed dredging because ships with our draw could not berth and take on fuel from standpipes on land.

We were given shore leave in the afternoon up to 1700hrs. We went ashore with our motorboat and once we began wandering through town I realized not too much had changed since my last visit. Were the shops were better stocked than during the war? Maybe, but I wasn't sure. It was hot, we had a few drinks, but the younger chaps couldn't handle the combined effect of heat and alcohol so they got drunk and wound up on the defaulter list. Fortunately, we did not stay long in Freetown and we soon set sail for our next destination, St. Helena.

This stop proved to be quite interesting but not necessarily for the reasons one would normally associate with the island. None of the ship's company had been to St. Helena and a history of the island was posted on the notice board in the passageway. It gave a brief description of the place where Napoleon had been exiled. That part was interesting but our interest began to wane when we realized that we had to clamber up hundreds of steps from sea level to the mountaintop where most of the Europeans lived. Down at sea level the heat and humidity were almost unbearable but higher up, relatively speaking, it was cooler and 'pleasant'.

After the paragraphs devoted to history and geography there was another paragraph that got our attention. VD rates were high, 80%! For those members of the crew who were less interested in history and more interested in the pleasures of the flesh, that announcement was not welcome. An intense discussion broke out and finally someone figured out that what the Royal Navy was talking about was the situation in all of Africa. St. Helena was not even mentioned on their list of dangerous ports-of-call. Things were definitely looking up but the threat of VD was something we could not overlook.

As we steamed toward St. Helena we were told that our ship was the first ship to make a stop since the beginning of the war. During the war years only the Union Castle boat from South Africa had made short calls to bring necessary supplies. There were only a dozen or so Europeans, the Governor and his administrative staff, the Medical Officer, the Church of England Padre with his Salvation Army band, and half a dozen Royal Marines. All these people had their families with them. St. Helena sounded like a nice quiet family island, a bump in the backwater of time that the war had overlooked. There were a few Europeans, there was rampant VD, and our officers advised us not to have any contact with the locals! Just the kind of port call no one wanted. Below deck we figured it would be a quick call and then back out to sea headed for South Africa.

We cruised quietly between Freetown and St. Helena. There was plenty of time to wash and paint the ship so she would look like a real peace time warship on a cruise to show the flag in foreign ports, a floating ambassador of his majesty. The ocean was like a peaceful lake, no wind, no rain, very inspiring and soothing to be at peace at sea. I loved the middle watch when the sky was covered with thousands of shining stars, watching the moon rise over the horizon.

We could even observe the influence of the moon over the sea. When the moon started to climb the sea began to ripple as if Mother Nature was waking up from a long sleep. Unlike wartime, we sailed with all the navigation lights switched on plus a few deck lights. Of course, this light attracted flying fish. Just as we used to do during the war, someone from the galley collected the fish that landed on deck. The next morning we had a welcome addition to our breakfast: fresh fish.

St. Helena rose from the sea on the horizon, a bare dark rock. When we got a bit closer the rock came into focus. All we saw were a few houses dotted here and there, just a few feet above sea level. What we would soon discover was what we could not see. The residential area was hidden on the top of the mountain. From our vantage point out at sea all we could see was a bare rock with no one in sight. Viewed from the sea, St. Helena promised to be a really great port call! Some mates even said they weren't going to bother to go ashore because from what we could see, it was probably likely there wasn't even a pub.

We dropped anchor. The water was deep around the island and we had to come in close to the shoreline because there was no guarantee the anchor chain was long enough to reach the bottom. Access to the island was on the east side, the side that was rarely exposed to winds. This was important because if we had to moor in deep water we didn't want our ship to be straining at her moorings when the wind came up. It was too dangerous; we might break free.

It looked as if the population had been observing us for a long time. Hundreds had gathered on what looked like a parade ground. All the personalities of the island were assembled. Some wore their dress uniforms, others their best Sunday clothes. The Salvation Army band banged and hooted, and lots and lots of young girls, pretty smiling young girls, were singing and dancing and making unmistakable signs to the men on deck securing the gangway. Maybe this wasn't going to be such a bad port after all!

When the gangway was lowered our motorboat was sent to fetch all the local notables onboard: the Governor, Doctor, Priest etc. The quarterdeck had been covered with a canvas to provide shade from the searing tropical sun. A table with glasses and drinks was set to receive our guests and from the way they acted, I really think they were genuinely glad to see us and to welcome us to their island, an island where time appeared to have stopped. It was an amazing scene and it made me think that this is what Cook must have seen when he was visiting far away islands in the South Pacific. As our motor boat left the island to return to the ship it was escorted by dozens of local canoes filled with young girls. I use the term 'young girls' within a context that has become quaint today. As far as we could see, the boats were filled only with young girls because there were no young men in sight. The girls sang and waved invitingly but they remained behind our motorboat. The governor had probably ordered them to remain out of reach. None of them attempted to come aboard.

We piped the governor onboard and he and the captain went to the captain's quarters to organize a cocktail party for the visitors. While they were out of sight the doctor and the priest were escorted on a tour of the ship. Curious, they looked into every nook and corner and even read the postings on the notice boards. The doctor stopped and read the now infamous VD warning notice. He exploded. "Where did you get this stupid information," he roared? No one had time to answer. "I'll have you know that since I've been on this island, and it has been several years now, I've not had one single case of VD." Oh joy, oh joy, what wonderful music to our ears. Was it true or was he just trying to spin a story and make his island seem better than it was? "When the war broke out all the young males left the island to earn a living on the African continent," he said solemnly. "As a result there is only a small number, mainly older people, who were left to satisfy the sexual needs of our female population."

At first he sounded clinical, as if he were addressing a group of doctors and not a bunch of sailors, but as he spoke, he looked around at us and broke into a big smile. Now he had our attention. Continuing his lecture, "The population is fairly healthy but I've had a growing number of cases of depression and these are due, undoubtedly, to boredom and a lack of a normal life." We understood the 'life' he was talking about. "Actually, not much has happened on this island since Napoleon was exiled here in the last century. You men are the first visitors we have had since 1940." If we could have sprouted wings to fly ashore the entire mess would have been airborne buzzing toward shore!

We went through the decorum as laid out in the Royal Navy instructions as to how to receive visitors onboard one of his majesty's ships. It really wasn't that long but for us it seemed like an eternity. Finally, the personalities clambered down the gangway and boarded our motorboat for the trip back to the shore. But this time, instead of accompanying our launch into port, the canoes came alongside our ship. The girls threw lines up to us to secure their canoes. Their 'invasion' had begun. Giggling women poured over the side of the ship and grabbed any man in sight and held onto him as if he was property and they were the new owners. Sometimes dreams happen and I think every sailor dreams of landing on a desert island where all the women want is sex, unlimited, unrestrained, frantic sex. Everywhere I looked men were flirting. I can't vouch for it but I heard that some of the women managed to find the captain's cabin.

For a brief period there was pandemonium. It was happy chaos, no violence, no drunkenness, only unleashed lust barely held in check. The officers finally brought order to the deck scene and 'invited' our female visitors to leave ship. As they began to shinny back down the side of the ship we heard the officers assuring the girls that shore leave would be granted later that afternoon. Their canoes formed a loose formation as they paddled back to shore, paddling, waving, shouting and laughing. We were almost in shock. "Damn, check and see if they've nicked something," the first mate said. Nothing, absolutely nothing, was missing.

It was a long wait until the officers left, late in the afternoon, to attend a cocktail party at the Governor's residence. Apart from a few suffering souls who pulled duty, the rest of the ship's company went ashore. What a welcome waited for us! We came ashore into a large crowd of screaming girls. In the middle, like an island of proper behavior fuming music, the Salvation Army band was pounding out hymns. The poor padre was having the devil's own time trying to keep his lusty sheep focused on him and the psalms.

Probably within a couple of hours the town pub had made more money since our ship landed than it had taken in during the previous five years. Everywhere you looked sailors had girls seated on their knees and when darkness fell the nearby beach was strewn with couples having sex. Most of the grunting and moaning was happy but every now and then the girls would start fighting. "I had him before you," a girl would hiss while clinging to her lover. What a sight, what a night, something to remember and laugh about when you are sad. At the edge of town the Salvation Army band continued to bleat and wheeze. Finally the padre marched his flock back to their quarters and no sooner was he out of sight than his singing sisters were seen high tailing it down to the beach to grab a man. They deserved their fair share of the fun

The next day I had recovered enough to visit the place where Napoleon had lived. Even the guide told us that he too had an affair with a lady living close to his quarters. Maybe it's the climate that does something to the locals to make them crave love so much. No, it wasn't the weather, just boredom, long grinding periods of absolute boredom.

The place where Napoleon was exiled was called Longwood and it was one of the best sites on the island. Often tour guides are willing to mouth the facts but our guide was different. Because he was genuinely interested in what had happened, Longwood became a residence where someone had actually lived. Little details were added to add 'spice' to his narrative. "Here's a hole Napoleon drilled in the shutters so he could observe the British soldiers drilling on the parade ground without being seen." His poignant comment that made me think of how proud a man Napoleon must have been. Now, whenever I see busts of the Emperor or heroic paintings, something in my mind triggers that visit and the little hole scratched out by a man who was once one of the most powerful human beings the world had ever known. Longwood was the only site worth seeing because the rest of the island was boring. There was nothing beautiful about the vegetation and getting around the island was difficult. In short, who ever decided to send Napoleon to St. Helena knew that there would be very little for the great man to do.

Boredom can be cruel punishment for a man of the world. I think that, even today, apart from the amazing welcome offered by the local girls, St. Helena remains a forsaken place. Sex aside, after a few days, boredom began to affect us as well. The locals did everything they could to get us to prolong our call but our orders required us to continue on toward Simon's Town. St. Helena had been fun, different from anything we could ever have imagined, but it was a sad place and when we left we actually felt sorry for those people locked up on their rock with no place to go and no one to visit them.

*****

The weather deteriorated as we got nearer to the Cape. Dark clouds, pushed by a cool and strong eastern wind, partially covered the sky. The sea also got choppy; deep waves hit the ship's side spraying the super structure as high as the bridge. Maybe our boring anchorage in St. Helena wasn't that bad after all. Until we entered the calm waters of False Bay the ship pitched all the way to our mooring in Simon's Town.

We saluted the flag ship, the cruiser HMS Nigeria, and our sister ship HMS Nereide. Our two ships constituted the South Atlantic Fleet. Our arrival was subject to the usual exchange of signals that were posted on the notice board. It was a simple and effective way to ensure that there was an official channel of communication onboard. The postings enabled the ship's company to acquaint itself with the rules and regulations of the South Atlantic station. Simon's Town was about thirty miles from Cape Town and there was an efficient railroad between the two cities. Apart from the married people who had their families in Simon's Town, the fleet crews spent their time in Cape Town.

Cape Town was well known in the navy and had a very good reputation. It was modern and equal to any city of comparable size in Europe. Even the South Africans had nothing in common with the other African peoples of West and Equatorial Africa. There were four distinct ethnic groups: Bantus (very black), Cape color of mixed blood some of whom were as white as Europeans, and the Malay who were Asian. The Europeans, a smaller grouping, were also divided into groups: European who included the Afrikaners or Boers, British people, and a number of Jews who came from various Eastern European countries and were fully integrated as South African.

Two days after our arrival, John Knight, Mac and I decided to go to Cape Town. The train trip only took half an hour and we enjoyed following the lovely coastline into the city. We visited the whole town from the central commercial area to sea point where all the hotels are located on a lovely beach that faces the cold Atlantic. Up until then the limited contact we had with the South Africans had been good. As far as we could tell they were happy and generous with the exception of a few Afrikaners who still had a chip on their shoulder, acting as if the Boer War had ended only a few years ago.

The disgruntled were a minority and they kept their aggression pretty well hidden, probably waiting for a day when they could come out in the open and let their political voice be heard and then claim to reflect the 'true' voice of South Africa. For the time being, they were satisfied with speaking to us in Afrikaans knowing full well we could not understand a word of what they were saying. Sometimes, though, their stubbornness brought out a mean streak in me.

Once I asked for a return ticket to Simon's Town at the railway station. The attendant stared at me and replied in Afrikaans. "I know fucking well you can speak English and you know that I don't understand Afrikaner, so don't waste my time and yours," I snapped at him through the spindly bars of his ticket window. "Do you want me to ask the policeman over there to translate for me what you are saying?" His face flushed beet red and he gave me my ticket without any further comment. But, this type of animosity between white was a rarity and it was practically non-existent in 1947. The race issue was another matter.

There was a clear separation between whites and blacks but not as strict as it became when the apartheid policy was introduced a few years later. That didn't stop the colored girls from trying hard to entice us. They used every trick in the book to invite us to their home to meet their sisters and brothers. In some families you'd see an array of colors: one or two girls absolutely white and the third very black. Later I would remember these families and reflect on the horrible dilemma that must have posed when strict apartheid was introduced.

The cost of living in Cape Town was about the same as in the UK but drinks were cheaper and this was probably a major factor contributing to the high percentage of alcoholism especially among the coloreds and the lower class of whites known as poor white. A little bit of information about the local economy and race relations, some sightseeing, and that was about all we learned on our first visit to

Cape Town. We slept at the navy club that night and took the early morning train to Simon's Town.

Life in port settled into a routine. Our workday started at 0800 with an ancient ceremony. We stood to attention on the upper deck, facing aft where the white ensign was raised. Over the screeching sea gulls we heard the bugle of the flagship, HMS Nigeria, and the whistles of the Nereide and Actaeon. At the end of the ceremony, we stood down and mustered to our workstations. Probably Lord Nelson had gone through the same ceremony as had generations before him.

I spent most of my free time reading my medical book that I found very interesting and a great help in improving my English. A little knowledge hurts. When I got to the chapters on gynecology and female diseases my reading slowed down. I kept quiet and swore to myself that I would not have anything to do with a woman other than having hygienic sexual contact. With my shipmates we went ashore weekends to Cape Town and had fun, drinks when possible with willing girls. This wasn't a bad routine and no one was complaining. It was peacetime and we had to do a bit of cruising to show the flag at various nearby ports.

We sailed to Mozambique, still a Portuguese colony, and we visited Lorenço Marques, the capital. I shut my eyes and thought I was somewhere in the Med. One factor was distinctly different from life in South Africa. There was no apparent color bar. The white Portuguese mixed openly and easily with the black Africans. For us, language was the only difficulty in this nice town because no one spoke English. After our stay in the capital we continued to Beira in the central coastal side of Mozambique. It was not very memorable, just another busy port; the town was very similar in many way to Lorenço Marques. On the way back, we made a three-day stop in Durban where we enjoyed our run ashore. The white population was mostly of English origin and we found they were easier to get along with than the Boers. It was almost a tourist cruise because we called into East London and Port Elizabeth before returning to Simon's Town.

Back in Simon's Town I was told that the proceeding for the divorce had started. I received a form to fill in from my wife's lawyer and my lawyer advised me not to answer it. It was 1949, time was passing and in two more years and I would be divorced. In the meantime our life of debauchery in Cape Town was going on at full speed. My life could be summarized as: work hard, study hard, play hard, and the rest didn't matter. I was happy. Soon after we returned from our cruise we were told that our next cruise was to the other side of South Africa, calling at ports on the Atlantic coast.

We headed north into the Atlantic and made a brief stop at Saldanha bay to carryout gunnery practice. Despite the fact that we were a peacetime navy, we were actually quite good. We performed as if we had already proven ourselves in battle. It stands to reason that a gunnery area is deserted and we didn't see a single soul. In order to break the boredom we organized a fishing competition because the Bay we were using as a gunnery run was supposed to be rich in fish. Organizing a competition is one thing but carrying out was another because no one had any fishing equipment so we had to improvise. We made our own lines and hooks, mostly bent nails, tied to steel yarn. A big chunk of meat was supposed to lure the fish. Fish are not known for being very smart and if they could talk they would probably have doubled up in laughter at the cruddy tackle lowered from our ship. It may have looked bad, and maybe it shouldn't have worked, but the catch was massive. The winner was a stoker who brought onboard a very large manta ray. His catch, added to our haul, meant that onboard the HMS Actaeon we had a fish and chips dinner.

We continued our trip up the coast with stops at Luderitz and Walvis Bay. These two ports were already important sites for diamonds and ferrous rock. In Luderitz we were invited to visit a diamond field that was located in a sandy desert. We went out in Land rovers and were told we could not leave the vehicle. A guide got out with a sieve and shovel, dug a bit, swirled the sieve, and brought it over to us to look at raw diamonds that he had scooped up in a couple of minutes! We were amazed and with this simple demonstration we could understand why the diamond fields were so well guarded. Walvis Bay was a big town that had been founded by Germans; it still looked German. All the pubs had German names but the war was pretty much behind us and we had a good welcome. So good, in fact, that many of our lads got drunk and were added to the defaulters list.

We then sailed to Angola and stopped at Lobito a typical Portuguese port, very much like Biera in Mozambique. All these visits always ended with a great cocktail party on the quarterdeck. The local notables hobnobbed with our officers but we, of the lower deck, were never invited. Our cruise continued further north up to a place called Boma at the entrance of Congo River in the Congo that is now called Zaire.

We took on a Belgian pilot to guide us to our next stop at Matadi. Only the pay master went ashore in Boma to collect sufficient local money for the ship's company to spend in Matadi. The trip from Boma to Matadi was very interesting because it was the first time that I sailed up a river with such a fast current. We were warned that there were a lot of mosquitoes in the area and that meant malaria. In response to the threat the medical orderlies made us take a slug of horrible tasting liquid quinine every day before lunch. Only with the help of a tot of rum was I able to push down that vile liquid. As we got closer to Matadi the pilot began to point out the river's dangers. In one instance we had to ease by some dangerous rocks sticking out of the rapids through which we were maneuvering. We dodged and held our breaths because there wasn't too much room to maneuver in.

We were finally given our berth that was very close to the centre of the town. On shore we were greeted by a school child's brass band playing a military march. A long bearded missionary, who waved his arms, as if the children could follow, led their little group. Two or three high ranking local personalities came on board to greet the captain and give him instructions and go through the formalities involved in visiting this charming town. We did not see many Africans apart from young children who came to gawk at our war ship. Our port call was a first time experience for them and they laughed and pointed, not quite able to believe their eyes. Under the river's surface another danger lurked: The water was full of crocodiles and we were told they would surely come to our garbage shoot at night. Even the governor was not exempt from their threat. One night he was out walking his dog close to where we were berthed. They were down near the river's edge having a quiet stroll and all of a sudden a croc shot out of the water and ate his dog.

Rene Dassac (in collaboration with Patrick K. Robbins)

When we got shore leave we decided not to stretch our legs down near the water's edge but, instead, to head toward a nice little hotel in town where we were assured there would be good beer. After all, we were in a country controlled by the Belgians. The beer was good, very good, we drank a lot and we also ate well which probably helped us to stay reasonable sober. Coming back onboard that night one of our messmates had his life saved by an African boy. Our mate was walking back to the ship and not really minding where he was headed when, in a flash, the lad stopped him just before he was about to step onto a black momba, one of the deadliest snakes in the world. We were all shaken and we gave the boy some pennies of the local money and continued our way back to the ship. In those final few hundred meters we watched every crack on the pavement and peered into every shadow.

Dinner at the hotel was interesting because we got a pretty good insight into how the Belgians treated the Africans; we didn't like what we saw. They still used the whip for what we thought were trivial reasons but the rest of the world didn't know about their brutal practices. The punishment they meted out was different than how discipline was enforced in the tip of Africa. The rest of the civilized was becoming aware of what was going on in South Africa. Down south the South Africans had a reputation for being harsh but, in the case of whipping, the whip could not be used except when ordered by a judge. On his orders a beating was limited to no more than three to five lashes administered in the presence of a doctor. This isn't as seaman's story because, as you will see later, I'll tell you about one of our hard case seamen got five cuts of the lash. The Belgians were brutal and apparently unrestrained by their judiciary.

When it came to civil administration in the colonies, I am not saying that we Brits were angels, far from it, but I never saw rank police brutality meted out for petty crime in British territories. Locals trained by the British and supervised by British officers, guarded delinquents. It was rare to hear of a British civil servant accused of brutality. The situation in the Belgian Congo was different: the Belgians were down right cruel. We made it back on board with no further snake scares but our shore leave opened our eyes to what was going on in the Belgian Congo. The world was oblivious to what we had seen and I am not sure, for that matter, any responsible world leader really cared.

We did not sleep well that night. Down below decks it was beastly hot and humid; mosquitoes were everywhere. Sleep, when it came, lasted for a few brief minutes, and as the night wore ones temper became shorter. Early the next morning the loud speaker crackled, "Hands fall in for leaving harbor. Special sea duty men close up." We were happy to get out of that hellhole but we didn't know where we were sailing. At Boma we released the pilot and headed out to sea. No mosquitoes, no dead air, it felt good to be away from the Congo. Once we were on the open sea the captain told us we had been recalled to Simon's Town at high speed to take part in two different operations. "We are going to be involved in one of two operations," he intoned. It was either the Falklands which Argentina was threatening to re-occupy or it was to head to the Gold Coast where a coup was underway. It only took four days to reach Simon's Town and onboard there was excitement. "Action," the youngsters talked excitedly. I didn't share their enthusiasm because I knew what 'action' meant. My memory was still very sharp on many points that I didn't bother to share with my peacetime messmates.

While our captain was on board the flagship HMS Nigeria to review his orders, we were busy refueling, taking on fresh food supplies, and preparing the ship to go into action. The Argentine propaganda machine was going full swing, churning out lies and drumming up support for the government's cause. "The British Lion is a toothless cat, give back the Falklands to avoid blood shed," they shrilled. We thought their hysterics were a joke, or were they telling the truth? Was the British Lion really capable of clawing up an enemy? Only a few years after the end of the last war, we were, once again, quite vulnerable in the face of a determined enemy.

HMS Nigeria was a tired old cruiser that might have to face a determined aggressor far away from home and far from the nearest South Atlantic support station. At the same time trouble started in the Gold Coast, now called Ghana. The frigate HMS Nereide was already steaming towards Ghana to take up station in front of the capital, Accra. We saw the HMS Nigeria sail past with her marine band playing on the quarterdeck. Almost in her wake the HMS Actaeon followed to take up our assigned station at Takoradi.

Being on station may have been a proper military decision but we had a major problem onboard, a problem that fortunately the rebels were not aware of because if they had been our task would have been much more difficult. Simply put, we had no marines and an inadequate number of small arms to fight a serious and well-organized rebel group. When we emptied all the lockers and scoured all the stores, all we could scrape together was some old .303 rifles and bayonets. This meant we could not advance beyond the cover of the ship's gun range. As long as we stayed under that firepower umbrella we were in pretty good shape. Out of range could mean being out gunned. Fortunately, as we shall see later, the bark and bang from our big guns were enough to calm the 'revolutionaries'.

It took us a few days to get to our station and that gave us enough time to select and organize some seventy men who could be spared to face the enemy. We organized ourselves into squads. Each squad had two signalmen who were responsible for maintaining continuous contact with the ship. In the meantime our radio men had picked up critical information concerning the enemy: their primary weapons were bows and arrows, weapons that weren't known for their accuracy beyond one hundred and fifty yards.

We were offshore Takoradi in the early morning soon after sunrise. We knew we were being watched. Our funnel smoke gave us away miles before we actually came into their sight. We steamed into their line of vision and began firing our three four inch guns. Star shells started bursting over the town that was just waking up. Our demonstration was designed to frighten them and let them know that we had superior firepower. Or, at least that is what we hoped we had because we didn't quite believe they were as lightly armed as the radio intelligence claimed. Fortunately, Takoradi had a small quay and we secured our mooring. Our field glasses scanned the town trying to pick out anyone who looked the least bit suspicious. Not even the cats were out. The admiralty intelligence briefs were incomplete and unclear. We tried to locate a particular part of town where the Europeans were likely to be holed up. No matter where we looked the streets were empty. If the town was not dead, it looked dead. All we got was hundreds of empty doorways staring back at us.

It looked as if the star shells had done their trick. They couldn't do any harm but they could scare and that was what we wanted to achieve: Let the enemy know that if he got in the way we would blast him into pieces so small even the ants wouldn't have any trouble carrying off their body parts. Because of our faulty intelligence we did not know that the European residence area of the town was on the top of the hill overlooking the port, above the commercial area and the native quarters. The screech and whap of the guns and exploding star shells echoed against the hill. Our volley was enough to put the fear of God into anyone within earshot.

Squads formed and started to go ashore with the first lieutenant whom we escorted to the British Commissioner. We formed up and began marching and I started to kid my lads. They had never marched into harm's way and I had and, being the most experienced, I had to do something to break their tension and work around their fear. "Remember, with our .303 rifles and bayonets we really are soldiers." Someone snickered, a nervous cough. "Don't talk unless you see someone hiding, look where you put your feet and don't fire your gun unless you have been ordered to." I sounded like a schoolteacher and they were still wound up. Half serious, half laughing, I went on, "watch where you put your feet, I don't mean that you could blow off your leg over a mine ... but you could slip on a dog turd, fire your gun and kill one of those vultures that has been following us." The first lieutenant did not share my humor, I thought I was in great form, but he told me to shut up and spread out my men at ten-foot intervals on both sides of the road.

It took us about half an hour to reach the Resident's house. We were nervous, waiting to be set upon or shot at. But as we marched up the road, something funny happened. Somehow people seemed to realize we didn't mean them any harm. Timidly, then more boldly, they started to spill out of their houses and wave to us. We started to relax and feel at little bit more comfortable with our new role as ground soldiers but when we got to the Resident's house he told us that just because they were waving at us didn't mean everything was returning to normal and that the situation was under control. "In fact I am sure that the minute you disappear behind the horizon, the mutineers will be on the prowl again," he said. "The reason why they are hiding now is because the star shells you fired had the desired effect on them." I guess it was a reasonable assessment. After all, he was paid to know what was going on. "They will have to be convinced that you are here to stay and that you mean business." Once again, the colonial mindset was at work. Use force and hint at an even a greater use of force if the situation didn't come right, cow the natives back into line, resume control and pick up where the situation was before the mutiny had broken out. That was his goal and we were there to help him. All good things done on behalf of the crown and country!

Our first lieutenant mulled over the assessment. "I agree with you sir," he said, "But, let me brief the captain." The radio crackled and the two men talked while the lieutenant held his hand over the mouthpiece in an attempt to muffle his voice. "We'll stay in touch via radio," was about all I could hear before the lieutenant signed off. We waited for about a half hour in the shade of the Residence and then returned to our ship without incident. Other squads began to trail in after us. They had fanned out through the town in an attempt to assess where the mutineers were holed-up. They didn't encounter any opposition and we all went back onboard to wait.

Before we disembarked with our old rifles, down in the mess everyone was giving his opinion on how we should deal with the situation. After our brief foray into town a bunch of sailors who had been pressed into the infantry had suddenly become a group of experts on urban warfare. If someone had stepped into our mess that afternoon he might have concluded that we actually knew what we were talking about. Now all we could do was wait to see what was going to happen next and kill time wondering if our officers really knew what they were doing. They didn't have any more experience handling a land operation than we did.

In the midst of our intense analysis, we heard the captain come on over the loud hailer. "All hands. The ship will remain on defense stations throughout the night. Man all light armaments. Search the area around the ship with the searchlights until dawn; follow a broken search pattern because we need to catch anyone trying to infiltrate our perimeter. Keep your eyes open. I have received reports from Accra that there have been some small disturbances but the army up there is in control of the situation."

We stayed in Tokaradi for two days. Nothing happened in the end. In the meantime HMS Nereide asked us to change stations with her. She was on station where there was no port. They were anchored offshore and caught in heavy rollers, a well-known problem on that part of the African coast. We sailed for Accra and passed the Nereide with a long exchange of signals. She left, and as if a hole had been carved in the sea, we slid into it and began rolling like mad. Within minutes we knew why Nereide had had enough of this miserable sea sickening anchorage. While we were on station in our miserable pitching bucket I actually managed to have a marvelous experience, a very funny pantomime typical of the colonial days in West Africa.

The small army garrison located in Accra contacted us and asked if we wanted to exchange cinema films with them? That was a good suggestion because we had already seen our collection so often some of the guys knew the script. The army sent a party to wait for us on the beach and they organized a native canoe to carry our group ashore. Each boat had six oarsmen and a coxswain to provide the rhythm. We watched them approaching the ship, wondering if they would make the 200 yards or so between the beach and us. The terrible rollers breaking on the beach tossed them about like rag dolls. Our problems were twofold: getting the canoe to us without capsizing and then returning to the beach without capsizing. Of the two problems we were more concerned about the second because we had to take the canoe back to shore! If the canoe overturned or swamped on the way out to us that was their problem, but if the same thing happened to us we were the victims. As we stood watching the canoe edge toward us we realized we there was even one more problem. If we made it to the beach without overturning, how were we going to get onto the beach without getting drenched up to our belts?

My party was in the first lot. The officer in charge of our little expedition was in our boat. He looked worried. Somehow we managed to jump into the pitching canoes. I got a seat in the center of my boat while hanging on to our box containing the films we wanted to exchange. From the way we were pitching and rolling I was convinced we were going to overturn before we left the side of our ship. Our officer stood behind me. The silly bugger was balancing precariously next to the half naked coxswain. He was a splendid example of all that is good in the Royal Navy: spotless uniform, creases where creases were designed to be and "veddy, veddy", well spoken. In his best Oxford accent, typical of many British Naval Officers, he ordered: "Carry on coxswain." The cox stared at him and smiled a big wide toothy grin.

The sea rose and fell under us violently pitching our canoe from bow to stern. As far as the cox was concerned, the officer could have been reciting the Magna Carta. The native didn't know what to do. The two men stared at each other waiting for the other to do something. A G.I. seated behind me piped-up. "Sir, he doesn't understand you." Before the officer could reply the G.I. said, "Just tell him to fuck off, Sir." Everybody started laughing. The cox barked an order to his crew. From deep in his powerful chest a low rhythmic chant rolled across our pitching canoe, "...rururu, rururu." At his sign oars sliced into the rollers and our little canoe raced toward shore. The beach started to close fast and I started my mental preparation of getting soaked. It was inevitable.

As soon as we were within jumping distance of the beach the crew started leaping out of the boat. Two held it steady while another oarsman reached over and plucked me off my seat and threw me over his shoulder. He carried me through the crashing surf as easily as if he were carrying a bag of chicken feathers through the market. My shoes never got wet.   Turning, I realized why my 'porter' had grabbed me before the others. I was obviously the lightest sailor that had to be carried through the surf. At least two natives were needed to lug ashore one of my messmates. Remember in those days, the same method was used to carry passengers from the lighters liners sent ashore. The passengers were lowered down to the canoes in big baskets and then their ladyships, sometimes rather hefty, were hoisted ashore on the shoulders of the natives. Considering the customs of that era, it was rather daring.

Everyone in our little party had a good laugh. Even our lieutenant managed a slight smile when the G.I. told the cox to "fuck off" instead of "shove off." Starting with that trip and until we left, anytime we used the canoes to go ashore we told the cox to "fuck off." He grinned and guided us ashore.

While we were on station the town remained quiet but the Governor was uneasy and he insisted that we remain on station because he was afraid the troubles would start as soon as we left. Our captain wasn't so sure but he decided to give the governor the benefit of the doubt and we weighed anchor as if we were leaving for good. Seen from the shore, it looked as if we were gone for good but in reality we had sailed just over the horizon, out of eyesight but we remained in radio contact with the governor's radio operator. The governor was right.

Two days after we left the governor radioed for help. Trouble had flared up again. Within hours we returned to our station and then began patrolling up and down the sea front in front of Accra firing volleys over the town so they landed outside populated areas but low enough to scare the daylights out of anyone underneath them. Our message started to have an effect on the troublemakers. After several noisy runs up and down the coast, whoever wanted to cause problems probably concluded that they were up against superior odds so they left. After a couple of days we left too, taking with us all two hundred and three rifles with their bayonets. We sailed down the coast to our homeport, Simon's Town, where we could go ashore and enjoy the good life.

A week after our return to Simon's Town, our flag ship HMS Nigeria steamed back into port after showing the Argentineans that the British lion still had sharp teeth. We were relieved that another armed conflict had been avoided but her departure to Latin America and ours to the Gold Coast were ample proof that world powers with possessions around the globe could never show any signs of weakness. It's hard to make politicians understand this because all they think of is budget restraint but when the shooting starts the consequences of budget savings are usually forgotten while the cost of human loss of life soars.

*****

Life went on nicely in South Africa. My divorce procedure was well underway. Slowly, but surely, my application was working its way toward the eventual final decree. Edith refused to join me. According to law, she had deserted me and I didn't care. I felt secure in my second life in the Royal Navy and I had no reason to give too much thought to what was happening to my private life.

Much to my surprise I was requested to join two groups of twenty men chosen from both frigates to spend two weeks in Johannesburg and Pretoria as guests of the South African army. We left Cape Town railway station at ten o'clock in the morning. It was winter but on the Cape the winters are never really bitterly cold, just cold enough to make you want to cover up. We had several compartments to ourselves. The train was very comfortable; the Cape Province countryside was beautiful. We passed through many huge farms and spectacular vineyards when we crossed the wine region. In the evening we had a nice dinner in the train restaurant and when we returned to our compartment we were amazed to see that each bunk had been laid out with blankets and bed sheets. This train was a rolling hotel and we were being treated like royalty.

The windows had begun to fog up and the attendant told us that the nights were sometimes cold, especially when we reached the plateau of the Kuru desert. In fact, we were very surprised when the next morning we found that the drinking water in the passage way was frozen! At that time, I had a beard very much like the one grown by the sailor on the Players cigarette packages. During the night when my mates thought I was sound asleep I heard them say that in the morning they would grab me and shave one whole side of my beard. I pretended to be sound asleep but I knew they would do it just for fun. My sleep was not all that deep that night and early the next morning I got up and shaved off my beard. When they saw me they asked me, "Why the hell did I shave it off?" I shrugged as if the answer should be obvious to even blind man. "There'll be army girls with the reception committee and I don't want to scare them off." We had a good laugh and that evening I finally caught a quick nap before we pulled into a suburb of Johannesburg.

Sure enough an army committee was there to greet us and the reception group even included some rather pretty girls. We were taken by bus to a nice hotel in the centre of the town. Johannesburg reminded me of an American town with its skyscrapers mid-town and its posh mansions in the 'Whites Only' suburbs. Although it seemed civilized, under the thin veneer of modernity there were aspects of downtown Jo'burg that astonished us. It was like the American wild west of a hundred years ago. So many people sauntered about town with guns stuck in their belts. We hadn't seen men toting weapons like this in Cape Town. Maybe it was due to the fact that there were so many millionaires or maybe it was because there were so many blacks from other parts of South Africa who had come to work in the gold mines, but whatever the reason, those gun toting South Africans sure made a big impression on us.

The South Africans we met were heavy drinkers; we had a job to keep up with them in the hotel's bar. Hand guns notwithstanding we found them to be a generally good and friendly people. During our stay in Johannesburg we were surprised to see a snowstorm. It only lasted for a couple of minutes, we didn't expect to be snowed on in Africa, but it was there for all of us to see.

After three days in Johannesburg the army put us on a train to Pretoria, the capital of South Africa. There we were taken away by bus to the army barracks where we were their guests for a couple of days. One evening our army hosts invited us to their club that was situated a couple of miles from the barracks. There were some army girls who wanted to dance. We had fun and I paired off with a nice looking girl who liked her drink. She was hot stuff and when we were dancing she held me tight against her and got me worked up. Both of us had had a lot to drink and about half an hour before closing time she said she wanted to go back to the barracks. "Do you want to go back with me? I've got my car outside," she slurred. "Yeah, sure, let's go," and we managed to weave off the dance floor out into the parking lot.

Half way down the deserted road to the barracks she stopped her car. I could just make out some trees to one side of the road but there were no houses, no signs of civilization. "What's she up to," I wondered? "What's up," I asked? I knew what I wanted but she was acting strangely as she shoved open the door and lurched upright into the night. "I want to puke," she replied in a funny way. "Where do you want to puke," I replied using a word I'd never heard before. I thought puke meant South African for sex. Before my hopes could climb any higher I saw her run behind a tree and heard her vomiting up all the beer I'd poured down her. I was dumbfounded and I guess I must have looked damn stupid but I started to chuckle at the prospect of my shipmates faces when I told them the story. I heard her scramble back to the car. She was deathly pale and didn't smell like peaches and cream. "I'm sorry John but I have been drinking too much and I don't feel too good." Talk about stating the obvious! "Don't worry; we'll meet up again tomorrow." She looked at me slightly cross-eyed. "You guys are being transferred to a nice hotel in town and I won't see you again. Let's exchange addresses and stay in touch." We managed to scrawl our addresses and she dropped me off in front of the barracks. When I told my story, the true version, none of my mates believed me because they thought I was being chivalrous and didn't want to admit that I had screwed her.

Just as my drunken army girl had said, the next day we were transferred to a hotel in town because we were leaving the next day and it was more convenient to go to the station from the hotel instead of from the barracks. In the evening at the hotel a strange thing happened. After dinner we went into the hotel's bar which was actually a very nice lounge. Three of us were at the bar and next to us was a chap about our age with whom we started talking. "Ah, so you were in the navy. So was I," he replied to our inevitable question about what he had done during the war. "I was on the German pocket battleship Graf Von Spee when it was scuttled off Montevideo. "I was interned there until the end of the war."

When he was released he decided to come to South Africa because he had an uncle living there. We talked a lot. It was a friendly conversation among men who had been enemies but now Fate had thrown us together in a bar in Pretoria. We were wearing our campaign medals. While he was asking what each medal meant, a chap came up and started to make a nuisance. He pretended to ignore the German. "Those medals, they're nothing but bullshit," he tossed contemptuously in our direction. My mate John Knight drew himself up so that he became as straight as a ram rod. For a minute I thought the evening was going to descend into one helluva bar fight. I could tell Knight was on the edge of losing it but he managed to hold himself in check. "Look mate, what do you know about those medals and …….. Where …. were you during the war?" He had lowered his voice. If words could ever be used to hurt someone, his were crushing body blows. I looked at the intruder. From his accent and attitude, he was a Boer and therefore anti-British. I managed to wedge myself between the Boer and the German. "You know mate," I said looking at the Boer, "I've got more respect for this German gentleman who fought for his country than for people like you who didn't do a damned thing."

Scrawny little me, I lit the fuse. All we needed was one swiping punch from out of nowhere and away we'd have gone. By now everyone in the bar had grown quiet. We were the center of attention. From the back of the room a couple of men shouldered their way through the crowd and came over. They took the loud-mouth by the arms and led him out. "Sorry mates, he doesn't know what he's talking about." Seconds before the room had been bristling and just as fast calm returned. We bought a couple of more drinks for our genuinely friendly German and then parted, making a great show of shaking hands and patting him on the back. Nobody cheered but nobody booed either. Wars can get started too easily.

The next day we took the train back to Cape Town. Our two week trip had been a good exercise in relation building between the South Africans and us, we had enjoyed ourselves and they had been outstanding hosts but it was, nevertheless, good to be back onboard and into our daily routines.

John Knight had a regular girlfriend. She was nice, white as any European, but her family was colored and her mother and sister were definitely darker than his girl friend. John was in love and started to talk about getting married. We tried our damndest to dissuade him because rumors were already rife that if the nationalists won the elections they would introduce what later became known as the infamous apartheid policy. If he married her he would have to leave South Africa because marriage between races would be prohibited. Even though she looked white, in South African terms she was colored. Defying us and following his dream, a few months later he married his lovely South African.

As for me, I hadn't yet got over my marriage debacle. The thought of eventually remarrying was absolutely out of question and I certainly wasn't going to marry in order to satisfy my sexual needs. I knew I was confused and hurt and my intense period of soul-searching was painful. I tried not to think about my failed marriage but the wounds of my relationship and divorce with Edith were still open and very painful. When I needed a woman it was for sex, animal lust, and for no other reason. I could not put Edith behind me. Yesterday's hurts were too deep to slough off easily.

While I was going through this turmoil our ship was chosen to take part in the International Medical Congress that was being held in Port Elisabeth. Enroute to 'PE' we stopped in Knysna which was a beautiful spot. The access was dangerous because it could only be made at high tide. Our stop was scheduled for only forty-eight hours but we wished it had lasted longer because once over the bar, it was like living in another world. At the entrance to the port there is a large sand bar that separates the turbulent ocean from the actual harbor that looks like a lake.

We did some sailing with our whaler boat and managed to turn it over twice. Insults and obscene comments were hurled down to us bobbing in the water and I guess the nicest that I remember was, "useless sods." I tried to hide behind the fact that I had not done any sailing since 1936 when I was in the French navy Boys School. No excuses were accepted and at least we not only had fun, we provided others with a jolly good show. After the sailing 'races' we challenged the other boats to rowing races and actually managed to elicit some applause and genuine shouts of approval. Winning, I guess, managed to outweigh losing and at least for those of us on the water (sometimes in the water) we had a welcome break from shipboard routine.

All good things come to an end and we sailed to 'PE' where a big crowd had gathered at the quayside to watch us go through our docking and tie-up procedure. In the evening two shipmates and I went to a big hotel not far from our mooring and took a table close to a married couple. Somehow we got talking with them and it turned out that he was a well-known surgeon from Cape Town. While we talked someone was playing a nice piano just out of sight. One of us commented on how nice the music was and the doctor said with obvious pride, "She's our daughter." When she finished they asked her over and we introduced ourselves. She was studying French and her father told her, pointing to me, "He's French."

I said something in French, I can't remember what, and she stumbled through a reply in French and then blurted in English, "Maybe we can write each other?" We agreed and exchanged addresses. In view of my emotional state, that was a nice offer and I didn't give it another thought. After all, it was one of those things you say to keep a conversation going and there was no harm in being polite. She was seventeen, good looking and nice to talk to. It had been a very long time since I had met anyone so fresh and so innocent. Her mother butted into our conversation and invited me to visit them we returned to Cape Town. "If you want, you are free to spend weekends at our house." Blow me over! I couldn't believe my ears. For the next four days of the convention I managed to meet Sue each evening. A nice platonic friendship had been established, or so I thought. What I could not realize was this chance encounter would wind up having a huge influence on me for the rest of my life.

On the way back to Simon's Town we sailed head on into a terrific storm. Roaring Forties tossed us all over the ocean. As best we could, we battened down the ship and then prayed she'd stay afloat. In all my years at sea, that was one of the worst storms I'd ever gone through. With the watertight doors locked shut, all port holes and hatches closed, the raging sea smashed as high as the B gun mounting just under the wheel house. All we could do was pray and hang on. Wherever I looked men were vomiting.

The mess decks looked as if everything that had not been lashed down was broken. Yes, this was a bad storm but I had been through bad storms before. I had flashbacks to six years earlier when we rode out the storms in the North Atlantic during the long battle of Atlantic. In the face of ferocious headwinds on that trip back to Simon's Town our ship barely made four or five knots. She shuddered from bow to stern and a couple of times I succumbed to asking the sailor's classic question: will she break up? Fortunately, she didn't. No one was lost overboard but onboard the HMS Nigeria a sailor had a close call.

We didn't hear his full story until we reached Simon's Town. It was so preposterous that we barely believed it. HNS Nigeria was caught in the same storm at about the same place. For reasons I can't recall a sailor was on deck when he was swept into the sea on the starboard side as the quarterdeck went down a deep trough. When the stern came up again the ship rolled and slipped toward the starboard side just under the poor chap who was swimming for his life. He couldn't believe it because his ship rose up under him and he almost found himself standing securely on deck, not too far from where he went over. Other than being drenched and in shock, he was in good nick. His story got his name in all the Cape newspapers. You never know what's going to happen when you are at sea. If he had tried to position himself for a rescue there is every reason to believe the ship would not have been able to stop and retrieve him. In the hell we went through no man could survive overboard but sometimes, just sometimes, miracles do happen.

Back in Simon's Town, our captain, Commander Cuthbert RN, wanted to show up the flagship whose Marine bugler sounded the color at 0800 hours and at sunset. He asked if there was anybody who could play the bugle so he could show up the flagship. I volunteered for the job because I had been a good bugler at the Boys School in Brest. "Captain, sir," I began, "I need you to let me train for at least a week in order to get my lips hardened enough to give a perfect sound." He squinted at me and granted permission to my request. "Take your time and let me know when you are ready."

I started practicing in the forehead mess deck so that nobody could hear me outside the ship. Those first days were awful; I wondered why someone didn't kill me for inflicting sonic torture on my mates. It took me longer than I had calculated to get back in shape. After about three weeks I told the Captain that I was ready. He smiled as if he was going to make a practical joke. "Are you sure of yourself?" He was half laughing and half serious. "After all, I want you to play at least as well as the Marine bugler onboard the Nigeria. "Sir," I began, "I can play better than he can." I was smiling but I wasn't joking and we both laughed.

The next morning at 0800 we were lined up on the quarterdeck and the Captain ordered, "Stand to attention." As the Nigeria's signal flag began to drop, I started sounding the 'stand to attention' and I was just a couple of notes ahead of the Marine bugler who must have wondered what the bloody hell was going on. The captain's ruse worked perfectly every weekday except for weekends when I was on shore leave.

*****

One day I got a phone call from Sue and her mother asking me if I would like to join them for the weekend. "Thank you, it would be a pleasure," and she replied, "We'll come and pick you up on the following Saturday morning." Sure enough, both of them, mother and daughter, were in their Plymouth they was parked outside the dockyard gate. When we reached Cape Town she showed me the quickest way to get to their house that was situated close to Table Mountain. The house was nice with a fantastic view over the whole town.

They did everything to make me feel at home but I was nervous and confused because I was afraid my 'mess manners' would surface and I'd make a fool of myself by cursing or saying something vulgar. In the space of a few minutes I was transported, literally, into another world where I was the foreigner, a visitor and 'polite young man' who had to behave like a gentleman. That behavior meant taking a big step and it took a lot of effort but I made it.

They introduced me to their family. The parents had produced a son, William who was 12 and they adopted another lad, Reginald who was 11. Another person, a young lady called Esther, stayed with them most of the time but did not sleep at Sue's house. I got on well with their children but I had a funny feeling about Esther. There was nothing concrete, just a feeling. It was as if she either distrusted me or disliked me, or maybe even both! Try as I might, Esther and I had a strained relationship. Later, I found out that she became jealous of my relationship with the family, but I could not figure out what I had done to make her feel jealous.

I had not given up reading my medical books. Interest in medicine was beginning to push my thinking down another path: why not get serious and start university work so that I could become a doctor? I told Edith's father what I was considering and he encouraged me to keep talking to him because he wanted to help me arrive at a decision. He was patient and surprisingly frank because he told me that I had a better future by avoiding medicine. "Lad, you'll be much better off financially by using your hands instead of studying for years to become a doctor. You can turn your love of science into a hobby but I would counsel you against turning it into a profession." Ten years was a long time and I would have to work and study in order to pay for my studies. "Once you've qualified, you'll be known as a 'Poor Man's Practitioner' and you're going to have to work all hours and tend to patients who often don't have the means to pay for your services but you have to tend to them anyway." He was honest and I needed that kind of advice. Some of the romance involved with being a doctor started to fade away. "On the other hand, you could work for an electrical contracting company here." He paused as if to reflect on what he had just said and when he got my interest when he continued. "I even know many companies are looking for qualified people."

He invited me to think over our conversations, take my time, and not rush into any commitments I might regret later. In view of the mess I had got myself into with Edith, acting first and then thinking, I accepted his well-reasoned advice. I was caught between pursuing a dream, perhaps not a realistic dream but one that had guided me for a long time, and chucking it to pursue something totally different. I followed his advice and began weighing the two ideas. Slowly, it began dawning on me that his insight made sense. Because of him, a new opportunity was taking shape for me. Maybe, just maybe, it might work out and I knew that I had to follow up on his offer to help and seize the opportunity because it might not repeat itself.

I continued keeping a close relationship with the Keiser Family. They were kind and generous and they considered me as an 'adopted' member of the family. One day Dr. Keiser told me that he was the Grand Master of the Cape Town Freemason Lodge. "One of my brothers in the lodge is the general manager of a big electrical contracting company and I've told him about your skills and your situation." I sat up straight, as if someone had sent a shock wave up my spine. "He's proposed to take you on as an electrical fitter to start with as soon as you're released from the navy." I couldn't believe my ears; I immediately began making inquiries as to whether it was possible to be released even though I still had eighteen months to run on my re-enlistment. There was some money involved. I can't remember how much, but the little question of money wasn't going to stop me. The good doctor even offered to give me a loan.

Getting out of the navy was a bit tricky but I managed to quit the service honorably. For the navy to release me, I had to produce evidence that the reason for wanting to leave was to study and enter the medical University of Cape Town. The ship's surgeon confirmed that I wanted to study medicine and Dr. Keiser wrote a letter saying he was going to tutor me. To be fair, I was bending the rules and regulations but it was the only way I could make a clean break and start a new career. Was I being dishonest? Technically, the answer was 'yes' but, realistically, I had arrived at a turning point in my life and there was nothing to be gained by running out my time with the navy. With a bit of finagling I took big steps toward building my new future. It was exciting and I was eager to get on with my new life. In record time I managed to get all the signatures the procedure required and I dutifully submitted my request through channels so as to avoid any delays that could be attributed to 'faulty procedures'. Then, I began waiting. In a matter of days my request was granted and I was released from full time duty. The navy transferred me to the Royal Navy Reserve and I agreed to report to the navy once a year.

I will never forget the day I left the ship for good! The captain and my division officer wished me good luck. I saluted them for the last time and then strode down the gangway while the QM piped me off. When I was facing aft I turned and saluted the white ensign and all my shipmates waved me off. I waved back and felt overcome by a strange feeling that was difficult to describe because it was a mixture of sadness, happiness and fear. Waving back at them meant I was saying goodbye to men with whom I had shared so much. I had flashbacks to how desperately lost I felt when I was demobbed in Portsmouth. Finally, and in South Africa of all places, I was 'jumping ship,' leaving the only way of life I had ever known for something totally new. From the moment I waved back I was also ushering myself into the civilian world. I was scared.

*****

Sue and her Mother were waiting for me outside the dockyard gate. I dumped my gear into the Plymouth's boot and climbed into the back of the car. I reached forward and bent their heads into mine. "Please don't make me talk, just give me time to get over it." As we drove out of the dockyard I gradually began to get a grip on myself and for the first time I really felt as if I was one of the family. Back in the house the boys gave me a great welcome, much shouting and whooping, and I felt a wonderful new phase of my life was starting.

Within a week I was introduced to my new boss and I started working in the electrical contracting company Dr. Keiser had told me about, "Hubert Davis and Co." I was given a mate, a middle aged Bantu, a very good chap who was generous in his advice. He probably opened up to me more than he would have with a white South African because I was a foreigner and obviously not a native born South African. I soon made some good friends. One in particular, a man called Gibbs who was ex 8th Army Desert Rats. He came to South Africa overland driving a surplus Army lorry he had purchased in the UK. He taught me a lot of technical things about civilian electrical installation that were non-existent in the Navy. For instance, he showed me how to bend steel pipes without kinking them. He was a good teacher and I was a fast learner. In fact, so fast that I became the fastest of the lot and that caused a bit of a stir. The other good friend was Snowy, so called because of his white hair. He was also ex British Army, and another chap called Swanepool who wanted the two of us to start a contracting business on our own once I had fully assimilated into the South African way of life. We would often meet in town for a drink but the meeting I really looked forward to was when Dr. Keiser and I would meet at the Bordeaux Hotel in Green Point.

We'd swim in the cold Atlantic waters and afterwards we'd warm up on the shore. These outings gave me a chance to meet some of his friends from the medical profession. I learned a lot and what I learned humbled me because no matter how difficult my life had been, the men I met had lived through much worse. His friends had interesting but frightening tales to tell. Most of them were Jews who had either fled Germany or had been kicked out. Despite their harrowing tales, I learned a lot from them. They spoke quietly and earnestly about the need to be patient and diligent. Over and over they stressed how very important it was to work hard and reach one's own goals in life. For instance, just because they were doctors in

Germany that did not mean they could automatically practice in South Africa. They had to re-qualify and in many instances this meant learning English. They considered me as an equal in term of class. Because of that I became more open minded. I started to discover a world I knew nothing about. In spite of the fact that they must have had a very hard time in their earlier life, they never talked about it. If Dr. Keiser hadn't told me, I would never have found out about their backgrounds.

Admittedly, I knew absolutely nothing about Jews and I could not understand why the Germans had such a furious and burning hatred against them. The men that I met through Dr. Keiser were perfect gentlemen. One day, the doctor organized a cocktail party at his house. There were about twenty-five guests and I was introduced to a Dr. Laufbaum and his wife Paula. He was German born and his wife was French. She was in her early forties, beautiful and definitely hot stuff. Unfortunately, her husband was old enough to be her father. Meeting her was a chance to speak French and it was obvious she had been briefed about me.

The party took place in the garden and she kept drawing me away from the others to a dark place behind a tree where she began rubbing her body against mine. I was panicked because I didn't want to be seen but I was as excited as she was. She said she would phone me during the week to invite me for dinner at her house and gradually we walked back to join the others with our empty glasses in hand. No one seemed to have noticed what had happened, or if they did at least they did not let on.

A new story was beginning, a wild erotic relationship that was grounded in passion, sheer raw lust. She needed me and I needed her. That was the end of the equation. Her husband was a hard case. In spite of the fact that he had been kicked out of Germany where he had a well known practice in Frankfurt, at heart he still wanted to be recognized as World War I cavalry officer, a period in his life that apparently was the happier and more rewarding than his prosperous career as a doctor.

One evening he told me that the Boers were too stupid to talk to and that he had a strong dislike for the English. I had to put up with him because he and his wife had worked out a little game of their own and

I was having fun. Every evening I spent with them the doctor managed to leave us alone for about a half hour. "Have to see a patient," and he left the room. Then we went at it! I know it sounds strange, but my relationship with them continued until I left South Africa. The good doctor was always courteous and selectively blind to what was going on between Paula and me. Now that I am older and wiser, I hate to think about what must have been going through his mind when he shut the door and trudged upstairs leaving us alone?

Although I was leading 'the good life' my mind really hadn't settled into a new routine that I could call 'a normal civilian life'. I began wondering about what I was really doing in South Africa. Did I really know what was keeping me? I wasn't running any more from my memories of my marriage, if you want to call it that, to Edith. By the time I met Paula my divorce had been granted and I was a free man. The lawyers handled all the paperwork. When I received their final notification I read the letter carefully, folded it, and filed it among my personal papers. At least that piece of Life's great puzzle had been nudged into its proper place.

Even though my recent past was a painful period in my life, in the struggle I learned a lot about myself, how far I could push myself and how far I would allow someone to push me. During the war there were no limits; there were only absolutes. Either you survived or you died. In civilian life there are limits but generally they are self-imposed. My torment with Edith helped me to discover new limits in myself and I believed that someday and somehow those awful months with her would do me some good but it was awfully hard to see how and when.

Despite my mind being a jumble of conflicts and contradictions I managed to look out at the world and admit that I had learned why others do many things that may have seemed strange to me but were important for them. I would never have thought someone could sit on the loo and compose a piece of music. The human family includes all men and women from all walks of life, even me. I was slowly beginning to admit that my life was like a huge puzzle. Some of the pieces in my puzzle were missing and when the time came, I would have to carve them out of my experience and fit them into place.

When they finally fit together I would have a picture of my life and it would make sense.

I couldn't hurry the maturing process even if I wanted to and I could not pretend as if the process wasn't happening. It was confusing and I was caught up in something that I could not quite understand. There was no doubt that 'something' was happening to me but I was incapable of stepping back from my daily routine to gain perspective. Accepting that I was in flux was difficult.

I had always been in control of myself but the person I knew was someone who had lived his life in a regimented world. Civilian life was different. I was expected to create my own regimen and that became an enormous responsibility because I had no prior experience to use as guidelines. Where was I headed? Damned if I knew! Even my love life had to be created. I could not use my failed marriage as a benchmark for any new relationship. Edith was part of my past that I did not want to dredge up. That painful period, all those little puzzle pieces, slotted into place; they were the old part of the puzzle. Now there were many new pieces that I couldn't seem to fit in anywhere. I knew I was struggling with giving meaning to my life and I struggled to see the bigger picture. At least I was certain about one point: There was a lot of contradiction in my life. Many pieces didn't seem to want to fit. I didn't know where to begin or how to push them into place and make a picture of my life, of where I wanted to go, that really made sense to me.

Professionally, I was doing quite well and I had greatly improved my knowledge of electrical contracting. With Swanepool we did a few jobs on the side during weekends and after work during the week. Financially, this was good because it helped me pay for the flat I was planning to let which was, for want of a better term, a love nest. Paula was beginning to get worried about our relationship. We didn't know how long the good doctor's blind eye would be turned away from us. It was a matter of time until something unpleasant happened and we both wanted to prevent that but still keep up our relationship.

In the meantime something happened that ruined my relationship with the Kaiser family. Paula was also worried about the effect Esther was having on me. I tried to be friendly with Esther but every attempt I made was rebuffed. Was she after me, was she a spoiler, was she psycho, or was she a bitch? I couldn't figure her out. Paula said Esther was jealous of me but I couldn't figure out what I was doing to make her jealous.

At first I took no notice but then I began getting hints from what family members said to me. There were definitely subtle changes in attitude towards me that made me believe someone thought I was beginning to play too important a role in their family. But, who could it be? I was on great terms with everyone. The only person I could think of was Esther. I wracked my brain to see if I could recall doing anything to her that warranted her stabbing me in the back. Try as hard as I might, I drew a blank but I was convinced Esther was up to no good. Apparently she would say something about the family and me, cite a little incident, two of us having breakfast together or laughing at a private joke, and then she'd make a gesture to indicate her bewilderment. Perhaps those little gestures were a hint at something more sinister. She was too clever to be drawn out. Once she sowed doubt she dropped the topic. But, the damage was done. Did anyone know what she was trying to say? No, but she succeeded in poisoning the atmosphere.

The Keiser family was not the type of family in which the parents encouraged their children to talk openly and get whatever was bothering them out on the table. Strict and structured, there was no way to bring this phantom problem out into the open. Once I caught on to what was happening I decided I had to get away from Esther. She was sabotaging me and I was not prepared to fight back, especially when I couldn't figure out what was upsetting her. If I was 'the problem' that meant I probably had to leave.

Some people in life may be born mean. I think Esther was one of those hapless people who drew pleasure from life when she was being nasty. The war of nerves heated up. Esther began getting at me through Sue's brother, hinting, if not outright telling him, that Sue's mother and I were having an affair. None of what she said was brought to my attention. I heard details of how she undermined me much later but in the meantime I knew something was seriously wrong. There was nothing factual that I could put my finger on. The situation began eating at me because I began developing strong guilt feelings and started to have doubts about myself. The pressure inside me was too much for me to handle. I knew that I had to move out.

The doctor and his wife were disappointed when I told them that I was going to leave. Using my work as an excuse, I explained that I was beginning to work on jobs that finished very late and some of the jobs were in a village about fifty miles from Cape Town. They accepted my story at face value. Gracious and good people, they invited me to come for Sunday lunch with the family whenever I had the time. I accepted their generous invitation. On those occasions when I did have Sunday lunch with them we really enjoyed being together again.

My mental turmoil and was about as turbulent as the South African political scene. The situation was deteriorating; the nationalists were becoming more aggressive. An election was coming up and they built their campaign around a program requiring complete racial separation. It was an awful proposal that would mean trouble for the country and for me. In the Cape Province, where the nationalists did not have a majority, we could not imagine how their policy could possibly appeal to enough voters to win the election. But, what we failed to realize was that the national party was strong in other parts of the Union, especially in areas where there was a large concentration of Boers. In those areas, like the Orange Free State, Transvaal, Bloemfontein, etc., they were still fighting the Boer War!

*****

I began making back-up plans, something I didn't want to do but, in view of the situation, something that I knew I had to do. During one of the national holidays, my friend Gibbs suggested that we go up to Southern Rhodesia and have a look around. "Just in case," he said, "we have to get out of here fast."

We took the train from Cape Town to Bulawayo where we hired a pick-up to continue our journey onto Salisbury, now called Harare. We drove through rolling fields where a labor-intensive crop, tobacco, was planted. Large-scale industrial farming had not yet begun. We looked around but our short stay was enough to convince us there was little opportunity for men with our skills. Someone told us that if we were out to make a quick quid it was possible to make a bundle hunting crocodiles. Fashion trends had changed and crocodile skins were in great demand. It was a hair-brained idea neither of us would have come up with on our own but it intrigued us. We went up to have a look at the Zambezi River and Lake Kariba and we saw a lot of crocodiles. Suddenly, the far-fetched notion of becoming big time hunters started to move from a hair-brained idea to a solid plan.

As we drove around the lake and through marshes, we were oblivious to the mosquitoes descending on us like black clouds. We were young and hearty and we didn't give them a second thought. Slapping and cursing, we thought of them as a minor nuisance on our road to great riches. But, Nature has a way of forcing people to change their plans. Gibbs came down with a terrible malaria attack and I had to race him back to Salisbury for treatment because there were no medical facilities out in the bush. He pulled through but we abandoned our plans. The thought of quick wealth was a nice dream but staying healthy for the rest of our lives was much more important than money.

Back in Cape Town, I met up with John Knight who had been released from the Navy. He was married to the color girl I mentioned earlier. Love and politics don't always mix. Unfortunately, the local political scene turned against John. The general election brought Dr. Malan, an ultra nationalist, into power. His party wasted no time putting Apartheid laws into practice. This was a disaster for the Cape Province because it had a large colored population. Many were accepted as white and John's wife fell into that category. Being accepted as white and being classified white were two entirely different concepts. John's wife was not classified as white. Under the new laws, she was a 'colored person' in a racial category that was neither white nor black. With the National Party in power, John either had to divorce her or leave South Africa.

John found himself in an impossible position and I resolved to help him at all cost. I began calling around to anyone who I felt might possibly be able to help him. Finally, Dr. Keiser came up with an idea: get him a job in Rhodesia. That was easier said than done but Dr. Keiser made a series of telephone calls. Finally, I contacted the vice consul of Brazil whom I knew through the Royal Navy

Association and he, in turn, put me onto the High Commissioner for Rhodesia. John and the commissioner met and shortly thereafter John took his family to Rhodesia where he began working for the Railway Company of Southern Rhodesia. He left with his wife and his first child, a lovely little girl with blond hair and blue eyes for whom I was the proud godfather. We stayed in touch for a few years. I knew he became the stationmaster in QueQue, they had another daughter, but once I returned to Europe we lost touch and I don't know what happened to him.

Apartheid meant many new laws governing race relations. With the new government cohabitation between blacks and whites was forbidden. Colored people were caught in the middle. Most white households had colored servants and nannies. In fact, I thought the lifestyle of the white population depended on easy access to blacks and the coloreds. When it came to sex and having fun, if you wanted to have a good time with a colored girl all you had to do was to hire one to do your housekeeping. This was because the Cape colored girls were very, very fond of white men. They were good in bed but they talked too much. In the new South Africa, if they shot off their mouths and began bragging about their white boss, both the girl and the employer were likely to wind up in jail for breaking the racial laws.

Fortunately, I didn't have to run the risk of breaking any regulations because I had many white girl friends. If I was satisfied with my private life between the sheets, I was becoming increasingly uneasy about how the new government was running the country. No one could deny that the Nationalist Party era ushered in a period of nasty social-political tensions that made daily life more dangerous. Now I sensed there was a dangerous undercurrent. For want of another word, it was a 'fear' that came into being simultaneously with the arrival of the Nationalists in power. Coupling political fear with my own growing frustration, I slowly concluded that I was getting nowhere in terms of having the kind of settled civilian life that I craved.

I began hatching a plot to leave South Africa and settle either in France or the U.K. For security reasons, and because I did not want to hurt all those good South Africans who had been kind to me, I did not tell anyone about my plans. But, as usual, there was a snag. I was short of cash. Yes, I had worked hard, but I had not managed to put away as much as I would probably need once I left South Africa.

One day I went to the Port Authority to see the Port Captain. "What are my chances of shipping out on a merchant ship as an electrician?" He thought for a moment. "Your chances are slim as an electrician but you might get a berth as a seaman. Do you want me to put you on the list?" I said 'yes' and gave him my telephone number. "This isn't going to happen overnight. You've got to be prepared to wait weeks or months before your ship comes in." I began waiting. It was impossible for anyone to tell that I had a secret agenda because I worked as if nothing had changed. Behind my façade, I held firm to my plans.

About two months later, at seven o'clock one evening as I came into my flat, the phone rang and an unknown voice asked, "Are you Mr. J. Powell?" "Yes, I am John Powell", I replied but I couldn't recognize the speaker's voice. I had completely forgotten about my arrangement with the Port Captain that I had made two months previously. "Are you still interested in leaving?" Out of the blue, the voice made sense! He told me that if I still wanted to leave there was a vacancy as an electrician's mate on a tanker. "The man you're replacing has been hospitalized." He instructed me to come to the port as quickly as possible because the ship was leaving at 0100 and there was a lot of paperwork to complete before I could leave the country. My mind raced and I made my decision: now or never. This is my chance. "I'll be there in thirty minutes," I said and hung up. I looked around my little flat and told myself that my life in South Africa was over. By 2200hrs I was onboard the S.S. Chisholm Trail a 17000 ton tanker that came from Abadan, bound for La Plata in Argentina. From there she was supposed to go back to the Gulf to refill and then sail to the UK.

A mess boy showed me to my cabin. The man I was replacing was its previous occupant. He, in turn, landed in the hospital because his cabin-mate broke a bottle over his head! Just my luck! Mr. "Heavy Hitter" was none other than the same person I was expected to share a tiny space with on the open sea for a very long time. When he came in he muttered something unintelligible before crawling into his bunk.

Taulus

I expected someone worse but he appeared okay. Until I got to know his ways, I was always on guard. We kept out of each other's way. We stood different watches and we had different work schedules. Most of his friends were in another cabin; they pretty much kept to themselves.

Most of the crew was Welsh. Once again, fate threw me together with the Welsh. First, when I had to take an English name I was told that Powell was a well-known Welsh name. Second, on my first ship the HMS Belmont, I was the only non-Welsh sailor in my mess. On this merchant ship my cabin mate was a Welshman!

I was back in my element: at sea. When the last hawser was lifted off its stanchion I felt the deck shudder. It was 0100 hours and we were headed for La Plata. I was headed for 'home', wherever that might be, and the promise of a new 'life' but I didn't have the vaguest idea what I was going to do. I was running, from something to something, but I was neither excited nor frightened. Just like during the war, I resolved to take each day as it came and leave the ship in one piece.

The Chisholm's tanks were full and the weather was fair so she remained steady. She barely rolled or pitched which was a relief because I had to find my sea legs again. Becoming a crew member meant I accepted specific obligations. I just didn't sign on for the trip to Argentina. I was actually bound to the ship because I signed articles of engagement that tied me up for two years. Only if we sailed to a port between the latitude of Hamburg and Brest would I be allowed to apply to apply to leave the ship. This was a pretty good deal because I was told we would be back in the UK within six to eight weeks.

Maybe it was typical of that period in my life because politics, turmoil in the Middle East, got in the way of my plans. When we arrived at La Plata we were told that the Iranian Prime Minister, Mossadeck, a fiery politician at odds with the U.K. government, had indefinitely closed the Abadan refinery in Iran. That was bad news because Abadan was our next stop before sailing back to the U.K with a load of Iranian crude. Since we were contracted to the Anglo Iranian Oil Company we had to follow their orders. They told us to go to La Plata and unload our cargo and then sail across the river and anchor outside Montevideo to avoid paying port mooring fees while waiting

Rene Dassac (in collaboration with Patrick K. Robbins)

for our next sailing orders. My plans to get aback to Europe were great. The only problem was reality kept interfering and screwing up my dreams.

I went ashore a couple of times and even went to Buenos Aires, a sprawling dirty city that reminded me somewhat of Marseille. It had the same mood, same noise, just a different accent. Montevideo was a different story. Hundreds of prostitutes strolled up and down the sidewalks offering their charms at extremely low prices. Prostitutes in port cities are as much of the landscape as cranes and hawsers but the docks were almost sagging under the weight of literally hundreds of professionals looking for a trick. The law of supply-and-demand was driving down the price of their 'service' fees which was great for the customers! I couldn't figure why there were so many girls on one side of the harbor and not on the other. A bartender set me straight: he told me that the girls were Argentine. Eva Peron outlawed their trade and kicked them out of BA. The girls packed their bags and took the ferry across the river into Uruguay. On the other side they caused all kinds of problems with the local trade because they were new, and numerous, competitors who were prepared to turn a trick for less than their Uruguayan sisters. Eva succeeded in becoming unpopular on both banks of the river.

We waited ten days at anchor in the Plata River. Most of the crew wanted a port call in the U.K. so we were all hoping that our ship would be sent to another oil producing port in the Gulf and then on to the UK. At last the signal came: Proceed to San Pedro, California via Cape Horn. No one I have ever talked to rounded Cape Horn and called it an easy trip. Under the best of conditions Cape seas pound ships mercilessly and some don't make it. The prospect of a rough passage was something I could live with but the fact that we had to round the Cape drove home another message: post-war Britain was broke. We could have gone to California via the Panama Canal but that passage was paid in dollars and our owners, like all of Britain, did not have dollars to spare. Paying back the Lend-Lease program was expensive. Foreign exchange controls were in effect and the government was not releasing precious dollars unless they absolutely had to. The cash crisis led me to another reflection: if a country wants to avoid aggression it must never lower its guard no matter how peaceful the world might appear. In more ways than one, we were living the consequences of our pre-World War II lessons.

We were glad to be at sea again even if it meant rounding the Cape with empty tanks. We sailed along the coast of Argentina and secured the upper deck to get ready to face the Cape's fury. The afternoon before we reached the Cape I was off duty and was sleeping in my cabin when the wind shifted and shot through my porthole. Because I was asleep I was unaware that we had filled the ballast tanks and this had lowered the ship considerably. When I went to sleep my porthole was open and well above the water line. When ballast was added the ship lowered. Seawater began splashing through my porthole onto my bunk and into the cabin. I managed to wrestle the porthole closed and secured it but the cabin deck was awash with several inches of cold water. Cursing I began cleaning and drying the cabin and about half way through my cabin mate came and helped me finish the job. We were both lucky because we could have had a serious problem if both of us had been out of the cabin and unaware that our porthole was open.

To no one's surprise, the weather deteriorated as we entered the Cape straits. It was so bad that walking the catwalk between the bridge and the aft meant you had to calculate how two waves would break before you could cross from the central structure where the officers and the bridge were to the aft castle where the crew was quartered. Although the weather was rough, it was nowhere near as bad as what I had seen in the north Atlantic during the war or in the Indian Ocean with the roaring forties. I kept reminding myself that I had lived through worse and experience taught me that there is an end to every storm. You just had to ride them out. Sure enough, once around the Cape and into the Pacific the weather changed so we could ride gentle waves all the way to California.

Immigration and Customs Officers came aboard in San Pedro. We were issued with visitor's cards so we could move in the dock area without any problems from the authorities. That was welcome but we had to put up with a meticulous inspection from the customs officers. They went through the ship from top to bottom, searching for drugs, tobacco, anything they considered to be contraband. They even sealed the cold room with the meat that had been bought in Argentina.

The reason? Argentina had hoof and mouth disease. During the four days in port we stocked up on American beef that was better quality and no one complained. At the end of the fourth day we had filled with crude and headed south to Australia. Before we left, I went ashore with the ship's steward who had all his teeth pulled in Cape Town. He wanted to see how much dentures would cost in America but the dental surgeon we contacted soon put him straight. Dentures in Australia would be cheaper than in the States.

After the visit to the dentist in Long Beach we caught a bus and to Los Angeles. It was a warm Sunday afternoon and the town seemed empty but we found a bar that was open in mid-town. The barman asked us where we were from, one topic led to another, and when we commented on how dead the city seemed, he replied, "It's Sunday most folk take their boats and go out fishing or just go out to the beach, maybe even out to the country to "relax after a good brunch". Talk about good living! We went through the employment section of the huge Sunday newspaper, the Los Angeles Times. We couldn't get over the number of pages advertising well-paid jobs. I stared at the toothless steward; he stared back at me. Both of us were thinking: "Now's the time to jump ship and start a new life."

Neither of us said anything for a few minutes. I was seriously considering melting into the California countryside and starting a new life in a country where jobs were going begging. Reluctantly, I finally had to admit that jumping ship was a bad idea. In the end, reason prevailed. The steward didn't agree with me at first and only when I reminded him jumping ship meant becoming fugitives and that meant spending the rest of our lives in hiding. "You want to start here, go to the U.S. consulate once we get back to the U.K. and do it the right way," I counseled, almost surprised at how reasonable I sounded. We didn't stay in touch and I wonder if he ever followed up on my advice.

Our wonderful stay in California was too short. The S.S. Chisholm Trail crossed the Pacific Ocean to Melbourne where we emptied our tanks before continuing our long trip to the Persian Gulf. In those days Australia had begun a massive immigration policy. They were so desperate for immigrants, especially Europeans, that in some cases they even paid part of the cost of travel to Australia to insure that these new Australians would stay because Australia is not everyone's cup of tea.

Sometimes the Aussies are a bit raw, rough in some people's minds, but they are nice people, heavy beer drinkers who have to live with funny laws. For instance, in order to obey the pub hour operating laws they drank themselves silly. In those days the pubs closed at 1800 hours. This meant that when the dock workers finished the day shift they would race to the nearest pub, order four or five pints at a time, lug them onto a table, down them as fast as possible, stagger out onto the street and vomit. Within an hour they were pickled and happy. Later in the evening, for slightly higher price, you could go to a public house and order a drink and enjoy it until closing time. Hopefully, as I am writing this, the laws have changed.

We left Melbourne and crossed the Indian Ocean to Bahrain on the Persian Gulf where we refilled with a cargo of crude oil bound for Cardiff in the UK. I think all the crew, the captain included, was glad to be on our way home at last. We'd been sailing around the globe for four and a half months and we were happy with the prospect of setting foot on U.K. soil. From Bahrain we sailed around the bottom of the Arabian Peninsula and steamed up the Red Sea, through the Suez Canal, across the Med, and through the Straits of Gibraltar out into the Atlantic. For many of my shipmates this was 'just another trip' but for me I could not help but remember a different time in my life, a time when being out to sea was a life-or-death gamble. Under our ship lay the remains of warships that lost their wager. At least, I was alive to remember those years.

Before the British coast came into sight something unpleasant occurred. It was a silly event but it shows how easily life onboard can turn into a confrontation between the captain and his crew. Everyday at precisely five minutes before lunch, the apprentice cook made his rounds through the ship ringing a hand bell to call the crew to lunch. It was routine and minutes before he began our stomachs were growling loud enough to tell us lunch was almost on the table. One day, to break the routine, the head cook, he liked to be called 'chef', unscrewed the handle of the bell before his apprentice began his rounds. It was meant to be a practical joke but it turned sour. Following a well-worn routine, the young apprentice went out on deck, shook the bell vigorously, and the bell flew into the sea leaving the lad holding the handle. The chef burst into laughter at the sight of the boy holding the handle and staring into the sea. He raced back into the kitchen, "Chef, what do I do now?" The kid was frightened. "See that big bell up there," the chef pointed to a big bell hanging just below the bridge. The boy nodded. "Quick as you can, run up and ring that." The lad swung into action and hammered the big bell.

All hell broke loose. The poor lad didn't know it, but that particular bell was to be rung only in case of fire. Within seconds officers and crew raced to the bell. "Where's the fucking fire," the first officer screamed at the boy. Already behind him fire fighting teams were breaking out the hoses, straining to see smoke. The lad stammered out the truth and the captain went mad. "You'll bloody well pay for this," he screamed at the boy. "You're going to pay for the bell out of your salary and then," he really had worked himself into a towering rage, "once we get to Cardiff I'm going to instruct the union steward to seek punitive action." Within just a few seconds, two or three minutes at the most, the ship's company had split into two warring camps: the crew versus the captain. Some of the officers were in silent agreement with us but their careers depended on keeping the captain happy.

Back in the crew quarters arguments broke out on what was the best way to defend the boy against union reprisals. We were still arguing when we arrived in Cardiff. Instead of a relaxed crew looking forward to a few days of port call, we were tense and angry. The captain turned vicious. Using every bit of authority vested in him as master of the ship, he turned the port call into a nightmare. Somebody would pay for the joke and he was going to have the last laugh. Twice he ordered the ship far out to sea to drain and clean the tanks until they were completely gas free. Each trip out was a long and tedious exercise and it really wasn't necessary because we could have completed the cleaning process in one operation on our way up the coast. Back in port he ordered 'abandon ship' exercises. We went through each step even to the point of lowering the lifeboats and rowing around the ship until he ordered them to be brought up, secured, and then he ordered the boats down and we went back around the ship. He kept us at it for two days and then paid us off. I've never left a ship hearing so much grumbling and bitterness. A stupid practical joke turned sour. By taking revenge the captain destroyed the entire goodwill of his crew. I went down the gangway and headed straight for the station where I caught a train to London to see my RN shipmate Watson with whom I stayed a couple of days before leaving for Paris.

*****

As the train headed into Paris I realized that I still hadn't made up my mind about finding a job and settling down. For starters, I didn't even have the vaguest idea of where in France I really wanted to settle. I could go anywhere I wanted to but with so many cities to choose from, I didn't have the foggiest idea where I wanted to live. Confronted with having to decide what I was going to do with my life, I couldn't make a decision even if someone paid me! I was torn in too many directions and this kept me edgy. Two of my sisters had married since I saw them in 1945. Genevieve married a barrister and lived in Epernay and my younger sister married a staff manager at Moet & Chandon and lived in the same town so I decided to go to Epernay that was close to Paris. That seemed to be a pretty sound decision. I figured with two married sisters in the same town, wouldn't their husbands lend a hand and help me settle? My plan sounded easy enough but there was no way for me to know that I was underestimating the difficulty of settling down in France and living a civilian life.

Frenchman by birth and upbringing, I was a stranger in my own country. Often I caught myself referring to my fellow citizens as "them" or "they." They ate different food and held their knives and forks different than what I was accustomed to, their pace of life was different, and even 'their' way of speaking wasn't a mixture of French and English. To 'them' I was different, a Frenchman from a different world. People were genuinely nice to me but I was the outsider looking into 'their' country. Logically, my reactions didn't make sense because France was also my country, I had as much right to live there as they did, but I could feel that I didn't fit into 'their' way of doing things. Fitting into 'their' ways was maddening but what really got to me was the fact that I didn't have a bloody clue about how to find a job in my own bloody country!

My sisters were very happy to see me. They put me on show for all their friends to see because I was the family hero. It wasn't too difficult to see that they were also trying to introduce me to many unmarried girls my age in the hopes that I would fall in love with one of them, settle down, start a family and stop what they called my life of 'great adventure." They went to work finding me a job. At last, through their friends and connections, I got a job with a local electrical contractor.

The contractor put me to work as an electrician's mate. My boss was a pretentious young idiot who treated me as if I were his apprentice. I knew more about electricity than he did. From the beginning I began having that sinking feeling that comes when you know you've started something that is going to turn out wrong. In order to placate my sisters I put up with the idiot for a few days but the tension was rising and my fuse was beginning to sputter. He was the 'boss.' From his superior position he thought he could do what he liked with me.

One day our strained relationship finally snapped. I couldn't take him any more and I let my self-control slip away. "You," he snarled, "pass me some screws." He used metric dimensions that I couldn't immediately visualize because I had learned my trade in inches. "Hurry up idiot," he barked when he saw I was confused. I looked up at him on his ladder and lost my temper. I grabbed the ladder and began shaking it. "Come down here you little bastard and repeat that to my face and I'll show you which one of us is an idiot." By now the ladder was beginning to sway. He started clutching at the wall, clawing at anything for a grip. His face was white; he was speechless with fear. I could see his legs quivering. We stared at each other. If he'd come down I'd have torn him to shreds. It was all over. "I'm not going to dirty my hands on you." Just to make my point I shook the ladder again. The moron knew he was at my mercy. "I'm going back to live with civilized people," I said and collected my tool bag. As I walked out he was still up on the ladder staring at the spot I just vacated.

Out on the street I had to accept a fact of life: I couldn't stay in France, at least not then, maybe, even never again. We, "the French and I", were too far apart for me to connect with 'their' way of life. My sisters and their husbands had been good to me. I couldn't walk out on them. Recognizing my responsibility toward them meant I had to find an excuse for going back to the UK without hurting their feelings. There was no way they wouldn't hear about my dust up with the young idiot. Somehow I resigned myself to facing up to the music. They lived in Epernay, it was their home and their community. I was an outsider. They deserved an explanation that was honest but not brutal. After I was gone they had to live with the consequences because I was their brother and I had 'caused' the problem.

At dinner that night I gave them a fair explanation of what had happened, omitting the rough language, and then slipped in, "I'm going back to England to get a job with a British firm in France." I went on to explain, actually I was sort of weaving a story, that I had more to offer a British company than a French company and it would be easier for me to work with a firm that needed both my skills as an electrician and my knowledge of the two languages. I was logical and managed to convince them but they were sad to see me go. "Will we see you again?" Their question was honest and I struggled with an answer. "Yes, and I'll write you and we'll stay in touch wherever I go." I sounded so sure of myself, so clear in my thinking. It was good acting on my part. In front of them I kept the proverbial 'British stiff upper lip' but I left for London with the grinding knowledge that I was turning into a failure at nearly everything I touched.

Going to London was a way to get out of France to another destination but I didn't know where I was heading. It was easier to run from a place than it was to go somewhere and be excited about it. Not only was I running, I didn't even know how to find a job that could use my skills and experience. Watson, my faithful and steadfast shipmate, kept saying, "Not to worry, it's a question of time, you'll get something." His encouragement kept me sane. He had made it, why couldn't I? I looked at him and his wife. Both had good jobs in the hotel business. He had done a marvelous job integrating into the west end where he worked and in the Elephant and Castle, the area where he lived. Forget about his past, listening to him you'd take him for a pearly because he spoke with a very strong cockney accent. In the evenings in his local, when you listened to him, you couldn't possibly think that he was a Frenchman. "He's made it, why can't I?"

Rene Dassac (in collaboration with Patrick K. Robbins)

After a couple of weeks with no income, I wound up eating too deep into my savings. Alarm bells began ringing in my ears telling me to wake up and do something. The fact of the matter was plain for all to see: there were no job offers. Unlike the job markets in the States and in Australia, the British job market was dead. A constant run of rejections from hiring companies started to eat into my ego. Staying in London and hoping for a break was ludicrous and dangerous. Not only was I unlikely to get a job any time soon, I wasn't sure I could take the mental pressure much longer. "Watson, I'm going to see the port captain in the east end dockyard and maybe he can get me back on a ship." My back was up against a wall of my own making. I responded to the challenge in the only way I knew how. Go back to sea. "You're wrong mate." He argued with me late into the night but I had made up my mind.

The next morning I went to see the port captain who, it turned out, was a good old merchant navy seaman who'd heard enough hard luck stories to fill a library. "It's time you seamen realize that it's no good to wait till you are broke to look for a ship." I was down and I really didn't want to be kicked around but I had to put up with him because he was my last hope and I was running out of luck. "I've only got two ships at the moment. Both are looking for crew but I warn you on one of them, it's so damn dirty that grass is growing on her deck." He gave a loud cough as if to expel from his lungs the sludge his mind had seen. "So far only a few sailors have accepted to sign her articles." I thanked him and started down to the wharves.

The 'Peter Star' was a shocking sight. An Anglo-Greek Company owned her and they were obviously operating on the principle of investing only to keep her afloat. The port captain hadn't lied. To my mind, it would take a good three days of hard work to make her look like a ship worth sailing on the high seas. It was true: grass was growing on her deck. Not a lawn, mind you, but prairie grass that had sprouted from the grain she had been carrying. After she made port and off loaded her cargo, the crew had left before sweeping down the decks. Grain that had spilled from the holds germinated in the cool wet London climate to produce lush green sprouts. Now all we needed was a shepherd and a cargo of live sheep.

I went to the captain's cabin and pounded on the door. He seemed like a good bloke and he told me that the Peter Star had a contract to take a cargo of tractors, cars, and other machinery to Australia. Once in Australia he was convinced he'd get a return cargo back to the UK. "We begin loading tomorrow and, if all goes well, we'll sail the next day during the night." That sounded pretty good to me. "Sign the articles and I'll give you a five pound advance." That sounded even better so I signed and rushed back to Watson to get my gear and say goodbye to my little London family.

I got to my cabin, fortunately quite clean unlike the ship's decks and organized my work shift with the boatswain. He was not a bad bloke but he was rough and rather dumb. As best as I could figure out he had a limited education. I'd met enough of his kind in the navy and I managed to get along with him reasonably well. But not everyone in the crew was as lucky. This immediate post war period was the beginning of an era when ship's crews changed from being largely European to crews wherein the majority came from the third world. We had a fair number of Egyptians among the crew and he openly detested them. I was a Brit so he felt more at ease with me.

We worked very hard to get the vehicles secured in the holds that also contained several luxury Jaguar motorcars. There were also many crates of whisky. Surprising no one, the dockworkers managed to break open a crate without breaking the bottles and then they shared the 'damaged goods' among themselves. This was the first time I had seen open theft in peacetime. During the war we tended to 'borrow', but I was assured that this peacetime 'accident' was quite normal. Insurance would cover the "loss." The deck between the fore and after castles and in front of the bridge was loaded with crates of tractors, bulldozers, and other farm equipment, to a height of eighteen feet above the deck. This made the ship look dangerously top heavy.

The English crew was composed of proper cockneys, a happy lot always joking and easy to work with. We sailed out of London after midnight because we had to catch the right tide down the Thames and into the channel. We sailed close to the French coast. The captain had calculated his risks sailing a top-heavy ship and decided to favor caution. He wanted to be able to reach the safety of a port in the event we ran into heavy weather that might prove too dangerous for our top-heavy ship. Despite some misgivings on my part, all went well and we sailed right up to the Suez entrance of the Suez Canal without any problems. At Port Said we waited eighteen hours before entering the canal with the pilot. I was on the wheel when we went through the canal. The pilot asked me if I was ex RN. "Yes," I replied, "why do you ask?" Looking straight at the canal and not at me, he replied, "It's the way you answer my orders. Typical Royal Navy."

We went down the Red Sea, across the Indian Ocean and called at Freemantle where we unloaded part of our deck cargo. Before we could unload we had to wait three days because of a strike. The Melbourne Cup was running when we got to port. For the Aussies, horse races were more important than unloading our ship. All physical work had either ground to a halt or, if it moved at all, it barely moved. Office workers crowded around their radios or called in sick, while the Aussies enjoyed their days at the races. It was fine for them but it hurt our plans for heading back to the U.K. Because of the strike delay we lost our cargo and it was given to another ship which meant problems for us. If we couldn't get a cargo on time and to where we wanted to go the rest of the trip would be affected. In maritime terms we were a 'tramp freighter' and this meant we had to accept any cargo and sail to any destination the owners told us to. We called at Melbourne and Sydney to get rid of the remaining cargo but in Sydney bad news hit hard: We had no cargo to take to the UK. If that was not bad enough, there was no likelihood of any cargo being nominated for the UK in the near future.

The captain got one offer: a run up and down between Sydney and the Pacific islands carrying iron ore. The money was tempting but the captain was dead against it because, he said, "Once we take on that lot we're stuck for two years." He began searching for a short run cargo to get us out of Australia and back to the UK and finally he found a solution. We could get a cargo of wool in New Zealand but to go there meant we had to leave with a cargo. After searching for a full day he found a cargo: five bales of Job cigarette paper to take to so we set sail with a cargo that could easily fit into a suburban home garage. I don't know if the captain got a dressing down from his company board of directors but we got a full load of wool from Christchurch and Napier to take to the U.S.

While we were in Sydney I met a Frenchman. Naturally, we began talking about France and I told him how hard it was for me to find a job in France. "When you go back, you put an advert with your CV in the weekly L'Usine Nouvelle." Not a bad idea. At least it was a fresh approach that I had not heard of and I was excited. "I guarantee you will get more than one offer. You're different. You speak English." I kept thinking of this and it suddenly struck me that I had not realized how few people in France could speak English especially technical English as well as I could. He made sense and I had a serious chat with myself and called myself a 'bloody cunt' to be stuck on a ship in the middle of the Pacific. What really bothered me was that when I left Epernay and headed back to London, I didn't follow my intuition: play up the fact that I spoke both English and French and furthermore, my English vocabulary included a full range of technical terms that would make me attractive to anyone in the huge field of engineering. His idea was 'new' insofar as it crystallized some of my thinking but I had not sat down and put 2 + 2 together before I went back to sea. Now, after a chance encounter, I was motivated to break out of my circle of failure-hope-failure.

From then on I set some goals for myself and began steering my life instead of having it steered for me either by the forces of chance or by living in the routine of shipboard life. I convinced myself that if I used all my brains and connections I could get a good job in France. In the meantime, I resolved to save as much money as I could in order not to depend on others in the period when I left the ship and finally found a job with a good salary that would enable me to live properly.

From New Zealand we crossed the Pacific to the Panama Canal. This was part of the world I had never seen before and I very much appreciated doing something new. We crossed the international dateline. The captain was no fool. To the dismay of the crew he made sure to cross it on a weekday so he didn't have to pay overtime if we had crossed it on a Sunday! We also passed some islands that were lying so low above the surface of the ocean that we were almost on top of them before we saw them. That little experience made me realize how extraordinary navigators our ancestors were to sail across these archipelagos without radar and all the navigating instruments found on modern ships. And, I could not help but think about how nice it was to sail and not have to worry about the freezing cold, or worry about being sunk by a U boat, or a mine, or any one of a million things that can happen to a ship during war. The Pacific can be a ferocious ocean when provoked by Mother Nature but we were lucky and we had lovely weather all the way to Panama.

It was my first time through the Panama Canal and I learned something rather fascinating, at least for me, it was. On one side you enter the first of five lock gates and then proceed to a lake that you cross and then you go down four lock gates into the Atlantic Ocean. I'll leave you with a question that we debated hot and heavy as we crossed Panama: is one side of the two oceans higher than the other?

We sailed into the Caribbean, a sea that is dotted with lots of islands. This meant lots of shipping, vessels of all sizes and shapes, and this meant extra vigilance during our watches until we turned north and headed into Philadelphia where we unloaded our wool cargo. Once again, just like when we landed in California, Customs and Immigration boarded and they began their routine.

I laughed at the immigration officer. He was the epitome of a civil servant, the mindless and humorless little man whose sole purpose in life was to read from his procedure book and enforce rules and regulations that often made no sense. It may have been crazy to us but, from his perspective, he never forgot that scrupulous adherence to the enforcement process guaranteed his paycheck. He was a good family man and he wanted to get paid every month.

One of my crewmates gave him a typical cockney reply. To understand this scene you've got to imagine a cockney speaking his English and an American bureaucrat speaking civil servant American. The questioning went something like this. "What is your name?" The cockney blurted, "Johnson, sir!" "Have you ever been in the United States of America before?" The cockney blurted, "No, sir!" The civil servant paused and moved his pencil tip down the page of questions to the next questions. "Have you ever been extradited from the United States of America before?" The cockney stared at him. "If it pleases you sir, how could I have been extradited because I just told you I have never been in the US before." The immigration officer's eyes never left his sheet of questions. Without losing his temper, and in the same dull monotone he had probably used all his professional life, he said, "Please answer my question with a 'yes' or 'no'." I wondered how many times that brave little bureaucrat had heard the same reply?

I went ashore just for a few hours to have a few beers and a good American steak. Two days later we sailed to New York where we unloaded the rest of our cargo and cleaned the holds. Maybe it started a couple of weeks before, I can't remember when, but the boatswain and I began to snap at each other. I accepted him in his position of authority but he was unnecessarily rough and crude with the crew and his way of handling us was helping to create an atmosphere below decks that was bound to explode. Something was building between the two of us. Even though I tried to keep out of his way, we were on a collision course.

While we were cleaning the holds I lost my temper and told him what I thought of him. He made us sweep the holds without spraying the floor with water. Sweeping kicked up huge dust clouds and we began to sneeze and cough so hard we thought our bloody lungs were going to fall out. Some of the guys started to complain but he wouldn't listen to us. I snapped. "If you end up with TB one day you'll have only yourself to blame." I was madder than hell and my lungs were burning. "This is a case to be squared up with the union." He pretended not to hear me so I wetted a handkerchief and tied it over my nose and mouth to make a mask. It was July and it was hot and humid, the sort of suffocating summer heat New York is famous for. We finished cleaning the hold and I went ashore with an Egyptian greaser.

He was a nice guy and we got on well right from the beginning. He liked to talk politics and, without going into too much detail, I am sure he must have been a Nasser supporter and not a loyal servant of king Farouk. We went to Central Park and then over to the heart of Broadway where we had a few beers and hamburgers and then we went to a laundry whose address he got from a local newspaper. The laundry sold unclaimed goods, especially shirts, and I was amazed at how cheap they were; some of them were as good as new. I bought a couple of shirts for myself. After this short visit to New York we sailed for Montreal.

Rene Dassac (in collaboration with Patrick K. Robbins)

I was on wheel duty going up the Saint Laurent. When I entered the wheelhouse the pilot was already there. Someone must have told him that I was a Frenchman because he started speaking to me n French. "Stay in Canada," he suggested. "Canada needs people like you and you can get a well paying job," he continued. "I'll help you if you're interested." I murmured something and focused on the canal ahead of me.

True, there were opportunities all over Canada and it was known to be a land of promise but....and this was a big, 'but,' the icy Canadian winters scared me. Before leaving he gave me his address and I promised to contact him if I changed my mind. We were tied up to the grain-loading quay and once the loading started it lasted for a day and a half. Life in Montreal was very similar to life in France but with no food rationing. I could have been tempted to try a new life in Canada except for the fact that Montreal was a huge refrigerator in the winter.

Our grain cargo was loaded and we sailed for Bremen where we could pay off if we wanted to and I chose to leave. We got to Bremen in ten easy days under a fine blue summer sky. This was the first time I had visited a German town. It was still completely flattened. Living conditions were awful. From what I could see most of the population was living in temporary wooden huts. I was battle hardened and although I felt sad for them, it was hard to drum up a lot of compassion.

I got my railway ticket and traveled overnight to Antwerp and then I took the ferry to London. I was a man with a mission, I knew what I wanted to do with my life, and I only spent two days with Watson while I waited to get my full pay and my official discharge certificate. With money in my pocket and a powerful determination to turn around my life, I caught the train for Paris.

At last, things were beginning to look up. I had managed to turn my back on the sea and stopped running from myself. Sometime earlier, probably after meeting the Frenchman in Sydney and then during one of those interminable nights in the mess when I was off duty and listening to the mindless chatter of my crew mates, I finally decided to turn away from the regimentation of life at sea onto a different course. I had a vague idea of what kind of life I wanted for myself and it didn't include spending the rest of my years floating around the globe as a merchant seaman. No, those days were over. They had served their purpose. Now I wanted something different, something better, and I was going to get it. No matter how severe the setbacks, and there were bound to be some, I was determined not to go back to sea.

Rene Dassac (in collaboration with Patrick K. Robbins)

CHAPTER SEVEN: STEERING MY OWN COURSE

As soon as I got to Paris, I phoned my brother-in-law, the barrister to see if he could help me. "I've got a friend in Sevres, known him since I was a kid, he knows you're coming and he'll put you up until you get settled." "What kind of a guy is he," I asked because I felt uncomfortable pitching up in a total stranger's house." My brother-in-law paused, "If this'll help, he's a mathematician who works in the international division of "Poids et Mesures." In other words, he had a huge brain.

I took the train out to Sevres, a short trip from Paris. His wife, Christiane, met me at the door. Thank God she didn't sneeze; she was hugely pregnant. She was kind and welcoming but she was a cleanliness freak and I suspected her penchant for neatness was one of those bizarre reactions women sometimes have before they deliver. Everything in the flat had to be spotless. Instead of walking from room to room, I slid across the immaculate floors on cloth pads that had been made especially for their flat.

That evening I met her husband, Georges. He was generous and immediately he made me feel at home. Within a few minutes I realized he was an extraordinarily intelligent and refined man who was happy to carry-on a conversation at length on almost any topic. All I had to do was ask a question and then he took over and pursued the answer through to its logical conclusion. At first I was taken aback by his long monologues but I realized that he probably needed to talk to someone in the evening because, as a researcher tucked away in a lab, he was so concentrated on his projects that he never had the opportunity to enjoy a casual conversation. It was as if, once he came home, he stepped out of his mental hole and embraced the world.

Once I was settled into my bedroom Christiane helped me draft my curriculum vitae for the magazine, L'Usine Nouvelle. It was easy for her because she was a secretary in the Ministry of Health and Social Security. After we got the CV ready to be sent off she also helped me on more personal matters. She told me how to get my French identity card and also how to apply for a French Passport. After we got through all the paperwork she took me around to meet her family.

Her father was a dental surgeon. Dentistry ran in the family because her brother was also studying to become a dentist. I got on well with both of them. Her brother later introduced me to a number of people who became my friends. My life was in a transition period and the family atmosphere they helped to create was good for me. Gradually I began to regain confidence in myself and, within a week, I felt happier than I had felt in years.

*****

The ad in L'Usine Nouvelle worked. I got five job offers. Instead of having to take one and make the best of it, I was able to take the offer that fit best with my professional background. I became the technical agent in France for Lucas, CAV and Gerling: Lucas provided automobile electrical equipment, CAV made diesel injection equipment and Gerling supplied automobile shock absorbers. At last, I was working and I was happy although my salary was rather meagre. It was fair and I resigned myself to give the job a chance. My colleagues were fine people and I got on well with them. Another Frenchman and I shared an office. He represented British motorcycles, BSA, Sunbeam, Ariel. The office was small but my colleague's attitudes were open, unlike the work environment I would likely find in most French companies.

I met the president and he liked me. One day he came into the office and looked at me. "I've got a diesel motor yacht and I wonder if you would look after it for me during the winter?" "What kind of engines does she have," I asked? "She's got twin Perkins 100 HP." I thought for a moment. "I've no problem with diesels but I don't know anything about Perkins'." He appreciated my honesty. "Good to know. I'll arrange to send you to the Perkins factory in Peterborough England for a quick course on their engines." I leapt at the opportunity. "In the meantime," he continued, "I'm going to Ouistreham this weekend. The boat's undergoing some minor repairs and maybe you'd like to come along and have a look at the boat."

The following Saturday we left Paris together in his Jaguar saloon. Once we were on our way he settled back into his seat and became very cordial. "When we're out of the office you're my friend and you have free access to the boat. You will have your own cabin and I'll show you where the food and drinks are stored. There is a young boy staying onboard and he is not a bad cook." I settled back in my seat and thanked my lucky stars at having landed so well. At last I found that there were also some good civilized people in France!

That trip set the stage for how I spent occasional weekends on the boat during the winter. I'd go up to Normandy, start the engines and run for them an hour or so in order to keep the batteries fully charged. I didn't even have to drive. My boss assigned his chauffeur to take me out to the coast and, of course, we used the company car! The chauffeur was a great bloke and we shared some memorable lunches in the local top restaurants. Life was good and I was really enjoying every minute of it.

As promised, I went to Peterborough to take the course on diesel marine engines which the president had arranged for me. Completing that course was another good point to add to my C.V. While I was over there I went up to the London export head office of Lucas and then I went to their Birmingham factory. I really got along well with the U.K. office staffs. So well, in fact that they even asked me to join the Lucas technical racing team in France for big events: the 24 hours Le Mans race and the 12 hours Riems race. At the "Salon de l'Automobile" in Paris I was part of the Lucas team. Every time representatives from the UK came to Paris I was requested to take them out in the evening to tour the town and take them to good restaurants and nightspots like the Moulin Rouge.

When I looked critically at this phase of my civilian life I concluded that this new career was also teaching me many new lessons. It was as if I was going to school and being paid to learn and push myself in new directions. I was learning the export business and how to sell my services. Hesitant at first, I finally admitted that I was in an exciting world that was totally new, challenging, and I liked what I was doing!

Fairly soon after I joined the company a new English chap was hired to handle the sales and public relations for the motorcycle side of the business that was expanding rapidly. His name was John Cooper and he had served in the African Rifle Regiment in Kenya where he had been living with his family before the war began. He still had some friends in the army who were serving in the outskirts of Paris.

Through one of his friends I was able to purchase a small M.G. "E" type. At one time it belonged to a German airman during the war. Somehow, and I'm not too sure of the details, it had become the property of a British soldier who had to sell it before being rotated back to the U.K. The car was registered under a S.H.A.P.E. number; that was probably why he could not take it back to the UK. Not quite a wreck, the body was in poor shape but it ran well provided, of course, that I took into account that it used petrol and lubricating oil in equal amounts. It had been used for off-road racing and it was fitted with special tires that looked like tractor tires. Anyway, it was cheap and I fiddled with it to keep it running and I had lots of fun roaring around the countryside.

By this time I had met a Franco-Italian contractor, Arthur, who was a master tile mason. He couldn't write French correctly but, by God, he could count. We made a deal. "You can stay with me in my big house but you have to write my tenders and invoices." It was a fair deal and I moved from the Leclerc flat to Arthur's house.

Arthur was a likeable fellow and very successful with women. He had a mistress living just across the road from his house and his love life became quite complicated. His mistress, separated from her husband, was a midwife and very jealous. From behind partially closed curtains she watched Arthur's house to see if any women that she didn't recognize came into his house. Sometimes he tripped up and when Arthur got caught with another woman in the house he blithely told his mistress that the woman he was with was actually coming to see me; he was merely 'escorting her'. His ruse worked.

One evening I came home with a secretary from our accounts section. We spent the night together and the next morning Arthur's mistress saw us leaving together. In her mind that was enough proof to satisfy her that Arthur was not lying. The secretary was great fun but we had to call it off because we couldn't be seen coming back to work together.

Arthur also had another girlfriend. She and her husband ran a grocery shop and Arthur was her dream lover. In return for his services she supplied him, free of charge, with lots of tinned food. Every Monday, sometimes even on Sunday, I'd go pick her up at a pre-arranged rendezvous point and take her back to Arthur's. By then I knew how to play the game and where to look. I'd glance up at the mistress' window as I ushered the shopkeeper's wife to her rendezvous with Arthur. I didn't mind offering my services but I never found out what his mistress must have thought of me.

Sometimes John Cooper came out with us in the evening. By then we were well known in Sevres. We usually started in the same pub in Sevres where I was called "L'Anglais." This was one of Arthur's tricks because he told everybody that I was an English friend who spoke French like a real Parisian. By the end of the evening we wound up in one of the hot spots in Paris on Rue Pigale. Once or twice Arthur and I spent a weekend with my sister in Epernay. We drove there in his car which was more comfortable than my small MG which was open to the wind and rain.

At last, life was nice and I enjoyed every minute of it. Maybe I was riding too high, but while I was 'up there' in mood, I really enjoyed it. Just before the Christmas and New Year holidays I met three American servicemen who had come to Paris to see the town. They were posted in Germany and came over for a few days. They asked me to show them, 'the real Paris', and since we were about the same age I knew what they were looking for.

We used their VW to tour Paris from the Champs Elysees to Montmartre, Pigale, into the Folies Bergere, the Moulin Rouge, and we finished at five o'clock in the morning eating onion soup in the Halles. We were exhausted. They accepted my invitation and we went to my house and fell into a deep sleep until early afternoon when we woke up with bad heads and fuzzy memories. We chose the 'hair of the dog' cure and managed to shape up after a few drinks and a good meal. They went back to Germany with good stories.

In the spring of 1952 I had a surprise visit from Dr. Keiser. Since leaving South Africa he and I had managed to stay in touch and our correspondence was amazingly regular. He told me in one of his letters that he was coming to Paris for a three-day medical conference. "We so regret your leaving the Cape so quickly," he wrote. When we met for a drink he told me, smiling, that Paula missed me. I didn't really skirt the issue but I had to draw a line through my past so I explained to him that I wouldn't have made as much progress in my civilian career had I stayed in South Africa and, furthermore, I could not agree with the racial policies of the Nationalist party and government. He nodded in agreement, presumably on both points, and that led us into a long discussion about the situation in South Africa.

It was obvious that he was worried about the social and political policies of the new government. Any sane person knew, sooner or later, the white government was heading for big trouble. It was only a matter of time until the lid forced onto non-white majority of the population by the white minority would blow off. When, nobody could tell but I told him that if troubles started he could count on me to give him all the help I could. He thanked me and I knew that, in my own small way, I had begun to repay an enormous debt that I owed this fine man and his family.

****

Shortly after seeing the doctor I met the woman who would become my future wife and our meeting would change my life and personality completely. We met on a Friday evening. When I came back from work Arthur told me that he was going to see an old Franco-Italian lady. He murmured a name and I vaguely recalled the woman. Keeping track of his trysts was beyond me but I thought I remembered his lady friend had children. Arthur wanted me to meet her eldest niece. Why not? It was Friday night and I really hadn't planned to do anything special. "All right," I said and went upstairs to take a nap.

Arthur was always looking out for me. I was totally unaware of his intentions but, behind my back, Arthur had been plotting for some time to get me married. Of course, living with him all those months he knew a lot about my personal life, my hopes and hurts and even my dreams. "Maybe we'll see her niece who just happens to be staying with her aunt and then, if she's cute, we'll go out for the evening." I had a funny feeling that I was being set-up but the penny hadn't started to drop. He gave me a vague description of the girl, enough details to tease me but not enough to satisfy my curiosity. According to him, the girl was separated from her husband but he wasn't sure why they separated. One fact was certain: her estranged husband was living in Spanish Morocco. "Rene," he began with a wide and knowing smile, "she is really beautiful." I returned his smile. Then I finally woke up and recognized what he was up to. The sly bastard! He was setting me up. Later that evening we picked her up at her aunt's house and took her to the Latin Quarter.

I wasn't expecting much when I walked into his lady friend's house. Arthur and I were good friends but our tastes in women were different. Some of the women I brought home for him were not, at least to my way of thinking, raving beauties but to hear him describe them you'd think they'd fallen out of the glamour pages of Paris Match. It was Friday night, and what the hell? There were worse ways to spend an evening, I thought. Even if she isn't a raging beauty, she might be fun.

"This is my niece," Arthur's lady friend said. I couldn't believe my eyes; Arthur hadn't been kidding. The girl standing in front of me was truly beautiful. Her blond hair was folded back in a style that I called 'Scandinavian' to frame her lovely blue eyes. Was she Scandinavian or Russian? I was stunned, almost immobile, which was quite unusual for me because I knew I was good at chatting up pretty girls. I couldn't answer my own question and I couldn't take my eyes off her. My God, she was a blond goddess. She could have dropped off the dark side of Mars for all I cared. "My name is Annie," she said offering her hand in a warm firm handshake. Her family name was Italian. "Why an Italian name," I managed to stammer?

What lay behind her answer was sad but interesting. "I was born French," she began. At an early age she met an Italian, fell in love and got married. Italian law governed their marriage contract. Unfortunately, after one son, she discovered her husband was cheating on her. He would not give her a divorce because Italian law forbade divorces. Partly to hurt her, partly to try and control her, he remained in Spanish Morocco and kept their son. She had arrived in Paris only a few days before and was looking for a flat, "anything but just something, somewhere so I can start a new life."

The forces of Fate were working. It only took a couple of minutes and then it struck me: the woman standing in front of me was going through exactly what I had gone through with Edith. She was struggling with loss and deception and the need to redirect her life into something that really mattered. It sounded like a mirror image of what I had lived through in the years leading up to my divorce from Edith. Does misery love company or did we have a lot in common? Her experience was almost a mirror image of my own life; she was grappling with great personal loss but she refused to give up.

As I listened to her I began dredging up a lot of rubbish in my own life. In a flash I remembered those painful years between my marriage and divorce. Back then I needed friends to help me get my life in order. This woman was no different than me. She needed friends and support to get her through her awful period of hurt and despair. "Maybe, just maybe," I thought, "Maybe I can help her."

I know this sounds funny, because I had no ulterior motive, but I suggested that she come stay with me and share my flat until she found something suitable. "Believe me, and I have tried, finding a flat these days in Paris is simply impossible." She looked at me probably suspecting the obvious. It was 1953 and I explained that whole parts of France had been destroyed and millions of people were still looking for lodging. "It isn't ideal but most young married people are still living with their parents because they have no place to go." She nodded as if to tell me she understood what I was talking about. She added, "Finding a place to stay is hard enough, but doubly hard for me because I've severed all ties with my family." I must have looked very bewildered. "I married an Italian and had to become an Italian citizen. That's two big marks against me and my family won't take me in."

She was matter-of-fact explaining that she got a special work permit to remain in France. "My brother was with the First Army and he fought right up to the Eagle's Nest in Germany. I had no problem getting my papers." For once the faceless bureaucrats of the world seemed to have had a heart. "It sounds good to me. At least, it's better than where I am now. Let me see if it'll work out."

Shortly after midnight we went back to where she was staying. Lord, what a pitiful place; it was more like a ruin than a flat. One look told me that she wouldn't stay sane in that hovel. The walls were cracked, the windows didn't shut and it reeked of mildew. "I'll pick you up tomorrow morning with my car." She agreed.

On the way back to our place Arthur was positively wild with joy. The evening was a wonderful success and he kept praising me for acting like such a fine gentleman. I let him natter, occasionally grunting a "oui" or "non" just to let him know I was listening. All I wanted to do was think about Annie. The next morning I took her and all her belongings to our house in Sevres.

She got a job not far from where I was working and we often had lunch together. Of course, my comings and goings with a new and beautiful young woman resulted in a lot of staff gossip. Even the director pulled me aside and asked me, almost breathless, "She's beautiful Rene, is she Russian?" I assured him she was French and after a few days the staff calmed down and I started to settle into a routine that resembled something like a normal life. I even introduced Annie to my sisters and they adopted her immediately.

My brother-in-law, the barrister, had bought a practice in Clamecy near Nevers. I remember helping him move all his furniture to Clamecy during an ice cold winter weekend. It was as cold inside the house as it was out, maybe even colder because the stones had soaked up the cold and it seemed like it needed ten warm days in Hell for them to thaw out. We went downstairs in the basement to fire up the old coal-burning boiler in the hopes of warming up the house. Of course, there was no coal pile. After all, this was winter, the war was barely over and Europe was short of coal so we didn't even have coal dust to light. We rummaged around in the barn and found some wood and paper and managed to get a fire going but shivered through the night until the following day. I can't remember whether we even tried to go to a hotel. At any rate, the town was so small it probably didn't have a hotel!

Taulus

Annie and I liked to go to Clamecy in the summer. My MG was the curiosity of the village. Our little car would grunt and croak its way down narrow cobble streets and everyone would stop and gawk. Little kids ran alongside. Dogs barked at my steaming and puffing little car. One Sunday evening when we were heading back to Paris we got stuck in a traffic jam. We were wedged in between a civilian sedan and a big SHAPE sedan. Of the three we were the smallest but my little MG was belching huge blue clouds from its scrawny little exhaust pipe. I could see the SHAPE driver's face and he wasn't happy being stuck behind a smelly little Brit in a rickety wreck! We didn't care because Annie and I were having a wonderful time. Could it be, I wondered, are we falling in love?

By now we were desperately looking for our own flat. Where we were was 'OK' but Arthur had become a problem. Annie did not dislike him but she did not trust him. To complicate matters, she did not approve of the way the house was kept. Before Annie, Arthur and I lived according to a bachelor's definition of cleanliness and order. True, the bathroom and the toilet left much to be desired and I could appreciate that Annie wanted more privacy. After much hunting, we finally found a place but it was only temporary.

The landlady was Portuguese. To avoid paying taxes she did not declare us as lodgers. It wasn't what we wanted but we didn't have the luxury of choice so we had to take it but with a lot of misgivings. Her house was in the Paris suburbs, convenient for each of us. We were given the first floor 'apartment'. The landlady took the ground floor. We had, in addition to our tiny bedroom, a small kitchenette and a bathroom. Maybe it was because she was playing around with the law, or maybe it was because of the way she lived, she was a nosey and suspicious widow. We found out that whenever we were away, she'd tour through our apartment poking into our private papers. We didn't announce the fact that we weren't married, it was nobody's business except ours, but she probably found out by rummaging through our papers.

Shortly after we moved into our new lodging, I had to go to the London export office and then to the Birmingham factory to attend to a meeting of the Europe agents. This trip was a good opportunity for me to take Annie with me and visit my adopted country. She had never been to England and she saw it with fresh eyes. It rained nonstop during the entire week we spent in Birmingham. Not just a few drops, but a steady cold downpour from which there was no escaping. It drilled the pavement without letting up. The foul weather was too much for her; she returned to Paris on her own. Even a wet and dreary Paris was a burst of sunshine in comparison to water-logged Birmingham.

Before going back to Paris I took a day off and went to see my old port division in Portsmouth. While I was walking down Commercial road I heard someone calling my name. The voice came from behind me; it was one of my shipmates on HMS Actaeon, Norman Webb. I could see by his striping that he was a petty officer on the aircraft carrier Bulwark. "We're in Le Havre next week," he said and I gave him my office telephone number because he said he would be allowed a couple of days to visit Paris. He had an interesting story.

When he joined the Actaeon in 1946 he was an ordinary seaman, one of those in my mess I thought was a good and disciplined seaman. I must have had a good reputation as far as he was concerned, because he started to ask me for advice. "I'm thinking of leaving the navy," he said. That surprised me because in seven years he had been promoted from ordinary seaman to the rank of petty officer and that was a series of rapid promotions, faster than anything we experienced during the war. Now he was a radar operator, married with two children, and what looked like to me, a nice career path to follow. Why chuck it up now? He had asked me a difficult question and I began clawing through me brain trying to figure out what kind of answer I could give him.

We went to his house and I met his wife and children. It made me feel good to see how happy they were. "Frankly, if I were in your shoes, I'd stay in the navy." They listened to me as I described my transition from navy to civilian life, with all the difficulties I had to overcome to land a job which was not much better than his. "You know, for a long time I regretted not staying in the navy. Yes, I wasn't going to get rich but I had a fair wage and decent accommodations for my family both at home and abroad."

My thoughts and my experience, maybe the quiet way I spoke with reason instead of with a lot of emotion, started to have an effect on them. "Keep in mind, the navy is going through a fantastic modernization program. What's that mean for you? To keep you and your mates they'll have to make sure your salary is attractive if they hope to hang on to you and also get new recruits to handle all the fantastic equipment they are introducing." By the time the evening ended I think I managed to sway him. His wife was obviously convinced with my line of reasoning and I left thinking that I had been able to use my experience to help someone answer some of the most difficult questions in his life, "what am I going to do with my career and how am I going to provide for my family?"

My trip to the U.K. was over and now it was time to go back to Paris. "Webb, give me a call when you get to Paris and I'll come in and meet you." We shook hands warmly and I took the night train from London to Paris.

When I got back to work in Paris, back into my routine, I realized that I was happy and that my transition to civilian life really was working out better than I had expected. My professional life was challenging, everyone liked me and by that I mean customers, colleagues and the management of the company. I even became popular with a friend of one of the director's. He was president of a big electrical cable manufacturing company. One day when he was out on his boat off the coast of Brittany he ran into trouble and called the office and asked to speak to me. "Rene, the diesel has stopped and I can't get it started." I had to think fast because that part of the coast was very rocky and he was drifting toward shore.

Years of experience kicked in and I remained calm under pressure. "Do you have any idea why your engine has stopped," I asked half expecting him to yell at me. "Yes, I forgot to refill my fuel tank." I breathed a sigh of relief. "You've got an air lock between the filter and the injection pump." Calmly, in very simple language, I told him how to get rid of the air lock. I made him repeat the steps to me to make sure he had understood. "Call me as soon as you get the engine running again." He assured me he would and within thirty minutes he called. "Rene, the engine's purring and I'm heading back to port." He sounded jubilant and I went back to work and forgot the matter until a week later when I received a crate with a dozen bottles of champagne. It was his way of saying 'thank you.' Annie and I enjoyed popping the corks!

My job required me to travel all over France. On one of my trips I was sent to Lyon to sort out a guarantee issue on some Lucas equipment and I took advantage of being in Lyon and went to see some of my family. Uncle Gabriel was still in his apartment and I invited him to a well-known restaurant, Chez Nandron on the Place des Cordelier. We talked a lot, mostly about my career and me and he was very impressed with my success. We owed each other a lot. He had the courage to let me follow my dream despite major misgivings. Could a child really know what he wants to do? The question haunted him and it wasn't until well after the war ended that he finally let himself off the hook: he'd done the right thing. And, from my perspective, if it hadn't been for his courage and support, I might have wound up differently. Would we still be talking to each other, would we be able to enjoy a good meal and a fine wine, would we admire each other? Yes, he was a tough old bird, and yes, I knew in my heart that he was a good man who looked out for us when we were very young and vulnerable.

My sister Paulette was still living with him. A good uncle, he was worried about her not yet being married. "Maybe I'm part of the problem," he said. "She probably doesn't think that I can get on with life on my own and she doesn't want to leave me." Perhaps there was some truth in what he said but I detected a sense of guilt that was borne out of his over-riding sense of duty to his sister's children. "Don't you worry," I said, "I'll talk to her and we both know that the time will come when she will decide or find the right man to share her life with." He perked up with my response and we ended our lunch on a happy note.

Back in Paris, I began to wake-up to the realities of my new settled life as a civilian. My salary was not what it should have been in view of my qualifications. Furthermore, our accommodations were far from satisfactory. I was slowly beginning to realize that I wasn't "going" anywhere. On the whole, life was good but it was a struggle and I could not see the end of my tunnel for many more years. To improve our life meant moving, again, but another move was less of a threat and more of a possible opportunity. Well paid jobs existed abroad in places we now call 'third world cities.' I was still fascinated with Africa and whenever there was a film about Africa I would take Annie to the cinema.

The wheels of change began turning. I started talking more and more about moving from Paris to another part of the world, to somewhere where we could have a nice house and a good salary. One day, after another film about Africa, I asked her, "Would you like to live in a country somewhere in Africa?" She bowled me over, "I'd love to." "Really," I asked to make sure she knew that I was serious? "Of course, "she replied and I promised her that I would start looking into the possibility of moving.

I decided on a job search strategy that involved several phases. First, I needed to know if there was any chance of improving my lot within the company. Casually, over lunch and after work at the café, I spread the buzz that I was thinking of going back to my old profession in the electrical contracting business. Other than some of my close colleagues on the staff, no one seemed to care. Their indifference helped me make up my mind and I then began the second phase of my strategy.

I put an advert in the "Usine Nouvelle." Within less than a week I received a letter asking me to meet with the UK manager of a recently created Electrical Contracting Company operating in Nigeria called Nigelec. The letter said I would have a meeting with the UK representative, a Mr. J.F. Catto. The letter gave a brief explanation of the company and this helped organize my thoughts. Nigelec was financed by U.A.C. (United Africa Company) who was the British shareholder and C.F.A.O. (Companie Française de l'Afrique Occidentale) the French shareholder.

Mr. Catto was based in Liverpool but he came to Paris to interview me. The interview went well and it was obvious that he had read my C.V. because he asked intelligent questions. "Why do you have two names?" I explained my two names and my dual nationality and I could see that he was impressed. "Nigeria is a British colony," he said and then went on to explain that it would be better for me to use my English name and passport because this would mean that I would not have to report to the local authorities as an alien. From the way he talked I knew I had the job. "After a three month trial period you will be able to send for your wife and we will transport her to Nigeria at our expense." That was wonderful news but I could not tell him that Annie and I were not married. Remember, in those days, living together as an unmarried couple was a big social sin that no one wanted to acknowledge.

Nigelec offered me a contract and I signed. As soon as I signed they told me to report to the CFAO office to collect my return air ticket and get the necessary work and immigration papers. "Your boss in Nigeria will be glad to see you. He's a former RNVR officer, a chap by the name of Charles Guest. He will meet you at the airport in Lagos." The interview went better than I had expected. The salary was good, they gave me the title of 'supervisor', all fine from my point of view but I felt sorry about Annie who had a long wait in Paris all by herself. Being separated was bad enough but getting her out to Nigeria was also a problem. We were unmarried and Annie had to travel with an Italian passport and use her husband's Italian name. I kept juggling solutions to my problems as I headed back to the office to type my letter of resignation.

My employer had been good to me and I was determined to leave on good terms. I explained the main reason for leaving was purely personal, that I had enjoyed working for the company, and wished them well in the future. No sooner had I signed the letter and delivered it to the boss's secretary, and my phone rang. It was the boss and he asked me to come to his office. We had a good meeting and I repeated my story because it was the only story that I had. He appreciated the problems I was facing, the problem of decent accommodations and that I really wanted to get back to my original trade which was the electrical contracting business. We parted on good terms. On my last day when I went in to say good-bye he asked me to come see him whenever I came back to Paris. They had been a good company to work for. They treated me well and I reciprocated with hard work, loyalty and honesty.

My contract specified that the duration of the first tour would be for two years. At the end of the tour I would get four months home leave in Europe. It was the usual overseas contract because it also stipulated that the company would provide accommodations. On the material side: money, career, housing, the prospect of a new start in

Nigeria was definitely attractive but on the personal side, I knew that being separated would be difficult for both of us. Annie was not particularly happy to have to wait for three months before she could join me in Lagos but there was no other solution. I summoned up all my powers of persuasion to reassure her that the time would pass fast, that I would write every week, and that I would behave myself.

Despite my efforts to keep my emotions under control, parting was a painful experience. Added to our own personal problems was the fact that I had to say goodbye to all the friends I had made during the previous three years. Arthur took it quite hard and I began to wonder whether I had made the right choice. Would life in Nigeria be better? I tried convincing myself that it would but, to be honest, I wasn't so sure. Was I nuts going back to Africa? In any case, I had closed the door at the company and opened another. Right decision or wrong decision, there was no turning back.

Rene Dassac (in collaboration with Patrick K. Robbins)

CHAPTER EIGHT:
OFF TO NIGERIA

The day I left was a sad day. Annie and I went to the Air France station where I got a taxi to take me to Orly. She clutched my arm so hard it almost hurt and I could tell that she was ready to burst into tears at any moment. I couldn't talk because I had a huge lump in my throat. Just when I thought it couldn't get any worse, fate intervened, and it did get worse. I kissed her goodbye and peeled her arm off mine and turned to get into the taxi. She still had her hand on the door and as I pulled it shut I caught her fingers on the edge of the door. Fortunately I wasn't pulling that hard but I succeeded in leaving her in tears anyway.

All the way to Lagos I wondered how badly I had hurt her, and couldn't forget her tears. The more I thought about saying goodbye the worse I felt. Now I realized how much I loved her and I knew I could not live a happy life without her. That realization comforted me on the long trip to Lagos.

We flew a super constellation on a twelve-hour jaunt with stops in Nice, Algiers, Niamey, Lome, Cotonou and finally Lagos. When I got off the plane every bone in my body ached. After customs I collected my bags and went out to the arrivals hall where Chas Guest was waiting for me. He held a piece of paper with my name, "J. Powell", written on it. It was night. We drove through the still busy city to the Central Hotel where we had dinner and began to get to know each other. I knew straight away that I was going to get on well with him. He was a good navy man. We shared experiences and, as I recall, many whisky sodas before parting.

The next morning a company driver, who I learned later was called 'Flash' because of his fast driving, picked me up and took me to the company house in Yaba, a suburb of Lagos. The house already had five occupants; all were company employees. I was shown to my bedroom and then I was introduced to my housemates. We had breakfast together and engaged in meaningless chit-chat.

Flash drove three of us to the company's downtown office where I was introduced to other members of the staff. The accountant, on loan to the company from CFAO, was a Frenchman by the name of Febvre. He gave me a run down of the company rules, some cash with which I could open an account at UBA (United Bank of Africa). Every month my account would be credited with my salary. "How long am I going to be living with the other five," I asked and explained that I planned to bring my wife as soon as possible. "I understand. We've got a block of flats under construction. They're reserved for married couples. All we can do at this time is to ask you to wait." At least there was the prospect of something better but I knew that in Africa things never quite worked out according to plan. Nevertheless, I could put our housing concern aside and focused on my work.

We had a big contract in Lagos to complete. It was a lighting installation at the newly built coal-and-fuel power station. I was assigned to this project and began working with a chap called Bob Conchie. We became best friends. Although he was younger than me, he had done his national service in the navy and that, in addition to our professional interests, helped us to cement our friendship. In the power station we worked night and day shifts. Our contract contained a stiff penalty clause if we did not complete our portion on time. There was no leeway and that meant working around the clock.

Unfortunately, in those days there were practically no qualified Nigerian electricians. Bob and I had to do most of the installation work by ourselves instead of delegating it to our subordinates. The strain on us was considerable. Our only alternative was to select and train a group of young Nigerians. The decision to train someone was the easy part of the solution. The hardest part lay ahead of us: finding competent young men we could train rapidly. We found a solution at the local polytechnic college. The technical teacher chose six young men who were apprenticed to us while they continued their studies. Our solution worked. Within a couple of months each of us had trained three young men to whom we could delegate much of the routine installation work. A good bond developed between my chaps and me. I am proud to say they stayed with me for many years right up until I left Nigeria for good.

Our boss, Charles, often invited Bob and me to come over for a drink in the evening at his flat and a friendship developed between the three of us. Camaraderie, a chance to relax, took the strain off both Bob and me because we were finding it quite difficult to live in an all bachelor community. At first it started off as a standard corporate type of accommodation but as time wore one it degenerated in steps from a reasonable B&B to a brothel. The company was landing more contracts and this meant more people had to be accommodated in the same house. It was like a ship's mess but without the discipline. Living on top of each other created tensions and these often resulted in heated arguments.

*****

Within three weeks the residents of bungalow were divided into clans. The Irish clan was made up of Mick Haud, Pat Kelly, and another whose name I have forgotten. They squared off against the Welsh lot: Shepherd, Walsh, Baxter, Conchie, Powell, Lemesurier who was from Guernsey, and Greenwood. Fortunately, those who were up country required our assistance and this meant that some of the boys left Lagos. Shepherd was sent to the Cameroons to install a coffee plantation including all the machinery, generator, and overhead distribution lines that fed all the houses of the plantation staff. Unfortunately, Shepherd was too inexperienced to work alone in the bush. Bush work was not easy. Once you left Lagos you had to improvise at every step of the operation. Often this meant that you had to have a good knowledge of basic mechanics. Shepherd wasn't up to the job.

Guest sent Shepherd there because the plantation was prepared to accommodate him and his wife. Shepherd was a friend of Guest since the days when they worked together in Wales. The plantation manager was a Dutchman by the name of Mulder. Soon after Shepherd's arrival he and Mulder started clashing. Mulder was from the old school and knew how to survive in the bush and he didn't give Shepherd any slack. The latter's inexperience showed and within a couple of months I was asked to take over the job and complete the installation. I was a hands-on type of man unlike Shepherd whom the Nigerian workers used to call, 'the man in white – super white.' He was always spotless because he never got his hands dirty.

Nigelec couldn't afford to have that kind of cock-up. Guest called me and asked me if I could stop what I was doing and take over Shepherd's job. "Are you sure you can do it?" I thought for a split second. "Charles, remember that I've worked in the bush in South Africa and I know I can handle this job." He seemed relieved but before he hung up I shared a point with him that was going to be crucial to my success up country. "Charles, I want my wife to join me up there." The way I sounded must have made him realize that I wasn't negotiating. I was stating a basic condition that had to be met if he was going to get me to take over Shepherd's mess. Guest paused for a moment to collect his thoughts. "That's a policy request that's outside my authority limits but I will take it up at the next director's board meeting." And he did.

At first the directors were against it. "Gentlemen, this request is somewhat extraordinary but I must emphasize that Powell is the only man we have who can get the job done. There's simply too much at stake not to grant his request." Guest prevailed in the end but the directors agreed only on the condition that I complete the necessary paperwork with the Immigration Office. They wanted to have nothing to do with my problem. Furthermore, none of them thought that I would be able to bring in the woman with whom I was living. We were not married. Fifty years ago living together as an unmarried couple was simply unthinkable. They were convinced no civil servant in any ministry in Her Majesty's government would ever accept such an outlandish request.

But, they had probably never run up against a man as determined as I was to bring Annie to Nigeria. Wedding license or not, she was coming and all I had to do was find a way the bureaucrats couldn't refuse. Charles and I began pouring through official statutes trying to find anything that had to do with the huge and controversial topic, "unwedded wife." We were both members of the RNVR club and they had stacks of regulations. Finally, when we were beginning to think there was no way around the immigration officials, we found an answer.

Guest arranged for me to meet the governor's secretary to discuss my request. On the day of the meeting I took great pains to get dressed in what I called my 'gentleman's suit.' My RN club tie stood out smartly on my starched white shirt. I took one look at myself in the bathroom mirror, straightened my hair and tucked a folder with my navy service papers and letters of commendation under my arm. I looked just as smart, and I was just as determined, as any fancy expert lawyer strutting into the City.

I was escorted into the office of the British High Commissioner's secretary by a marine guard. No cute little blond, the Commissioner's secretary was a huge, he must have been nearly seven feet tall, red haired Royal Marine officer. He was waiting for me. For anybody less determined than I he might have been intimidating but I merely saw him as a potential obstacle on my way to success, someone who had to be dealt with and got out of the way. To speed things along I cut short the ritual, meaningless, polite formalities. My slight foreign accent was actually an advantage. I could almost read his thinking, "Where in bloody hell does this guy come from?"

The marine officer secretary looked at me. Rather, he started to stare me down. "You are Mr. John Powell?' I stared back at him just as I had stared at countless officers and responded crisply, "Yes, sir." He paused, stared, and cleared his throat. "What can I do for you?" For a split second I wanted to hit him with both barrels but I restrained myself because surely he had read my request and surely he understood the decision that I required. I played the game and began an explanation of my needs that would have made any barrister proud to call me a colleague. "Sir, I am about to be sent to the Cameroons by my company to erect a coffee plantation. Accommodations are provided for my unwedded wife and me. My company's board of directors agrees to my wife joining me provided the immigration services issue an entry permit for my wife." That was it. Short and sweet, he knew what the problem was and what he had to do.

He continued to stare at me as if I had asked for an impossible request. His face relaxed and I knew what was coming. He was going to turn me down. "You must understand that we cannot agree to this request." Drawing himself upright in his chair, he uttered the standard defense all bureaucrats use when they want to wiggle out of a decision: "It's against all rules and regulations." His face relaxed and he probably thought he was off the hook. "Why, just imagine. If we were to do this for you, we would have to do it for everybody." Harrumphing at the thought, "We cannot take such responsibility." Instead of speaking in everyday English, I added just enough Cambridge accent to give me stature without overdoing it. Instead of a Mr. Nobody trying to put on a show, I was a serious gentleman who knew what he was talking about.

Like an animal that doesn't know its being stalked, he walked into the trap I had set. It was my only chance but it was a trap with big teeth and he was not going to wiggle out easily. "I understand the importance of responsibility. In 1940 I was only eighteen and I took the responsibility to join the navy and I was sent to sea and fought until the end. I know something about responsibility." His face hardened; I saw his jaw begin to twitch but I continued my verbal attack. "When I left the navy I was told that if I ever needed help I could always count on the navy. Remember, we are a big family." Then I began closing for the kill. He couldn't stop me because I had earned a right to make my case. Citing a King's Regulation number also used by Lord Nelson, I continued. "Lord Nelson said that an unwedded wife is entitled to the same benefits as a 'wedded wife' provided that she is recognized by her surroundings as a wife living with her husband."

When that fact was laid on him I thought he was going to fall out of his chair. I saw him flinch and then I went for the kill. "Even he was not wedded to Lady Hamilton but the navy recognized his relationship." I reminded him that I was 'still navy' because I was a member of the RNR. "I cannot marry my wife because she is married to an Italian with whom she is legally separated. Divorce is not allowed in Italy. If it were, she would be divorced and we would be married. Think about the honesty of this request. Sir, I beg you, please take my case to the governor".

My trap snapped shut. He stood up. Instead of a scowl, something akin to a smile that almost radiated admiration, started to spread across his disciplined military face. "As a marine officer I will support your request. Please wait for me here." He disappeared and I sat quietly in his huge empty office staring at his papers and wall hangings. I was relaxed because I knew that I had argued my case well. That was it. There was nothing else I could do to get Annie into the Cameroons.

He came back after spending about half an hour with the governor. As he came into his office he did something that was very British military. He gave me a 'thumb's up'. "Your request is granted but the governor asks your cooperation." For a moment I thought there was going to be a hook from nowhere, something I had not planned on. "The governor would very much appreciate if you would not brag about his decision to your friends." I understood the governor's request and I assured his secretary that I would keep quiet. I was a military man and I had given my word. Nothing more could be asked of me but he had one last bit of administrative detail to tell me. "A document will be sent to your office for you to sign. It must be returned to me and then we will start the immigration process."

I thanked him and left feeling proud as Punch. Pride for what I had accomplished and pride in the British system that was still capable of looking out for the 'little man'. His, "Good luck," was still ringing in my ears when I reported to Charles. When I told him how it went his face broke into a big smile. "Imagine the look on the directors faces when they hear this. Just imagine how they'll feel when you prove to them that your meeting with the governor wasn't a waste of time after all!" I was happy but I also knew that it would take a long time before the paperwork was completed and Annie could join me.

I immediately wrote Annie and gave her the good news but I also had to tell her to be patient. "It takes time, lots of time, to get things done here, but in the meantime stay in touch with the Paris Office of CFAO. They'll tell you when to come and collect your air ticket and fix a departure date." It was another seven weeks before she boarded the plane and headed out to Lagos.

As soon as I ended work on the power station I was asked to go to Enugu, a coal mining town in the Eastern Province. Before leaving I bought a used Austin Minor to take two of my apprentices and me to the new assignment. They were now good electricians and trustworthy. I was sent to replace Michael Hoad, the fighting

Irishman, who had always been nice to me. For some unknown reason he had been transferred to work with someone else at Ibadan. Before going to Bamenda in the Cameroons, I was told to contact Mr. Cornwall on arrival and he would show me around the job I was to take over.

Driving in Nigeria was never easy. Lorry drivers who thought they owned the roads were the biggest problem. The view from behind their wheel was uncompromising: a private passenger vehicle was an unnecessary obstacle on their road. Why did they consider a public thoroughfare their road? The answer was simple: right-of-way on the road belongs to the driver behind the wheel of the biggest vehicle. According to their logic, lorry drivers owned the road. They barrelled down the middle, forcing you to cling to the edge on your side of the road. None of the verges were stabilized. It didn't take much to have an accident. For starters, all you needed to do was to let your left front wheel slip off the road. With a simple unthinking flick of the wrist you were almost certain to lose control and maybe even lose your life.

Although we left very early in the morning, we did not reach the queue of vehicles waiting to be taken on the ferryboat to cross the Niger River before 1500 hrs. We arrived at Enugu at 1700 hours and I went straight to the rest house to meet Michael Hoad. I spent the rest of my assignment in the same rest house until I had completed Michael's work. I sent my lads down to find the living quarters of Hoad's men and then Mick took me to the club to introduce me to his Irish friends.

We stood at the bar and started a beer drinking session. Boy, could these Irish boys swill their beer! They became louder the more they drank. I looked over and saw Mick and his friend in a heated discussion. There was too much noise to figure out what they were saying but from the looks of it, whatever was bothering them was going to be resolved with punches. Sure enough, all of a sudden I saw Mick take out his false teeth and put them on the bar. Mick and his mate, in time honed Irish tradition, were going to have a go at each other. I shot across the barroom floor and put myself between. "For fuck's sake Mick, what's going on?" I'm no hero and I know the best way not to get into a fight is to walk away from it. I had come to the bar with him to meet his friends and now I was about to be caught in the middle of a fight.

Mick could see I was pissed off. "It's my first day here and I'd really like to have a quiet drink together in peace." Mick stared at me. The toothless hole in his face gave a twisted grin and he stepped back and put in his teeth. "Sorry John, I forgot it's your first day here." Their dispute, whatever it was because no one bothered to tell me what it was all about, had been settled peacefully and we all sat down and continued drinking as if nothing had happened. I'd seen this happen before. The Irish are strange people. Somewhere inside their heads there's a little on/off lever and when it is flicked they switch from being nice and courteous to each other to pounding each other mercilessly.

After completing Hoad's work I went to the new cement factory in Nkalagu, 25 miles from Enugu and started the handover procedure from Cornwal to me. It was a complicated contract because it involved doing the entire electrical installation in the factory. Fortunately for me, Cornwal had done most of the work and it was well done. Before leaving he gave me some good advice. "Watch out for some of the building contractor's staff because he's hired a lot of trouble makers." When I asked him what was causing the problems, he shrugged and came out with the not surprising: "Beer and women." After work they'd go to the canteen, get drunk and start fighting. Later in the evening some of the local female students would knock on the men's doors offering to tuck them into bed for the night. It was a typical bush scenario and I kept my distance from the canteen and the girls. Whether Cornwal had resisted the girl's knocks on the doors was his story to tell and I didn't ask.

I was given a sleeping area that was nothing more than a bedroom built out of wood planks; there was a hose pipe shower and a cracked ceramic flush toilet. The shower water was bright red because the open cistern filled with red dust that swirled with the slightest breeze. It was like rinsing off in red sludge. The locals didn't have showers because they used the river. Within a couple of days I began to use the river too but I did not know how dangerous that could be.

There were some Cypriot contractors who, just like their island, were divided into two camps: one Greek and one Turkish. They spoke the same language and they hated each other. Working in the bush was hard enough but with those tensions I decided it was safer and wiser to only go to the canteen for lunch and breakfast so, I left them alone. After work I went down to the river for a quick wash, changed clothes and went to the club in Enugu where I had friends from CFAO. At the end of every week the CFAO manager would give me the pay packets so I could pay my staff on time.

At the club I met a doctor, a specialist on tropical diseases, who had been sent out by UNESCO. He was French and a keen fan of good motorcars. He even had a sports type Jaguar and from what others said, he drove like a madman on the dusty roads around Enugu. Unfortunately, after I left, I learned that he had been killed in a motoring accident on the road between Enugu and Lagos. One night he and I were having a drink together and, quite casually, I let it slip that I bathed in the river. He reacted as if I had shoved a bee's hive in his face. "Stop! Stop! That particular stretch of the river is renowned for having some particularly dangerous tropical diseases." In spite of my tan, I must have paled when he implored, "Watch your urine. If you see any signs of blood come see me immediately. The parasite crawls up your penis and eats away your bladder and kidneys." It was his turn to shock me and I stopped using the river and became quite happy slopping around in red sludge. At least my urine didn't turn red.

Annie was fed up waiting. Every week I heard the same complaint: she went to the CFAO office several times a week and several times a week she got the same answer: "It won't be long now, just be patient and wait it out." Being separated for months on end was hard on both of us. Enough was enough. I managed to get a phone call through to Charles. "Charles, I need your help to get Annie out here. We're going around in circles and we're tired of waiting." He was a good boss who knew how important it was to maintain the morale of men who are out in the bush in hardship posts. "John, you have my word, I'll step in and speed up things." I believed him and before we hung up he told me that I would be transferred soon to a coffee estate near Bamenda in the Cameroon. "Why," I asked. "It's Shepherd again. He's had a row with the plantation manager and he's going to be kicked off the site if we don't get him out first." I must have sounded down because before we hung up he assured me that Annie would be coming soon and that he would be at the airport to meet her plane. That cheered me up and we rang off.

We had agreed that Charles would send Annie to Enugu and that I would come down from Bamenda to fetch her at the airport. In the meantime, I made preparations to receive my replacement, Lemesurier. Also, in those final days I managed to sell my Austin. In preparation for my transfer Lagos had sent me a Land Rover with a driver. This wasn't a luxury; it was a necessity. The roads were awful and to get anywhere you had to spend time calculating your trip. At the foot of the mountains the roads narrowed into rutted tracks and traffic was regulated to odd and even days. Odd days meant everyone drove up into the mountains and through the rocky passes; on even days traffic came the other way. The road was simply too narrow for two vehicles to pass and there was no room to pull over. On one side were towering cliffs and on the other side there were yawning chasms.

I explained all this to Annie because I knew that she was adventuresome and would accept the challenge of going into the African bush but I thought, a little pre-arrival conditioning in letters, would certainly help to soften the inevitable rough spots she would encounter once she got off the plane in Enugu.

*****

After months of waiting I was now ready for the big adventure and I left Enugu with lots of projects in my head. There was still a lot to do to prepare for her arrival, 'my wife'. A lad had been sent by the plantation to show me the way and I followed in the Land Rover. Night fell before we arrived but the lad took me straight to the house the plantation had let for me. From what little I could see, I concluded that a huge forest covered most of the mountains. The roar of our cars and the glare of our headlamps startled the night animals and insects. The pitch black outside my new house was filled with cries and calls, brush rustling against prowling animals and the steady whir of thousands of insects trying to poke through the mesh netting covering the windows. We were probably in the middle of nowhere. The trip up involved crossing many narrow bridges on a miserable road that was almost impassable when the rain turned the dust into slippery red mud.

Night in the heart of Africa is black. There are no shades of gray. With nightfall a solid black cloud drops over the land when the sun sets. Even in full moon light the night is black. In the jungle moonlight gets stuck in the treetops and never falls to the ground to shine on man and animal. We kept the car engine running because I had swung the car around to face the front door. I groped through the door and found a petrol lamp. There were no other sounds except the jungle noises and the car's idling engine. The driver and my electrician left after bringing in my suitcases and kit bags. "We'll be back tomorrow morning to take you to the plantation," the driver told me before driving away into the night.

The light thrown off by the petrol lamp was strong enough to illuminate most of the room. Typical for this part of Africa, the walls were made of mud bricks; the ceiling was a patchwork of palm tree branches woven tightly when the house was first built but now, after a few months, some of the branches hung from the ceiling, Nature's chandelier without candles. Dust was everywhere. It filtered through the roof, down through the palm ceiling, and into every place we stepped. Because the doorjambs were fixed to the ceiling, slamming the doors brought down clouds of dust, so thick that I began coughing and sputtering.

There was only one bedroom. It contained a narrow single bed, a metal contraption that sagged in the middle and squeaked loudly when I sat on it. Indoor plumbing included a latrine and a homemade shower but neither had water hooked up to them. A cooking area, some might even call it a kitchen, was located outside. Someone had been cooking with green wood because the walls were covered with thick black smoke. Dust stuck to some of the rougher parts of the wall.

For a moment I had genuine second thoughts about my job, the dust strewn overgrown hut that I was supposed to call home, and my sanity in wanting to bring out Annie. The nearest rest house was twenty miles away in Bamenda. It could have been on the other side of the moon. I had no car and no place to go except inside myself to find a new resolve to push on. After all, I had been through a lot worse. At

Rene Dassac (in collaboration with Patrick K. Robbins)

least, I wasn't being shot at or floating in the middle of an ocean waiting to be blown out of the water.

Once I got a grip on myself I fumbled around in my kit bag and found a tin of sardines, my 'welcome' dinner. I went out on the porch. It was cool at 4500 feet. Just as I started to relax my sixth sense told me that there was someone else near the house but I couldn't see him. When I finally made out a human figure, he was moving toward me with his spear pointed down. My driver had forgotten to tell me that the house came with a guard. We tried to communicate but he only spoke his tribal language, Housa. Smiles bridge a lot of gaps. I quickly concluded that I had a good man looking after me. I went back inside; the mosquitoes were fierce and I was tired. Making my bed was a study in frustration. Whenever I pounded the mattress to shake out the dust it merely rose and then fell back on me. As I drifted off I made a mental note to get a petrol-operated refrigerator and I guess I fell asleep making a long list of things I needed in my new home.

Early the next morning a Land Rover came to pick me up and take me to the plantation. What a change! The plantation manager gave me a warm welcome. I smelled breakfast before I saw the table. "Here, sit down. A man can't go to work on an empty stomach." Breakfast was good, just like in Europe. There were eggs and meat, butter and bread, and lots of coffee. He needed to talk to someone; all I had to do was be patient and listen. He began by describing the assignment and he gave me a very clear idea of what was expected of me. As he went on he relaxed and did not hide the fact that he and Shepherd were cross-threaded. "Do you know him?" he asked. I admitted that I had met him a couple of times but I really couldn't say that I knew him well enough to discuss him. Without telling him, I knew that his reputation was not all that good and I caught myself wanting to tell him that I wasn't surprised. But I kept those thoughts to myself as we went out to begin touring the work site.

We walked through several sites. Of course, I met men whose names I promptly forgot. Something struck me: these men know what they are doing. I could tell right from the beginning that I was going to have a different relationship with them than what they had experienced with Shepherd.

"Now that you've met your men, off you go to check in with French customs and the gendarmes." It wasn't every day a Frenchman pitched up in the middle of nowhere. It was a good suggestion because we immediately established the kind of camaraderie that occurs when foreigners band together outside their home country. In addition to friendship, it was important to be on their right side because all the good fresh meat and vegetables were found on the French side of the border and I wanted to be able to cross without unnecessary searches or delays.

The next major step in the project was to install a large generator but it was not due to arrive for another week or ten days. The manager advised me to use the lull to get myself organized and I followed his advice. I took a driver and a lorry and arranged to go to the waterfalls and fill up my water drums for the house. It's amazing how, in the civilized world, we take water for granted in our houses. When you don't have it, and have to rig your own plumbing system, you don't waste it. Getting water was an adventure.

When I got back to the house the local schoolteacher dropped by to introduce himself. In fact, he was my neighbor but I hadn't seen his house on the way in. He was a Christian from the Ebho tribe that was concentrated around Enugu. Very kindly, he let me know that I was a bit of a curiosity since I was the only white man in the village. We talked local customs and he pretty much laid out what was expected of me. "As for food," he said there was a market every Sunday in the center of the village where local women sold baskets of local vegetables, some were new to me but there were many I recognized.

Markets are a part of village life that was pretty much to be expected but my first trip was a bit of an eye opener: all the women were naked except for those who had babies wound around them. Each child was firmly held in place with a dirty cloth. Vegetables were safe to eat if you washed and peeled them but the meat and poultry was something else. The meat was usually butchered on site in the market; all chickens were sold live and then butchered. You really had to be hungry for meat because all the meat that was hanging on display for sale was crawling with flies. The meat looked like it had been wrapped in a fly motif plastic film that moved and buzzed when the butcher approached.

Rene Dassac (in collaboration with Patrick K. Robbins)

My neighbor looked around the house and quickly offered to send me one of his pupils to clean the house. Elisabeth was only twelve years old, had brothers and sisters, and within a very short time after Annie's arrival they became very good friends. I was grateful because there was no way that I was going to be able to come back from a hard day on the job and shovel out my house. While I was congratulating myself on this stroke of good fortune, the lorry came to take me to the waterfall.

Six used petrol barrels clanged in the back of the truck as we lurched through the bush. "Have you cleaned them well," I asked and the driver told me they had been cleaned and rinsed. "Can you smell petrol in them?" He looked straight ahead. "No, they are empty." So much for that line of reasoning, I thought. We drove up to the foot of the mountain and then he reversed the truck under the waterfall. He didn't stop when the water began splashing over the cabin. He decided to do two jobs at once: fill the barrels and wash his lorry. The fact that his lorry was mud caked when we left the waterfall was irrelevant because, at one time while we were getting soaked, it was clean. It only took about a half hour to fill the barrels and lurch off again down the dusty track back to the village.

After we off-loaded the barrels and hooked up 'the plumbing' I decided to treat myself to a nice shower. There's nothing like taking a shower in a new house and stepping out of the shower stall to say, "I'm home. This place isn't so bad after all." When I opened the faucet my nose confirmed my worst fears: the storage drums had not been thoroughly cleaned. The water and I smelled of paraffin, not too much, but enough to make my eyes smart until they got used to it. Actually, it was just enough to keep the mosquitoes away without making my skin bubble. Yes, the drums were empty; no, they were not clean enough to be safe to use for drinking or cooking. Even after boiling and filtering there was still a telltale odor.

Stench or not, and I think I probably smelled like anyone else who has just begun the process of breaking in his storage barrels, I decided to pay a courtesy call on the French customs post. I dressed smartly and set off for the border crossing.

Draw a line in the dirt. Nigeria is on one side and Cameroon is on the other. The Nigerian border officials were operating out of mud huts but when I went in to introduce myself they began laughing, a jovial hearty welcoming laugh. I had only been in the neighborhood a few days but they knew everything about me. Bush news travels fast. I explained that I wanted to go across to the French customs post. They escorted me up to the barrier and made sure the guards were instructed to let me pass whenever I wanted to.

On the French side, in Cameroon, everything was different. The building was made out of breeze block. It was well maintained, clean and orderly. Instead of mud huts the customs officers lived in proper houses. The gendarmes were real gendarmes, not a bunch of stooges in uniform. They spoke French well and were very courteous. After all, they had been trained in France and were proud of their training and their heritage. I was ushered into the chief's office and he stuck out his hand. Welcome. We were expecting you Monsieur Powell."

He presented me to the gendarmes and the customs officers as if I were someone special. After a few moments of polite conversation the chief of the detachment took me to his house and introduced me to his wife. She was warm and welcoming and they insisted that I stay for lunch, a gesture that I very much appreciated. It was a typical French lunch: aperitif before the meal to whet our appetites, in this case Pastis was served along with a little bowl of black olives.

Over drinks he gave me a general picture of life in what he called, "this forgotten place." I still remember those plaintive well-chosen words and I still wonder what it must have felt like to be a gendarme in a part of the world that was so far removed from the rapid changes that were taking place in postwar Europe. At lunch he noticed I enjoyed a glass of wine and he said, "I'll give you some wine to take back to Santa. When you run out, come see me and I'll give you some more." Here we were in the middle of nowhere and this officer, a total stranger, was almost offering me the shirt off his back.

When he found out that I was waiting for my wife to join me the conversation turned to practical aspects of life in the bush. "Take her to Tchang. It's only about eighty kilometers from here but it has everything, almost like any French town the same size." I asked him why Tchang was so much better off than the other towns and he explained that during the war, all the food supplies for Douala and other towns in the south came from the area around Tchang. "In fact, it's still used as a rest center for people who want to escape the heat, especially if they're trying to recover from malaria." Because of its high altitude the climate was excellent. The conversation wandered but with each new turn he gave me solid advice.

He suggested that I stop in at his house before I went to Tchang for the first time. "I'll make a list of foodstuffs you need to buy. With a list you won't run yourself ragged and you'll know where to go." Then he gave one of those little nuggets of advice that make the difference between living comfortably in the bush or merely hanging on until the next transfer. "Take as much whisky as you can carry." He explained that the range of whiskies was better in Nigeria than in the Cameroon. As a result, the locals would pay through the nose for a whisky no one else had. The difference in price, between what I paid for it and the price I sold it for would largely pay for my foodstuffs. He chuckled when I thanked him profusely and I promised to invite them to dinner as soon as Annie arrived. What a great afternoon! I met him totally by chance. But, getting to know him made a huge difference in how 'comfortably' we were able to live in the bush.

I never thought that Africans living so close to each other could be so different. All we had to do was step across an invisible line drawn in the dirt road, a line demarcating one country from the other, and the changes were incredible. There was no comparison between the quality of the French trained civil servants and their Nigerian counterparts. The French trained Africans had 'class'; the Nigerians did not.

Back on the plantation I worked hard to show Mr. Mulder that I was determined to complete the job satisfactorily. In the beginning he hovered over me like a hawk, watching my work methods and how I got along with my staff. He didn't try to tell me how to do my job but I knew that if I had made a mistake he would have swept out of nowhere to let me know that he was still around. Not too long after I began working I realized he was showing up less frequently. Whew! That was a sign that he was satisfied with me. I was happy for that little progress but by the time I finished installing the machines inside the factory building we realized that we had run into a problem that no one had anticipated.

We had been working flat out to get the site ready and nobody was aware that we were not going to offload the lorries carrying the generating set, its components and fuel tanks unless we had a crane. The power station was about five feet above ground. Damnit! We had no way of lifting the equipment from the lorry beds onto the site. If the site had been lower we could have unloaded the lot by putting pipes under the crates and rolling them inside. It would have been hard work because the equipment was heavy. The flywheel weighed five tons, the crankshaft weighed close to a ton and the Ruston horizontal pistons and engine weighed three tons. There was no easy solution but we kept working on finding a solution. Finally, we came up with an idea that Mulder approved. We built up a runway ramp and then reversed the lorry up to the edge of the powerhouse. The truck bed was at the same level as the powerhouse. It was difficult but we managed to roll the equipment off the bed and onto the powerhouse floor.

We still needed a block and tackle; the plantation's chain block was adequate but we did not have a tripod. Lifting was a problem; positioning the equipment was another matter. The set was designed to fit according to detailed plans that had been drawn up by a local contractor who was supervised by a Scottish engineer on the plantation. There was a home made lifting tripod in Bamenda. I went to check it out. "It will do," I concluded and brought it back with me. Things started to look up. With the lifting tripod in place I could hook up the chain block and begin the assembly process.

Even though we were fitting big pieces of equipment, we could not forget that this installation required precision engineering. Everything had to fit down to the last millimeter. There was no margin for error. The crankshaft had to be perfectly positioned on its three support bearings. All my life's professional experience was used: my crash course with Perkins diesel engine in Peterborough and my fitter experience during my apprenticeship in the French navy in Toulon helped.

It was painstaking work. Mulder watched me from a distance. It took me a full day to get it perfect. Mr. Mulder gave a grunt of approval but to be safe, he called for a specialist to check out my installation. My ego didn't get in the way. I understood his concern and I fully agreed that he needed to be covered because, in case the crankshaft was not set properly, there could be a lot of damage.

The specialist came the next morning, lugging two trunks of testing gadgets. He began his work and you could feel the tension in my team. Nobody had winged it but we all knew that we had been working under primitive conditions and what we assembled was far from primitive machinery. He fiddled, measured, and generally poked around. I hovered behind in case he had any questions but he was happy to talk to himself.

When he finished he wiped his hands on an old wipe-cloth and started smiling. He was amazed. "How could you do such an accurate job with only a piece of chalk?" It wasn't a gratuitous question. He was genuinely curious. There he was, a master engineer with considerable experience, standing in front of me a skinny little man with a funny accent. My only 'technical tool' consisted of a piece of school blackboard chalk given to me by my neighbor, the school master. "It took me a full day to adjust the bearings," I said and he whistled softly. "I won't doubt that," he replied and then commented on the fact that I had done an outstanding job without the help of any sophisticated equipment or a trained support staff. "It's an outstanding job." I felt great.

Mulder's great shoulders fell with relief. From that moment, his attitude changed immediately. Instead of being worried about whether the installation was going to be done correctly, he began sharing his other big concern. "Now that's done, will it work?" I had become a competent person in his mind, not just any employee sent out by head office to do a job. He even said, "Now I know what you meant when you told me that you were not Mr. Nigelec but John Powell." Obviously, I had truly earned his respect and I felt great.

The moment of truth arrived. I walked over to the control box and flipped the switch. The engine began humming as if it had always been there. We waited for about fifteen minutes because if anything major was going to go wrong, it was likely to happen soon after start up. Nothing happened. Mulder turned to us and motioned outside. We followed him into his house for a well-earned celebration drink. Mulder was almost beside himself with joy and I began to appreciate the incredible amount of pressure he must have been under while we assembled the rig. "By the way, your boss, Mr. Guest, is arriving in Victoria tomorrow. Take one of the trucks and go down and fetch him." That was a nice break and I looked forward to getting off the plantation for a short break.

Driving on the French Cameroon roads was a piece of cake compared to the Nigerian side. Guest was shocked at how primitive my living conditions were in Santa. He promised to get me a kerosene-powered refrigerator as soon as possible. Somehow, I can't remember how, Annie's arrival came into the conversation. He knew that Annie would be coming in a couple of weeks and he assured me that he would meet her at Lagos airport and make sure that she was sent up to me as quickly as possible. "Go to Enugu and buy whatever you need to make her happy," he instructed. He was probably thinking to himself, "get her anything to keep you here but as soon as I can I'm getting you out of here." Before he left he must have done some real soul searching because he promised me that as soon as this job was finished he would send me to a nice place in the north: first to Jos and then to Kano.

At last, the telephone call that I had been waiting for finally got through: Annie was coming! Lagos called the plantation to confirm that she was arriving at the Enugu airport the next morning at 11:30. Good news in Africa often comes sandwiched between layers of bad news, or at least bad circumstances. The road to Enugu was closed that morning to outgoing traffic and open only to oncoming traffic. Of course, I had to go in the opposite direction of the traffic flow to get to the airport. There was only one solution: travel at midnight when no one else was on the road. Put another way, I'd run the gauntlet to Enugu in the opposite direction before the traffic flow was switched at 0600. According to my calculations, if I got on the road at midnight and drove without breaking down or being stopped, I could make it beyond the traffic flow barrier with an hour to spare. Driving was the least risky part of the trip. My personal security was another matter.

I traveled alone with my spear and a machete. Just in case! Up until then there were no known cases of whites being attacked but life in the bush is a hard teacher. One of the lessons you quickly learn is to take precautions before there's a problem because if your worst fears become a reality, you are prepared. It's like carrying a shovel and a length of tow rope in the back of your truck. You don't plan to get stuck but if you do, you're prepared to get yourself unstuck.

I probably didn't have to fear about my physical safety because at that time the white man was almost immune from violence originating in the native community. There were very few whites and the blacks said, jokingly for the most part, that if a white man went missing the police would start searching for him because there weren't that many of us in the community and we were easier to find. For once, there was safety in being a minority! I didn't like traveling with 'weapons' but at the same time I recognized that I am not the type of person who is going to stand by idly if someone tries to rob me or hijack my truck. If a fight starts, I told myself, I'll try and outrun them but if not, I'll take them out one by one.

Traveling at night was not as bad as I thought it was going to be. In fact, darkness actually worked in my favor because I could see headlamps far enough ahead of me to give me time to find a place to pull over and let the other vehicle pass. I set off confident that I'd get to Enugu in one piece. Actually, I only had to pull over once, and as the lorry barreled by I am sure the driver didn't see me. I was close to Enugu when dawn started to inch across the night sky and I finally caught myself relaxing. It had been a hard drive but I had made it through the worst and there were only a few more miles to go. All of a sudden I felt the car lurch. A puncture! I was in the middle of the road with no place to pull over. As I braced the car and wrestled with the flat tire I began cursing and ran through every word in my well-developed Royal Navy seaman's vocabulary. If the trees had ears and manners, I must have caused a few to shed their leaves. Not only did I want to get off the road before I got run over, I wanted to get to the rest house, have a shower and maybe even a haircut, before meeting Annie at the airport. Somehow I managed to switch the tire and race into Enugu before 0600 and into the rest house.

*****

With only a few minutes to spare I managed to get to the airport, cleaned up and properly dressed. I went inside and started mixing with a few Americans who were there to pick up some of their fellow countrymen who were making a film in Enugu. I think one of the stars was Eartha Kitt or someone like that. We scanned the sky and then a little dot appeared. It was a Dakota, the air workhorse of Africa. Twin Pratt and Whitney's thundered across the sky. If it had been trailing a plow it wouldn't have surprised me because that squat wonderful plane was known affectionately as a flying tractor. When the door banged open I strained to see Annie coming down steps.

There were three big guys, Americans, standing behind me. All of a sudden they started jostling each other. "Look at her. Now, that's some fine woman!" Annie was beautiful, a burst of sunlight walking toward me. Who is the lucky guy? As she came closer I saw that she had a new hairdo but there was something wrong. Was it my eyes or what? Annie's blond hair had turned pink! In a space of seconds I got mad, started to laugh, and caught myself when one of the Americans burst out, "Damned if she isn't French." Obviously for him, French women were meant to be beautiful and Annie, even with pink hair, was beautiful. People stared as I ran to her.

We drove into town to the rest house where we had lunch with the general manager of CFAO General Stores and the general manager of CFAO Motors. Both were French and they came from Nice. They were married but their wives had gone back to France with the children for a holiday. They were good men and they cared a lot about making our stay in the bush as comfortable as possible. "There's a lorry leaving this week carrying food stores to Bamenda and we put a double bed mattress onboard. We've also arranged for one our colleagues in Lagos to buy you a refrigerator and bring it up to you." That was very nice of them. They didn't have to get involved with that level of detail but they did and their concern for our well-being paid off. From the beginning I was loyal and hard working but now I was just that much more loyal. I vowed to give even more of myself because with bosses like that looking after me, I was going to show my gratitude in ways that would reflect favorably on them: highest quality workmanship.

After lunch Annie and I went back to the rest house. It had been built to European standards: plaster walls, mosquito netting, overhead fans, indoor plumbing with lots of hot water and a shiny wood plank floor that was kept immaculately clean by a house boy wearing a white jacket with brass buttons. "Annie my love, don't get too comfortable," I said. "Where we are going life is pretty basic." From the way she looked at me I thought that maybe she believed I was joking with her, joshing a bit to set the scene because we were going to leave a town and live in a village. It was not a village by French standards; it was a Nigerian village. The gap was too big to try and explain so I decided to give her an example. "When we get home, you've got to become a baker." That was news to her. That example helped me drive home the point that we were like pioneers in the Far West: we had to rely on ourselves to turn our bush house into a little paradise.

Back in town we bought bags of flour, tins of butter, and tins of cheese, tinned milk, tea and coffee. The more we bought the more excited she became. After long hours in town we'd return to the rest house, take a swim in the pool, and spend the evenings with our friends. Life was good, life was gentle, and life was quite civil. I let her enjoy it because I knew that at the end of the road in Santa, life was very different. I hoped the shock wouldn't be too great. By the end of the week we had stocked up with enough provisions to get us through the first few weeks until we could cross the border into Cameroon and get fresh meat and vegetables.

We left Enugu on a Friday afternoon in order to reach Santa before midnight. This meant we would spend the last hours of the trip going through the deep forest in total darkness. I'd done it before, so had others, but it was not something I would have chosen to do if there had been other options. There were none. Like a pilot inspecting his aircraft before a long trip, I circled our vehicle and looked at it with a critical eye. Our provisions were lashed down in the back of the Rover. Nothing was likely to fall off. I checked the tires. They looked good but you never knew what you were going to hit once tarmac roads turned into rough dirt tracks. When we drove out of town into the bush we turned our backs on the easy life of an expatriate in exchange for a life on the frontier. We began living our new life.

Just as the sun was setting we pulled into Manfe and I stopped by the river so Annie could see the hippos lumbering out of the water. In the tall tree tops above us monkeys screamed as if they were trying to warn us of a lurking danger. Annie stared first at the glistening hippos and then up at the monkeys scampering through the dark green canopy. She was smiling and her head turned as if watching, in slow motion, a tennis game being played on two courts: the river and the trees teaming with chattering little hairy people-like animals. We got out and stretched and had tea from our thermos and a few sandwiches. Our little tea break was as nice as it was necessary: I knew the next leg of the trip would be more difficult.

The road narrowed and began twisting as we lurched up through the foothills into the mountains. Sunset was brief, a pause between day and total darkness. Our headlamps sliced through the night. Rising on a small crest I stopped and turned off the motor and extinguished the headlamps. We sat enveloped by forest night sounds: insects whirring and buzzing, high-pitched shrieks and hoops from animals wrapped in the thick cloak of the forest. Annie was tense but not scared. She strained to differentiate the cries and wondered what kind of animals could make such weird noises.

We got back into the car and began grinding up the mountain. We drove slowly because it was pitch dark and there were potholes deep enough to snap our axle if we were foolish enough to try to speed over them. Each pothole meant changing gears, slowing down, grinding up the other side. I couldn't see her but I began to sense that she was getting tired. "How much further?" she asked. I didn't give her a straight answer but I pointed to a mountain crest that we could barely see etched against the night sky. ""It's just over there," I lied. If all went well, we had another three hard hours ahead of us. Fatigue was getting to me and I began speeding up which was the wrong thing to do.

No sooner had I deluded myself into thinking that we were going to be able to maintain the luxury of speed when we rounded a corner and pitched into a deep pothole. Those were the days before seat belts. The shock was violent and Annie shot up from her seat and hit her head on the ceiling of the cabin. Because I held the steering wheel in a death grip I only bounced but from the sound of it, she had to be hurt. "Feel your head," I ordered. "Are you bleeding?" She ran her fingers through her hair and massaged her scalp. "No, I'm okay," she replied laughing softly.

I exhaled a huge sigh of relief. Yes, there was no physical damage. I managed to chalk that event off to good luck and nothing more. She could have gotten a nasty gash; we were miles from any medical care. And no, I didn't have to worry about her spirit. Her laughter told me that she would be able to cope with life in Santa where she would have to live by her wits and ingenuity. In Santa her ability to improvise would mean the difference between merely existing or an exciting life. How calmly she took her first 'bump in the bush' taught me a lot about her inner strength.

After five long hours lurching and pitching through total darkness, five hours of not seeing another human being, we drove into the village. I stopped the car in front of our house. Miracle of Miracles, the night guard was not sleeping. He must have heard us grinding through the bush. He smiled as he approached the Rover muttering a greeting that neither of us could understand. I was too tired to show Annie around. It was after midnight. Every bone in my body ached from fighting the Land Rover. The guard helped us unload, lighted the kerosene lamps, and left us alone in our new home. We were dusty and tired. Naturally, Annie wanted to wash. She didn't complain about the petrol-perfumed water. It was warm. After our showers we collapsed into a deep and well deserved sleep.

We woke up the next morning with what felt like broken backs but we could actually move. Despite the trip, we felt amazingly fit. After a solid breakfast we gave the house a good cleaning. I thought I had left it clean but dust always got in everywhere. If there wasn't a lot of space to clean, there was a lot to do. By the time we got to our bedroom we were tired and thought of taking a nap but then we looked at our narrow single bed on which we managed to sleep the night before. We exploded with uncontrolled laughter.

When we arrived we were too tired and it was too dark to be discriminating. Somehow we had managed to wedge two bodies onto a very narrow cot that had served me well when I was on my own but it was too small for the two of us. One night was enough, we agreed on that, but where would we get a new bed? It wasn't as if we could hop in the Rover and go into the village and choose a new bed. Getting to the nearest mattress store meant driving for eight hours.

Obviously, something had to be done about this if we wanted to get a good night's sleep.

After lunch, while we were pondering the bed problem, we heard a lorry creak up in front of our house. Actually, we smelled it before we saw it stop. He was carrying a load of tinned food, vegetables, and stockfish. The sun beat down on the fish. The ice that the fish was packed in had melted and the fish was oozing into filthy water sloshing on the truck bed. A large new mattress was perched on top of the load, perhaps to protect the fish from the sun.

There are times in Africa when your dreams don't quite work out. This was one of them. Our dream of a good night's rest stank of stockfish. There was no way we could wash out the smell. Ever the ingenious couple, we decided to leave it outside in the sun in the naïve belief the sun would burn out the stench. All we did was to help our corner of the village smell like a seaside fishmonger's shop. Annie had an idea. "Let's spray it with eau de cologne." Brilliant idea! Anything that could take away the stench was worth trying. It did have an effect. Now the mattress smelled as if a high class Parisiene had fallen asleep in a fish shop.

The human nose has an uncanny ability to adapt to bad smells. Over time, the human race becomes incapable of detecting a persistent bad odor. It becomes part of our waking day and we don't think about it. In a couple of days we couldn't smell our fishy mattress. Life moved on. At least, part of our life moved on. The mattress didn't fit our scrawny single bed frame. Turning it first one way, then the other, the mattress flopped off the frame and almost touched the floor. There was no way we could sleep on that contraption.

In the end, I went down to the plantation and collected three empty wooden boxes and a couple of planks that were as long as the mattress. I maneuvered the boxes, planks and bed frame into place and secured the base with rope. It wasn't elegant, but it worked and we were the only family in Nigeria to have a double bed that stank of stockfish and eau de cologne. We never got rid of the smell but we slept well. Maybe the fish-and-perfume mixture was a secret sleep potion that we should have tried to bottle and sell.

Rene Dassac (in collaboration with Patrick K. Robbins)

During the first weekend after we arrived I introduced Annie to the Mulder family. They were gracious and told her that she was welcome to visit anytime she liked. An added bonus, their two daughters spoke a little French. Her first Saturday in the bush was pleasant and I promised to take her shopping the following day.

Sunday was market morning. I didn't tell Annie about the market other than saying we were going to buy some fresh fruit and vegetables. I couldn't bring myself to tell her this market was not quite what she was accustomed to in Paris. I parked the Rover and we began walking toward the first stalls. There were mounds of lovely fresh vegetables with smiling native women beckoning us to come and buy. Annie's eyes were straining to stay in their sockets. Ample naked black bodies framed flashing white smiles when the vendors beckoned us to their stalls. We wandered through the market, stopping and talking, slowly filling our baskets. By the end of the morning Annie was quite nonplussed. Winking at me she said, "This could never happen in Paris. It's too cold."

Our neighbor, the schoolteacher whom I had invited for a drink when I first arrived, followed up on his offer to send one of his pupils to keep Annie company and help with the house. Elizabeth was about twelve years old, a gangly but gentle youngster. She came to our house on Monday carrying a small basket of fruit. She was an engaging young girl and within a very short time Annie and Elizabeth became close friends. Having someone to share her day with was important for me because every day I left Annie on her own and headed for the plantation. My days were long but if she had been left on her own, Annie's days would have been longer and that is not healthy when you live in an isolated bush village.

One evening something quite strange happened. The night watchman knocked on the door and asked me to come out. "There's a madman who wants to set fire to your house." After years living with extreme danger, I thought I had heard it all, but this was a first. I reached behind the door and grabbed my spear. The night watchman stared at the madman. Neither man moved. "Tell that nutter to fuck-off or I'll ram my spear through his neck." My trusted night watchman was petrified and mute. The madman stood as if anchored to the ground. "Go to the village and bring me a policeman," I yelled at the night watchman. He scampered off into the dark while I stood poised to skewer the madman if he so much as twitched.

A few minutes later our constable huffed onto the scene. "Don't worry, he's nuts but he's not dangerous. I can't do anything. He sort of wanders all over and I guess this is the first time he's visited you." That may have been a good answer from his point of view but it left me with a nutter who wanted to burn down my house. "Very well, I'm going to Bamenda to get the chief of police." I turned my back on the trio and began walking toward my car. That galvanized them. The constable grabbed the madman and shoved him off into the dark in the direction of the village. Once the loony had loped off into the night the constable came back to me. I was sitting in the driver's seat prepared to leave. He was smiling, almost laughing. "Don't worry. There's no danger. You've been set-up. The village chief was trying to scare you into hiring some of his tribe." The penny dropped, the switch turned, and I sheepishly admitted to myself that I had fallen for one of the oldest con games in the bush: create fear in the white man and sell him protection.

I decided to play their game. Before going to bed I wrote the chief a note full of flowery phrases, explaining that I could not hire anyone to help build an addition to my cottage because I didn't have the necessary material, and that I would seek his guidance and assistance to recruit reliable workers, and that I respected him and looked forward to living under his protection. My note did the trick. The chief and I became good friends. He even offered me the use of two of his horses. I had never ridden in my life but I appreciated the offer and was happy that he became my ally instead of my enemy. The village was his little kingdom and I was his guest. Even grown-ups can play games.

We settled into a routine. Despite the fact that we worked hard, we also learned that in the bush expats also play hard. One Saturday Mulder sent his driver to deliver a letter inviting Annie and me for tea. Quite proper and quite British, thank you. We had our lunch, showered and dressed for what we thought was going to be an afternoon event. We were wrong. Mulder's tea party turned into a rollicking party that lasted until Tuesday morning. When we arrived at the plantation the Mulder's and the Scottish engineer and his wife met us. So far, so good, we thought. We engaged in idle chat, some work, some stories, and settled in for more tea. After about an hour of tea, cars started pouring into the plantation. They came from all over the Cameroon, even eighty miles away.

Drinks began flowing after all the guests had arrived. A buffet appeared, the music got louder and we danced until our legs started giving out. Late into the night, perhaps it was early morning, we managed to slip away and get a few minutes of rest in one of the armchairs before returning to the hilarity. All the food helped to keep us somewhat sober but in the middle of nowhere, who cared? We certainly didn't. Annie could not believe her eyes. Here she was about as far from civilization as she had ever dreamt of going and the bush people, just like the two of us, were partying as if there were no tomorrow. We left sometime early Monday morning, showered, and slept the rest of the day. No tea party we've ever been to since then matched that 'quiet afternoon' in the bush.

My work in the plantation factory was almost finished. The heavy work was behind us but I had to stay for another three weeks. We were in the tense trial period. Our installation had gone well; there were no major problems but until the client signed off, and my reputation was on the line. Mulder didn't want to let me get too idle. He asked me to refit a seven tonne lorry. Parts were no problem; they came from the CFAO garage in Enugu. The motor stymied me because I was a diesel man and the lorry was a petrol motor. The plantation engineer pitched in and agreed to help me because he had the experience I lacked. Two determined men overcame problem after problem and kept coming up with solutions that amazed even both of us. We completed the refit, flipped a coin to see which one of us hit the starter and I lost. He pushed in the starter and the big monster let loose with a lusty roar. Specialists couldn't have done a better job and I felt proud of myself and my men.

One day our young Elisabeth told me that her father's maize grinding machine was broken and he couldn't start it. The consequences were serious because ground maize was their food staple. For the natives, when there was no machine, there was no dinner. I went to see his engine. What a sight! It was filthy and decrepit. For someone with my background, equipment had to be clean and maintained in perfect working order. There was no other way. Like it or not, that's the way I was trained. Looking at that wreck I knew that I simply couldn't walk away. The problem was obvious: mud, dust, and gunk clogged the pump and nozzle.

I grabbed a rag and a wrench and went to work. In no time at all I stripped the engine, cleaned the parts with some kerosene, reassembled it and shined anything that I'd missed on the first go. It looked great. Little Elisabeth raced to get her father. He came stumbling after her and when he saw his 'new grinding machine' he almost fainted with joy. He tried to pay me. "Thank you but friends don't accept payment." It was a pleasure to be able to help him. He had been so kind to us and we were fond of Elisabeth. From that day until we left the village, every morning Elisabeth showed up carrying a basket of fruit on her head.

We were almost finished but I asked for more help to get the job done. Fortunately, someone was available. Patrick Kelly was sent to help me. Now the pressure was on us. I had to finish and get up to Jos, a mining town in the north, as soon as possible. A critical job was underway but the electrician had been sacked for incompetence. My reputation was well established and I wasn't surprised to receive my new transfer orders.

Pat was a nice young Irish chap. I couldn't go to Enugu to fetch him but I sent a lorry to meet him and load his motorcycle. He was a good worker and a lot of fun to be with and he was exuded a wild adventurous spirit. Nothing was too zany for him to try at least once. The three of us, Annie, Pat and I, took off one day to 'walk around the summit' of the mountain that overlooked the plantation's coffee trees. It is hard to say whether we were irresponsible or nuts, I suppose a mixture of both qualifiers is appropriate given the circumstances. We set out on our adventure armed with a couple of spears and a vague idea of where we were going. We needed the spears because we were told the area was full of wild animals especially baboons that were often very dangerous if they thought they were being provoked. God looks after his innocents. I learned that lesson during the war when He was on duty with me. He was there that day when we ploughed our way through the forest.

Rene Dassac (in collaboration with Patrick K. Robbins)

We walked about twelve miles before we finally reached 'civilization' which was the part of the plantation where the workers were housed. Below us we could see the residential area. Even from a distance of half a mile, that part of the plantation looked neat and orderly. We stood in the African quarters and saw little Europe with its manicured lawns, wide streets, swimming pools and little pink children playing in the gardens. All quite civilized, we thought, and we set off down the steep hill giving no thought to our safety. We made our way slowly down the track. Except for the stone deaf, anyone could hear us coming. After much longer than we thought it would take us, we struggled into the plantation only to be confronted by Mr. Mulder who was a couple of hundred meters away. He was very agitated.

When we got closer we realized he was yelling at us; he was positively raging. What he was bellowing about made our knees start shaking. Fear and not fatigue made us quake. Mulder, in no uncertain terms, told us that we had come through a very dangerous part of the jungle that men went into only when they were armed and even then they didn't stay any longer than they had to. It seems there were all kinds of dangerous animals in the forest we had wandered through including a herd of very dangerous buffalo, huge animals with wide horns that they used like battering rams to crush their prey or their enemies. Thick forest for them was about as challenging to rip apart as a mosquito net was for us. And, in addition to their great bulk, they were fast and absolutely fearless. Even experienced hunters respected them. "The first shot better be a kill shot or you'd better have a tall sturdy tree to climb and wait him out," someone told me on another occasion. Armed with two spears and hiking boots we thought we were invincible.

Mulder calmed down and offered us beers and a ride back to our village. Both were accepted with gratitude and, to be honest, we were also a bit sheepish. Our happy walk could have turned into a disaster. Fortunately, that Special Spirit, Someone Else, was walking with us. We were oblivious to what dangers lurked in the forest. Our only worry was whether we would make it down the steep descent into the plantation in one piece.

My tour in the Cameroon had been a good experience. I had to learn to operate on my own because I was far from any support the company headquarters staff might have been able to offer. Through trial and error I managed to gain confidence in myself and to make decisions entirely on my own. I had taught myself a simple formula to apply when I had a problem: weigh both the pros and cons, look at them closely, build on the pros and overcome the cons. It sounds simple but it wasn't so easy at the time when I was both learning and working.

Taking everything into consideration, perhaps what I was teaching myself was how to be independent. An idea was beginning to take shape but I was in no hurry to rush it along. I'd take my time, keep learning but, for the time being, I had developed an idea that started acting like my own private inner compass. It gave me direction and the little voice associated with the idea was telling me: someday I might be good enough to become either my own boss with my own company or a senior contract manager in charge of big jobs. I liked that idea. It was 1957 and I gave myself a couple of years, three at the most, to reach my goal.

*****

While I was still in Santa I got word that Charles Guest wanted to meet me in Enugu to brief me on the mess I was about to step into in Jos. Our client was a big oil company, Mobil Oil, and the Nigelec supervisor had managed to make a cock-up in a very short time. Not only did he have trouble with the professional aspects of the job, he proved himself quite adept at infuriating our customer who just happened to be one of the biggest companies not only in Nigeria but in all of Africa, maybe even in the entire world. Guest had confidence in my ability to step into a bad situation and set it right. He thought of me from the perspective of a Royal Navy officer. He was confident in my integrity and in my ability to size up a situation and get the most important things done in such a way that the 'entire crew', as he put it, would be satisfied.

I was chuffed he thought so highly of me but at the same time I cautioned him not to get his hopes up. Talking about sorting out a mess was a lot easier than actually getting it done. He agreed and told me another aspect of the job that had escaped me. I would represent the company in the entire north of Nigeria. This was a huge new responsibility but he assured me he was confident I would be able to overcome the challenges he described. I thanked him for his compliment and the confidence he had in me but I had my own very private doubts that I didn't want to share with him.

Twisting cable into place is one thing but representing a huge company is quite another story. During our meeting he took time to give me an overview of where the company was going in Nigeria and what future role I was likely to play in their ambitious plans. He also said that after we finished two years in Kano the company would give us four months home leave. We talked a lot during those two days and we also drank a lot. Maybe one helped the other. As I left him I counted at least two empty whisky bottles and a pile of empty beer bottles. It had been a good meeting.

On the way to Enugu I felt the heat and humidity beating down on my car harder than usual. We were at the beginning of the rainy season; my body was trying to tell me there was a storm brewing. The steering wheel was gummy to the touch. The first rains fell when I started back to Santa. For months the sun baked the red soil until it became a compacted surface almost as hard as a well-built motorway. The first rains were often the most dangerous because the roads became so slippery that it was like trying to drive on a surface of green soap. Once they were wet I knew what would happen. In a few weeks the surface would crack and then the roads turned into a long and treacherous series of mud holes. This was the 'slippery season' before the 'rainy season' and I fought to keep the Rover from spinning out of control. I started up the mountainside just after sunset. It was dark. In my glow of my headlamps the leaves looked like they had been painted with luminous paint. The first rains had just washed off months of accumulated dust to give the forest a surreal glow.

A light rain was still falling and I felt reasonably confident about getting home to Annie in one piece. All of a sudden, while I was in the middle of the forest in pitch darkness, a thunderstorm unleashed its fury. I drove with eyes in the back of my head, on the sides and on top. Suddenly, I heard an almighty 'crack' and smelled the sharp tang of fresh ozone. Lightning cut a tree in half just as I was passing. It crashed down on the flat bed behind my cabin missing me by a few inches. The impact was so violent that I lost control and my Rover spun off the road, careening toward a ravine. My left wheel hung over the ravine. The motor hadn't been damaged; the gears worked but I couldn't get traction. I sized up the situation quickly and concluded that there was nothing I could do. I had to sit and wait for help.

After a couple of hours I heard a lorry grinding toward me. It squished to a stop. The tree was blocking them too. There were several men and they began chopping furiously on the tree. Sure enough, they cut a section just wide enough to let their lorry pass. They started to move while I stood in the pouring rain blocking their way, pleading with them to throw a cable around my hitch and pull me out. Sods! No one 'understood' me; they lurched past. I had been there longer than they had and I knew what was probably going to happen on 'my' road. It was a sure bet. As soon as the driver changed gears his lorry slid off the road. We were both stuck. Now we needed each other and I tried to explain that to them. If they cleared the tree from my path, my four-wheel drive could pull them out. If not, I told them, we were going to sit out the night together until another lorry came and helped both of us. A strange thing happened. In a flash the lorry driver who moments earlier couldn't make sense of what I was saying suddenly 'understood' me.

Bitching and moaning, they set about to clear the tree that was blocking me. After about a half hour in bucketing rain, they wrestled the tree off the track and lifted-pushed my Rover back onto the road. I kept my promise and attached my steel cable onto the back of his lorry. They started pushing and I began pulling. Mud flew; spraying man and forest for meters around us but their lorry managed to inch up onto the road. The Africans began whooping and hollering, singing and dancing, and carrying on as if they were into the second barrel at a good wedding party. I left them and continued on to Santa and managed to get home before dawn. It was still raining but I had survived.

*****

Events moved fast and soon it was our turn to leave. We were excited but we were also a bit nostalgic. Life in Santa had been good. We made friends in both the African and expat communities, we learned how to turn hardship into fun, and we had a routine that we liked. A new assignment meant new challenges and new unknowns. We knew we were up to the challenges but we were, nevertheless, just a bit reluctant to let go of 'our' little corner of Africa. Annie took responsibility for preparing all the gear we were going to take with us and I became the family loadmaster. We crammed the boot so full you couldn't squeeze in a toothbrush. I checked out the lorry and loaded a drum of petrol, cases of tools and then managed to squeeze in the Morris Brake. It needed a complete refit. We drove by the Mulder's, and had our last cup of coffee together before starting our trip to Enugu.

I knew what condition the roads were in and I drove carefully. Annie seemed relaxed, maybe ignorance is bliss, but I was tense because I was afraid of what the rain had done to the road surface. There were no culverts, no man made drainage ditches to channel the water off the road and back into the forest. When the rainwater came barreling down the mountainside it hit the road so that all its force was channeled into the narrow strip linking Santa to Enugu.

My car led our small convoy and my staff followed us in the lorry and the Land Rover. We drove slowly down the middle of the road. There was only one incident. We were on a slippery slope that led down onto a narrow wooden bridge that spanned a raging torrent. We inched toward the bridge but my car started a slow slide. It was headed off the road. The slope was too steep for my tires; the red clay mud was as thick and slippery as the industrial lubricant I shot into hammer mill bearings. I yelled for help. Fortunately, the lorry and Rover managed to stop without sliding. My staff piled out and grabbed the sides of the car, three on each side. They braced the car down. Just in case, I kept my door open. We crabbed down onto the bridge where I was able to get traction.

We crossed the bridge slowly and I slid and spun my tires through the mud up the other the side. The other two vehicles following me had proper tires and they made it across easily. When we found a safe spot, I pulled over far enough off the road to allow other vehicles to pass. We needed to refuel and I decided to take advantage of the stop and told my men to take a lunch break. After lurching, pitching and slipping, it felt good to stand and stretch.

Annie was tired. Our car had springs, it was reasonably comfortable, but I had to admit long hours on that road made for a punishing ride. There was no way to relax except when we stopped. I looked in the car. Annie was resting and I didn't want to disturb her so I took my ice box and went up the road a bit to eat my sandwich away from the petrol fumes. I found a soft spot with some nice grass, kicked the brush to make sure there were no snakes or spiders, and sat down to eat. About half way through, when I was actually enjoying being in the midst of a beautiful wild forest, I heard movement in the brush behind me. I looked down the road and did a quick head count. All my men were there and Annie was still in the car. Whoever it was had to be big because I could hear branches snapping as he lumbered toward me. I turned slowly, wishing I had a spear or a gun, wishing I were sitting behind the wheel of our car with the doors locked.

A black head rose out of the bush and stared at me. I was no zoologist but I knew that head belonged to a big male gorilla. Wide nostrils quivered as he raised his massive furry head to let his shiny brown eyes focus on me. Evolution Papa, the big gorilla and I eyed each other warily. He made deep hooting noises which I interpreted as him telling me he was as surprised as I was to meet on the side of the road in his forest. I did not try and engage him in conversation; I probably couldn't have opened my mouth anyway. Fear and surprise rendered me mute. He was about as tall as me, heavier and from the way he acted I think he was simply curious about the strange looking monkey in front of him. The stand-off didn't last long but it lasted long enough for me to start thinking about getting out of there fast but I knew I had to leave calmly so I would not provoke him into attacking or just coming over and giving me a great big happy gorilla hug that would have broken every bone in my body.

I bent over and picked up my icebox and backed away. He looked around, turned and crashed back into the brush that he had come from just moments ago. I yelled to the lads. At first they thought I was joking but from the way I was acting they knew it was no joke. We repacked our vehicles in record time and drove away, happy to leave the gorilla to go tell his friends about the albino with short arms and funny hair.

We reached Enugu late in the afternoon. Annie and I went to the rest house; my staff went to their quarters. The next day the staff continued on to Lagos while we remained in Enugu for a couple of days.

Those few days were a welcome break. We needed to get the car serviced and I needed a haircut. Annie had done her best to keep me looking somewhat respectable but I was shaggy and welcomed the hand of a professional. After a haircut and a break in the real world, I looked like a gentleman who was ready to take on all the trouble the general manager of Mobil Oil in Jos could possibly throw at me.

His nasty reputation was well documented. Putting aside the fact that my predecessor had been sacked, industry sources confirmed to me that Mobil's man was a hard case. I did not look forward to working with him but I kept telling myself that I had faced a lot of tough people in my life and no one had yet to get the better of me. There was always a first time, though, because bad luck happens. But, something inside told me that whatever was waiting for me in Jos my upcoming assignment was not going to be the venue for my first failure to turn an opponent into an ally. It might happen later, perhaps, but I kept reassuring myself it wouldn't happen now.

The road from Enugu to Jos was not much more than a mud track stretched around potholes. We weren't contending with just a few little indentations in the surface. No, those potholes were big enough to cover the width of the road and deep enough to snap an axle. I knew the drill. Just as dawn was breaking we drove out of Enugu and began lurching toward Jos. With any luck I thought, we might make it into Jos before dark. The thought of spending a night in the forest did not appeal to me.

The part of eastern Nigeria we were driving through is thick forest until the river port town of Makurdi, the last port on the Cross River. Out of Makurdi we started to climb toward Jos. Getting there was going to be difficult but Jos had its own reward: at 3000 feet above sea level it was renowned for its fine climate. Annie was the perfect tourist. While I wound our way slowly around the potholes, she admired the well-kept farms many of which were run by Europeans. Every conceivable kind of vegetable was grown in those gardens. And, luxury of luxuries, in Jos there was the prospect of buying butter and cream and even going to a butcher's shop and buy meat that had been cut by proper butchers and stored in sanitary conditions. This was a tantalizing prospect, a real step up from fly infested slabs of bloody beef hanging under a banana leaf.

We came into Jos a bit before dusk. As we drove in it was obvious that Jos was a rich town built around a successful mining industry. Tin, silver and bauxite were extracted in and around Jos. Of the three, the later was the most lucrative because it was sold to the United States atomic energy program and payment was made in dollars. In those days the dollar was the king of the world's currencies. Miners were making fortunes and they spent their money lavishly. There were big hotels and swank clubs, even a lovely golf club that would have been envied anywhere in Europe. With wealth came a certain civic pride. Money was invested to keep the city clean and the roads were in excellent condition.

Reservations had been made for me at the Jos Anglo Club, a hotel and club mostly used by expatriate miners. Compared to our living conditions in the village, this hotel was an island of great luxury. Often in remote areas where there are expats, behind the veneer of civility there is another world, a world of sharp passions and people with strange characters.

The hotel owner and his wife were well known for having colossal rows. They never tried hiding the fact that, with no forewarning, they'd have a go at each other. When the urge came, they just let rip much to the dismay, disgust, and sometimes amusement of anyone within earshot. He was a hearty fellow. One day several years later they had a particularly heavy go and he died. He didn't curl up his toes on the spot but it was soon enough after their bout to make tongues wag. True or not, the rumor mill churned out the story that she had found a way to poison him and not get caught! From poison to passion, the step was short.

There was a French couple and she, according to local lore, was busy screwing half the male population of Jos in addition to sporting in public with her French lover. At night the French woman and her husband would come to the club. He spun off to the bar and began drinking himself into a coma. Out popped her French lover. The two swayed on the dance floor until the early morning. Then her lover, always the gallant, helped her steer her husband home. How long the lover stayed after his act of charity was a topic of earnest speculation. Everyone in town knew what was going on. It was such an open topic that people had quit laughing.

We soon learned that the French couple was not the only couple involved in extra-marital escapades. Apparently there was a lot of wife swapping going on in Jos and I had to explain this to Annie and put her on her guard. New woman in town, I knew that she was being eyed by some of the couples that we met. Even the notorious French couple tried to become friends. Fortunately Annie wasn't naïve; she didn't like the French woman. Using skills unique to women, she tactfully wove her way out of the snare set by the French woman.

Sex and petty disputes aside, life was good. After a few games at the table, the club invited me to join their snooker team. They needed me because they had accepted a challenge with another club about twenty-five miles away. As the team captain explained, they wanted some new blood. I told him I was rusty; he replied, "You'll do well." He was right. I racked up a good score and our team won the challenge!

As much as I enjoyed the game, I was not sent to Jos to play snooker. Shortly after our arrival I contacted the Mobil Oil manager. He wasn't all that bad. It was true, he was tough but he had a right to be demanding because he was responsible for a big operation and he could not be let down by any of his service providers. It didn't take me long to become very friendly with him. It helped that we both played snooker at the same club. After each game we stopped and had a couple of beers and talked and he opened up. Very soon I had gained his complete confidence.

The perimeter security lights were one of the problems my predecessor had failed to sort out. At first sight the overhead lines were properly connected but the lights didn't work. What baffled me was that none of the fuses had blown. This was highly unusual. I took a piece of paper and began to diagram the problem, just as the Navy had taught me to do many years ago. I could hear my instructor's voice ringing, "start from the source of supply and follow the whole circuit until the point of rupture is reached." Good instructions back then were just as good now, I told myself.

The underground cable was energized right up to the first pole on the perimeter lines. At that point I ran into my first unknown. The current was okay on the underground side but not on the overhead lines. I checked the connections for both and they were correct. Why didn't the current pass, I kept asking myself? The overhead lines were aluminum; the underground cable connected to it was copper. The aluminum connectors to which both the aluminum lines and the copper cables were connected were covered with a thick non-conductor paste that had been created as a result of a chemical reaction between the two conductors. The electricity did not connect because my predecessor did not use special connectors. They were not readily available but by then I had developed contacts with the Public Works Department and they helped me out. In Mobil's eyes I was a real hero but, much to my chagrin, success meant that I was going to be transferred because there were no new contracts coming up in Jos.

I was directed to go to Kano to relieve our employee who was due for leave. He had been in Kano for a year. Twelve months was enough for him. He did not like Nigeria and unfortunately for the company, he did not want to renew his contract. It was the company's loss because he was a good and competent supervisor. We drove down to Kano, through Kaduna, the university town of the North. It was a nice looking town but we didn't have time to stop and admire it. The closer we came to Kano the more we began to notice the difference in climate and vegetation. It was hotter and drier than in Jos. After the cool climate in Jos, the heat and dryness really hit us hard. Everything was dusty. Even though the road was tarred most of the way it was wind swept and dust swirled on the slick surface. A hot wind blew dust across the surface and up onto our windscreen. We kept the windows shut to keep out some of the dust but by closing the windows we were denied any cross ventilation. It was suffocating; muddy sweat streamed down our faces. By the time we checked into the hotel we looked like we had fallen out of a sandblasting furnace. The Central Hotel had air-conditioning and a good shower; within minutes that bad trip became a vague memory. We had just enough time to cool off and clean up before we met the man I was to replace.

*****

Greenwood met us at the hotel for dinner. Although I had never met him before, it took just a few moments for me to conclude that he was superior to many of the lads I had met in Lagos. He was frank and open, well spoken and intelligent. He knew what was going on and he gave me a good description of the situation in Kano. "Why, aren't you going to renew your contract?" "I've had enough of this country," he replied. Once he got back to the United Kingdom he was going to look into possibilities either in New Zealand or Australia. Fair enough. Nigeria was not everybody's cup of tea. At least he was honest and had the courage to act on his convictions.

He picked us up early the next morning. I asked Annie to come along because it was an excellent opportunity for her to see the town and also have a quick overview of some of the sites I would be working on. By now I knew the ritual of taking over a job. I had to appear to be a 'boss'. My authority had to radiate from me, from the way I acted, and from the way I conducted myself on site. As a new man on a job, the first question any employee would ask was, "Does this bloke know what he's doing?"

Instead of joining him in his Peugeot pickup truck, Annie and I followed him in my own car. Driving on my own in a private sedan, with my wife, meant in the eyes of the African's that I was 'somebody'. First impressions count not only with the Africans, I said to Annie, but also with the European managers. After all, I was going to meet the CFAO general manager. He would size me up and I wanted him to know that I was every bit his equal. In the past few months I had seen that CFAO staff tended to look down on Nigelec staff. Their condescension clearly placed us slightly above the African staff but considerably below the CFAO management. Of course, they never let on but their actions spoke more than their words. We set off. Our car followed closely behind Greenwood's battered pick-up.

Greenwood was shrewd because he started the trip where it meant most to Annie. He took us to his house that was going to be transferred to us. It was a nice house on the northern edge of Kano. Our closest neighbor was a Fulani village. Colorful? Yes ... but ... thousands of flies swarmed around their cows and poultry. The air was black with millions of buzzing biting bodies and there was no escaping them. They flew into our eyes, nose, ears, and hair, crawled across our face, and chased each other up and down our legs. "If you're new to this part of Nigeria, don't forget the Fulani are well known thieves. Anything that is not nailed down is going to go walkies."

Thieves and flies, our spirits began to sag. Furthermore, Kano was terribly hot during the dry season. It could easily reach 40°C by mid-morning. By nightfall the sun has baked the earth. When the sun set heat continued to radiate from the earth for hours. Standing outside was like standing inside an oven either with the lights on or with the lights off. At least our bedroom had a ceiling fan but all it did was shovel invisible mounds of hot air from side-to-side. The heat was too heavy to move. To make matters worse, we had to sleep under a mosquito net. Our body heat was trapped inside the net. The squeaky fan was all but useless. Air conditioners, something we accept as standard appliances today in the tropics, were hard to find in 1957 and very expensive luxuries. Two years later every expatriate house had at least one or two!

After swatting our way through the flies that acted as if they owned his house, we went to see the general manager of CFAO. He was an older man, perhaps twenty-five years my senior. Instead of returning to France to fight, he spent the entire war in Nigeria making lots of money by over-charging everything he could. He played on simple market demand in a war environment where scarcity drove up prices.

He was not a bad old chap. I figured I could work with him but I couldn't trust him. There was something about him that reminded me of all the fervent followers of the fascist Vichy government that I had met. He thought I was English because of my English name. But, when I explained to him how I had acquired my English name, I could feel his attitude changing. There was still a noticeable uneasiness between French citizens in those early post war years. I was sensitive to that uneasiness because I had to keep my feelings in check when I dealt with men who, for whatever reason, had chosen a path different than the path I took during the war.

After our introductions, and going through ritual inane pleasantries dictated by protocol and good manners, we got down to business. He droned through a long list of instructions, most of which I forgot within thirty seconds, summarized the internal regulations of the company, and finally advised me to go meet the manager of the CFAO garage. "I'm sure he'll be happy to meet you." What a relief. I think I'd have welcomed talking to a totem pole merely in order to get out of his office. Greenwood met me as I came out of the big man's office. We visited a few more contract sites and he also introduced me to my staff of laborers and semi-skilled help.

The laborers were local and I didn't know what to make of them. They were from the Yoruba tribe and I had not worked with them before. From what I saw I quickly decided to ask the Lagos head office to send me the three electricians that I had trained months ago. I trusted them; we worked well together. They knew what I wanted and I knew their limits. Furthermore, because I trusted them I felt comfortable giving them supervisory positions over the Yoruba tribesmen. It had been a trying morning and I was tired and fighting with my emotions. The jobs were demanding but I felt up to them. However, the living conditions were different and I did not feel as comfortable as I had hoped I might.

After our quick tour and the meeting with the boss, we had lunch at the Central Hotel. After lunch we went to meet the CFAO garage staff. Things started to look up. Thank God they were a lot like me. We were roughly the same age and had similar backgrounds. Three of the most outgoing quickly adopted me into their little 'clan.' The general manager of the shop was a Frenchman called Le Guilloux, the Texaco representative was Paul Bordry and there was another chap, Dupuis, who used the shop to manufacture ground nut shelling equipment. His little operation was a gold mine for CFAO. These three men introduced me to all the people who mattered in Kano. Red-blooded types, I also saw that they were very interested in Annie. She was one of the few good-looking white women in Kano. She knew that her good looks had not gone unnoticed and we laughed about calling her 'the belle of Kano'.

It didn't take long to go through the formal steps to take over the contract from Greenwood. We'd had only a short time working together but we had succeeded in forming a good relationship. I took him to the airport. "I'm happy to be leaving Kano," he said while flies romped on his shirt. The last thing I heard him say was, "Good luck," and I wondered if that was a formality or he knew something about the place that he had not shared. Time would tell. I was on my own.

I left Annie to look after the house while I was working. We had a big contract located between the Housa city and the new international airport outside Kano. It was a large orthopedic hospital financed by NATO. Why NATO? The answer was strategic: the West was fighting the Cold War and it was spilling into the Middle East. Military planners concluded that if war broke out in the Middle East there would be huge casualties. They needed a site away from the conflict in a country they controlled. Kano's new international airport had been built to handle large military aircraft. To no ones surprise, the importance of the hospital and the airport served to drive home the fact that even in remote parts of Africa, the battle between the West and the Soviet Union was serious business.

Maybe it sounds flippant, but I was simply too busy organizing my life with Annie to even stop and think about another war. I had my own life, we were living well but in a developing country where there were enough daily challenges to keep our thoughts focused on getting through each day instead of wasting time thinking about problems that might blow up in another part of the world. I worked hard making a name for myself at work and becoming acquainted with as many people as possible so that we could enjoy a pleasant social life.

The idea of creating my own company was still very much in my thoughts but I didn't let it get too far. Every day I learned something new and this told me that I still had a lot to learn before I was capable of running my own show. From casual comments, chance encounters, I learned that my professional reputation was good and that I was respected for being trustworthy and competent.

Stepping out into local society, Annie and I joined the Kano club and the golf club. To be admitted you had to be sponsored by two members in good standing and you had to be a white European.

Rene Dassac (in collaboration with Patrick K. Robbins)

Segregation and racial distinction was an accepted part of life in Nigeria at that time. The color line was so carefully drawn that it excluded Lebanese and Syrians. Because they were not classified as Europeans the Arabs built their own club. Many of our club members were wealthy business expatriates with interesting backgrounds. One chap, for whom I did some work later on, had made a unique contribution to the war effort. He bought the RAF a Spitfire and was awarded an OBE in gratitude for his largesse.

Officially, the war was over but unofficially in many ways, even more than ten years later, it was still being fought. I was working in an orthopedic hospital where the building contract had been awarded to an Italian company but the works surveyor was a Scotsman, ex Eight Army desert rat. He fought the Italians in Libya and he could not forget the war despite the fact we were living in the post-war era. He detested Italians without exception. There was a youngster in the Italian crew who had been too young to fight in the war. I happened to be friendly with both the Scot and the Italian lad. Without fail, every single day the Scot, Macintosh, sought out the lad and heaped abuse on him. He'd call him a 'wop' to his face and referred to him often as 'a fucking idiot.'

Macintosh was nasty. Whenever their paths crossed, the lad began shaking. I felt sorry for the kid. He was a good craftsman but he couldn't speak enough English to confront Mac and ask him why he was being singled out for his abuse. Mac shot off his mouth and Mosca just stared back. He knew he was being humiliated for no reason. Finally, I decided to get involved. "Mac, what's eating you?" He looked at me as if I were as dumb as a brick wall. "Listen." He put his hand on my shoulder as if to steady himself because his body was beginning to quiver with rage. "John, I can't help it. I still hate these bastards now as much as when I fought them in Libya. All I have to do is see one of those fucking wops. When I see one the hair on the back of my neck gets bristly and I feel my adrenalin pumping in." We were both warriors once, and I had a right to speak my mind and I didn't hesitate to share some of my personal feelings. "I'm no fan of Italians either, but this kid you're beating up on is too young to have had anything to do with the war. He wants to do a good job and you're making his life miserable." Mac looked at me as if I had revealed some kind of a deep truth.

He didn't continue the conversation but immediately after our chat he got off Mosca's back. Yes, he criticized the lad's work but I think Mac would have criticized the person who invented the circle if he'd been an Italian. Mosca's boss came to see me and thanked me for stepping in. "John, if you hadn't got involved, I think those two would have tangled. I've got enough problems on this site without two guys starting World War II again."

Shortly after we had put the Mac-Mosca crisis behind us, Mosca went down with a bad malaria attack. He was off work for a few days and when he came back he was nothing but skin and bones. I told Annie about the lad's condition. She had a wonderful feminine solution that worked. "What he needs is a big plate of spaghetti with lots of mincemeat and tomato sauce. A bowl a day for two weeks and he'll get back to normal." The club served spaghetti. When we knew it was on the menu we invited Mosca and made sure he was served huge portions in a large bowl. Sure enough, in a couple of weeks he returned to his normal weight. The lad never forgot us. Without being heroes, what we did was just a small insignificant step to help heal deep wounds the war left on so many of our community.

Fate began working in my favor. At the club I met the man who was to become my best friend. Later he helped me start my own company. He was the son of a rich Swiss trader who retired and left his business to his son born in Africa of a Fulani woman. He had been given a European name, Philip Gaydoux. He enjoyed all the benefits of having a wealthy Swiss father including his father's nationality and the chance to be educated in Switzerland. When I met him he was still a bachelor with a formidable appetite for the opposite sex. In those days the air hostesses often had a rest layover in Kano.

There was only one decent hotel in town and the Kano club had a nice swimming pool. Need I belabor the obvious? The club's pool was a magnet for every bachelor. With the thermometer stuck at 40C the hostesses could hardly refuse an invitation. Sometimes passion led to romance and even marriage. Some of the expats wound up marrying their hostess girl friends. In fact, I knew one Frenchman who met a South African hostess and they got married and she became a French citizen.

Rene Dassac (in collaboration with Patrick K. Robbins)

At the bar and at the snooker table I met many business people. Once they learned about my background they encouraged me to start my own electro mechanical company. More than once I heard the same refrain: "The North is expanding rapidly and a man with you skills doesn't have any competition." What they said was true but I knew I was not yet ready to strike out on my own. I kept reminding myself that I still had a lot to learn. My current position was like being in school because I could watch people around me make mistakes and learn from them. Their mistakes became my lessons and I learned a lot. Even Annie pushed me to start my own company but I resisted the temptation and held steadfastly to the course I had charted for myself. In the end, I was right not to jump too soon.

At the peak of the dry season, which sometimes lasted seven months, the country was covered with dust blown down from the Sahara desert. My French friend Dupuys, some other hunters and I, would get up very early in the morning on the weekends and go out to a lake, Ringim, which was more of a swamp than a real lake. But there was enough water to attract all the migrating ducks that flew between Nigeria and Europe. There were hundreds, even thousands, of ducks of all sizes, shapes and colors. It was a hunter's dream. Maybe our brains became unsettled because, looking back, we took absolutely stupid risks to get a good shot.

One morning Dupuys and I crept slowly through the water to get to a flock of ducks that appeared to be sunning themselves just out of our gun's range. We were oblivious to the leeches, snakes and ticks in and around the lake. In due course, Nature got back at me. That morning a leech attacked me by gnawing a hole through my heavy cotton trouser legs. I managed to get him out in one piece but the wound had to be treated by a local doctor because it created a bad ulcer. Minor injuries aside, the risks we took were worth the effort because after every trip we came home with at least a dozen ducks. They were delicious.

*****

It had taken time but I was finally beginning to admit that I liked Kano. Yes, it was hot and dusty, yes we were living in an outpost with all the usual difficulties, but our friends were great and the work was interesting. The hospital contract still had another three months to go and when that was finished either I would stay on in Kano with another contract or I would be shipped somewhere else until my home leave came up. In the meantime, as far as I could see there were no new contracts on the horizon.

The prospect of being shipped to another site was eight months away and I realized that if I was going to stay in Kano I had to find another contract. I began looking around for work. That process was a good test to see if I was capable of starting my own company and drumming up new work. Up until now, someone else was responsible for bringing in new business. My job was to complete the contracts developed by the business managers. Now I was put to the test.

I thought it would take me a long time to secure a good contract but I was surprised to see that the first one came easier than I expected. Leads started to develop once the word was out that I was looking for new work. Within three weeks the manager of the local Total Oil Company contacted me. He wanted a price for installing all the electrical wiring in a distribution park they were building not far from our home. I got the drawings from Total and worked out a price. Some of the components were not available in Kano so this meant that I couldn't determine the cost for those particular items. I called Charles Guest and told that I would send him the drawings. "You can complete my cost build-up and pricing and at the same time I'd appreciate your reaction to this proposal. It's my first time." He was supportive but he told me that he would develop the pricing himself and then send it directly to Total. I could understand his logic.

The company had a business development process and a pricing model. I was starting from scratch and it was too big a job to entrust to me. In reality, I thought I knew what I was doing but I also was honest enough to tell myself that I was taking a big risk. Quite often, improper costing led to ruinous results because once the customer accepted the quotation, there was no getting out of it. Charles offered to take some time with me on my next visit to Lagos to show me how to build up a proper cost proposal. I accepted his answer at face value but now my interest was whetted and I became ingenious in finding ways to get books that taught the A to Z of the electrical contracting business.

In the meantime I continued working hard and playing hard. Every Saturday night Annie and I went to the Kano Club for dinner and to enjoy the pleasures of a typical British dance floor. I had to teach Annie the English way of dancing including, the slow waltz, the slow and quick step, and others. Unlike today when you can show up just about anywhere dressed any way you want to, on Saturday night both men and women had to be properly dressed. Ladies wore evening dress and the gentlemen were required to wear a necktie. Keep in mind that it was sweltering in the club and on the dance floor it was even hotter. There was no air-conditioning. Ceiling fans turned slowly, shuttling the heat from one side of the club to the other. Cold beer and a commitment to decorum kept us 'cool'.

We had great fun. British colonial rules were strictly applied because we had to set a good example for the Nigerians to copy. This meant no swearing, the exercise of proper manners, and the men's collar buttons closed at all times. Dancing in the club ended at midnight with "God Save The Queen." That was the formal part of the evening. By then the party was just beginning; nobody wanted to stop. The informal evening began when the dancing moved outside around the pool. Stiff upper lip and decorum were tossed aside. Ties came off, collars were opened, and men began telling bawdy stories provoking gales of laughter. One half of the evening wasn't 'better' than the other. Each served its purpose and it was right not to mix the two. We had fun at both.

We were happy. During weekends I taught Annie how to drive using the company pickup. She learned fast and I managed to get her a driver's license with the help of just a little bit of 'dash', Nigerian slang for what is known today as baksheesh. Was I doing the right thing, was I ethical and honest when I bought her license? Our Puritanical stage didn't last long in Nigeria.

Corruption was endemic in Nigeria. It was present at every level of society, in every business and in all government departments. It was so widespread and commonplace that everyone thought it was normal. To explain how widespread, the only comparison I can make is with the Anglo-Saxon expression, "Thank you." We use that expression all the time and don't even think about it. We quickly learned that the Nigerians were corruptible all the time and didn't even think about the morality of taking and giving bribes. It was banal. "Thank you for that observation."

It took us no time to recognize the system and to learn to live with corruption. Relative to what happened after independence, corruption in the late 1950's was mostly limited to making minor payments in order to take the rough edges off getting something done, like getting a driver's license. Following all the steps in the rulebook meant a lot of time and frustration had to be invested for a nominal return. Easing the administrative wheels with a squirt of 'dash' made life easier for everyone. We didn't feel we were corrupting the system or the players. Dash was part of life. It was something expected from you; something you did because no one really lost any sleep about this time-honored practice without which the Nigerian economy at all levels would probably have ground to a halt.

Illness reminded us that we were mortal and living in Africa. Annie had a bad bout of malaria. Her fever rose quickly and then she began vomiting. I had seen malaria before but I'd never seen it attack someone I loved. I asked the doctor, a British surgeon, if it wouldn't be better for me to send her back home. "Wait on that decision," he advised. "We're going through some kind of an epidemic and even I'm suffering." He proscribed strong anti-malaria tablets for three days. "Keep her in bed and let her sweat it out." He was right. After three days she felt better but she'd lost weight. Shortly after her first bout with malaria she came down with another medical condition. Annie told me that she was pregnant. We were delighted.

The next three months were a whirlwind of activity. I managed to end all the contracts I was working on and we survived, just barely, a long round of farewell parties. When we left there were many well-wishers and we said, honestly, that I was going to do everything possible to get reassigned to Kano. The two-year tour that we completed had been a good experience for us. We grew as individuals and as a couple. Accepting hardships, we learned to work around numerous large and small difficulties. Each time our wills were put to the test we met the challenge.

Before we left Lagos Mr. Guest confirmed that Nigelec wanted me to contract for another eighteen-month tour when we came back from our four-month leave of absence. We were delighted. This meant that

Rene Dassac (in collaboration with Patrick K. Robbins)

we could look to the future with confidence and serenity. Life was good, very good. We had one tour in Africa behind us as a couple. Through good times and tough times, we managed not only to stay together but we also knew our relationship was growing and maturing. Annie was carrying my child and I was over the moon. And, after a period of home leave that we definitely needed, we knew that we were going back to a good life back in Africa. We were grateful and we were excited.

*****

We stayed in Paris for a few days to see all our old friends. It was good to be back in France. Grudgingly we had to accept that we had been away for a couple of years and life in Paris had managed to get on without us. At first, we acted like tourists in the city we both loved and knew. There were many old sights and sounds we 'saw' almost as if we were seeing them for the first time. Once we overcame those first feelings of awe, we quickly succumbed to the excitement about being back. Walking down noisy streets smelling fresh bread, wandering through street markets where female vendors wore blouses and jackets, splashing through fresh rain on cobblestones instead of wading through red mud, we were electric with joy at being back in France.

Cities have important monuments but what really counts, what makes life tick, is friends. Georges Leclerc and his wife Christiane, two wonderful people who had been such a great help to me when I started work in France, were first on our list to meet. They were so glad to see that we had succeeded. All of us started talking at once and, I am not sure we made sense. If someone had been trying to listen in on our conversations I'm sure he'd have concluded we were slightly crazy. We went out to dinner together, they were our guests, and we filled the restaurant with happy babble. Even Arthur was still there. We had quite a few good laughs remembering all the good times we had shared together. We were on a high.

While Annie shopped I went to see my old boss. He greeted me like a long lost friend and he gave me a lot of his time. I told him about the opportunities I saw in Africa but I realized he did not share my enthusiasm. "Rene," he said, "I respect what you have achieved and I appreciate the importance of the information you are sharing with me but, honestly, I can't bring myself to try to expand our business into Africa. We can't handle a foreign operation." He was honest and I realized that in life sometimes you have to meet men who look into their souls and tell you what they see in order to understand how rare and how good honest friendship is to savor and hold, to cherish and nurture. Not all friends, certainly not all men who were your former boss, have the guts to tell you what really counts: to tell you the truth.

Annie and I were two whirlwinds sweeping our way through Paris. I caught up with old friends and business connections. She, the other wind, streaked through downtown Paris getting lost in shops for hours because she was busily planning for our new family. One night she said we had to go see my sisters and I knew she was right. Sooner or later, you have to turn off one tap that's pouring out a lot of happiness and open the flow of another that's going to pour out the same but into another bucket. I knew she was right.

Champagne, a region that we considered as part of the soul of France, called us back to Epernay. We took the train from Gare de l'Est. Judging from what I saw from the train window, France was doing well. The road that ran parallel to the train track for most of the trip was in good shape. Gently rolling fields were full of grain and the countryside, often fought over, was lush in peacetime.

We wanted to buy a car but this was still a period in which buying a car wasn't as easy as it is today. Then roads were not crowded with lots of automobiles. In fact, owning a car was seen as a form of social and economic status. We weren't interested in status. We needed wheels but not at any price. Our goal was to put down a reasonable amount of money for a car, a vehicle that we thought of as nothing more than a pile of steel on wheels that someday would fall apart. Living in Africa had helped us become very pragmatic!

When we got to Epernay I began poking around in the various small garages and I finally I bought a used Citroen 15. Before I parted with our cash I climbed over and under the car. When I came out from looking at its undercarriage I said, 'she's in good nick.' The owner wanted more money than the car was worth and I haggled with him. We could have been in Africa for all I cared. In the end he came down and sold his car for a price we both felt was fair. Years in Africa had sharpened my bargaining skills.

We spent a week in Epernay. To appreciate that week you have to put our visit into context. This was the mid-1950's and for many Frenchmen and women their most exciting adventure was to go to another town, perhaps only a hundred kilometers away, and then tell their friends and family about their 'major' excursion. Then we arrived on the scene. We were fresh from Africa, charging back into the lives of our family and their friends as some kind of outer space aliens who had just negated the Flat Earth theory. Years before we chose to reject their concept of civilization and live below the Equator in a strange country, among blacks and foreigners, and be happy. In their eyes we were visiting family, returning heroes, and, I guess they probably thought, sort of weird. No one, at least among their friends in Epernay, had ever done anything so outrageous and so exciting. To them we were buccaneers, explorers, exotic tribesman from the white race who had returned from the dark side of the world or even, perhaps, even the dark side of humanity. We were alive, we were happy, and we kept them laughing at us and with us.

I got a lot of questions about my British name. My sister's French friends simply could not grasp how one human being could have two names and two nationalities. At first it was difficult to explain because we had to accept each other's recent past. I didn't lecture and there was no formal discussion but they questioned me until, at times, I thought I was going to lose my mind. By discussing my name and my past we gradually allowed our minds go back to the awful period we were all trying to put behind us: the war. Perhaps we didn't recognize it as such; talking was part of a healing process that could not be stopped. The process had its own rhythm and took its own time. We were both actors and observers. Talking could be painful sometimes; there was no way to avoid realities we could not forget.

I couldn't tell my story without opening up and baring my soul. As I spoke, I tried to keep myself under control but I knew each time the topic came up that I would relive a part of my life that was painful. Some memories came back to me in the middle of the night and I had to fight to get back to sleep again. France was at peace and I tried to put my war years into context, accept them for what they were, and move on. That was easy to say than to do. I knew those years would always be with me; there were thousands of memories waiting to surface. Even when I walked down a street and was thinking of nothing in particular, something would pry open doors to my soul that I wanted shut. In my soul I knew that I had changed my name because I was willing to die for what I believed. Years after the war, it was a hard story to tell but I told it anyway. I was a Brit, I had an English name, I fought for the crown, worked abroad as a Brit, loved coming back to France, felt proud to be a Frenchman in a France that was better than the France of 1940, and I was in love and a father to be. Eh alors, how much do corks cost this season?

My family loved having us visit. The last time we'd met my sisters saw their brother as a young man in great turmoil, someone they wanted to reach out to and touch and love and calm down, someone who was at war with himself. The Rene they saw on our first trip back from Africa was a different man, a happy man. I was certainly a strange buccaneer adventurer in their eyes but I had mellowed and I could feel they loved us. One night I heard someone say, I can't remember who, "How wonderful to see him so happy. He's civilized." It was a good week but the vacation clock was ticking and we needed to head south.

We needed to go to Spain. The purpose of our trip was part pleasure and part personal. There was a lot of Spain we wanted to visit. After all, we were tourists. But there was also a personal note. Annie wanted to visit her son who still lived with his father in Ceuta in Spanish Morocco, just opposite Gibraltar. With mixed emotions, sadness at saying goodbye to family, and genuine excitement about taking a motorcar trip down to Spain, we left my family in Epernay.

Traveling by road through a country that was in the throes of post war reconstruction is interesting and it taught us a lot. In general, the living standards were improving. In the rural areas there were more electrical and telephone cables than before we left, the roads were in much better shape. Judging from the appearance of the villages it was obvious the Marshall Plan was working. No, there was no doubt in our minds; life in France was definitely headed in the right direction.

*****

Rene Dassac (in collaboration with Patrick K. Robbins)

What we saw were improvements primarily confined to physical change. Western Europe was still trying to understand how to live together. In political terms, the Europe we saw still needed to grow up and learn to live with other nationalities. Our biggest problems almost always involved civil servants, mindless gnomes tucked into every layer of society. Anywhere there was a civil servant there was bureaucracy and often indecision. Petty bureaucracy often made our life difficult on that trip.

We were stopped when we tried to cross the border into Spain. Customs and Immigration officers could not quite grasp the idea of a French-English person driving a French registered car was someone whom they should allow into Spain. In their eyes, I was not normal. Seething, I shared their frustration because it was all I could do not to tell them they were a massive pain in my backside. The flunkies couldn't think in terms of shades. I was trying to explain gray and they could only see black-and-white. Fortunately, there was an intelligent Spanish immigration officer on duty. He saw his men were struggling and he came over. Within less than a minute he was able to put together the jigsaw puzzle pieces of our lives and wave us through. "I've heard of cases like yours," he explained to me, "but you are a first and my men simply can't grasp it. Welcome to Spain." I was grateful for his welcome because it was sincere but my fuse was sputtering. Annie even congratulated me at keeping my temper. I grunted a surly, "Thank you," and looked for a place to have a drink.

We spent our first night in Sigdes, a lovely little seaside town. The hotel was quite reasonable. In fact, it was a much better deal that what we could afford in either France or the U.K. The food was good and inexpensive and I finally was able to relax and drink a toast to the Spanish customs officer. We started laughing at what we would have done if he hadn't been there? How would we have crossed the border? With another sip we shrugged off our 'border difficulties' and agreed to relax and enjoy the rest of our trip. We didn't have to meet a time schedule and this meant we could drive at our own pace. This was important because Annie was in her fourth month, the Citroen's suspension was not very gentle for a pregnant woman, the Spanish road system was barely adequate, and I wanted to avoid the prospect of rushing Annie into a Spanish hospital.

Taulus

Spain was still under the tight control of Franco's dictatorship. Compared to what we had just seen in France, the Spain we visited was poor, very poor. It lagged far behind either the U.K. or France in terms of social and economic development. We drove the length of the country and we did not see even one tractor. Farmers were using horses and oxen to drag steel plows. The countryside was out of another age, maybe the nineteenth century. When I was a kid I saw the very same plows ... but they were on display in our village museum! Our car passing through the countryside caused quite a commotion: farmers stopped and gawked. Automobiles, especially a French car with French plates, were still a rarity.

*****

We got to Algeciras and checked into a hotel. Annie took the ferry to see her son in Ceuta. I stayed behind. She needed private time with Marco who was a teenager, perhaps fourteen years old. He and Annie managed to stay in touch by writing letters. The break-up with her ex-husband had been messy and he was not about to allow her visitation rights to her son. Instead of being a decent chap about it, he did everything possible to keep the two apart. What he underestimated was a mother's ingenuity.

With the help of some of her friends who still lived in Ceuta, Annie managed to let Marco know she was coming to see him. They met in a friend's house and spent the entire day talking and getting caught up. Marco had grown. He was now a handsome teenager. Despite the trauma of his parent's break-up, he was a nice lad and one of his best friends happened also to be the daughter of one of Annie's best friends. Because of them a confidential communications channel had remained open for years. It wasn't as if Annie could pick up the phone and talk to him whenever she wanted to but that relationship meant she was not completely cut-off from Marco.

A bit later, perhaps a couple of months or so, Annie's friends moved to Switzerland at a time when the Swiss were importing Spanish workers. Once they got settled they asked Marco's father if he could come to Switzerland and live with them. There was work for youngsters and more of a future for Marco than if he remained in

Ceuta. His father agreed. Once Marco was settled he found work and began a new life in Europe.

While Annie was in Ceuta I had a look around at the various places where, during the war, the Germans used to spy on the movement of ships through Gibraltar. Admiral Canaris was the chief of the German intelligence, the Abwehr. He stayed at the best hotel in Algeciras where he had a nice view over the port. It may not be true but it makes a good story. Someone wrote that Canaris sat on his balcony with his binoculars and spent hours watching allied ship movements! I also went to La Linea, a small town only a few hundred yards from Gibraltar airport.

It was in this Spanish port where the Italians had made a clandestine workshop that was hidden inside a wrecked half-beached cargo ship. Under cover of the crippled ship they were assembling midget submarines designed to stick mines on the hulls of British ships and also to mine the entrance to the harbor. It was an ingenious plot that never succeeded. By sheer chance, one day a British naval officer was scanning the Spanish side when his binoculars stopped at the hole that was made when the cargo was hit. Through it he saw movement and light. He reported this finding to the intelligence officer who ordered the wreck to be put under constant surveillance.

They waited patiently. Instead of removing cargo, they observed a suspicious steady stream of lorries that were off-loading crates onto the ship! That was strange. Without letting on to the outside world, the British uncovered an ingenious and potentially disastrous plot to be carried out by Italian frogmen who planned to attack the closed harbor by cutting through the steel protective net. The wreck was their staging area. British patience paid off. As soon as the midget subs were seen moving outside the hulk the alarm was raised. Destroyers patrolling the Strait responded immediately. Something went wrong on the Italian's side because the subs started to blow up as they approached the allied barrage net. To make sure that none of them survived, the patrolling destroyers began a terrific depth charge run. There were no survivors.

I stood and looked at the Rock remembering it in different times. Those years seemed both a long time ago and, oddly, they also seemed like only yesterday when we entered and left the harbor never knowing what was going to happen to us. We fought and lived from minute to minute, from day to day, taking horrible losses in the early days of the war when we were fighting alone. I shook my head to try and clear my thoughts but it didn't help. I wanted to visit the Rock but there was no direct crossing point. Politics got in the way of simplicity. To visit meant I'd have to take a ferry over to Tangier and then catch a British ferry back to Gibraltar. That was too much trouble so I decided that someday we'd visit the Rock when the politicians had sorted themselves out. I'd done my bit to preserve democracy in order to give the politicians the opportunity to talk a problem to death. Talking was better than shooting.

When Annie returned we left Algeciras by the west coastal road. We drove past places that brought back more wartime memories. Cape Saint Vincent! Seeing the Cape meant that as soon as we got past the Cape we were approaching the safety of the waters around Gibraltar. Driving may have been hard on my nerves but I couldn't give in to my feelings too much. The roads were awful. By the time we reached Grenada we were ready for a rest. We took time to sightsee in an amazing city that reflected five hundred years of Moorish occupation. Spanish summers are hot. When we got to Seville we thought we were back in Africa.

How were we to know? It was obvious that we had misjudged the weather because we had not counted on it being so hot. Annie was very big. The combination of the heat and the driving were taking its toll on her. Our plans had included returning to France via Portugal but she wasn't up to it. We spoke with a Spanish doctor who advised rest. "Once she's rested, drive back to France slowly and be sure to stop frequently so that your wife can lie down." We heeded his advice and left Seville under a scorching sun. When we got to Burgos we enjoyed the 'cooler' weather; it was hot but it was also twenty degrees Celsius less than Seville. From Burgos we headed to the French border and then up to my sister Genevieve who lived in Epernay. As soon as we got to my sister's Annie was confined to bed until she had no more uterine pains. By the time we were ready to get our return flight to Lagos she had recovered fully and she was in great shape for the long flight back to Africa.

*****

Rene Dassac (in collaboration with Patrick K. Robbins)

The African jinx struck again! During our absence work on the Nigelec flats was to have been completed. Naively, we believed the deadline would be met. After all, weren't the builders working for Nigelec and didn't Nigelec always get their jobs done on time? Disappointment isn't quite the proper word to describe how we felt. We were stuck and frustrated. The company apologized profusely. To their credit they had arranged for temporary housing in a suburb of Lagos that was 'unpleasant', to put it mildly. Awful was perhaps a better description. That suburb was noisy, dirty, and insecure.

Nigerians were known throughout Africa for being masters in the ancient craft of thievery. If you compared them to Renaissance artists, they were individuals who did their apprenticeship and studied under great names before they went out on their own. For example, one Sunday afternoon I was taking a nap. While I was asleep they stole my white shirt with gold cuff links. I had hung my shirt on the metal frame that held my mosquito net in place. The frame was at least eight feet from the bedroom window. Like all windows in Nigeria, there were heavy steel security bars to prevent intruders from crawling in. I hadn't counted on the thief's ingenuity: he took a long stick to ease my shirt off the frame and hauled it back through the window. I hated that house and I was very uneasy about leaving Annie alone while I was away at work.

We managed to find an English couple living in the same neighborhood and the two wives got along well so they went shopping together. Fortunately, we moved to the company's flat two months later. It was big and clean, new and comfortable. The block of flats we lived in was reserved for married couples. This meant that Annie spent her time with English wives who spoke no French. Her English improved so well that she found out that some of the words she heard me use were not appropriate at a lady's tea party. Settling in took a bit of time but soon we were well established and enjoying our new home.

Lagos was booming. It seemed like on every corner something was being built. Office blocks, apartment houses, petrol stations, warehouses, they sprouted like weeds in Lagos' headlong rush to modernize. Nigelec was getting a big share of the electrical contracts because we had earned a good reputation for getting our jobs done on time and within budget. Looking back on it, in that period when everything was possible and there was more business than contractors, even I have to admit that they were easy years. Business rolled in, we took our share, and in turn shared some of our business with two other British contractors.

Life in the apartment complex was good. We were all pretty much the same age, roughly from the same background, and some had children but many others were like us. Either they were waiting for their first-born or they were coping with the strains of parenthood. During the week the men worked hard and the women stayed busy with the babies and toddlers. The weekends were spent playing and partying. We were young and living for the moment. Who was worried about the future? None of us were and that was for sure. Life was so much fun that we thought our wonderful life style would last forever.

My neighbor Ken Briggs was a character. He and I were assigned to supervise the contract Nigelec had with the Dunlop tire factory. Ken and I got along well. Although he was married and apparently a devoted husband, he was a chronic skirt chaser. Often I covered for him to keep him from getting into trouble with his wife. His interests were eclectic. For a time he was keenly interested in female personnel from the aviation industry. Any new airhostess arriving in Lagos was fair game as far as he was concerned. I kept a watch on him but in the end, work got in my way. Another big job had been launched on the other side of Lagos and I was asked to supervise it in addition to the Dunlop job. It was demanding to try and be in two places at once but I did manage to work with Ken.

On weekends we used to go to the beach with his wife and Annie. When his wife became pregnant they were faced with the dilemma we all faced: to have the baby in Lagos or go back to the U.K? In the end they decided to have their baby in the U.K. Fortunately for them, he could accompany her because the end of her pregnancy coincided with his home leave. When we managed to think of something other than pregnant wives, what really interested us on the weekends was to go boating. But, neither of us had a boat so we had to wheedle invitations from boat owners to spend time on their boats. That tactic worked for a few months but it started to become a chore for us and probably a bore for the owners who must have started silently to dread our phone calls.

Without a boat we were limited to going to Victoria beach but that was not the most pleasant way to spend a day by the water. The beach was crowded with young Nigerians who were noisy and unpleasant. If they weren't bothering us they were trying to steal from us or hang around and beg until we gave them a few coins to go away.

No boat and bad beach life meant only one thing: we needed to build a boat but neither of us had a clue on how to build one. We got a drawing from a builder in the U.K. and started to build it in our garage and then take it to Tarkwa, a pretty beach that was only accessible by boat and better than Victoria with is strong rollers and obnoxious bathers.

Annie was huge. Delivery was imminent so I followed her doctor's instructions and took her to the Creek Hospital in Lagos. By anyone's standards, the Creek Hospital was a good medical facility. It was well equipped and run by English nurses and doctors. After a brief consultation the doctors informed us that they expected her to deliver during the night. It all sounded quite normal and routine but as the evening wore on it became obvious that Annie was having some difficulty because the baby had not turned.

Instead of presenting head first, the baby chose to arrive feet first. I couldn't spend the night and day at the hospital because we were in the middle of a big push and I was needed on the job. At about ten the following morning I was called to go to the hospital to see my son! Can you imagine? My firstborn was a boy! I was over the moon. When the news spread in our block of flats everyone decided to share my joy. The arrival of our son became the excuse for a huge 'congratulations' party.

I raced to the hospital not quite believing my luck. The hospital staff told me that I had to sign a paper stating that I recognized the baby to be mine. With this written acknowledgement my son would be given my name. Remember, there was still a minor legal complication in our relationship. Annie's passport indicated her name was that of her previous husband from whom she was not divorced. He was Italian and, according to Italian law, divorce was still illegal. Technically, she was still married to him and therefore it was important for me to make sure that the baby was given my name as it appeared on my British passport. I proudly wrote my son's name: Philip John Powell. That was half of the nationality issue resolved. The other half was quite easy because the French consul in Lagos was a friend.

During the war he had been the chief of naval intelligence for the Free French Navy and he knew his way through the administrative thicket. He advised me to register little Philip also a French citizen. I went through the routine of filling out more forms, getting official stamps and signatures, and …. Voila! We had a new little Frenchman. I was both a happy 'daddy' and a very proud 'papa.' Philip's arrival began the process of new babies invading our apartment block. Shortly after Philip arrived Ken and his wife went on leave. While they were away they became parents of a baby girl: Julie. In theory, the two babies would have each other as playmates.

There was so much work that I really didn't have time to stop and enjoy my new son. Wiring the tire factory was a difficult project that took a lot of time. Time wasn't a commodity in great abundance. Because I was involved with two projects I turned into a long distance runner, loping between sites. We'd solve a problem on one side of this huge project and then I would be called to go to the other side of town and give the boys a hand. I kept fit racing back and forth. My legs had to be in good shape for midnight patrols with my new son. At night while his exhausted mother slept, young master Philip and I had little walks while I fed and burped him.

He was a good sleeper. This meant that I was only up once a night to walk with him after he downed his night ration. This was my first time at being a father and I like to think that he and I developed a pretty efficient system to get him back to sleep. As soon as he had fed I'd prop his head on my shoulder and pat his back waiting for a couple of good burps. We'd pace the floor and I'd whisper navy songs into his little ears. It worked every time. He'd let rip with a couple of good sour burps, I'd continue my sea chants, and soon he'd drop off into a sound sleep.

Maybe I didn't get as much sleep as I should have but what I lost in sleep I gained in time with my son. Through him and because of him,

Rene Dassac (in collaboration with Patrick K. Robbins)

I relived part of my infancy. During our nighttime 'strolls' I grew closer to him. Of course, he couldn't understand a word I was saying but I talked anyway. A wonderful bond was growing between the two of us, a bond that has lasted until today. Starting at an early age I realized that I couldn't get angry with him. As a father I was becoming a softie and I never really changed throughout our entire relationship. Maybe I was over compensating for what I had lacked in my childhood but I wasn't fussed about how I felt. He was my son and I loved him and was proud of him.

Our tours had been cut from twenty-four months to eighteen. When Ken Briggs came back with his wife and their baby daughter we got busy again on our boat-building project. Instead of working together on one boat we decided to each build a boat so that we had a backup in case something went wrong with one of the boats. A friendly competition grew between us to see who could get his boat finished first. There was no winner: both boats were completed about the same time. We worked every weekend. Even our wives were pressed into service. Once the planking was on they helped with the sanding and painting. Each boat was fitted with a 45 HP outboard. He chose a Johnson and I chose a Mercury outboard. The boats looked great but would they float?

We launched them, made some trial runs, hauled them out of the water and made adjustments to the keels to keep them horizontal at full speed. If we had to say so ourselves, they were smart looking boats and we were proud of our efforts. Ken used his boat mainly to practice water skiing. I was not that interested in water sports. Our boat was a comfortable transport to get us out into the lagoon where we often found quiet beaches for our picnics. I made a removable cabin that gave us the opportunity to have lunch and take a siesta in the shade. The Nigerian sun was very hot. Philip's skin was still too tender to be exposed to it. We had lots of fun.

We invited Charles Guest to join us one day for a run on the lagoon. I opened the Mercury full throttle and we raced across the surface, carefree and happy. Charles, seated in front of me, was acting as lookout. All of a sudden I heard him yell, "Look out. There's a big plank ahead." I swerved sharply to the right and slowed down. The 'big plank' was a huge crocodile that had been sunning himself.

When we got a little too close for his comfort he lowered his head and dove out of sight. Knowing that big fellow had friends, family and neighbors, we were careful not to give into our desire to take a swim off the side of the boat. As far as he was concerned, Charles and I were food.

****

Much sooner than we expected, our tour ended. We began preparing for home leave. Following a well-established custom, we sold all of our property except for some personal effects that we wanted to keep. There were plenty of buyers for our refrigerator, air-conditioners and car.

Before leaving I ordered a Ford Chambord to be delivered duty free for our arrival at the airport in Paris. It was a beauty: black with ivory trim, shiny and very luxurious. And, you know something? We earned that car the hard way. We took risks and went to a part of the world most of our friends and family in France couldn't even spell. For them, what we were doing in Africa was completely unthinkable. In return for taking those risks we were paid well. With the money we made we also earned the right to be good to ourselves when we had the opportunity.

When we got back to France we didn't act like wealthy 'colons' returning from their colonial paradise but when friends complimented us we felt good about 'showing off' just a little. Deep inside, I was proud to be able to show my relatives and friends that I had succeeded in creating my place in the world. When the sun shines it shines on all of us. On that trip home we absolutely glowed.

I saw my old boss and office friends. They spilled out of their offices to greet me and went outside to admire our new car. They were happy to see me and, I suspect, just a bit envious of my material well-being. Some of the girls I had gone out with before I met Annie were still there and they were still single. From the way they were acting, I was still a hit with them. Unlike other home leaves, this time we spent most of it with my family in France. We visited them in Paris, Epernay, Lyon, Clamecy and even a short trip south to show Philip what France really looked like. He had gotten to an age where he tried to copy everything that I did and his antics gave me a lot of laughs.

I needed something to take my mind off Africa. Before I left my boss, Charles Guest, pulled me aside and advised me to have a good rest. "I think the situation is going to change in Nigeria after they gain their independence." His face was grave. "What do you mean," I asked? "It's hard to put words to ideas that have been bothering me for many months. It's more a feeling, something telling me that life is going to be a lot more difficult for us once the crown hands over to the locals." At the best of times life was not really that easy. After a few months you learned to live with daily irritants, with the fact that nothing ever really worked properly, and that no matter where you turned someone had found a new way to hit you up for dash. I took his advice to heart and had a good rest in France.

CHAPTER NINE:
A DIFFERENT NIGERIA

Independence was scheduled for 1 October 1960. There was feverish excitement among the Nigerians. When I talked to them I had the impression that, for many, it seemed as if they were watching a great stage on which a huge curtain was soon going to be lifted. On the one side was the past: Nigeria under colonial rule. Everything that was bad, everything that they didn't like was on the colonial side of the stage. But, when the curtain was lifted to show the future, there would be a fantasy in the new Nigeria after 1 October 1960. All the wrongs many Nigerians felt they had suffered under British rule would be righted and everything in the country would work famously.

I had my doubts about a new order unfolding when Nigeria was left to Nigerians. Was my skepticism beginning to show? Had I been in West Africa too long? I didn't share their enthusiasm but I began to appreciate Charles Guest's apprehension about the kind of life we were likely to lead in Nigeria in the future.

Nigelec had a huge order book. I was given several sites: the High Court of Justice, The Western House - the first 24 floor building in Lagos and a block of three floor flats for government representatives to stay in when they came to attend sessions in the House of Parliament in Lagos. There was also another big program to install street lighting for the entire city of Lagos. The lighting project was so important for the nation that Nigelec ordered all staff to contribute their spare time to the lighting project in addition to the other projects to which they were normally assigned. "Between now and 1 October 1960, you are authorized to work whatever hours are necessary to enable us to fulfill our commitments." There was no question about using our leisure time. We had jobs to do and they would be done.

Rene Dassac (in collaboration with Patrick K. Robbins)

Today, over forty years later, I cannot understand how so many young Frenchmen complain about their thirty-five hour workweek.

Each week consists of one hundred and sixty eight hours. During that period in the run-up to independence I often worked over one hundred hours a week and I didn't complain. As I write these lines I have to remind myself that I was born in 1922. Maybe my generation was made of stronger stuff than the young men and women of today. Is this generation weaker and more fragile than we were? I am not sure I have an answer to that question but it strikes me that one of the major differences, between the time when I worked and now, concerns how the employee viewed/views his job.

In my time we lived our work and looked at working as a lot of fun. Sure, it was hard and we put in long hours in less than perfect surroundings, but we had fun. Am I correct in observing that today many employees look at work as a form of punishment to be endured until they can retire? If my observation is correct, their boring life is a far cry from what we enjoyed.

Everyone in the company felt involved. Our commitment and involvement made living during that period exciting and fulfilling. We knew we were struggling to keep projects on schedule but we didn't complain about how hard life was for us. If you want the salary you have to be prepared to make sacrifices. The office staff brought us food and drinks and cheered us on. Despite the strain, we were genuinely happy. When the staff showed up with their food and drinks baskets we'd pause, tell stories, and laugh at some of the predicaments we had got into during this crazy period when there weren't enough hours in the day to do everything we needed to complete. It was a period in our lives when we were at war against the clock. Pushing ourselves to the limit brought out the worst and best in us. In spite of the difficulty, we managed some genuine laughter.

One incident was particularly comical. We had to install a very big transformer: 11KV to 300V. Of course it was not going to be installed in a part of the building where we had easy access. It had to go into the basement of the Western House, the famous 24 floor building. There was no loading ramp, no easy way to slide the transformer into place. Instead of being able to use mechanical lifting devices we had nothing to rely on except our own raw muscle power and determination: No matter how difficult, we were going to install the transformer.

I called together all my electricians and their mates who were in the same building and explained to them what we had to accomplish. No one was leaping with joy. It must have been close to 50C and the humidity was 100%. It hurt to breathe, there was no fresh air and the place already stank of mildew. We began pushing and pulling and I began to curse and cajole my team. Two thousand years earlier we could have passed for slaves working on one of the Pharaoh's tombs. Necessity is the mother of invention; I found verbal resources that I had almost forgotten. The best of the 'Royal Navy below decks' vocabulary came out with accuracy and ease. We grunted and groaned. Cokes and beer sweat streamed out of our bodies. It looked like we had sprung leaks. Our clear body fluids were draining onto the floor and into each other.

One bloke said he was straining so hard that, "I'm going to vomit my guts." Slowly, ever so slowly, the beast scraped forward. We had only a few centimeters to go before it was properly positioned. I yelled, "Heave." The muscles of twenty men tautened for one final effort. Suddenly, one of the big blokes cut a fart, a long lazy full-bodied mellow fart that began with a low roar before rising to a high pitched squeak. It was dark, we were all bent over, and I yelled, "Who made this fucking stink?" The headman continued pushing but replied in his Pidgin English, "I've never heard this stink before." His reply was so spontaneous, so utterly incongruous, that I burst out laughing and so did everyone else. Even today when I think about that awful time in the bowels of Lagos' first skyscraper, I cannot help but laugh at that crazy incident and my headman's wonderful reply.

One had to have a good sense of humor to work with Nigerians. Sometimes they could drive you mad but at other times they could easily laugh at themselves with you. The Hausa in the North had a good sense of humor. They gave nicknames to all white men. Mine was "Feetela" which means wire in Hausa; I got it because I was so thin. I could live with that but the CFAO manager's was a bit more graphic. The Hausa called him 'turkey' because he had a lump of red skin hanging off his chin. Keep in mind that none of the names were malicious. Whatever name they gave was either related to your work or to your apparent relationship to an animal or a bird.

Tension mounted the closer we came to 1 October. Troublemakers began circulating rumors; increasingly the rumors began to have racial overtones. The most frequently heard rumor promised the Nigerians a better way of life at the white man's expense. In short, all the Europeans would be thrown out of the country and the Nigerians would take over their houses. We didn't need this kind of tension but we didn't let it slow us down. Too much had to be done, we were running out of time, and we couldn't stop and let their post Independence Day dreams worry us. Nevertheless, the fact that rumors could start and circulate merely underscored the latent resentment of the blacks toward the whites.

No matter how much we could justify our contributions to their country, we were still seen as white masters representing a colonial past. Fortunately, the army and the police were well trained and prepared for any eventuality. When they paraded down the Marina in full force there was no doubt in anyone's mind that Nigeria, for the time being, had a credible force to ensure law and order.

When 1 October 1960 arrived there was an outburst of great rejoicing and there were celebrations everywhere. Amazingly, there was very little drunkenness or civil disturbance. Nigerians let off steam and went back to their daily routines.

Or, so it seemed. Our lifestyle was relatively stable for about the first eighteen months after independence. The apprehension of the first few weeks gave way to the gradual realization that nothing much had changed. Business, for us, continued to boom. We got the electrical installation contract for the Nigerian navy barracks and this included the signal school and an asdic that was on the frigate which the Nigerians bought from Britain. We got this contract because we worked closely with Admiral Way who was in charge of the fledgling Nigerian Navy. He was an honorary member of the RNVR club to which many of us belonged. Because of my career in the navy I was given the task of making a system for the students to read and send light signals. This was actually a copy of the system we had in Brest when I was a boy and very similar to the type used in Portsmouth by the Royal Navy.

Admiral Way, although a Nigerian citizen, was actually a native of Sierra Leone. During the war he had been a maritime engineer in Free Town. He enjoyed the company of other men who had spent part of their lives at sea. His 'war story telling sessions' were usually accompanied by some very serious drinking sessions. After several particularly wet sessions in the RNVR club Charles Guest and I had to help him home. His size wasn't a problem although he was big. His problem was his wife. She was a tough old girl who scared the hell out of us. We knew that if she heard him coming to bed drunk she'd raise the roof. We became close friends because we succeeded in getting him home and to bed without arousing her ire. As far as he was concerned, we were very reliable suppliers. Little debts sometimes have big payoffs!

Every year at the anniversary of the battle of Trafalgar the Royal Navy veterans had a big celebration and dinner at the airport hotel. The High Commissioner was invited to attend and serve as the chairman for the evening's events. He sat at the top end of the table that was formed in the shape of a U so that every dinner guest could see him. The seating format and the entire evening were conducted according to Royal Navy tradition. Dress code was strict: evening dress and miniature medals were obligatory.

I wore five medal ribbons and Charles Guest wore his. Between the two of us we had the most medals after the High Commissioner. We lined up in the entrance hall waiting for his arrival. I was fourth in line. He shook my hand. As I whispered my name he stepped back. A feint smile broke across his face. "You should have been a sea lawyer." I smiled and appreciated his uncanny ability to remember my petition to allow Anna into the country many years earlier.

He worked his way down the line of men, pausing every now and then to say something to many of them. He took his place at the head of the table. We followed to our assigned seats, remaining standing until he was seated. Two stewards went down the sides of the table serving each guest from large decanters of dark red port. Following tradition we waited for him to lift his glass and say, "Gentlemen, to the Queen." He remained seated as he proposed his toast. Some might think this odd but the tradition of remaining seated for the

Rene Dassac (in collaboration with Patrick K. Robbins)

Royal Navy toast stems from the time when the king came onboard to thank Nelson's crew for their victory at Trafalgar.

Apparently the king was below decks and he rose to propose a toast. He had forgotten the deck to ceiling distance was lower than what he was accustomed to in a room in one of his palaces. His majesty rose...and he banged his head into the ceiling. Recognizing his error the king decreed that from then on, when at sea, guests would remain seated to toast the crown. Hundreds of years later we maintained tradition. Even our drinking was governed by tradition. We were not at liberty to drink when we wanted to. All eyes on the top of the table, we drank only when he drank. Fortunately, he was a good drinker! Some might think this ritual to be a bit stuffy but I was happy to see it was being maintained and proud to know that I had earned the right to be part of it.

Once we had completed our work at the naval barracks Charles Guest and I were invited by the Admiral to take part in the first sea trials of the pride of the Nigerian fleet. Their frigate was an old lady who had seen better days. But, putting aside her age, she responded well to all the rudder trials. Even the engine room behaved very well after a few minor adjustments. We spent a full day at sea and returned to berth at the naval base in Apapa.

It was nice to have been back to sea again. I had good memories of my life in the navy. Even when I included the hell of war, I concluded that those years spent at sea had been good years and I had no regrets concerning the choices I made. After all, if I had not invested the time then, I would not have been standing on the deck of a Nigerian frigate as their guest. Above decks the ship met Royal Navy standards but below decks the boys had a lot to learn especially when it came to sanitary conditions in the mess decks, and in fact, sanitary conditions in general. The conditions I saw would never have been allowed in the Royal Navy.

*****

One day I was called off the site where we were working and told to go to the head office because Charles Guest wanted to see me. I walked into his office and he said, "You're off to Victoria in the British Cameroon." I stared at him thunder struck because I had no inkling that the company was considering me for another assignment. I started to sputter and he replied, "Take Anna and Philip." Good! At least the family side was sorted out but what was I supposed to do up there? "We got a good contract in Bouea to do the electrical installation in a German built castle that is going to be turned into a museum."

I almost laughed at the prospect. First I fought the bastards and now I was going to wire them. He explained that all the wiring had to be done with pyrotenax cable. This was a special cable that was widely used in historical buildings in order to minimize the risk of fires. "All the equipment is already on site," he assured me. According to him the local government that was responsible for the castle would provide me with the drawings and installation instructions.

I raced home and broke the news. Anna took it well; just another challenge and another chance to see a part of Africa we didn't know. Packing for two adults was easy compared to packing for a baby. We managed to squeeze everything we thought we might need into two suitcases and headed for the airport.

The trip only took an hour but it was very turbulent. I forget what kind of plane we were flying but I remember that it was small: only twelve passengers. Philip was lashed into his carrycot that we tried to steady on our knees. The little aircraft bucked and dove, shimmied and rolled from side to side. While the wing tips were soaring and plunging the pilot was fighting to keep her steady. I kept looking at my watch. We'd been airborne for almost an hour and I knew that he was beginning to circle for his approach.

All of a sudden, the plane dropped out of the sky. It was as if we had been sitting on an invisible platform in the air when, with no forewarning, the hidden hand that had been shaking us got tired and pushed us off the platform. The plane dropped sharply; I was sure the pilot had lost control. "This is it," I thought, "This is what it's like to die in a plane crash." Just as quickly, but I thought it took him a lot longer, I heard the engines roar as he poured on the power. He lowered the nose and we made a 'firm' landing.

Getting off planes with small children takes time so we waited to allow the other passengers to disembark ahead of us. The pilot came to the cockpit door and stretched. As if anticipating my question he told us that we had hit an air hole. "I thought we were going to end up in the drink but I managed to hold onto to the stick and fight her back into a horizontal position." He apologized about the landing but I reminded him that any landing is a good landing if you walk away from it. He laughed in agreement.

In the airport Mr. Harper was waiting for us. He was as white as a sheet and managed to stammer a perfunctory greeting. "I was watching your approach when, all of a sudden, the plane just dropped out of the sky. I thought you were goners." Anna and I thought we'd come through the ordeal rather well but I caught a glimpse of my face in a mirror above the bar and knew that our trip merited a huge drink to steady our nerves and compose us after our brush with death.

The drink, or rather drinks, helped. Harper invited us to a quick lunch at the airport. Despite what we had just gone through, we were hungry. He and I talked about the project while Anna tended to Philip. He gave me the project plans with a pile of other documents and took us out to the car and driver they had laid on for us. We headed away from the coast up into the mountains to Bouea. The town was located high up in the mountains and was often cloud covered. Mt. Cameroon, an active volcano, was not too far away. At night we could hear the volcano rumbling and, when the wind changed, we got a whiff of sulfur. It actually erupted once while we were there but the lava fell on the opposite side of the mountain away from Bouea.

An Italian company managed a huge timber operation and this meant the town's economic life was dominated by only one company. The boss was a Neapolitan, hugely rich and charming. He and his wife became the only couple with whom we managed to establish a 'visitors' relationship: short-timers who are tolerated by the locals because we were novelties, new faces on the street. We stayed in the local rest house that was quite comfortable considering how far Bouea was from the rest of civilization. Anna spent much of her time visiting with the Neapolitan's wife while my time was totally taken up by work on the castle, known locally as 'the schloss.'

The Germans built it when the British Cameroon was a German colony. As one might expect, the 'schloss' was built to last. The entire structure had been built with granite stones; all the door and window hinges were made from steel that had been melted down from guns and artillery that was used during the war to colonize this remote African country. Access to the castle was at the end of a road. It was barred by a large steel gate that opened onto a big garden, a well-kept green lawn, and there were lots of roses and tropical plants. African squalor was on one side of the gate; the splendor of Imperial Germany was on the other side. The two sides stared at each other.

On the Imperial side, the road from the gate was divided. On the right it led up to the castle that was built on a small knoll, perhaps ten meters higher than the gate. On the left it wound down to the garden and back to the gate. The doors opening into the castle were made out of native timber.

To get to the main door you climbed six wide stone steps, each carefully carved from gleaming granite. The reception room was large and austere. There were two windows on either side of the main door into the reception. The walls, solid granite, were unadorned except that the lower part was covered with beautifully carved mahogany panels that were to cause me enormous problems because I had to install cabling and wall sockets without 'damaging' the wood. Opposite the main door there was an imposing granite fireplace. A large imperial eagle was carved into the panel above the mantle. If I stood quietly and let my mind play games, I'm sure I heard the walls speaking formal German.

There was nothing cozy or friendly about the room but at the same time there was nothing particularly hostile about it either. It was built to impress, to convey authority, to convey permanence, and to grant power on all those who called the 'schloss' their home. Large stairs led from either side of the room up to the living quarters on the first floor. I was impressed but I was also stressed. Somehow I was expected to bring the advantage of electricity into a building that had been built before electricity had come to this part of Africa. As usual, they hadn't given me very much time.

I searched deep in my brain to find a way to install my cables so that they were invisible because I was forbidden to make major modifications to the actual mahogany panels. In other words, I couldn't drill where I wanted to grouter cable tracks. My local labor force had never been confronted with this type of a challenge, and as a consequence, they were useless trying to find a solution. To begin with, I actually had to invest time to make them understand what I was trying to do. Then, because the work was so delicate I spent more time giving them close supervision than I spent installing cables and sockets. I've forgotten the details of how we got the job done but I managed to complete it without damaging anything.

Because time was limited I worked every Sunday. One Sunday, when I was alone in the 'schloss', something very strange happened. Late in the afternoon, as I was finishing a section, a man came in. I could tell from the way he walked, his dress and his bearing, that he was no ordinary European who just happened to wander in. "May I visit?" he asked politely. I explained that I had instructions not to allow any unauthorized person into the building while the renovation of the castle was in progress. He replied in his quiet firm voice, "I appreciate that there are rules and if my request were not unusual, I would not ask your permission." He continued before I could collect my thoughts. "You see, I am the last British resident of this building. I've made a brief business trip to Cameroon and I've come back here in the hopes that I could be allowed to visit the living quarters on the first floor." The request seemed reasonable enough.

Looking at him I concluded that he was not the kind of person who would sneak up behind me and beat me over the head. I am sure he sensed my misgivings and to reassure me, he continued. "A minor point of history, I am sure, but you might appreciate that I was the person who relieved the German resident after hostilities were terminated in 1918." He was gracious in a quiet manner and I agreed to his request. "Certainly, go ahead but I am leaving at four o'clock and locking the door. You'll have to be out by then." He bowed slightly and went upstairs and I went back to my work.

I was too absorbed with what I was doing to keep an eye on my watch. In fact, I'd forgotten about him. When I finally decided to quit at four o'clock I remembered that he had not come down. Or, if he had, he'd slipped out quietly without me noticing. I packed my toolbox and went upstairs to find him. He was crying in front of one of the bedroom windows. He must have been crying for a long time because his cheeks were still wet. I looked around. There was no one else; he had not heard me coming. It had been years since I'd seen a man cry and I felt uneasy. As gently as I could, I began speaking. "I am about to leave and I will have to close the castle." He turned to me, brushing at his cheeks. "It's here, in this room, that I lost my wife. Only three days after she arrived," he blurted.

I was horrified to be alone with him, wrapped up in the fury of his grief in this stark room with granite walls and two windows. "It's cursed. Did you know that the German governor who lived here before me lost his fiancée only a few days after she set foot in here?" I was speechless. "No woman has ever lived in this residence since it was built." He stared at me as if he had imparted a major truth, a warning perhaps not to meddle with forces greater than either of us would ever understand. Offering his hand he thanked me for letting him visit. "Good luck," he said as we shook hands. I heard his boots clunk down the stone stairs, slowly, as if marking a farewell to the last moments of the time he shared with the woman he loved.

When I got back to the rest house that evening I told Anna what happened. I think the hair on the back of my neck was standing up and it took me the better part of the evening for me to calm down. Anna never set foot inside the castle. I told her all about what it looked like but I was not going to tempt fate.

*****

When you stood on the hill the castle was built on you had an almost panoramic view of the valley below where a sea of banana trees stretched for miles. The Germans had built rail spurs and stone bridges to take the bananas to be processed and then shipped. The fruit industry was profitable but not as profitable as the timber industry. That had developed more recently but it lacked the infrastructure and organization that the Germans had built for their banana plantations. To get at the timber the forest operators carved roads out of dense bush and then loaded the logs onto trucks that were driven by Nigerians or Cameroonians. They drove like madmen.

Most of the drivers learned to drive the hard way: they were self-taught. If they were fortunate enough to survive their inevitable accidents they found employers who needed their 'skills'. The drivers didn't believe in road safety. Instead of easing a truck loaded with tons of mahogany down the mountainside, they took over the middle of the road and raced at full speed. Braking the truck with its gears was a skill very few either knew about or cared about. What was important to them was to get paid at the end of each run. It came as no surprise that there was a terrifying loss of drivers and trucks. The Neapolitan boss of the timber company told me, on average at least once a week, they lost one truck with its crew and load. Most accidents occurred at high speeds. When the logs moved they broke their restraints and crushed the men in the cabin to a pulp. The bends on the road down to Victoria all had gouges, scrapes, and even sometimes crumpled wrecks.

In one sense, the carnage on the road was a symptom of the gradual disintegration of social order and civil infrastructure in Nigeria. The overwhelming percentage of fatalities involved Nigerian drivers. They were plentiful, most had bought their licenses, and for them driving was a great big game of chance: they either lived or died. If they lived they got good money and they could spend it they way they wanted. If they died, they were dead which was what was going to happen anyway. So, why not drive logging trucks? The pay was good. Nigeria had become a land of 'if's': If more care had been spent by the Nigerian government training its drivers, if the market in illegal licenses had been stopped, if traffic codes had been enforced, the horrible cost in human life and materiel never have been incurred. Sadly, the situation hasn't improved because it is still dangerous to drive in towns like Lagos, even now in the 21st century.

I was beginning to realize that the path to realizing the potential greatness of Nigeria was obstructed by a logjam of "if's." Anywhere you looked it was easy to see that something good could happen in the country, "if only." If the roads were safer more goods could be moved at lower cost, if the standard of living improved there would be fewer poor and malnourished citizens, if tribalism were eradicated the nation would pull together and become a beacon of hope in Africa. If only the Nigerians were able to confront and rise above the "if only" in their lives.

When I finished wiring the castle Mr. Harper came over to inspect the job. He was pleased; the city authorities accepted the work. We left

Buea for Victoria and spent a few days in the local rest house where we met an interesting, but sad, English gentleman. According to the locals he belonged to a wealthy English aristocratic family who sent him to Victoria in order to get rid of him and his drinking problem. He pitched up in Victoria where he drank away his life.

Every week he received his allowance and every week he drank his way through it. His family paid for his rent and bar bills in the rest house. When sober he was interesting and polite. Obviously well educated, he could speak knowingly on many subjects. For him, Victoria was the end of the line. Abandoned by his family, his daily life was drinking until he destroyed himself. I don't know the causes for his illness but I was bitter at his family letting him go. Wouldn't a bit of compassion have brought him back from the narrow abyss in Africa on which his life was perched? I'll never know but when we left I think we had helped him because he seemed genuinely glad to have made our acquaintance.

Back in Lagos life was different and not necessarily all that better when compared to life in bush or in smaller towns. Lagos was hot and humid and very noisy. The pollution from all the diesel trucks and open cooking fires attacked your eyes and throat. It bothered us, the adults, because we knew what was causing us to feel so rotten but it didn't bother the children. If they 'hurt' that meant they were feeling normal; they had been born into pollution and had grown up with it. Certainly, it didn't stop them from playing hard all day.

Philip was now four and he played with Julie in our compound's garden. He switched from English to French and back again so naturally and that made us happy that he was learning both languages without having to study them. The garden surrounding our apartment complex became their playground. In the dry season it was dusty but in the rainy season it was a bewitching sea of mud puddles. At the end of the morning they were covered from the tops of their little heads down to their bare feet with brownish red mud, glorious squishy mud that seemed to cake the sides of the bathtub like a new light ochre porcelain layer.

While they were outside the day guards kept an eye out for snakes. It was not unusual for the guards to catch and kill them much to the delight of the children and the sheer horror of the parents. Most of the snakes were relatively harmless but some were poisonous. It's hard to be ambivalent about snakes and if there was any doubt we supported the guards who believed, with few exceptions, that the only good snake was a dead snake.

The night guards had a special challenge. When night fell pythons, big fat snakes with huge heads, began slithering through the bush,. I had heard stories about pythons in town but I dismissed them as nothing more serious than what a relaxed imagination could conjure up after a few too many beers. That fantasy served me well until one morning I crossed the night guard as he was going off duty.

He pointed to a brownish green mound at the base of a palm tree. At first I thought it was merely a pile of leaves left by a lazy gardener but when I approached the mound began twitching ever so faintly. It was a snake, a huge python, and quite dead. The night guard had surprised it, perhaps the snake had surprised him, and he killed it. I went to my truck and rummaged through my toolbox to find a tape measure. Eyeballing the snake was not enough for me to be fairly confident in telling a true 'big snake' story. I needed facts. He straddled the snake and lifted its mid section while I slid the measure under it and cinched it tight. We didn't measure it once, but three times in three different places. The guard was laughing and I felt a bit queasy. The snake's circumference was measured a 'mere' forty centimeters.

I didn't go back into the apartment and tell Anna. Some experiences are better not shared. It wasn't my secret that I wanted to keep from her. A long time earlier I had learned in Africa that sometimes it was better not to share with Anna everything that happened during my workday.

I told the guard to get rid of the snake and he obeyed willingly. The next morning he told me that he had cut the snake up into pieces and sold it in the market to the Africans for fresh meat. Perhaps he saw me shudder but it didn't stop him from reassuring me that he would stay awake because if he found one python there was bound to be another one. Perhaps the next one would be ever bigger he said breathlessly, almost overcome at the prospect of making even more money.

Taulus

*****

We were tired and fortunately we left on home leave soon after the snake incident. The trip out of Africa was something we looked forward to. Twice we took the French line from Pointe Noire in the French Congo to Marseille. We really enjoyed those trips. Once, when we boarded the SS Mermoz, the chief steward looked at my British passport and stopped reading when he saw that I was born in Tarascon. "You must speak French," he said and I replied, "of course." He called over our cabin steward, a Frenchman who spoke little English and who had complained about having an English family to look after. "Jean Marie, ne t'en fais pas, ton Anglais est de Tarascon," and everybody laughed. Because of that little exchange my story spread and nearly everyone in the crew knew my background.

One evening I was having a drink in the bar and I noticed the barman was staring at me. It didn't make me uneasy. As a matter of fact, I thought his face was familiar but I couldn't place him and I was too relaxed to want to try. He cleared his throat to get my attention. "I think I have seen you somewhere, but I cannot recall where it was." I shrugged. "I have always been in the French and English navies. We could have come across each other either in Toulon or in Portsmouth," I ventured. He laughed. "It was Portsmouth. It's where we had our Free French Petty Officer club, in the South Sea." His memory was better than mine because I couldn't remember his face but he was a link to another era. He rummaged around and showed me some pictures of his friends in the U.K. but I could not recognize anybody I knew. Anyway, we became very good friends much to Anna's dismay because almost every night he invited me for drinks. We whiled the time away into the early morning telling war stories.

In 1962, the board of directors decided to gradually discontinue the contracting business and close down. Guest and I expected this would happen. Management was not up to the task of running an operation in a country as demanding as Nigeria. Before the war the management group had limited experience as general merchandise traders. They really didn't know what they were doing running a contracting business in Africa. One symptom of their problems was obvious to anyone who looked closely at how the company was run. They recruited people who did not have sufficient electrical contracting experience. Furthermore, their staff was often left on their own far away from the head office. Stuck out in the bush somewhere, without any knowledge of invoicing, accounting, or even basic management, their 'forgotten' often succumbed to the corruption that was endemic in the country; they took off with the cash they were entrusted with.

Guest tendered his resignation and advised me to do the same. "Hand it in and come with me to London. I'm going to the head office of Rashly Phipps Electrical Contracting Company." He explained that he had already found a job before he left Nigelec. Moreover, he assured me that he had already intervened on my behalf. Phipss was prepared to hire me to take over a big job in Port Harcourt because their supervising engineer had resigned.

All these changes happened fairly fast. The prospect of a new job was both good news and bad news. The good news was obvious: I had a job but the bad news concerned Anna. Anna had gotten tired staying at home all day so she scouted around for a job. She was successful and had just begun working for USAID running their guesthouse. She was very well respected. They paid reasonably well. We were planning to bank her salary because some day we wanted to buy a house in France. I went to see the American in charge and explained the situation to him. He understood our concerns. We agreed that he would keep Anna's job but we had to find someone to fill-in for her while we were in London. With one less variable in the equation I tendered my resignation. Within a month we were off to London.

I did not know how long I would have to stay in London so I sent Anna and Philip to stay with my sister in Epernay. I stayed with Guest in his mother's house at Ipswich, about sixty miles from London. I spent a couple of weeks there with his mother. She was a sweet old lady who was well into her nineties. Her mind was sharp. One day she told me that I reminded her of her other son who had been killed by the Japanese in the Pacific. From the way she treated me I am sure that sometimes her mind must have slipped and she thought I was lad who died during the war. I took her shopping in the village and always bought her bunches of flowers and a few bottles of stout that she enjoyed drinking with me at 11 o'clock before lunch.

In the meantime I met my new directors who obviously had been thoroughly briefed about me. It only took only a few minutes and we found we were talking as if we had known each other for years. I signed my contract and went back to Lagos via Paris where I picked up Anna and Philip.

As fate would have it, Guest and I went our separate ways. I had looked forward to working with him again in Nigeria but Phipps sent him out to Hong Kong. Apparently he did quite well. He met a wealthy Chinese woman, had a successful career, and died in Hong Kong.

Back in Lagos Anna returned her position as head of the USAID rest house. Philip was happy to be back. We had a two bedroom flat in Apapa, the port town of Lagos. The house was well situated because it was not far from her job and the Phipps head office. For a while I was assigned to the office helping to cost the many contract tenders the company was involved with. I was also working on various other sites when necessary. It seemed they put me into jobs when they needed to make up time because they were often behind schedule. The company was busy and I was trusted. From the way work was coming from all over the country, I knew that we were not going to be in Lagos for too much longer. As much as it hurt me to have to do it, I advertised my boat and sold it very quickly.

Phipps was stretched to the limit. They operated throughout Nigeria, Ghana and Sierra Leone. I knew what havoc that kind of business could mean to a company and I hoped they wouldn't make the same mistake as Nigelec: as soon as they stretched too far they would lose control because they probably wouldn't have the right people in the right place. Within a few months my fears were confirmed: The chap in charge of Sierra Leone disappeared with 30,000£ of the company's money.

That huge loss was a wake-up call for the company. They took drastic action and began closing down in areas where they knew there was no control. It was about this time that I was sent to Kaduna to replace a chap who decided to quit. By the time I got to Kaduna, he had already left. Without him there it made sorting out the job more difficult. Fortunately, the Nigerian headman knew a lot about the job. He showed me the list of jobs that had been completed for which we had never been paid. This headman was worth his weight in gold.

He and I went to inspect the primary job we had with the university to make sure everything was under control and also to be sure the job was progressing correctly. I left him to supervise the job. At first I didn't think he understood that I really meant what I said: he was responsible for supervising the job and making sure it was completed in line with our contract. I looked him straight in the face and told him that he had my full support. What else could I do to encourage him to step into a position of genuine responsibility? It didn't take him long to show me that I had made a good choice. Watching him on the job was a real pleasure. It was obvious from his attitude and the way he worked that he was happy to have real authority and my trust. I left him to get on with the job but I visited the site every day.

My worst headaches were the paperwork. The office work was in a mess and I had to sort it out in order to identify all those accounts that had been completed but never billed. I knew that administration and paper shuffling wasn't my strength but I was smart enough to recognize that weakness and admit because I didn't like doing something that was no excuse for not doing whatever I found unpleasant. I operated like that when I was in the navy and with this new assignment there was no reason for me to change my ways. I was on my own; Phipps gave me responsibility and authority. Therefore, it was up to me to get the job done quickly and correctly. I didn't know why we hadn't been paid so I proceeded cautiously using every bit of diplomacy and tact that I could muster. At all costs, I needed to avoid head-on confrontations but I also needed to get to the bottom of the mess left by my predecessor.

One of the first chaps I met looked at me and started smiling. "We were waiting to get invoiced." After a few customer calls I realized most outstanding accounts were pretty easy to collect and I developed a collection strategy. I began with a feeble excuse to explain why we hadn't billed the account. I briefly referred to my predecessor, explaining that he left in a hurry for 'family reasons,' and then I steered the conversation onto the main topic: we wanted to get paid for services rendered.

Not too many want to pry into other people's lives. That old chestnut, 'family reasons,' was nice and convenient. My primary goal was to walk out with a check and let the customer know we wanted to bid on any other contracts they might be preparing. Fortunately, I didn't have to visit all the outstanding accounts. I think word began to spread that I was the 'new man in town' and that I was determined to collect monies owed the company. We wrote many clients. Very soon all outstanding invoices were billed and payments started rolling in.

Our bank balance was improving week after week. One day, totally out of the blue, I got a phone call from the London Office telling me to go to Kano the next day to fetch the chairman and the contract manager. That was a strange request. Admittedly, I hadn't been with the company long enough to have a good feel for how management worked, but normally they were pretty good about giving us advance notice any time executives went on field trips. Why hadn't there been any forewarning about this trip? I recognized the voice on the other end, Ron English, so I asked him, "What's up?" There was a pause and he whispered, "They'll tell you to close down all the operations." He hung up before I could ask any more questions. He was obviously running scared. There was no doubt in my mind from the way he acted: the purpose of their visit was serious and very hush-hush. The way I saw the situation, the two top executives wouldn't come out to the field on short notice just for the sheer novelty of taking a trip to Kaduna, another backwater in West Africa.

The next day I picked up the two directors at the airport. On the trip back to Kaduna they were pleasant but non-committal. They asked the usual questions, the eternal: "How are things going", as if I could answer that one in a few short sentences. I told them that I was spending most of my time collecting for completed jobs. "Our accounts receivable ledger has been decreased by ten trading days," I said proudly because I was expecting them to want to hear more. For the next few miles they asked a few lame questions to try and keep up their end of the conversation but their heart was in it. That was strange. Why didn't these two men want to know more about the company's improving financial situation? I couldn't put my finger on it but something else was bothering them; they hadn't come clean with me.

We thundered down the dusty road in uneasy silence. "How about the political situation," one of them asked? Okay, now I knew what they were after! They were running scared. I told them what I thought of how the country was evolving. Pushing aside the complex problems of tribal rivalries and simmering ethnic violence, I told them that as far as I was concerned the biggest problem in the country was rampant and fast spreading corruption.

They weighed my response carefully when I concluded, "Corruption and stealing are a way of life here." I was half laughing and half serious. They laughed with me but it wasn't genuine laughter. Sometimes laughter is merely a diplomatic gesture to mask frustration and resignation. Perhaps, what I said was not what they wanted to hear but it was an honest appraisal from their man on the ground. Did my response confirm their deepest fears? If you gave the situation two seconds thought, there was nothing to laugh about. For the rest of the trip our conversation drifted but I knew they would probably pump me for more information once we got to Kaduna.

I had them booked into the Kaduna Hotel. After they checked in we drove straight to my house that also served as my office. We had some drinks and a snack and then the boss got to point. "John, I want you to finish what we have in hand and as soon as possible and then close down the operation. We've lost enough money as it is." Before I could answer the chairman continued, "If possible could you farm out the remaining work to a local contractor to finish?" He had his little presentation carefully thought through; he knew what he wanted me to do. "As soon as you have finished I want you to go to Port Harcourt and take over the work from Fraser. He has personal problems and has to leave as soon as possible." They watched me carefully to gauge my reaction.

I am cool under fire. "I can do what you want me to do but you need to understand that in a very short period I can recover about £12,000. In addition, the two houses that the company owns can be sold to CFAO for another £10,000. They are desperate for decent accommodations." They listened carefully. I gave them more details about money that I had collected from jobs that had never been invoiced and described how the university job was nearly complete. I had even figured out how I could give some of the collection work to a good lawyer who would collect on our behalf. "We can even generate more cash by selling all the excess company furniture," I said. It was a silly detail but it got their attention. Their response, a form of grudging amazement, told me they had not done their homework before leaving London. "We did not know there was still so much money outstanding."

Blow me over. I thought the company was in business to make money, not lose it. His stupid response confirmed to me what I suspected all along: they were mismanaging their opportunities because they didn't understand their operations. If my little operation needed cleaning up, what about all the other sites that I didn't know anything about?

As if to answer my own question they instructed me to take two weeks to clean-up Kaduna, transfer the cash to London, and then head down to Port Harcourt. Once again, it was a repeat scenario: clean up the small jobs, get the money, complete the power station which might take a few months, and then wait-and-see what might happen. I didn't own the company but I was really irritated although I didn't let my emotions show. So much business and so much goodwill were being thrown away just so they could cut and run. It was 1963 and I didn't like what was happening.

I was left with the unpleasant job of closing down the company in the north and Port Harcourt and I was on my own. The two directors told me to use my own initiative, gave me a little pep talk that really didn't come from the heart, and then they flew back to London. At least I didn't have to worry about what they expected from me. That much was clear but when I went back to work I was uneasy.

I knew myself well enough to admit the deteoriating political situation was beginning to get through to me. Rumors were flying and most focused on the rampant corruption in the government. Of course, I told myself, this isn't a European style work environment but there was opportunity if the company was prepared to pay the price. Perhaps the chairman and board had concluded the price the market was asking was too much to pay in worry and management time.

Were corruption and the inability to have a reasonable work environment the real reasons for the company's decision to close down? I wanted to say, "No", but I wasn't absolutely convinced my response made that much sense.

I wasn't plugged into the government but I felt reasonably comfortable thinking the rumors were worse than the actual situation. Was the company over-reacting or was I just being blind to reality? I had a judgment call to make. On reflection, I felt they were over-reacting. Arguing against myself, I asked whether I was I in a good position to understand the strategic decision they shared with me. Probably, I wasn't. I had learned to shrug off a lot of what was wrong with the country. My conversion process worked for me because it enabled me to survive and live off the land in spite of all the difficulties.

It was possible, I had to admit, that I had become too close to the daily grind to see the larger picture, to really see what was happening. I wanted to say I was comfortable with my assessment but that would be a lie. Something was bothering me and I couldn't put a finger on it. Later, much later, I learned their early assessment of the rapidly deteriorating business environment was accurate. Events would prove I was the optimist and they were the realists. Subsequent events would show that I was too close to what was going on to have a decent perspective. To their credit, they had the advantage of many sources of business intelligence and that helped them to see the forest. I only saw the trees.

I phoned Ron English and Blackwood in Lagos to find out more about what was behind the company's decision. "It is politics and the military." Telling me that was merely repeating what I had already heard: a military coup was brewing. They had received the same intelligence estimate from the London board of directors. Putting politics to one side, I thought about my personal well being in the event of a coup. I did not feel personally insecure because I had good personal relations with all the Nigerians with whom I worked. But, I couldn't assess the real impact of how a coup was probably going to affect me.

From reading the newspapers and talking to other men who had survived coups in other parts of the world, I knew that one of the most critical phases in the life of an expat was during the period immediately following a military takeover. Everything was new. A new set of rulers meant building new relations with the authorities. Walking into any government office in post-colonial Nigeria and expecting to get something done quickly and efficiently was a pipe dream.

In the new Nigeria access to government ministries had to be developed. Contacts inside and outside the government were all that counted. After a coup there were bound to be new faces and that meant building new relationships. Until new patterns emerged there would be great uncertainty. Unless I was wrong and had misunderstood the likely mechanics of a post-coup Nigeria, I would have to live with uncertainty and that was not a good operating environment.

While operations were winding down in Kaduna I took a few days off to inspect some of the other sites I had been instructed to take over. In Port Harcourt, Fraser was on the verge of a nervous break down. His wife had left him with their two young children; she had run off with a Danish engineer. All Fraser wanted was to return to Liverpool with his children, stay with his mum and start divorce proceedings. I guess it could have been worse for him but I didn't see how? He left me to finish a huge job that required me to be on site every day. I was lucky. Usually when you inherit a mess isn't there always something well hidden that needs urgent attention? Fraser was an orderly and honest chap and there were no nasty surprises.

Even the office work was in perfect order and he had managed to train a competent office staff. I shuddered to think of what the Port Harcourt job might have been like if he had been a bad craftsman and a weak administrator. He was a good professional. We planned the handover steps. Each of us knew what the other was expected to do. He focused on his work and I admired his courage but felt sorry for him. Beyond feeling sorry, there wasn't much I could do to help him on the personal side. Given the circumstances, he was holding up well enough for me to leave but I told him that I would be back in a week. I tried to cheer him up, but there wasn't much I could do for him. Sometimes in life you walk into situations and there is really not too much you can do for the other guy. Fraser was in one of those situations. All I could do was hope his kids wouldn't suffer too much and that he'd get out of Nigeria in one piece.

Back in Kaduna I transferred all the cash to London as instructed and gave the house furniture to the lawyer along with the remaining small invoices for him to collect and send to the Lagos office. I loaded all my gear and drove to Port Harcourt, a town I thoroughly disliked.

Port Harcourt is situated between the Niger River delta and the ocean; it is one of the most humid cities in the world. The rainy season lasted for six to eight months. The road system was appalling. Elsewhere in the country, in the dry season the roads were reasonable but Port Harcourt had to be different. In the dry season the roads were bad because it was so humid the road surface became nothing more than a layer of oozing thick red mud.

I was given a duplex flat that I shared with an American oil company employee, a southerner, who killed his spare time playing poker. Every night he turned our apartment into a casino. I'm not a card player. To be social I agreed to be taught different games but I couldn't be enticed to the table. Watching them play was more fun for me than playing. One of the players was from Louisiana, a big man with a foul mouth. He was a redneck, one hundred percent genuine U.S. born and bred. He spoke another kind of English, a strange language that was funny and pithy, a language I'd never heard from other Americans. He also drawled. Words oozed out of his mouth, often as tangy as chewing tobacco spit. He liked me probably because I didn't play cards and probably because he'd never met a Frenchman who spoke English well. He held his cards close to his big burly chest and muttered a lot to himself. During one game he looked up at me, muttered something that I couldn't understand, and then he repeated so everyone could hear: "Goddamn cotton picking cock sucker." I laughed when he asked me, "How do you say that in French, John?"

Fraser introduced me to the engineer in charge of the whole project and to the other contractors involved in the installation of the 20 MGW Brown Bovary gas turbine. The contractors were Swiss but the engineer in charge was an Englishman who had worked for a French cement company in the south of France at Golfe Juan. Besides being a good coordinator and excellent at working with different nationalities, he was a great help because he advised me on certain aspects of the job that were beyond my competence level.

It was a lot of work; I wound up spending many days on the site. There are only so many hours in the day and this meant that while I was away on the turbine site I had to leave all the other small jobs in the hands of one of the Nigerian headmen I trusted. Thanks to him we closed down all the small jobs in town; the power station was twenty miles away in the bush.

When the dry season came Anna sent Philip to stay with me until I was ready to go back to Lagos where we planned to stay until the company closed down and we all left to go to France. Before I left Port Harcourt I phoned the London office to ask them what to do with some leftover material. I made a list that included a huge drum of 11 KV cable that had been sent in excess to our requirements and also some miscellaneous house furniture. The household effects were no problem. The person I talked to told me to take what I wanted and sell the rest. It was a good deal and a nice way for London to thank me for doing a good job closing down their operations.

The chap on the other end of the line read down the list without making any comments. When he got to the cable I thought he was going to explode. "For god's sake," he whispered into the mouthpiece, "don't bring up the copper cable." "Why not," I asked. It was company property and it was very valuable. "Look John, I'm the one who made a mistake in pricing that project and if they ever find out about the cable I'll lose my job." Fair enough. There wasn't much to be gained by pursuing the matter, but I couldn't just leave it there. "What am I supposed to do with it?" He didn't even pause and I was happy to follow his instructions. I sold the copper cable and all the left over lead from the high tension cable to a scrap dealer and those transactions made me a lot of money. I played the game. As far as the company was concerned, I followed head office instructions and sold their assets so that made them happy.

Philip and I left for Lagos after the sale. Unfortunately we were delayed in Lagos because the military staged a bloodless coup and departures were being delayed for security reasons. In technical terms the coup was a success but we wondered how long the new president Gowan would be able to convey a new sense of security? He was a

Christian; his father was a Protestant preacher. I knew the man rather well because I had worked on jobs in which he was involved.

One time after he became president I happened to be out of the office when he drove through Lagos. A large crowd had formed on either side of the street to stare and wave at the motorcade. I was standing in the middle of a bunch of Africans when the new president passed. He saw me in the crowd, recognized me and waved at me. There was no doubt that for a brief moment that day, on that particular part of the footpath, I was definitely 'the' man of the hour because I knew the President and he obviously knew me.

That little bit of relationship may have been helpful but it didn't reassure me that I could leverage it and somehow avoid the political turbulence into which the country had slipped. Having friends in high places is fine provided they stay there and provided they don't do something stupid and get themselves either killed or overthrown, or both. I shrugged off my connections and stayed focused on my work.

I wound up staying a couple of months in Lagos with Blackwood, an electrical engineer. He had a typical London cockney sharp accent and he was constantly smiling. If I closed my eyes I could imagine him behind a barrow in Covent Garden. Open them and I looked straight into the face of a very black man. When he kept his mouth shut he blended into the African population in Lagos.

One day we had a meeting at one of our sites in Lagos. We were waiting for someone who had not shown up. Finally the architect said, "Does anybody know where Mr. Blackwood is?" Silence. Blackwood identified himself with his ever-present smile. The architect was flustered. "Oh, I am so sorry. It never crossed my mind that you aren't Nigerian. You sound like a cockney over the phone." Blackwood continued to beam. "Sir, I'm a born and bred Londoner but don't worry. I know that the color of my skin, particularly here in Nigeria, can be confusing!" Everyone burst out laughing and the architect started the meeting. His good humor defused a situation that could have turned ugly.

*****

We left for London shortly after this funny incident. At the head office I was told that the Director of "Drake and Skull" wanted to see me about a possible tour in Nigeria. My friend Guest had talked to them on my behalf before leaving for Hong Kong. The director and I met. He was a gentleman and a former high-ranking officer in the British army during the war. He was an attentive listener and asked a lot of good questions. I was truthful and direct. He concluded that the situation in Nigeria was too unstable to warrant them offering me a job. "We'll have to wait and see how this plays out," he said. We agreed to stay in touch and I promised to call him as soon as we got settled in France.

The three of us left for Cannes. There was no particular reason why we chose Cannes other than the fact that we knew winters on the Riviera were warmer than the long gray cold endless winter days in the north. We had to find a place to live. Unlike right after the war, the housing market had improved and we contacted several agencies to see if the had any apartments for rent. One agent was particularly nice. After talking to him about the real estate market and a possible career change, he told me that he knew someone who wanted to sell her real estate agency. Was I interested? It wasn't a silly question.

Maybe, I thought, based on our conversations, another opportunity was unfolding and I could be looking at an opportunity to start my own business in France. It was one of many ideas and at first I wasn't interested because I didn't know anything about the real estate business and I couldn't really fancy myself selling property. But he sowed the idea and like a good salesman, he persisted. A few days later he arranged a meeting between a lovely old lady who told us she wanted to sell because of age and ill health.

I met Hervette Perret, a charming lady and a tough businesswoman. She was a genuinely nice person and we got along well right from the beginning. In fact, a business relationship turned into a personal relationship because she became a very close friend and almost a member of our family. Sadly, she was widowed. For reasons we never found out, her son and other members of her family had abandoned her. She took great pains in teaching me the real estate business. I learned fast but she used to tell me that I was too soft with customers.

One day she gave me a chewing out that I will never forget. I told her that I felt sorry for a chap who wanted to rent a flat. He was a baker who was occupying the house owned by a former boss who was living in Casablanca. That worked well until the owner said he was returning to France for good and wanted his house back. We had a flat for rent but the baker couldn't come up with the deposit: three months rent in advance. He was quaking when he came to see me. I believed his story so I made a deal with him: I would lend him the equivalent of two month's rent and he would pay me back over the first four months of his rental contract. He listened to me not quite believing his ears. His lined baker's face began to crumple. He took my hands in his and began thanking me; tears welled up in his eyes. I felt good about helping him and Anna was present when I signed the deal. She agreed with me. When Mme. Perret learned about what happened she exploded. "Never, never, never, trust them. They'll make you cry, they'll try and make you believe their stories, they're all actors," she shouted at me. Of course, she was right. But, the baker was an exception and he paid me back on time.

We were making enough money to live comfortably but we were unhappy. Real estate was not our future and we couldn't escape the pull of Africa. Hardships were real in Africa, there was no denying that fact, but life in France was driving us nuts. After living in Africa, daily life was dull and France had become very bureaucratic. The country was wrapped in red tape. To get anything done we had to fill in reams of paper and deal with surly little government employees who delighted in making our lives miserable by working to rule. But, and this was also a possibility that we recognized, maybe we weren't giving France enough of a chance and we were actually talking ourselves into going back to Africa.

One day I called Drake and Skull if there were any openings overseas. "Yes," provided we agreed to return to Nigeria. It took us no time to weigh their offer and accept it. They told me to get to London as quickly as possible so they could begin processing my papers. I told Anna to start putting out feelers to sell our agency. Even Madame Perret helped us by developing a list of interested buyers who were real estate professionals. I signed my contract in London; they gave me an air ticket to Lagos via Nice and Rome. I was due to leave in ten days. It was short but ten days gave me enough time to sign over power of attorney to Anna and begin the paperwork to sell our little company. Mme Perret was sorry to see us go. We had become her only family. She had been very helpful getting us launched in our new venture. We invited her to spend time with us once we settled in Africa and she readily accepted the invitation from her "new" family.

*****

I left Nice early one Monday morning for Rome where I was to take an Alitalia night flight to Lagos. We left Italy on time but after only two hours we were ordered to return to Rome because Lagos airport was closed. Guess what? There had been another coup. After the usual confusion that Italians love to create and apparently revel in, Alitalia put up the transit passengers in a hotel in Rome. We were two to a room. My roommate was an American who worked for an oil company in Port Harcourt.

We were irritated at not being able to get to our assignments but we concluded, rather philosophically, there wasn't a damned thing we could do to but make the best of a bad situation. We began killing time walking around Rome. I have never walked so much in my life. Even my military career marches must have been shorter! Worse still, it was July and Rome was stinking hot. We'd walk, feel thirsty and duck into the nearest bar for a drink, go out and walk some more, and then head back into a bar. In the end, what little of Rome we didn't see wasn't worth the effort finding. Despite the walking I was getting nervous because I didn't have much cash with me. The company told me that I would get a lump sum on arrival in Lagos. That is, if I got to Lagos.

After three days the airline called all the passengers on my flight to a meeting and announced they could not continue to pay for our hotel rooms because there was no way of knowing how long the airport would remain closed. I was stuck in Rome. Alitalia agreed to pay for a limited number of phone calls and I called the London office and explained the situation. After a brief discussion we agreed that I would return to Cannes and wait for an improvement in the situation. To complicate matters, London was jittery and concerned about my safety in Nigeria. The press was reporting unrest throughout the country; the short-term situation was too unsettled to be called 'safe.'

Back in Cannes I waited for another week. Finally, London called and gave me permission to leave. I rebooked myself, called London with a new ETA, and flew to Lagos without any further delays.

Lagos was under martial law. The army and police were in control of all movement of public and private transport. Temporary barricades had been erected everywhere. They were new but some things don't change. As usual, getting through the barricades without a shake down meant a little dash money came in handy. I stayed in Lagos for five days and was given the drawings and the contract documents for the electrical installation of the new central bank in Benin. The company booked me into the Ikoye Hotel and advised me not to go out at night. There were a lot of expatriates in the hotel and I knew some of them from my previous stays. Being locked up in the hotel had some benefits because in the evening I was about to pick up additional tidbits of information about what was happening throughout the country.

I left for Benin early in the morning with a pick-up and a Nigerian driver. In view of some of the stories I had heard at the hotel, I was nervous about driving outside of Lagos. But, we only saw two or three police barricades at the entrance of town. When they saw my white face they waved us through. The trip was uneventful. After I got booked into the rest house I went out and had a look at the site and met the headman. He seemed like a nice chap and we agreed to meet the next morning.

I spent the evening in the local club, had a few drinks with the local white men and one Nigerian army officer. He was reassuring and told me that the army had the situation under control. Drawing on what I saw on the way to Benin, he wasn't telling stories. But, my sixth sense and experience told me that the calm we appeared to be enjoying was too complete to be normal. I knew there was still a lot of tension. This most recent coup had not solved all of Nigeria's woes. I was convinced that it was only a matter of time until riots would erupt.

Furthermore, I didn't trust the people in Benin. They were a mixture of Yoruba in the west and Ibo in the east on the other side of the Niger River. Not that I could do much, I was sandwiched between the two and I didn't like being there. I was in a hurry to finish and go to

Kano in the North where I knew lots of people. But there was another factor, I felt safer with the Hausa and Fulani. I rushed the job in Benin but as the job wound down troubles erupted in the north and I had to wait in Benin for the situation to calm down before I could leave.

When there was a brief lull I took advantage of the relative calm and left Benin with my pick-up and driver. Before leaving I asked around and was told that many of the petrol stations en-route had been torched so I took three extra jerry cans of petrol. On hindsight, I took unnecessary risks leaving during the lull. The situation was neither quiet nor secure. By the time we reached Bida and Mina, south of Kaduna, I realized the situation was not at all good. The petrol stations had been burnt to the ground; most of the town's inhabitants had fled the area. Those remaining behind looked like they had dropped off the dark side of Mars. They were wild men. My driver was scared and begged me to leave quickly.

I agreed about leaving but not in a great hurry. We had to keep our heads and leave naturally. He was too scared to argue and I managed to calm him down. "Trust me. If we show them we're nervous and try to roar out of here, they'll swarm us and kill us." He nodded but the whites of his eyes were so wide he looked as if someone had glued a white plastic strip over his eyelids. Calmly, as if we had no other cares in the world, we filled our petrol tanks and drove off leaving the Martians staring at our dusty pick-up. It was hard to tell who was more scared: them or us?

Life appeared more normal the further north we drove. This was partially due to the fact the Nigerian army had military barracks spread throughout the area and also it was probably due to the fact that the Hausa were less jumpy than the tribes down south. I was glad to be back in Kano. It wasn't Cannes but it was nice to be back in a town that I knew and among Nigerians that I could work with.

Peter Walsh met me and gave me the keys to my bungalow. It was a two-bedroom house with a nice living room and kitchen, completely furnished and air-conditioned. I showered and went into town to meet all my old friends and I was warmly welcomed. Many slaps on the back led to a serious drinking session at my old watering hole, the Kano Club.

Rene Dassac (in collaboration with Patrick K. Robbins)

The house included a cook/steward, a gardener, and a night watchman who slept all night. After some delay I managed to get a phone call through to Anna and told her to get her entry visa ready and come as soon as she could. There was nothing to keep her there now. She was delighted to know that it was safe to bring Philip because there was a new French school in Kano and he would have plenty of playmates. Kano wasn't perfect but relative to most other cities in Nigeria it was more pleasant. At least, that's how I felt.

I went to see the architect in charge of the Kano university contract. He had a double barrel name, Guilmer-Raylor, and we had a long talk. He was frank and open. His primary concern was getting electrical contractors to come to Kano and then getting them to stay on the jobs he was supervising. It seemed like every time he had a problem and needed additional help he had to wait weeks before someone was sent from Lagos. His complaints were worded in such a way that I suspected he was sounding me out to see my reaction, to see whether I could offer him a solution. A year later his questions came back to me and my hunches were borne out. I put out a call to the former electricians I had trained in Lagos; they were Yoruba. Within a few weeks they were back with me. I felt a lot better having my work crew instead of strangers. We trusted each other and in those trying times, trust could mean the difference between life and death.

As far as my work was concerned, everything was running smoothly. But, like most of the married men who were separated from their families I spent too much time in drinking sessions in the Kano Club. The nights could get very long but when you were with friends and around the table, time seemed to pass more quickly. It was time for Anna to join me but more trouble was brewing.

Everyone knew there was trouble in the ranks of the army. That was nothing new. A disgruntled army was something we had grown accustomed to accepting. What made the situation more serious was not the extent of the disgruntlement but where the discontent was located. Instead of grumbling troops it was the senior officers turn. Any interested outsider could see that the senior officer corps was split along tribal and religious lines.

There was one faction, primarily Muslims from the northern and southwestern states, and part of Benin that was allied to General

Gowan. Their opponents had rallied around General Ojuku, a Christian Ibo from the eastern states. They refused to be governed by northerners whom they felt were inferior and poorly educated. This group wanted to break from the federation and created a separate state in the southeast called Biafra. Small in size, the proposed state was rich in mineral wealth. It included all the oil production in the river states in the Niger Delta as well as the coalmines in Enugu, their proposed capital.

General Ojuku's men acted like conquerors in the north and they didn't go down well with the Hausa who were becoming angrier at being treated like second class citizens. Tribalism, the gnawing disease of modern Africa, had broken out in pandemic force. It was only a matter of time, no one knew when, before the disease swept across the nation. Festering and feverish, tribalism had almost broken out into a full-blown attack on the body politic of the young nation. Any incident and the nation would erupt into full-scale civil war. We waited and wished we were somewhere else.

When the Ibo assassinated the Sardona of Sokoto the festering abscess broke. Hatred and destruction spewed across the young nation. The Sardona was a Muslim cleric, comparable to a Christian archbishop. The Muslim population exploded when photos were distributed showing the Sardona lying dead on the floor with an Ibo soldier's foot on his head. Hausa got dragged into the mess. As expected, there were flash points everywhere. The Hausa chiefs realized the great danger to their people and ordered them to remain calm. Ordering people to obey is easy but getting them to follow your orders is another matter. Events began spiraling out of control. The northern tribal chiefs met in secret and gave the Ibos a week to leave the north. Ojuku's soldiers had already left. Was this a masquerade used to signal the secession of the new state they called Biafra?

The expatriates in the North were told by the local chiefs not to evacuate. We were assured that even though something bad was certainly going to happen, the eventual clashes did not involve us. Many Ibo left in droves by whatever means they could find: rail, lorry, cars loaded with bags strapped to the roof. But, and this was a tragic miscalculation, many stayed secure in their sense of superiority. After all, they were Ibo and who would harm the mighty Ibo? The

Hausa wanted them out. Ugly rumors flew about town. Rumors were repeated, embellished and then repeated as true statements of fact. I tried to understand the depths of depravity to which the local population had sunk but it was impossible for me to sink my thoughts to their level of blind hatred and sheer stupidity. One rumor said the police had found a cooked Hausa child in the suitcase of an Ibo headed south. As inter-tribal hostilities flared, stealing increased because the Ibo needed money to pay for their transport south. Even I was a victim!

One night I came home from the Kano club fairly well loaded. My night watchman had not yet started to sleep when I came in. I showered and fell into a deep sleep. The next morning when I awakened I was stupefied to discover that my room had been cleaned out. My clothes were gone, my brief case with my papers, even the bedroom curtains. From the way I felt I wondered whether I had been doped during my sleep. I put a towel around my waist; at least they'd left me a towel and I went to the police station in the pick-up they hadn't nicked. There were too many police barricades to travel safely in a stolen vehicle.

When I entered the police station barefoot and furious, my towel clutched tightly around my skinny waist, the duty officer looked at me and smiled. "I was expecting you Mr. Powell." By now my head was clearing but I couldn't figure out how he knew my name. We'd never met and I hadn't had any run-ins with the police. "Your neighbor's steward saw your personal papers on the side of the road in front of your house and brought them to us." He reached into a desk drawer and took out a Manila envelope with my passport, papers and my war medals. "You weren't the only house visited. The Ibo are desperate for money." We chatted for a moment. I actually felt comfortable standing there all but naked. What I couldn't figure out was why I didn't hear them.

"Did your eyes burn when you woke up," he asked? Come to think of it, they did. He laughed and explained that they used a special smoke and blew it through the air conditioning system to knock me out. "Even my night watchman took off," I complained. The policeman assured me that if the watchman was a Hausa he'd be back with an excuse but it was up to me to check out his excuse. Thanking him I drove over to my friend Dupuy's house and asked him to lend me some clothes. After breakfast I went home and asked my steward if he had heard anything during the night but he shook his head so that was a dead issue as far as his involvement was concerned.

The next morning Dupuy came to get back the clothes he had lent me. The night after I was robbed his steward, an Ibo, cleaned him out and disappeared south with all his clothes and money. Maybe he was behind both thefts; we'll never know.

We laughed at this strange turn of events. By taking his best trousers the day before, I managed to 'save' them for him when it was his turn to get robbed. Our little incidents were a prelude to something worse that was about to happen. We heard rumors and we almost believed some of them. Tragically, the lurid rumors were tame compared to what actually happened.

Two days later violence broke out on the deadline date the Hausa had given the Ibo to be gone. At daybreak we heard lorries rumbling into town. They were filled with Hausa armed with machetes and truncheons. They surrounded the Ibo part of town, 'Sabon Gary', a distinct community that was primarily Ibo but there were also some Yoruba. The killing began but only Ibo were killed; the Yoruba weren't touched because the Hausa had not told them to leave. I witnessed some of this when I drove into town with some of my Yoruba lads. They were reasonably safe going into town on their own but, as a white man, I wanted to accompany them to make sure they would not get molested. Before leaving I checked with some friends and they assured me that expatriates were not the targets. The Hausa were after the Ibo who threatened to destroy the Nigerian federation. I favored General Gowan because I felt he was honest and he wanted to avoid bloodshed but I underestimated the power of the tensions that had built up.

When I went to the post office to collect the mail for the company and the staff I witnessed an event that would, in my mind, represent everything that was happening elsewhere in the country, in villages and along roads far from probing eyes. As I turned down the street where the post office was located, I drove past a crowd of men, women and children that had gone berserk. They were chasing an Ibo. He saw my car and ran toward me for protection. Too late, the crowd swarmed over him. As I accelerated away from the mob I looked up in my rearview mirror. A huge Stilston spanner appeared from out of nowhere and shattered the back of his head. The impact was so violent one of his eyes shot from its socket and hung briefly on his cheek. It was the last I saw of him as he fell to the ground under the feet and fists of his pursuers. For a split second I saw his body being stomped under a forest of bare feet and then I could not see him.

I slammed on my brakes and got out and made a gesture, quite futile actually, of disapproval. A man stepped from the stomping ground and walked toward me. "Sir, please don't intervene. This has nothing to do with you." He was right and I was too late. I slipped the pick-up into gear and I could see the crowd in the rear view mirror finishing off the boy. Hatred, blind hatred, unleashed a flurry of arms and feet. Underneath their blows a human life was pounded into paste. How many thousands of times did that identical event occur throughout the entire federation? Can anybody ever answer that question?

After I collected my mail I drove through the back streets to Guyou's house. Other friends and acquaintances had gathered there. Philip was well informed about what was going on and he relayed to us what his Hausa politician friends had warned him: stay indoors, don't play hero and try to protect the Ibos. If you go out after dark drive with the car's inside lights on so you can be identified as a white man, and sit as low as you can.

We were in a residential area that was quiet. Eerily quiet in view of what was happening elsewhere in the city. Some corpses of people who had been killed during the day were still lying in the gutters. Strangely, the phones actually worked. We began calling friends who lived in areas where most of the killing was taking place. Those who lived near the airport road were horrified. There was sporadic rifle fire so we told them to keep their lights on and lay down to avoid stray bullets. We arranged a pool of drivers to fetch them and bring them over to our relative safety.

We drove in two cars. Taking no chances, we drove with our interior lights on to let the mobs know we were white. As we passed screaming, rampaging mobs they would pause from their killing, wave and smile at us, and continue their carnage. Were we some kind of a parade and were they the happy onlookers, waving joyfully at the white man's cars, their machetes glistening wet with blood in the glow of the few working street lamps? Outside our friend's house there was a lot of shooting and screaming. We pounded on their barricaded door and managed to get inside. Five terrified women huddled in the middle of their lounge barely able to speak let alone stand. On the other side of their garden wall death was present only a few meters away. Our little group was all that stood between them and incomprehensible horror. None too gently, we bundled them into our cars and raced back to the relative safety of Gaydou's house.

That night we remained staring into the radio. We got the usual international channels. Other than the comfort we drew from knowing there was another world where, for the time being, it was less hostile than what we were going through in Nigeria, listening to BBC was futile because they knew less about what was going on than we did. We took advantage of the telephone lines still being intact and we contacted our colleagues throughout the north. They confirmed what we feared: the violence we saw was happening everywhere. The only difference was the intensity. Where there were more Ibo, the killing was worse than where there were smaller populations. Hollow-eyed, we were glad to see daybreak after a long and terrifying night.

By mid-morning we were able to take stock and piece together the bits of information we had accumulated in order to try and understand what had happened. We heard lorries grind their way out of town heading back to their villages. They were filled with weary and often bloody rioters. We managed to make enough phone calls to friends who were stuck in their homes to confirm that, to the best of our knowledge, no white men had been killed but everyone we talked to had horrible stories to tell. Since there was safety in numbers, we decided to drive through town in a convoy to get a first hand impression of how much damage the rioters had done.

Police were everywhere. For once, I didn't curse the roadblocks. It was almost comforting to see that armed police were patrolling the streets. The only trucks allowed through the barricades without stopping were those mobilized to collect the corpses. They were strewn everywhere. Try to appreciate the horror we saw. Imagine municipal sanitation workers in any big city in Europe arriving at a parade route after the crowds have gone. The broom-and-scoop squad stops, sweeps, and loads rubbish into their trucks before the streets and sidewalks are cleaned to look like there had never been a parade. The trucks we saw were performing the same job. Instead of pushing paper into piles and throwing it onto a truck, they collected bodies, body parts, and heaved them onto the truck beds. There were so many bodies that we gave up counting. Army engineers were in charge of the burial operation. Along the road outside the mud walls of the old city bulldozers were digging mass graves. Lorries lined up patiently waiting to dump their grizzly cargo.

I wanted to see what had happened to the university building site where the contractors had employed many Ibo. I passed one burial site without slowing down and pretended as if I hadn't seen what they were doing. When I got to the university, I met one of the managers who worked for the lead building contractor. He was in shock and could barely speak. Apparently all the Ibo workers had stayed on the site thinking that they would be safe there. When they heard the screaming hordes running from their lorries toward the main gate of the university, the Ibo workers panicked and ran away to hide wherever they could. They were no match for the mob. Outnumbered and terrified, in a matter of minutes they were surrounded and massacred. The British supervisors who had been caught on the site tried to intervene but to no avail. "White man, this is not your country. Stay away." Helpless against a huge and howling mob, they witnessed barbarity. While we were talking, Hausa men continued to gather corpses for burial in mass graves.

There could be no doubt: the massacre had been prepared like a military operation. First, there was the massive assault in the early hours of the morning. That lasted four or five hours and it involved the killing and burning of Hausa homes and shops. Second, posses sprang up throughout the city to hunt down Ibo and kill them. Each time we heard a shot another Ibo died. Finally, when all the Ibo had been found and killed, a clean-up operation was organized to gather the dead and bury them quickly in mass graves

Some people who employed Ibo stewards or cooks managed to save their lives. When the mobs began roaming they told their staff to climb up into the attics of their houses and hide until the mobs left. The Hausa were no fools. They knew the Europeans were protecting their quarry. Sometimes they loitered in front of some houses waiting for the Ibo to reappear. They screamed at the Europeans to turn over their staff but the common reply was, "You're too late. They all left yesterday." The Hausa didn't believe them but they didn't go into the houses. When you come to think of it, that kind of discipline was amazing but it also showed instructions had gone out to mob leaders not to interfere with the expatriates.

For many Europeans this horror had a special meaning because often their staff had worked for them for many years and were thought of as members of their family. In one case, the superintendent of the water works in Lagos was in the process of retiring when the rioting erupted. His cook/steward had been with him for twenty years. During the riots the steward's wife was caught and killed. The European asked him where he was going to go, what was he going to do? The old African looked at him and said, "I've lost my wife and I am alone. My family is dead. I have no place to go." In the end he went to Scotland to continue to serve his master.

Gradually, calm began to spread throughout the city. It looked as if we were returning to normal, as normal as a city can be after days of slaughter. But, the calm could not hide the sight and sound of corpse filled lorries. Day and night, for the next three days I saw them roll down the city streets, belching exhaust fumes. Their flat beds were loaded with bloated beaten corpses, often stacked in layers two or three bodies high. If they had been firewood their load might have shifted but since they were human beings with clothes and limbs akimbo wedged against each other, they looked like they were holding onto each other during their final ride. At least, I didn't see bodies fall off but I wouldn't have been surprised.

The lorries stopped next to the city walls and dumped their loads into open trenches that had been dug with earth moving equipment. Once a trench was filled with bodies a bulldozer operator appeared and pushed fresh dirt over the opening and then raked it smooth with his blade. Within weeks weeds and grass began growing. Less than two months after the horror there was a rich green strip next to the walls. Tribal justice had been meted out and now Nature was laying down a green carpet to hide the past.

Three months later I had begun to hand over the job at the university to the northern government. Our head office told me to give Peter Walsh any company material in my possession. Peter was finishing a job in Kaduna. The company told me to return to London because they were going to close down their operations in Nigeria. They said it was temporary but I could tell from the way they were winding up that they would not be back for a long time. I had mixed emotions about this. On the one hand, I could see their point but on the other, I could see there was opportunity for someone like me, someone with my skills and my ability to work with the Nigerians.

*****

An architect friend, Guilies Reyburn, called me and asked me to meet him in his office. He got right to the point because he knew that we were in a close-down mode. "Have you ever thought of starting your own electrical contracting company," he asked studying my face. I shrugged and laughed but before I could manage a reply, he continued. "There's plenty of work coming up now that the government has divided the country into states." What he said was true. Kano, Maidugury and Sokoto had become states. He asked me to look at the question from his perspective; he had plenty of work but he did not have reliable support from a contractor who knew the area. "Think of it this way," he continued, "I can give you a pretty good contract to get you started and I'll cover your expenses."

He described how we could work together and how important it was, from his perspective, not to have to rely on a company with headquarters a thousand miles away. His proposal became more tempting the more we talked. "You've got to give me some time," I replied, "because I've got to form and register a company and Lord only knows how long that will take." He laughed in agreement and we shook hands. As I walked out of his office into the bright sun I realized that I was about to take one of the biggest steps in my life. I was ready for it; the time was ideal and I knew that I would succeed. It didn't dawn on me at the time but later I realized that I had been preparing for this step all my life. Now was the time to seize the opportunity and live another phase of a commitment I made to myself many years earlier: take charge of my life.

I drove over to see my friend Philip Gaydou of Western Sudan Export Company and asked him to help me with all the paperwork. I desperately needed his help because he had a lot of experience pushing paper through the labyrinth called 'The Nigerian Civil Service.' Furthermore, he was very well connected with many influential people in the Northern Nigerian Government. I won't call it waving a magic wand, but whatever he did was as close as you can get to waving one in Nigeria. My request was quickly approved and I registered my company as: "J. Powell Electro – Mechanical Contracting Company Ltd." Gaydou even lent me one of his properties he was not using so I could turn it into my office.

I rented the house I had been living in when I worked with Drake and Skull and that meant I could send for Anna and Philip. True to his word, Reyburn got me a contract with an extension that was being built onto the new university. That job gave me the necessary cash flow to open a bank account at UBA. Fortunately another good friend, Sam Woodward, was general manager and he went out of his way to help me with the paperwork and to provide me with a lot of very valuable advice. Things were definitely looking up.

Rene Dassac (in collaboration with Patrick K. Robbins)

CHAPTER TEN:
ON MY OWN

I told Anna to come with Philip as soon as she could get tickets. In the short run, we had two variables going in our favor. Firstly, there was an apparent lull in political turmoil and the federal government had its hands full with the problem in Biafra. They were trying to secede from the federation; this would have meant the break-up of the nation. As long as there was a lull it meant that there was a chance for more business. Secondly, the near term prospects were good for my little company. In the long run, and no one knew how long that might be, if we took some chances there were more reasons to get back together again as a family than to remain apart. In the back of my mind I was pretty much convinced that the Biafra mess would lead to a bloody civil war but if it did break out it was too far from Kano to affect us.

Time flew. I seemed to be working day and night. When Anna and Philip arrived at Kano airport all our old friends formed a huge welcoming committee to greet them. There was no hiding it, Anna was happy to be back in Nigeria and we were happy to be together as a family. We sat around the kitchen table and decided what had to be done to organize our lives so that we were as comfortable as possible. Years of experience in the bush counted and, as best as we could, we shaped our environment to our needs. I can't remember all the details but what ever we did must have been right because we were happy.

During this period in Kano we learned to live with ever increasing corruption and the difficulty of getting work completed on time. I strained to keep my jobs on schedule and that must have taken a toll but I was too busy to count all my aches and pains. We were making money and, despite it all, we had fun. Daily life was full of "laughs" if you allowed yourself the luxury of laughing at yourself. One day the general manger of SCCA and his wife came to see us. She was a great cook and managed to make the most extraordinary meals using local produce. I don't know what prompted her thinking but she fancied having some veal. She became quite worked up about the prospect of a lovely veal stew.

As a first step, she bought vegetables from her favorite market ladies and then went to the butcher. "Do you have veal," she asked. The butcher cocked his head to one side and looked down at the filthy butcher shop floor. "Yes Madame, I have veal." She was delighted. "I'd like two kilos cut into chunks about this big," she said showing her clenched fist. "No Madame, I cannot cut the veal." Perplexed and perhaps irritated at having to sweep away hundreds of flies that were trying to land on her head, she replied curtly, "That's fine. Just give me one big piece and I will have my cook cut it into smaller pieces." The butcher was obviously agitated but he continued to stare at the floor before mumbling, "I cannot give you the veal Madame." Her fiery Italian temper boiled over, "Why not?" she yelled at him. The butcher lifted his head and smiled innocently before stating the obvious: "I will have to kill the calf." The butcher was a Fulani, a cattle herder. Killing calves is not in their culture. Once again, the WAWA principle reached out of nowhere to affect our lives. For those who don't know what WAWA stands for, it means: West Africa Wins Again!

My contracting business grew rapidly. There were several reasons it took off well but I think three were really critical: I was known and respected as an electrical contractor, I had competent Nigerian staff that lived up to my standards, and competition was weaker than me in most cases. I soon learned that growing a business is hard work and I had to be careful and not make the same mistake some of my previous employers had made: over commit and then under deliver quality work on time. It didn't take me too long to realize that I had to hire some expats to supervise jobs that were too far from Kano for me to handle alone. I began looking for competent people in the community. Unfortunately, they were not easy to find. I had to scrutinize every C.V. because I knew from reading between the lines that there was a lot of truth stretching when it came time for the applicant to describe his accomplishments.

Rene Dassac (in collaboration with Patrick K. Robbins)

In the end I phoned the general manager of the company in England that supplied me with most of the electrical material I was using. Bob Wynn was a very good friend, an ex merchant navy engineer. He listened to my problem and then he came up with a good idea. Why not place an advertisement in the Electrical Engineer Association monthly for the kind of men I needed? It was a good suggestion and we figured out how to handle responses.

We agreed that he would run the ad. As soon as I got an answer that sounded promising I would take the first available flight to London to interview the candidate. Within a week I got an answer and I left for London. The candidate was impressive: married with two grown children. His daughter was an air-hostess who was married to an American naval officer; his son was a university student. These were good signs. They told me he was probably a steady and straightforward man, just the qualities I was looking for. Like me, he had acquired British citizenship.

When the war broke out he fled Poland as a young boy and somehow 'walked' across Europe, around the Mediterranean, and joined the British forces in the Middle East. His C.V. was filled with solid accomplishments. He was the right kind of man I needed to take over some of the work in the field so that I could concentrate more time on pricing tenders and paper work in general. We agreed that he would come down on his own first and work as a bachelor until his wife joined him. That worked out well because his wife had health problems and could not have stayed the duration of a full tour. He signed his contract, got his entry visa and flew down to Kano to meet me.

Civil war broke out when the federal government failed to convince the Biafran government headed by General Ojuku to remain in the Nigerian federation. Federal troops were deployed around the Biafran border. As far as we were concerned in the North, the fighting was 'somewhere' else and it really didn't bother us. We had ample food and what we couldn't get locally we got in Zinder, a little town just across the border in the Niger republic. Lagos Port was working full time. On average, up to forty cargo ships were laying offshore waiting for a berth to unload. There was only one 'war threat' in

Kano. No one seemed to get too excited; in fact, the locals thought the incident was rather funny.

A commercial plane that had been converted into 'a bomber' flew over one afternoon to bomb the airport which was defended by a squad of machine gunners who couldn't shoot straight if you held their shoulders steady for them. The 'bomber', I think it was a vintage World War II Dakota, lumbered into sight. From where we were standing on the ground we saw the cargo door was open. The 'bombardiers' were pushing homemade bombs out the door with their feet. Their 'aim' was a bit off. Accuracy was impossible and all the bombs fell in the bush away from the airport. But there was one casualty. A Nigerian ran down stairs from his upstairs bedroom to get a better look at the plane. He started hopping up and down when the plane flew over and sprained his ankle. The local newspaper had a great time reporting his 'war wounds".

We did feel some changes to our life style but they weren't serious. Many of the younger men were mobilized and there was a shortage of local transport. As a result, we found ourselves reaching into the community and getting closer to the Fulani and Hausa peoples. We'd give them a lift or help out some other way in their daily lives. It wasn't much (in fact, I can't remember too many details) but I knew they very much appreciated our help

I became a very popular contractor and business kept rolling in. Once again I realized that the mistakes of others and my previous experience helped me. I recognized that I could not keep on expanding, keep on attracting quality contracts, unless I had another two or three expats. I started looking for another house for myself so I could free up the house we were living in for any new hires I brought in. As I looked around town I noticed that there was a big empty house. I liked the looks of it and found out that it had belonged to a bankrupt company whose assets had been seized by Barclays Bank.

I saw the manager and asked him how much he wanted for the house. He said something in the vicinity of £4000. That sounded interesting and he arranged for me to get a look inside. It looked promising but an Italian contractor friend, who knew more about houses that I did, looked at it and told me there was a lot of work before I could more in. He advised making an offer of a thousand pounds less. According to him a counter offer could be justified because of the amount of work that had to be done. It sounded fair to me; the bank accepted. We moved in after the repairs had been made and after Anna had worked her magic. It was ours and we were proud to live in one of the best houses in Kano.

The civil war ended gradually. No one knows why. Maybe it was just the simple fact that people got tired of killing each other so they went back home to their routines. For those of us who tried to inject numbers into the horrors that we witnessed or heard about, we guessed that the cost in human lives was somewhere around one million but we would never know the real number. No one would. Among the dead there were soldiers, what you'd expect in a war, but the real losers were civilians. Their losses must have been in the hundreds of thousands and most of them were Ibos.

It's hard to say something good came out of the slaughter. But, a new Nigeria emerged out of the blood bath. It was a federal republic in which ethnic groups had their own states. The federal government remained intact but the army controlled the government, not the other way around. Real parliamentary democracy was still a theory in Nigeria, an idea trying to find roots. To their credit, the military began to focus on development and many projects were undertaken, especially in the North that had been neglected for too long. Kano was a rich state and many large contracts were put out to tender. I got a large share of a big job, not because my company had a long track record, but it was because most contractors had their hands full in the south and they didn't want to send anyone up north.

I needed help and I brought out two expats from the U.K. One stayed only long enough to unpack his bag before he decided that he didn't like the climate and didn't like working in the bush so I bundled him on a plane back to the U.K. My Polish engineer, Rustetsky, understood my predicament and suggested that I hire Poles. "They're good workers and," he paused as if to clear cobwebs out of his mind, "they're poorly paid in Poland and anywhere they go will be better than working in Poland." He made sense and I trusted his judgment. I had to admit: if his fellow countrymen turned out as well as he had, it was fairly certain I would have a good team of expats.

I never regretted that decision. I hired a Pole by the name of Janiak and he arrived with his wife and two adolescent children, a boy and a girl. Contracts kept arriving almost faster than we could handle them. The company did well. We shrugged off politics as being just another fact of life. In fact, we became almost blasé with each military coup. The succession of military leaders didn't faze us. They were on top of the social heap skimming money from the public coffers into their pockets and we were somewhere in the middle of the social heap, making money and staying out of trouble and trying to find new ways to fight off corrupt officials.

*****

Within a few years after independence, it was obvious that corruption had become a way of life for them and us. For them, and this meant any official with whom you had to deal regardless of his level of authority, from the electricity board to the military junta, bribes were expected and there was no alternative to 'dash'. Corruption had got so bad that to get anything done meant first plotting a list of who was going to ask for bribes, and second, hoping to limit the bribes to just that list and not the friends-of-friends list that grew longer and longer. Part of our challenge as expats was to try and make sure we were bribing the right person so that he, in turn, would bribe the right person. Often, your money passed through several hands before 'the door was opened.'

By the time corruption became rampant most Nigerians had perfected the skill of trying to con expats into believing that the person with whom they were dealing 'was really honest.' Time and time again I'd advise gullible expats not to fall for that line and just as often, usually after money had parted hands and no service was rendered in return, they'd come back to me and whine, "But I thought he was different." The do-gooders fall from innocence was the hardest to watch. They simply could not make themselves believe that if they were honest their gesture would certainly be reciprocated and honesty would prevail. After they had been taken several times their halos lost their shine. They began looking at old timer expats, bitter and realistic, differently. In their eyes we were no longer ex-colonial devils out to fleece the poor unsuspecting natives. Actually, it was the other way

Rene Dassac (in collaboration with Patrick K. Robbins)

around: the wily natives were out to fleece the poor unsuspecting expats. I could give you hundreds of examples that were almost laughable if they weren't also often very poignant.

The Nigerian government was getting foreign aid from the Russian government. Fleecing foreigners was a national sport and it didn't matter whether the victim was capitalist or communist. Country of origin meant nothing to the men and women doing the shake-downs. Money was the only thing that mattered to them.

One case, among many, was particularly sad. A Russian doctor had been sent to Sokoto as an adviser to eradicate cholera that was rampant in some villages, especially in our part of Nigeria. He was a nice person who was devoted to his job. I actually met him a couple of times in the Sokoto club with his wife. He toured the infected areas and then asked for a meeting with the governor. The governor of the Sokoto state listened to what the doctor had to say. "This epidemic can be stopped but it will require your help," the doctor explained. The governor leaned forward as the doctor continued. "You must call on the police to put up cordons around each village and stop people from entering or leaving until the epidemic has stopped." The governor nodded as if he understood and then did nothing. There were no barriers but there were more deaths. Would the governor have changed his mind if an envelope filled with cash had come with the doctor's proposal? We shall never know.

The doctor refused to accept responsibility for the situation but he was powerless to prevent the epidemic from spreading. The doctor resigned, the government dithered, and the poor bitter doctor flew home alone. During those months of professional anguish his wife died. I don't know what she died of, probably not cholera, but that's not really the point. If the governor had acted responsibly hundreds of lives would have been saved. Instead, he avoided the issue and probably wasn't even aware of the fact that the Russian doctor had resigned and gone back to Russia.

The Governor of the Kano State was another character, a well trained bureaucrat who underwent an all too familiar transformation after he was appointed. It didn't take long for him to change from being a good administrator into becoming a mindless and corrupt little tyrant. When he took his post in Kano he was an unknown entity. He started off correctly. Money was invested in sprucing up the town; he had street lighting put on all the main streets. He was even nice enough to award the contract to me. Then he also awarded us the electrical installation for a five-story building, the State Secretariat Office. Later, when it came time to build a large reception building next to the Governor's lodge, I got the contract. To be trusted by the Governor was a great advantage, but, as was often the case, advantages also became serious disadvantages. Any time of day or night, no matter how trivial, if the governor wanted an electrical job done, I was called and I was expected to down tools and tend to him when any Ministry of Works electrician could have done the job.

In the beginning he also helped the farmers. We had good cattle in the area and someone explained to him that if he mixed local cattle with imported stock he would be able to increase the supply of fresh milk, cream, and butter. Within a few months the new livestock arrived and shortly afterwards we began to enjoy dairy products that were truly outstanding and widely appreciated. He even had an expensive breeding bull imported from France.

Our new governor was exceptional and for a while it seemed as if he could do no wrong. But, time and corruption, began eating away at him and he began acting like a pretentious and openly corrupt little king. He soon listened more to himself than to his advisers and he began making stupid decisions. He organized a huge barbecue in the park of the governor's lodge. That wasn't a bad idea but the choice of menu left us stunned. He had his prize breeding bull butchered and cut up for barbecue meat. The foreign breeding specialist was speechless and powerless to stop his prize animal from being killed. He warned the governor that he would complain to the federal government but the governor laughed at him. He was, after all, the government. The fools in the presidential palace hundreds of miles away didn't matter.

The problems didn't stop. He continued, unchecked neither by the locals nor the federal government. For example, they were making great progress at the agricultural experimental farm that was headed by a well-known English specialist. Under his leadership the farm was producing wonders by growing tons and tons of tomatoes. The specialist found a buyer in Switzerland who wanted to buy the entire production and process it into tinned products. The profit made by this new market could have been used to purchase farm machinery with the foreign currency that was earned. The governor dismissed the idea out of hand when the proposal was presented at a board of directors meeting. "Silly, silly project," he scolded. "Don't you know that with all the oil profits being made in the Niger delta this country doesn't need foreign currency from tomatoes?" The project died. Or as one of my friends in the club said glumly, "It withered on the vine." He chuckled at his own joke.

The governor's evolution was not unique; his decline into incompetent venality was the rule and not the exception. Along with nationalization of basic industries there was another program, a parallel track that began to eat into the size of the expatriate community. It was called Nigerianization: replace expats with Nigerians regardless of whether or not the Nigerians could do the job the expat was performing. In the beginning the electrical field was excluded but I was under no illusions. Sooner or later our time would come.

Corruption, Nigerianization, nationalization, the waltz of military coups led by officers who were out to fill their pockets quickly, proclamations that things were improving in Nigeria when, in fact, they were not, the slide into near anarchy was painful for everyone except for those on top who had direct access to the State's coffers.

Every now and then in a fit of righteousness, the military would clamp down on corruption. Of course, where they tightened was not in their own areas of responsibility but elsewhere when they found, all too easily, another and politically weaker corrupt Nigerian. He would be hauled before judges friendly to those in power and he would be given a 'fair trial' after which he was executed.

His execution was supposed to serve as a warning to others. I suppose a message of sorts did manage to filter down but it wasn't the message the leaders intended to send. It was: "if you are a stupid minor offender you will get caught and you will die. Get smart and beat the system."Naturally, the leaders did not turn their righteous focus on their own cliques. None of those on top were ever tried or convicted. The little guys were drummed through court, taken out on the beach, and shot in public. The public was not duped; it was docile. They knew that most of those executed didn't have anything to begin with so there wasn't too much for them to lose except their lives and those were often miserable. Maybe death wasn't too bad an alternative after all.

Getting adequate foreign exchange cover was a headache. It was becoming more and more difficult to import the necessary equipment to complete the various contracts we had. Opening a letter of credit was almost impossible and I couldn't operate without a LOC. The government resorted to auctioning foreign currency. As a businessman I needed FX to survive but the military needed the same money to fill their accounts in Switzerland and buy their fancy cars.

We drank in the New Year but I was in no mood to celebrate. I'd had a good run but I was coming around to accepting a difficult conclusion: It was 1978 and I had enough. The time finally came for me to stop and take stock. I had to find a way to recover my capital and repatriate it before I lost everything. The strain was too much for me to handle any more. Unlike others who had spent only a few years, I had lived in Africa long enough to know that I was struggling more in the work place than I wanted to and that was not healthy. Above all, I was no longer having any fun at work. For years it was all I could do to stay in bed in the morning. Every day I was bursting with energy and full of laughter. Almost without me noticing what was happening, my natural joie de vivre was being wrung out of my system. I was running out of steam and that was no laughing matter. It was time to call it quits. I wanted to retire.

*****

In a normal world it would have been possible to sell my shares and leave the country. But I wasn't running a business in a normal world. All I had to do was look out the window to remind myself that I was in Nigeria. Selling a business and leaving the country was too easy. In Nigeria, leaving the country required starting a long and complicated process of obtaining official approval documents and signatures. Each approval level became an opportunity for someone with signature authority to sign-off on my file provided he had been properly 'considered' by the applicant.

There was still some fight left in me so I decided to play the game straight. There was no way I could 'help' my file through a labyrinth of cloying and clutching little bureaucrats. Instead of playing their game I decided to present my various application forms so well done that no one, not even the head of the country, could find fault with them. I knew I had a strong case and my request could stand on its own even under heavy scrutiny. With the help of my banking friend Reginald Woodward, I filed all the documents necessary to transfer everything in my bank account in Kano to my account in London. That was the easy part. My worries began when my file started meandering through the various ministries.

The following eight weeks were hell. I had no other choice but to go to Lagos to see if my file was moving from office to office. In each office someone was expected to sign or put a stamp on the documents. It was painful to be at their mercy. Could I have 'facilitated the process' and move my file through more quickly? I didn't think it was possible. I understood the perverse logic in bribing and I knew how 'the system' worked. Bribe one person and you have to bribe everyone above him and everyone below him. They all talked and if one was getting a cut, the others expected equal treatment. Even in a corrupt system there are rules of conduct. More than once I began to think that I was going to lose everything I had worked so hard to earn. My hair turned from light gray to snow white. Furthermore, the trips back and forth between Kano and Lagos were expensive.

I didn't let on to the outside world the kind of toll this process was taking on my mental and physical health. Judged by my attitude, I was the usual happy-easy-going John Powell but inside where no one could look, my coping machinery was breaking down. I began aching in places that had never ached before; I was coming to the end of my rope and I was damned if I was going to fall apart in Africa. In the seventh week, as I came out of the airport in Kano, I saw an old Nigerian friend. We greeted each other warmly. He stepped back and looked at me closely as if I was an exhibit on display in a Middle Eastern mummy museum. "John, my good friend, tell me now, are you sick?"

He shouldn't have asked because I let him have it. I told him, in detail, what I was going through and the havoc it was wreaking on my health. He listened patiently. "You're a silly chap and if you didn't look so awful I'd scold you. You've been in Nigeria long enough to know that good friends can help solve problems." I looked at him dumfounded. "Go back into the airport and get us a booking for Lagos tomorrow and we'll go see my brother who is the chairman of the Central Bank." My alarm bells started clanging. "This bugger is just trying to get a free ride to Lagos," but I did as he told because I was at the stage when I had to try everything. I bought the tickets and the next day we went to see his brother.

My friend strode into the Central Bank as if he owned the place. I tagged along behind him. He went straight to the reception desk. "I would like to see the chairman," he said firmly. Before the receptionist could ask the obvious question, he stated his name. "We are brothers." A quick phone call and we were informed the chairman would receive us immediately. Only then did it really dawn on me that this guy was not kidding. The chairman really was his brother. As fitting for a chairman, we were shown into a large office on the top floor of the building. The brothers greeted each other warmly in a manner that was as much tribal as it was family. Trappings of office aside, behind closed doors family ties and tribal relations were what really counted.

The two men joked and traded barbs for about twenty minutes; it was the usual type of joshing one would expect to hear from brothers. Almost in mid-sentence, as if he had suddenly remembered our meeting was not a social occasion, the chairman leaned over to his brother and got serious. "I suppose you did not come with this gentleman just to visit me," he asked. On that cue my friend told him why we needed his help. Damn! Didn't he really lay it on. His oration on my behalf almost brought tears to my eyes until I realized he was talking about me. He explained that I was a good man who was now old and wanted to retire. For once, my white hair helped because I knew that Africans respect white haired old men.

He outlined my career and made sure his brother understood that I had made a contribution to Nigeria. I wasn't like many expats who saw their Nigerian assignment only as a means to make a lot of money and get out quickly. No, I had lived among Nigerians and had helped many of them from all walks of life. His brother listened attentively. "What can I do," he asked? My friend asked his brother to accelerate the clearance process. "He's been at it for two months, he's flown up and back to Lagos many times, that's costing him a lot of money, and he deserves better treatment." There it was: my problem was laid out for the big man to either see or reject. When my friend quit talking all I could do was hope he hadn't overstepped some invisible barrier and angered his brother. His error, if there was one, could easily have consigned my appeal to "documents lost" status inside an impenetrable bureaucracy.

The chairman picked up his phone and ordered the person on the other end to fetch my file and come up to the office with it "immediately." Within moments a low ranking civil servant scuttled into his office and placed my file on the chairman's desk. The chairman thumbed through it quickly and then looked up at the quivering little bureaucrat. "This file is in order. I cannot understand why it has taken so long." Pounding the shiny desktop with his big black index finger he barked "Put this file in order. Get it ready for my signature. Have it on my desk at ten o'clock tomorrow morning." Almost as if he enjoyed the power he held over the poor flunky, he barked again, "...and I won't tolerate any more delay." Clutching my file in his trembling hands the flunky backed his way out of the chairman's office.

I could have sworn he was bowing but I was afraid to stare for fear something might go wrong. I didn't like seeing the little fellow being beaten up but my file had taken a hiding from countless faceless bureaucrats and now Fate had swung in on my side. But, a little voice inside me to not get my hopes up too high. I was still in Nigeria and anything could happen in the next twenty-four hours. We could have another coup, the chairman could change his mind or drop dead from a heart attack, whatever, and I would be left alone with no allies trying to push my file through an administrative thicket denser than the worst jungle I had ever hacked my way through.

I held onto my benchmark for success: I would beat the system only when all the money in my bank account was transferred to London in the coming week. For Nigeria and for me, that was an awesome benchmark and even after an apparently successful meeting I was wary. I couldn't quite bring myself to believe the system would work. Nevertheless, I had to believe in something so I convinced myself that I was going to succeed no matter how high the odds were stacked against me.

The next day, at a few minutes to ten, my friend and I were ushered into the big man's office. He beamed and he handed me my file. He thanked me for helping Nigeria. I had an adrenalin rush that almost knocked off my eye glasses. I thanked him profusely. Clutching my file as if my life depended on, which in fact it did, I caught the first taxi out to the airport. When we got back to Kano I gave my Nigerian friend five hundred pounds. Without him I'd probably still be waiting for my money. Reginald Woodward, my banker friend, arranged for the contents of our account to be transferred to London.

I cannot tell you how good I felt. That money had more than financial meaning; it also symbolized everything we had struggled to set aside, the hardships we'd endured, the dreams we followed, the setbacks we lived through in order to keep on going and finally be 'wealthy' enough to quit working. There was a new life waiting for us in France and we had the money to be able to live reasonably well in the new phase of our lives that we still had to discover and create.

Anna and I began to sell everything we did not want to ship back to France. There were a lot of parties but none had as much of an emotional impact as the farewell party organized by all my Nigerian staff and expats. Naturally, there were a lot of speeches and gifts and I caught myself close to tears several times. Yes, we had worked together and the relationships we had developed were more than just professional. Across cultures and languages, we learned to respect each other and they thanked me for what I had done for them. We were happy to being leaving but we were sad to leave behind a wonderful group of men and women we knew we would probably never see again.

Just before we left, a rich Nigerian electrical contractor whom I had helped over the years asked me if I could open an office for him in France. He wanted me to act as his representative and buy material and equipment that I would ship to him. It was a good idea. After we negotiated most of the details I realized we couldn't take the project any further until I was back in France. He agreed he would come to Paris to finalize the proposal. There were several advantages to being his commercial representative. Not only would I still be able to keep my hand in the business I knew very well, it was also a way to make some money while I was settling into a new life in France.

On the eve of our departure, I really didn't know what I wanted to do with the rest of my life. From a financial point of view we had enough cash set aside to live reasonably well but, after years on my own, I had learned to respect money. After all, it was just as difficult to keep money as it was to make it. I realized that money had become a tool to work for me because if I didn't invest it we would lose it.

Although we were happy with the prospects of starting a new life, my Polish engineer was not happy at the thought of working without me. He told me that as soon as he could get his money transferred he would resign because he did not want to work with the people who took over from me. He was upset with the fact that my successors were suspected to be incompetent and corrupt. One man, an Indian, had been sacked from the NEPA (Nigerian Electrical Power Authority). Apparently he had used a false M.I.E.E. diploma. It wasn't unusual; I suspected it happened all the time. Anyway, I was almost one hundred percent certain that it wouldn't be long before our company would be nationalized. If that didn't do in the company something else would. Theft and armed ambushes were increasing and those two factors alone would certainly prevent us from working correctly. I felt sorry for Nigeria but, at the same time, I was glad to leave. We had our health, our wealth, good memories, a good marriage, our son was safe in France, and we had the prospect of a new life back in Europe.

*****

Anna and I took the 22 March 1979 British Caledonian flight to London to do some shopping and unwind. The last few months had been difficult and the strain was beginning to show on us. We needed a break, a chance to do something very different, and then get on with our lives. At our London bank we transferred some cash to our account at BNP in France that we had opened to pay for Philip's schooling and a pension I paid to my sister who looked after Philip while we were in Kano.

Taulus

Before leaving Kano, my Polish engineer Rustacki asked me to please see his wife who had been hospitalized in London with cancer. I promised him we would and when we finally met her we found that she was in bad shape. We talked, said the inane things one does in that type of situation, and she asked us to pray for her because she did not have long to live. It would have been easy to agree with her but we assured her we would and tried to cheer her up by telling her that cancer treatments were improving all the time and that she had to hang on because her husband would soon be back. We left her with a bunch of flowers. When we waved goodbye we knew, behind the frozen reassuring smiles on our faces, that we never see her again.

After we finished our personal business in London we went to Heathrow. It was still winter and to no one's surprise except us - we had forgotten what winters were like in northern Europe – we were told the airport was socked in. We began waiting because there was nothing else to do except go back to London. We dismissed that alternative because we didn't want to go through all the hassle of finding another hotel and losing our place in the growing list of passengers trying to get to the Continent. Our luck was with us; later that evening we managed to get a flight to Amsterdam. Once we got there, we hoped, the weather in Paris would improve so we could catch a connecting flight. How we made it into Amsterdam is anyone's guess; the fog was so thick we couldn't see the ground until we felt the plane's landing gear shudder on the wet tarmac.

With cloud cover as thick as pea soup, it was obvious we were stuck in Amsterdam. That wasn't a problem for us because we were in no hurry. We were beginning to discover a new dimension in our lives: Missed flight connections meant we had the luxury of filling our hours the way we wanted to and not the way we had to. We worked for years meeting deadlines and now, with our careers behind us, we no longer had a continuous commitment to someone else. Instead of rushing about meeting deadlines, we were slowly becoming aware of the luxury of doing whatever struck our fancy.

Landing in Amsterdam was our first test case and we weren't too sure how to react. We were torn between carrying on as usual which would have meant trying every trick possible to find a way to get to Paris despite the foul weather or telling ourselves we weren't in a hurry. Without having to rush somewhere to catch a flight and be at our destination on time, did we know how to take it easy and let things happen? Maybe another question was more pertinent: Was there anything stopping us from learning? Nothing appeared to stand in our way from doing what we jolly well wanted to do so we chose a nice hotel right in the heart of town. It had a good restaurant with plenty of seafood; we feasted on lobster and oysters. We couldn't recall when anything had tasted so good. We were back in Europe, not quite where we wanted to be, but at least on the right Continent, and we had a lot to look forward to in our lives. The lobster and oysters went down easily as did two nice bottles of Chablis.

After dinner we went for a stroll and decided to go into a Dutch pub for a night cap. It was noisy, smoky, and everyone was enjoying himself. Someone was playing an accordion and many customers were singing and dancing. We watched and laughed with them. Instead of letting us sit quietly and be casual observers, the revellers pulled us onto the dance floor and helped us join in their fun. That was a great evening and also an eye-opener.

Sharing their fun was a way for me to change my perception of the Dutch which, up until then, was not very favourable. The people in the pub were warm and friendly; I couldn't say that much about many of the Dutch that I had met outside of Europe. Too often the 'colonial' Dutch were harsh and arrogant. Locals were 'natives' in their eyes. Talk about being tight fisted when it came to money, I knew the Dutch could make the Scots seem like high rollers in comparison. Because of that night in the pub I had to admit the strangers we had fun with were different than most of the Dutch I knew, and to be honest, disliked. I learned something and I came to the conclusion that the people we met that night were very similar to Frenchmen in similar circumstances. It was a good evening and we left happy and wiser.

We were fortunate because the following day the weather lifted and we were cleared to fly, at last, to Paris. Our new car was waiting for us and we decided to drive straight to Cannes and get rested before we started our new life in France. We were excited and tired but we wanted to get on the road as quickly as we could load the car and head south. A couple of years earlier we had bought an apartment in

Cannes off plan. We owned it, more or less with the bank, but we had never actually set foot in it and we were eager to see it.

On the way down we stopped in Dijon where my younger sister was living. We had forwarded a crate from Africa that was waiting for us in customs; there was an even larger one in customs in Marseille but that one had to wait. When customs asked for my clearance papers I handed them a pile of documents the French consulate in Kano had prepared to prove that I was importing personal property. There were no problems and we headed off to Cannes somewhat heavier than when we arrived.

We furnished our flat and began the long process of 'feeling at home.' I'm not playing with words when I confess: just because you live in a house it is not necessarily a home. A house is a place in which you dwell. It has walls, a roof, doors and windows. Everything in it is functional. But a home is different because it has soul and character. In the beginning, our apartment in Cannes was our house but we were determined to turn it into our home.

*****

Our transition process to our new life in Europe had its ups and downs. One aspect of our new life that shocked us was the amount of paperwork the different administrations required. For a time it seemed as if all I was doing was filling-in forms and standing in endless queues. We registered with every conceivable government agency: civil service, national health, pension, and taxes. The list seemed endless. Fortunately my family had been concerned enough about our re-entry to take time and advise me how to work my way through the bureaucratic labyrinth and come out smiling. And,.with the necessary signatures and documents. Every time I went into an official office I felt my blood pressure rise but I restrained myself from venting my frustration. It took hours but in the end I managed to supply: parent's birth certificates, my own birth certificate, and countless other documents that were so numerous that I have mercifully forgotten what I supplied.

The paper chase took the better part of a month but it was worth it because, once I had all the forms filled-in and deposited with the proper authorities, I found out that I was going to get a good pension. I had forgotten that my pension was based on a points system and to get the maximum number of points I had to be sure that I had all the support documents. It was enough to drive me crazy but since I couldn't change the system I merely went along with it and played the system to my advantage.

As I wound my way through the civil service I realized that I had been away from France during a critical period in its history when it began an ambitious rebuilding and modernization program after the war. While I was away I looked at living in France through rose tinted lenses and I concluded that 'life,' in all its complexities was easier than either Africa or Britain. I had to remove my glasses when I came home. For example, in England it only took a couple of weeks of form filling before you could start up a business. In France, it took me three months and miles of red tape to cut through before I could start up my little business. I wanted to get going with the business concept I had cobbled together with my Nigerian friend before leaving Kano. After a couple of weeks beating the pavement, I quickly admitted there was no way we could start an export office in Cannes so we moved up to Paris. Then Cannes was not the international city it has become today and to get anything done, especially something complicated like an export business, one had to be in Paris.

Getting office space was no problem. Another friend from Nigeria days had a big office and he rented me desk space at a reasonable price. It was all I needed to get started. We rented a flat in the fourteenth arrondissement near the newly built Japanese hotel on the banks of the Seine. I knew that going back to work would require approval from the ministry of labor so I went over to talk to them.

I was dumfounded when the bureaucrat told me, after reviewing all my papers, that I could retire immediately with 78% of my salary and hold that until I reached the age of sixty-five. What this meant was simple: I could get my state retirement immediately. Since it was based on my highest salary I could live very well until I turned sixty-five. At that point I would tap into my private pension plan. I didn't argue with him; you don't argue with people who give you great gifts like that! Our personal expenses were under control, which was one of the lessons we acquired in Africa: live within your budget, so we really didn't have too much to worry about on the financial side.

Dealing with the family side, our son, was more of a challenge. We knew how to live in Africa but coming back to France we had to acquire new skills on how to live as retirees in France. Furthermore, we had to learn how to live together again as a family. We met both challenges head-on and succeeded but it was not easy at first. Philip had been called to do his national service and he chose to go into the navy. Time had flown. For us it seemed like yesterday when he was born and we were still young and carefree. Now he was a young man who had survived the rigors of living apart from his parents for many of his teenage years.

When he was about eight or nine we realized that we could not keep him in Africa. The schools were reasonably good but life in Nigeria was becoming more dangerous and more turbulent for expats. Not that he minded. He had a good group of friends and they were too young to understand fully what was going on around them. It was different for us. He was our only son and we knew we had to start making some difficult decisions about his education and his future. In the end, there was no choice: we knew we had to send him back to France.

Making that decision was difficult for all of us. Starting with his birth, we had grown together as a family. Perhaps the bonds we had created since he was born were not unusual for families with small children who were raised in remote areas but for us, his parents, responsibility for bringing up Philip had special significance. We poured into him the life experiences that neither of us had. Anna had not been able to guide and comfort Marco when he grew up and I felt cheated by my parent's early deaths. Far from being perfect parents, we made sure we gave him unstinting and endless love. Anna was stricter with him than I was. Philip realized discipline (firm and fair) came from his mum but my relationship with him was different. I knew that I was a softie (he did too) and I also knew that I was developing a relationship with him that could be called a bond of friendship in addition to having him recognize me as his father. When he was a little boy we were almost mates. That made child rearing somewhat difficult for Anna because she was raising a little boy and also scolding his father who acted like a little boy sometimes.

Our family life was happy and we were close to each other but we knew our idyllic 'African life' couldn't last forever. Even if he didn't go to France, and even if we found a miraculous solution to his education, he was growing up and sooner or later he would go his own way. Because of where we lived and how we lived, it was a foregone conclusion that he would have to leave sooner than when we wanted. He would have to leave when he was still a little boy. The thought of him leaving was almost too much to bear.

Lying awake at night we struggled with weighty questions about how we were going to function as a family. He was too young to leave home, we told ourselves. That was the truth and we could not overlook that fact. But, we also knew we couldn't use his age as an excuse to keep him in Nigeria. No matter how we turned the problem, there were no new solutions. We knew he had to send him back to school in France. But where was he going and under what conditions? Those were more vexing questions without easy answers.

After exhausting all possibilities we decided to arrange to have him live with my sisters. Staying with my sisters and their families meant he would avoid my experience. He was not shipped off to boarding school at an early age. Neither Anna nor I wanted that and my sisters fully agreed. Working as a family, we made sure that he was given love and support while we were far away. Sometimes he was in Epernay, then outside Paris, and finally down to Nevers where he got his baccalaureate certificate in 1978.

He spent his long holidays for us and those were magical weeks but at the end of each holiday we, he and us, had to face his return to France. It was hard on him and hard on us but we made it through those difficult good-byes. Once Annie visited him to see how he was doing while he was living in Epernay. He must have been eleven or twelve. At the end of her visit she had to take the train back to Paris and he wanted to accompany his mother to the train station to see her off. Annie was touched but her train was scheduled to leave while class was in session and she did not want him to be absent and get in trouble with his teachers. He insisted but she had the last word and set off for the station carrying her suitcase. He ran part of the way with her until he had to turn back.

Instead of going straight to school he ran into my sister's house pleading, "Quick. Run down to the train station. Wave goodbye to mother. Wave and wave until you can't see her any more." We cried when we heard that story. Kids look at the world differently than their parents. Who was right and who was wrong? We agonized with that question for months.

He got through his teenage years without too many mishaps and he became a fine young man. By the time we were settling into Paris he was in his first year in the Merchant Navy Officers School. He was doing well and he was getting good grades. He liked the navy and he even toyed with the idea of making a career in the merchant navy but when he started to explore the idea with friends who had become officers in the merchant navy he soon changed his mind. Conditions were bad and he was advised to look for a shore job. Most ships had re-flagged under flags of convenience and onboard conditions were worsening. The majority of the crews came from third world countries and they were happy to put up with conditions that were unacceptable to Europeans.

While we were in this transition period I went to Kano three or four times to price some jobs for my new partner. We got the business and with it came good orders for equipment and that meant good commissions for me. The business side was satisfactory but I didn't like what I saw was happening in Nigeria. It was clear to me that my partner's business depended on him making kickbacks to the current military government. We stuck it out for three years and, sure enough, another military government came to power and they were against the powerful growing business class who sought stability.

I used that coup as an excuse to close down the Paris office and take pre-retirement like my accountant advised me to do. Furthermore, I was not happy with how my partners were running the business. They managed the company as if they were still back in Nigeria. Skirting the law was a game for them. Not that we did anything illegal, I wouldn't have stood for it, but there was often a whiff of something rotten in some of the ways they transferred money or booked credits. In the end, my expert external auditor told me to wind down my participation slowly and pack in the company.

There was no reason for us to stay in Paris any longer. We planned our move back to the coast and I filled in all the papers necessary to end the lease of our flat. We drove south and this time we were pretty sure that once we settled, probably in the Cannes-Mandelieu area, it would be for good. In April 1981 Philip was released from the Navy and he came to stay with us. He kept busy doing odd jobs, and some temporary work, but his qualifications were highly specialized: navigation officer in the merchant navy.

While he was with us he received an offer from one of the cargo ships sailing under a flag of convenience. I didn't like the looks of it and I told him to not take it. Being out of work was beginning to take a toll on him and it almost broke my heart to see him so concerned. I knew that, as a father, I had to let him grow up and face the real world on his own. But, I also knew, that I did not want him to suffer some of the ways I had when I was growing up. No, I was determined to fight and make sure our son didn't get hit with more than he could handle.

Finally, I started calling all the friends I had in Britain to see if someone could help us. Bob Wynn told me to send Philip over to him. "I'll put him on a twelve month assignment with a diesel engine company. When he comes out he will know everything there is to know about the maintenance and repair of marine and land transport diesel engines." That sounded like it made a lot of sense. He continued and said that after the diesel training I ought to consider sending him to one of the electrical companies that I still had good connections with and have him learn H.T. and L.T. installation. After that, maybe it would help to have a spell with one of their branches that dealt with power generators.

I could see what he wanted to do: give Philip a wider technical education that would help him find a good paying job. It sounded like a good deal because he would be paid while he was learning. I told him not to worry about the cost of lodging; we would pay for his B&B accommodations. He perked up and in a very short time we saw him off to Farnsborough, Peterborough, and Newcastle. Eighteen months later he returned a new man. He was confident in his newly acquired skills and he began looking for a job. It was tough and after living and working in the U.K., he found it difficult to return to France and work in a country where he often felt himself to be an outsider. I could appreciate how he felt and I managed to share my experience with him to help him make the transition.

He landed a job with an electrical contracting company and he enjoyed it but after a few months his employer decided to reduce staff and move the company. Fortunately, he had a good boss who had been a lieutenant commander on a French aircraft carrier. He took an interest in Philip and advised him to apply for the position of maintenance engineer in a plastics factory outside of Geneva, Switzerland. He got the job and while he was there he met his future wife.

About the same time when Philip was getting his career started, an old friend contacted me. He had his own energy company and he was well known in the nuclear and atomic energy industry and research circles. We saw each other fairly often and he introduced me to an oil drilling and service company. They wanted to open an office in Paris and they needed a Frenchman on their board of directors. I had a nice job: sleeping shareholder. This meant that I attended meetings, enjoyed nice lunches, got paid and did nothing. But, there was an interesting spin-off because I had the opportunity to meet a lot of fascinating people.

Through these contacts I put Philip in touch with the Shell Oil Company and he was hired a maintenance engineer in Gabon. He's still at it and he's involved in this field from Nigeria to Cameroon, Gabon and Angola. Now he is married with two marvelous children, a son and a daughter who bring us happiness and sunshine in our retirement in Callian, a small village in the Var. Typical of a contractor's life, Philip and his wife have moved all over the world. We visited them in northern Holland where his son Olivier was born and several times in Gabon where his daughter, Marine, was born. When we saw their place in Nigeria it reminded us, fondly, of our life in Nigeria. He and his wife have led a good life and have raised two fine grandchildren.

Rene Dassac (in collaboration with Patrick K. Robbins)

CHAPTER ELEVEN: REFLECTIONS

Many chapters in our life were closing. Our flat in Cannes-Mandelieu was nice and comfortable but we had enough of living in a busy town. When we were in Africa, despite the difficulties, we found living in villages or small towns was more pleasant than life in the big cities. In a village there is more of a chance to take time to get to know your neighbors, to listen to what is happening, and to enjoy the rhythm that comes from people moving at a slower pace. Towns are full of strangers bumping into each other and rushing off without a minute to spare. We finally accepted being caught in that kind of lifestyle was something that did not appeal to us in our waning years.

Moving away from the coast and into the country was an idea whose time had come. Fortunately, we were in a good position to turn the idea into something concrete, like owning our own house. Many years earlier, perhaps a decade earlier, maybe even more, on the advice of a friend living in Nigeria, we bought some land outside the village of Callian in the Var. We bought a five thousand square meter section, in the middle of nowhere, covered with hundreds of oak trees. We didn't even know what it really looked like because it was terribly overgrown. If it hadn't been for all the acorns and brush native to northern Europe, we could have sworn we were back in Africa. We knew we had bought a parcel of land because the surveyor had marked it but all we could see was big trees and brush, some of which came as high as my chest.

For months we would pack a picnic and drive out to Callian to clear our land. Axing our way through the underbrush led us to discover many things: new muscles, and numerous 'restanques' or terraces. Once we cleared the land we decided to build a Swedish design house that has great acoustic and thermal insulation. Normally building a house in the backcountry is synonymous with waging a war with your builders. They never show up on time, nothing quite fits, and in the end you might get a house but it often costs more than your budget and your relations with your partner usually have suffered irreparable damage. Our construction saga was a happy event. Once the foundations had been dug the house was erected quickly with only the occasional confrontation with the building crew. We've been in Callian for nearly a quarter century. Our life among the boar and mushrooms is serene. There is just enough garden to keep us busy.

At first after we moved in I became quite active in the village helping with the local tourism board and pitching in when the mayor's office needed someone who could speak English. Volunteering was a great way to meet a lot of people. It didn't take long before we were recognized for what we are: a happy retired couple living a quiet life in a small village. There is nothing fancy involved with our life style. As happened so often in our lives, we met a challenge and made adjustments in the way we look at the world.

Now I've come to a period in my life when I have the time and the age to reflect on where I have been and what I have done. Most of my wartime shipmates have crossed the bar and many post war friends have also gone. I am still healthy and happy. Every evening at precisely 18:00 I treat myself to a nice whisky. Anna and I sit and talk, sometimes about old times, more often about what needs to be done in the garden. She's more of a gardener than I am but once she's dragged me outside I actually enjoy cutting and pruning or just watching nature. I've found that when I take time to poke around our land there is always something new to discover. Maybe that is the way I've led my life: pushing back the under brush and discovering something new.

When I was a child I couldn't have known a soldier's helmet was so heavy until I tried one on and had to tip it up from behind to see out. Were all officers born with eyes in the backs of their heads? My night in the brig was a discovery experience about the consequences of right and wrong. Every waking moment during the war was a chance to discover something about others or myself. Not all men are equal but we share more points in common than points that divide us.

Honesty is universal and it doesn't depend on a man's religion or race.

I met great yet simple men from all walks of life. Their greatness, when I took away the trappings of their profession, was linked to who they were and how they behaved toward their fellow man, not their social status. I've discovered that I could rise from the depths of despair about ever finding a woman to love, to living a long and happy life with my beloved Annie. Through her and with her I've discovered the mystery, the beauty and the frustration, of parenthood. Raising a child was an adventure, a daily discovery of new limits for both of us. To the best of my knowledge there are no schools to teach you how to be a good parent. Every day is another chance to learn something about human nature even when you become a grandparent and your grandchildren sail through mind-boggling computer problems with their eyes shut!

And I have discovered that I can have a good laugh when I stop and remember all the crazy things I did and the risks I took. Every time I see an advertisement for a trip to Tunisia I think about our swim to buy some wine. I wonder if that Tunisian is still alive; how many times has he told our story? Yes, my memory is still sharp and I can make myself chuckle because I can laugh at myself.

Is the act of discovery another form of fighting? I've often thought about that question and I am not sure my answer is appropriate for someone else. When I was a kid I took charge of myself and therefore I took charge of my life. It didn't take long for me to realize that if I was going to amount to anything in life I had to fight for what I wanted. The greatest bouts were not fist-to-fist with another person. No, the most painful rounds were those I fought when I was looking inside myself trying to figure out what I wanted to do with my life, trying to figure out why something wasn't working. Edith was a brutally painful period in my life that should never have happened but it did. I fought to retain my sanity when around me even friends were going mad with grief and hatred. I discovered I could fight back the urge to destroy someone or something because I had been deceived and used. The rage I felt then was kept inside. My emotional boilers didn't burst and that discovery taught me another dimension in my resilience and it gave me something to be proud about: my self-esteem was strong and I could rise above a broken heart.

Now I can live with the answer to the question about discovery and fighting. As far as I am concerned I could not have discovered so much about myself, about my fellow man, or about the world through which I traveled, if I had not fought to discover new depths in myself. Outwardly, my life has been a continuous series of grand adventures. Inwardly, in my soul, I have grown and I continue to grow.

Looking back, I can safely say that life was no bondage. My trip through life has been a mixture of hardships offset by fantastic happiness and grand friendships. Fate did not steal away my life from the course I finally set for myself. At times Fate almost succeeded but I fought back, turned the tables on Fate and carved my own path. Nothing has come easy. At every major step I've fought to achieve my fair share of what life can offer if you work for it. In my process of struggling I have known the richness of love shown to me and I have given love. I have seen heroism and I have seen Man at his worst.

After more than eight decades I can safely say I have led a rich and satisfying life.

Rene Dassac (in collaboration with Patrick K. Robbins)